MIDDLEBROW MODERNS

Middlebrow Moderns

Popular American Women Writers of the 1920s

Edited by LISA BOTSHON & MEREDITH GOLDSMITH

NORTHEASTERN UNIVERSITY PRESS

BOSTON

Northeastern University Press

Library of Congress Cataloging-in-Publication Data

Middlebrow moderns : popular American women writers of the 1920s / edited by Lisa Botshon and Meredith Goldsmith.
    p. cm.
Includes bibliographical references and index.
   ISBN 1–55553–557–7 (alk. paper)—
   ISBN 1–55553–556–9 (pbk. : alk. paper)
   1. American fiction—Women authors—History and criticism. 2. Women and literature—United States—History—20th century. 3. Popular literature—United States—History and criticism. 4. American fiction—20th century—History and criticism.   I. Botshon, Lisa II. Goldsmith, Meredith.
   PS374.W6 M53 2003
   813′.52099287—dc21   2002152469

Designed by Lou Robinson

Composed in Scala by Coghill Composition in Richmond, Virginia. Printed and bound by The Maple Press Company in York, Pennsylvania. The paper is Maple Tradebook Antique, an acid-free sheet.

MANUFACTURED IN THE UNITED STATES OF AMERICA
07 06 05 04 03   5 4 3 2 1

Contents

Illustrations   vii

Acknowledgments   ix

Foreword   xi
    JOAN SHELLEY RUBIN

Introduction   3
    LISA BOTSHON AND MEREDITH GOLDSMITH

I   Placemaking: Gender, Genre, and Geography

"Written with a Hard and Ruthless Purpose": Rose Wilder Lane,
Edna Ferber, and Middlebrow Regional Fiction   25
    DONNA CAMPBELL

The Cosmopolitan Regionalism of Zona Gale's Friendship Village   45
    DEBORAH LINDSAY WILLIAMS

Winnifred Eaton's "Japanese" Novels as a Field Experiment   65
    DOMINIKA FERENS

II   The Middlebrow and Magazine Culture

Feminist New Woman Fiction in Periodicals of the 1920s   87
    MAUREEN HONEY

Progressive Middlebrow: Dorothy Canfield, Women's Magazines,
and Popular Feminism in the Twenties   111
    JAIME HARKER

"Lost Among the Ads": *Gentlemen Prefer Blondes*
and the Politics of Imitation   135
    SARAH CHURCHWELL

III Women behind the Screens

Edna Ferber's *Cimarron*, Cultural Authority,
and 1920s Western Historical Narratives   167
    HEIDI KENAGA

Anzia Yezierska and the Marketing of the Jewish Immigrant
in 1920s Hollywood   203
    LISA BOTSHON

IV Women and Consumption

"An Unwonted Coquetry": The Commercial Seductions
of Jessie Fauset's *The Chinaberry Tree*   227
    SUSAN TOMLINSON

The Wages of Virtue: Consumerism and Class Formation
in Fannie Hurst's *Back Street*   245
    STEPHANIE BOWER

Shopping to Pass, Passing to Shop: Consumer Self-Fashioning
in the Fiction of Nella Larsen   263
    MEREDITH GOLDSMITH

Notes on Contributors   291
Index   295

Illustrations

Campbell's Soup advertisement   144

"If you turn your back on a statue . . ."   146

"Paris Now Contemplates the New Hat."   146

"This is Anita Loos . . ."   155

W. H. D. Koerner's painting *Madonna of the Prairie*   174

RKO's two-sheet poster for *Cimarron*   187

Miguel Covarrubias's caricature of Edna Ferber, ca. 1930   192

Acknowledgments

This work began in the bowels of Columbia University's Butler Library, where hundreds of American middlebrow women's novels had been tucked away for decades. These books gave us much pleasure during our dissertation years when we swapped and gossiped about them with joyful abandon. Our early readings of popular authors like Gertrude Atherton and Dorothy Canfield, as well as less well-known novelists like Emanie Sachs, provided us with reams of footnotes. It wasn't until the dissertations were safely defended that we began to realize that these women deserved a criticism of their own. So, first, we would like to thank our contributors—whom we found at conferences, through friends of friends, and via many calls for papers—for really giving life to a project we had been dreaming about for years. Thanks, too, to our editor, Elizabeth Swayze, whose unwavering support was critical to our confidence and ultimate progress. Susan Ward at the Boston Museum of Fine Arts was of immense help with some of our key illustrations. We also greatly appreciated the insightful comments of Melinda Plastas, Eve Raimon, and Siobhan Senier on early drafts of our introduction. After these good people, we would like to thank our partners, Mark Bergman and Pete Milligan, for the usual things, and, of course, Grinch and Ruby.

A version of Lisa Botshon's "Anzia Yezierska and the Marketing of the Jewish Immigrant in 1920s Hollywood" was published in *JNT: Journal of Narrative Theory* 30:3 (Fall 2000): 287–312. An earlier version of Meredith Goldsmith's piece, "Shopping to Pass, Passing to Shop: Consumer Self-Fashioning in the Fiction of Nella Larsen," was published in *Recovering the Black Female Body: Self-Representations by African American Women* (New Brunswick: Rutgers University Press, 2001), 97–120.

Foreword

JOAN SHELLEY RUBIN

In 1921, a forty-three-year-old Wisconsin librarian named Flora Neil Davidson pasted an excerpt from a newspaper column into her diary alongside accounts of her daily activities and favorite snippets of poetry. The column, addressed "To a Youth, Cynical" and signed "Anne Elizabeth," declared:

> Because I say "damn" and use lipstick, you were sure that I was a flapper; however, the fact that I hated F. Scott's type of youth, and that I hadn't been kissed was inconsistent with flapperism. But when you found out that I subscribed to the "Bookman" and read Huneker, you decided that I must be a "Young Intellectual," and were surprised that I hated "Erik Dorn" and preferred Whitcomb Riley to The Benets [*sic*]. . . . Now, why won't you believe that a person can be 20 and live in Chicago and yet have old-fashioned ideas? Please believe that I *do* hate studio parties and the "new" literature and blasé youths, and that I can like organ music and lolly-pops and Thackeray and still be modern.

This entreaty happens to focus solely on male writers. Still, it captures one of the most valuable features of the essays in this collection—namely, the effort their authors make to disentangle the modern outlook from its customary association with high literary culture. Davidson herself exemplified the need to do so; she presumably identified with "Anne Elizabeth" as a forward-looking woman of taste, yet her diary mingled lines from Riley along with quotations from youth's emissary, Edna St. Vincent Millay. Moreover, the column alerts us to an equally useful characteristic of this volume: its exploration of the ways in which figures whom avant-garde critics judged irredeemably middlebrow—such as the Benéts—played an innovative and even oppositional role for the large number of readers who (like Davidson) saw them as "new." The essays here assembled, in other words, importantly reevaluate both of the terms in the volume's title, *middlebrow* and *moderns*.

In their introduction, Meredith Goldsmith and Lisa Botshon sketch the contours of that reassessment with respect to the current state of literary scholarship. They note that the tendency among critics to associate middlebrow writing with the pernicious aspects of consumer culture has inhibited examination of the fiction that incorporated elements of both the serious and the popular. Their project, they explain, is thus in part an act of recovery. The volume's contributors restore middlebrow works to view because of the intrinsic qualities such works contain, rather than merely attempt to establish a counterpoint to the existing canon. Furthermore, as Goldsmith and Botshon observe, these essays—all devoted to fiction by women—bear the same relationship to American literary history as the late-twentieth-century feminist scholarship on sentimentalism; like their predecessors, the scholars represented here believe that gender bias has so structured critical categories that it has obscured the actual content and function of the novels and short stories they discuss. In particular, the contributors want to correct the propensity to gender high modernism as masculine and popular literature as feminine, a strategy for ignoring or dismissing both "the majority of female authors" and the wide audience of "middle-class female consumers" (see page 9).

Nevertheless, because *Middlebrow Moderns* strives to "situate the popular female authors of the 1920s in a variety of social dimensions" (see page 11), it also bears a relationship to scholarship in American cultural history that should not escape notice. Of all the periods by which historians have routinely divided up the American past, the decade of the 1920s is perhaps the one that has accrued the greatest number of stereotypes. As writers on the historiography of the era almost unfailingly point out, an early, influential source of those stock images was Frederick Lewis Allen's *Only Yesterday* (1931). The heart of Allen's chronicle was his description of the "revolution in manners and morals" that, in his view, permeated American society in the years following World War I. Allen's cast of characters consisted of those familiar figures—flappers, gangsters, bathing beauties, baseball players, and crooked politicians—who made the twenties "roar" with exuberance and prosperity. Another powerful version of that picture derived from F. Scott Fitzgerald, whose novels and essays appraised the "jazz age" as "the greatest, gaudiest spree in history." Both Allen and Fitzgerald saw modernity—the hallmark of the New Era—as inseparable from liberation, especially the emancipation of women from sexual repression and household drudgery.

Some influential historians, such as William E. Leuchtenburg, largely accepted that emphasis on the hedonism and quirkiness of 1920s culture, even when they profitably exposed the anxieties that underlay the period's political and religious fundamentalisms. By the mid-twentieth century, however, others had embarked on a reconsideration of the cultural scene. In the area of literary and intellectual history, Frederick J. Hoffman's *The Twenties: American Writing in the Postwar Decade*, first published in 1949, remains a monumental achievement in its integration of thematic narrative and textual analysis. Hoffman was convinced that "a period of years responsible for so many distinguished products in the arts . . . must have been more substantial than it is usually represented as being" (ix). As a result, he constructed a framework that allowed him to explore postwar disillusionment, regionalism, expatriation, faith in science, social criticism, and other outlooks that informed American fiction, poetry, and drama. His great success was his incontrovertible demonstration of the brilliance, energy, and moral fervor that animated American writers' perceptions of modernity.

Yet it is sobering to realize that just two of the authors Hoffman selected to epitomize the arguments of each of his chapters—Sinclair Lewis and Willa Cather—can be called popular—or even middlebrow—figures. Furthermore, Cather was the only woman in Hoffman's group. More to the point, the subjects of the essays in *Middlebrow Moderns* are almost entirely absent from *The Twenties*. Dorothy Canfield appeared with Cather as a counterexample to the dominant postwar ethos; Zona Gale occupied the same anomalous place vis-à-vis critiques of the middle class. Oddly, given Hoffman's scant attention to mass culture, Anita Loos earned a listing in Hoffman's biographical appendix, but she was never mentioned in the text itself. Neither Fauset nor Larsen (nor any other African-American writers) was visible to Hoffman's eye. For all of Hoffman's insights, American writing in the postwar decade was largely the province of Pound, Eliot, Crane, Hemingway, Fitzgerald, and the like. Modernity to him was virtually inseparable from aesthetic modernism. Given that white, male, modernist emphasis, we should not be surprised that Hoffman's work does not grace Goldsmith and Botshon's own bibliography.

Of course, Hoffman did not have the benefit of the enormous out-pouring of scholarship on women and minorities that, around 1970, began to shape a more inclusive, richer understanding of the American past. A signal contribution was Estelle Freedman's 1974 essay "The New Woman: Changing Views of Women in the 1920s," first published in the *Journal of American History*. Although Hoffman's interest in literature was outside her purview, Freedman explicitly questioned the legacy of Allen and Leuch-tenberg, arguing that they and subsequent historians had distorted the extent of women's emancipation while underrating women's political activities. Freedman's article set an agenda for investigations that would shed "literary stereotypes" and avoid the "excessive generalization" mar-ring studies of "*the* American woman" (393). Over the next twenty-five years, numerous scholars accepted that assignment with enlightening results.

Among synthetic volumes, one of the best recent examples is Lynn Dumenil's *The Modern Temper* (1995), which includes a lengthy section defining the "new woman"—here a synonym for the modern—anew. From Dumenil's perspective, neither emancipation nor a retreat from electoral politics was an accurate or complete description of women's ex-perience in the 1920s. First, she insisted on recognizing the multi-plicity of circumstances in which American women found themselves—circumstances created by the variables of race, ethnicity, and class. Second, Dumenil made clear the limits of sexual liberation even for middle-class white women, tempering her account of real change with observations about the persistence of traditional morality and the impact of images gen-erated by movies and advertising. Dumenil not only adhered scrupulously to a vision of a heterogeneous American society; she also displayed an awareness that one could live in that modern milieu, work in modern industry, buy modern consumer goods, and still find "elusive" the "mod-ern goals of equality and personal autonomy" (98).

Yet for all its strengths, in the matter of literature and the arts *The Modern Temper* was as dichotomized in its own way as Joseph Wood Krutch's despairing 1929 portrait of faith versus science from which Dumenil bor-rowed her title. Intellectuals here consist almost entirely of high culture figures, even if Dumenil's formulation admits to those ranks the members of the Harlem Renaissance and ethnic writers. At the other end of the spectrum, one finds mass culture, differently packaged and consumed depending on the class and race of its audiences. (Middlebrow culture makes only a cameo appearance as a commodity that promised personal fulfillment.) In other words, Dumenil's commitment to conflict and diversity—which served her so well in her retrieval of neglected social history— actually obscured a crucial part of the cultural story: the middle between the high and the popular. Overcorrecting for the focus of previous scholars on homogeneity, *The Modern Temper* omitted the white, Anglo-Saxon Protestant readers, male and female, who participated in the civic life of the Lynds' *Middletown*, shunned the Ku Klux Klan, worried about declining moral standards, and made Dorothy Canfield's novels best sellers. Flora Neil Davidson would have experienced no shock of recognition had she perused Dumenil's pages, yet in terms of race, ethnicity, religion, and perceived class affiliation, she belonged to the group that comprised most Americans of the period.

The same point can be made about another recent overview of the 1920s, Ann Douglas's erudite and provocative *Terrible Honesty* (1995). Douglas depicted the decade as a time when Americans rejected the precepts of the Victorian matriarch in favor of a masculine—and modern— sensibility that emanated from New York, welcomed emotional freedom, and celebrated it in the popular arts. Her formulation made no room for the unalienated Midwesterners Daniel Borus highlighted in reprinting the essays on "These United States" that appeared in the *Nation* magazine between 1922 and 1924: Americans who, along with their own belief in modernity, "valued past practices for their abilities to confer a valuable sense of order and rootedness" (4). Neither did it accommodate the conservative impulses Roderick Nash charted in *The Nervous Generation* (1969), a work unusual in its appreciation of diverse themes in the era's intellectual life.

Given the achievements and drawbacks of recent monographs, it is thus both satisfying and frustrating to examine treatments of the 1920s in recently published high school and college American history textbooks. Most have absorbed the revisionist emphasis on the limited degree to which farmers, immigrants, and racial minorities participated in New Era prosperity. Conflict between modern and traditional outlooks has become a central theme. The New Woman often is not merely a liberated flapper but instead confronts both professional opportunities and domestic constraints. The underside of the period—nativism, prohibition-related crime, bureaucratization—is fully evident. Yet, notwithstanding a few gratifying exceptions, literary production and reception continue to suffer from oversimplification. Textbook authors persist in counterposing the rise of mass media to a disaffected high culture—as if intellectuals never enjoyed the movies—and in implying that those two phenomena represent the entire scope of the arts in the 1920s.

That is why *Middlebrow Moderns* is so welcome. These essayists pay attention to an enormous body of writing and to its cultural significance. In mapping the ground between the high and the popular, the contributors have absorbed the lessons that historians (and other scholars) have taught about the importance of attending to the categories of race, region, ethnicity, class, and gender. Yet they have understood that those categories acquired some of their modern resonances through their transmission in conventional prose forms. That is, they have seen that the tensions and anxieties characteristic of American political and social life during the 1920s carried over into the literature that critics have predominantly dismissed as merely commodified and imitative. As these essays show, while the authors of middlebrow fiction usually—although not always—rejected aesthetic experimentation, the novels and stories they produced were sites for other kinds of questioning. Rose Wilder Lane, Edna Ferber, and Zona Gale, for example, voiced ambivalence about regional myths, especially those pertaining to women. Contradictory understandings of race and ethnicity marked the work of Winnifred Eaton and the packaging of Anzia Yezierska. The desires for wealth and refinement, for success in and freedom from the marketplace, competed on the pages of magazines and in the books of Jessie Fauset, Fannie Hurst, and Nella Larsen. One of the decade's most thoughtful—and popular—commentators, Dorothy Canfield, opposed inequality and the oppression of women by reaffirming her commitment to self-sacrifice, marriage, and motherhood. She and her colleagues among the "middlebrow moderns," grappled with such issues, as Jaime Harker writes, "within the ostensibly reactionary confines of middle-class literary institutions" (see page 120). In addition, some of the contributors to this volume have augmented our knowledge about how those institutions functioned, explaining, for example, the financial rewards of serialization or the factors that affected the filming of a book. In those essays, the creator of middlebrow fiction becomes a subject in her own right, adding a dimension to the history of women professionals and thus further eroding the image of the New Woman as a "jazz baby."

As Frederick Hoffman speculated long ago, the stereotypes of the 1920s that literary scholars and historians have tried so hard to dislodge may endure because Americans need to believe in them; they preserve a vision of innocence even as they conceal expressions of insecurity. It may be that the currently unsettled state of the world will even strengthen the allure of a mythical 1920s—ostensibly a simpler time not only because of the supposed harmlessness of its dance crazes but also because of the apparently clear-cut hierarchies of taste into which Americans neatly fit. Ambivalence is not easy to live with. Thus it may be prudent to concede that, despite the gains scholars have made in demythologizing them, the flapper and the expatriate may never lose their hold on the American imagination. Yet the essays collected in this volume should inspire future historians and literary scholars to continue reassessing the context in which those caricatures emerged and to place them in the company of other modern Americans who populated—and read—middlebrow fiction.

MIDDLEBROW MODERNS

Introduction

LISA BOTSHON AND MEREDITH GOLDSMITH

> Midway between these wholly atrocious and quasi-respectable evangels of amour and derring-do, there floats a literature vast, gaudy and rich in usufructs, which outrages all sense and probability without descending to actual vulgarity and buffoonery, and so manages to impinge agreeably upon that vast and money-in-pocket public which takes instinctively a safe, middle course in all things.
> —H. L. Mencken, *Smart Set Criticism* (166–67)

In his cynical view of the "vast" sector of the public that safely plots its taste along a middle path, cultural commentator H. L. Mencken reiterates many critical and scholarly assessments of what came to be known in the 1920s as "middlebrow" culture. Not quite "vulgar" and real enough to be deemed low culture, nor sophisticated or experimental enough for high culture, the middlebrow ostensibly offends the consumers and producers of both. Just as deleterious, according to Mencken, is the appeal of the middlebrow to sheltered, unoriginal consumers—the "money-in-pocket" masses—which is enough to disqualify it from "true" art.

Like most cultural classifications, the term *middlebrow* defies single or simple definition. As it came of age in the twentieth century and flowered in the 1920s, it has most often been defined by what it is not: lacking the cachet and edginess of high culture, the middlebrow has also been perceived to be in want of the authenticity of the low. The middlebrow is associated with other slightly soiled middles, including the middle class and midlife. As such, middlebrow culture has been linked to conservatism, both aesthetic and social, and perceived as analogous to the masses and consumerism. Dwight Macdonald's famous 1960 "Masscult and Midcult," for example, accused the middlebrow of reducing high culture aesthetics to mere consumables.[1] While disseminating principles of the avant garde to the general population would imply a democratization of culture, the middlebrow has been vilified for dictating precisely which aspects of high culture the masses should consume, such as in the case of the grande dame of the middlebrow, the Book-of-the-Month Club.[2]

In her groundbreaking 1992 work, *The Making of Middlebrow Culture*, Joan Shelley Rubin illustrates the ways in which the "midcult" has been scripted as threatening to both the "true art" of high culture and the "authenticity" of mass culture. Denigrated by Virginia Woolf as the "pernicious pest who comes between" (quoted in Rubin xiii), middlebrow culture has until recently been elided by many scholars of twentieth-century American culture who have "perpetuated the conventional dichotomy between 'high' and 'popular' culture, overlooking the interaction that went on between the two" (Rubin xv). The neglected third term in the interaction between high and popular culture was *gendered*: the "pernicious pest" that intervened between high and low was feminized, and the authors of the fiction that "outrage[d] all sense and probability" were often, like Hawthorne's dreaded successfully scribbling women, female. This anthology addresses the neglected aspect of this interaction specifically through an examination of the gendered middlebrow. We focus on a representative group of women writers of diverse class, ethnic, and racial backgrounds, politics, career paths, and domestic situations to illuminate the unique contributions of the commercially viable, "quasi-respectable," serious yet "pernicious" authors whom we deem *middlebrow moderns*.

While critics have fruitfully explored the interplay between high culture and a variety of popular sources such as advertising, popular music, and vaudeville, the naturalized binary opposition of high and low has encouraged critics to ignore the popular middlebrow fiction that was, in fact, consumed by a majority of readers. Moreover, much modernist scholarship that includes a study of the popular does so in order to provide new understandings of canonical texts rather than to shed light on the less canonical. Instead of using middlebrow culture as a straw horse for high culture, this anthology grapples with the middlebrow on its own terms, uncovering a richly textured area of cultural production. This study also recognizes the natural interdisciplinarity of the middlebrow as it highlights a group of women writers who successfully made transitions between literature and the burgeoning technologies of magazine publication, book clubs, advertising, radio, and film, institutions that deliberately targeted "middle" audiences for maximum distribution and profits. Additionally, this volume provides an early-twentieth-century counterpart to major feminist scholarship of the previous two decades, which revised the role of women's nineteenth-century sentimental fiction in the American canon. Much as feminist critics intervened in the masculinist discourse of nineteenth-century American letters by heralding the previously scorned sentimental writers, our work seeks to reframe the American modern period in terms of popular women's writing.

Attention to the popular women writers of the 1920s prompts a reconsideration of the way modernist literary studies have not only reinforced hierarchies of culture but also segregated and separated authors from differing ethnic and racial groups. Middlebrow literature, when it receives critical attention, is usually defined as a principally white and Protestant literary phenomenon. However, many authors who gained the attention of the "majority readers" (quoted in Rubin xii) of the 1920s came from a diverse set of social, racial, ethnic, and regional backgrounds. Despite the differences in their roots, middlebrow writers were hardly ethnically exclusive in their approaches, calling upon immigrant culture, the vogue for African-American expression, and the local color tradition of American literature as sources for their material. Fannie Hurst and Edna Ferber, for example, were both products of midwestern German Jewish culture. In their work, however, they treated questions of Jewish assimilation (Ferber's *Fanny Herself*), problems of racial passing (Hurst's *Imitation of Life* and Ferber's *Show Boat*), and working-class and ethnic disenfranchisement (Hurst's *Lummox* and Ferber's *Giant*, among others).

Many popular women writers of the era also maintained active cross-racial and -ethnic dialogues and exploited the possibility of multiple ethnic identifications: Anzia Yezierska developed relationships with Zona Gale and Dorothy Canfield Fisher, while Chinese-Canadian writers Edith and Winnifred Eaton wrote under the Chinese pseudonym Sui Sin Far and the Japanese-sounding Onoto Watanna, respectively. While an examination of material history—author interviews, correspondence, and reviews— reveals the degree of racial, ethnic, and regional intermingling that informed the literary production of the era, few studies have directly engaged such comparisons. Studies juxtaposing Anglo-American modernism and the literary output of the Harlem Renaissance (Michael North's *The Dialect of Modernism* and Ann Douglas's *Terrible Honesty: Mongrel Manhattan in the 1920s*, among them) have turned critical attention to the black-white interactions that characterized both Anglo-American and Harlem Renaissance experimentalism, but with the effect of erasing the ethnic contributions to the literary culture of the era. On the other hand, a few feminist studies of early-twentieth-century U.S. literature have argued for the common political concerns and rhetorical strategies linking women writers across differences of race, class, ethnicity, and region; among these are Elizabeth Ammons's *Conflicting Stories: American Women Writers at the Turn into the Twentieth Century* and Carol Batker's *Reforming Fictions: Native, African, and Jewish American Women's Literature and Journalism in the Progressive Era.* While *Conflicting Stories* makes an important intervention into the masculinist tradition of modernism that would ignore these writers altogether, its relative inattention to material history prohibits the book from demonstrating the extent of 1920s women writers' redefinition of the modern. Batker builds on the work of Ammons and others but reintroduces class into the analysis of comparative women writers. *Middlebrow Moderns* proceeds in the direction that these works have suggested but broadens their comparison by examining writers from the wide variety of professional and class positions that constituted the middle—magazine short story writers, popular novelists, and Hollywood scenarists, among others. By bringing together popular women writers of a variety of backgrounds and working in a variety of media, this collection sheds new light on the cross-racial, -class, and -ethnic engagements that characterized the 1920s literary marketplace.

Middlebrow Moderns consolidates emergent scholarship on these women authors, shifting the focus of this early period from high modernist paradigms by illuminating these writers' significant contributions to the culture of the era. As a group, they participated in and advanced the cultural debate over domesticity and women's work, marriage and reproduction, assimilation, consumer culture and capitalism, and the rise of new technologies. Creating a multifaceted literary response to the pressing issues of their era, these authors negotiated a delicate balance of commercial success and (albeit grudging) critical respect. Neither "high" literary producers nor "low" dime-novel creators, the women writers we attend to here succeeded in the marketplace: published by major presses, they made bestseller lists and bridged gaps in an audience increasingly fragmented by economic, racial, ethnic, and regional differences.

Edith Wharton comments on the rise of middlebrow fiction through her novelist hero Vance Weston in her 1929 novel *Hudson River Bracketed.* As Wharton writes, Weston's first novel, *Instead,* "was one of those privileged books which somehow contrive to insinuate themselves between the barriers of coterie and category, and are as likely to be found in the hands of the commuter hurrying to his office as of the wild-haired young men in gaudy pullovers theorizing the void" (309). Weston's bridging of "coterie and category" places the author in a dilemma relatively new to the twentieth century: the commercially successful serious artist. As the "high" modernists sniffed, such a category could not exist; to be a serious artist, one could not, should not, or would not be commercially successful.

In both content and style, *Hudson River Bracketed* registers Wharton's struggle, from the early 1920s on, to adapt her own work to a changing literary marketplace. Magazine deadlines for *Hudson River Bracketed* intensified the pressure on Wharton to write quickly; in response, she overwrote, producing a novel of over 500 pages that failed to achieve critical success (Lewis 490–92). Although Wharton had been celebrated by critics of the previous two decades, her reputation among the literary elite suffered in the 1920s even as she achieved increasing popular acceptance. Wharton's reading of Vance Weston's short-lived fame voices her ambivalence about the costs of her commercial success: the vogue of *Instead* engenders Vance's artistic stagnation, preventing him from finishing his next novel. Unlike her hero, however, Wharton continued to produce more work and also sustained negotiations with the two worlds of readers that consumed her books.

Wharton's case illuminates some of the ways in which writers of her time could and did permeate the boundaries of "high" and "low" in their writing and thinking. For example, though she was traditionally viewed as an adamant foe of popular culture, Wharton deliberately appropriated the themes and strategies of popular fiction writers, particularly as she realized that the production and consumption of literature were in flux. In her identification of Anita Loos's popular 1925 work *Gentlemen Prefer Blondes* as "the great American novel" (Lewis 468), she displays her ability to bridge a variety of tastes, engage a range of audiences. Wharton's engagement, however pessimistic, with the blurring of literary boundaries was hardly unique to her cultural moment or, even more importantly, to the very visible group of middlebrow women writers who rose to fame at her side—writers like Loos, Fannie Hurst, and Edna Ferber. While writing scores of best-selling novels and often attaining critical success, many of these writers also enjoyed a potent cultural authority: Eleanor Roosevelt once named Dorothy Canfield Fisher as the most influential woman in America.

In his seminal work on modernism and mass culture, Andreas Huyssen maintains that "[m]odernism constituted itself through a conscious strategy of exclusion, an anxiety of contamination by its other," an "engulfing" mass culture gendered as feminine (vii). In the 1920s United States, this "engulfing" mass in part took the form of middlebrow women authors, whose very success triggered their rejection by the canonical writers of their time as well as by recent scholars of the early twentieth century. As critics have noted, high modernists had a range of motives for their rejection of both women and the popular. For instance, Ann Douglas argues that male modernist authors, guided by their fear of the Victorian matriarch, repudiated women through a persistent rhetoric of matricide (*Terrible Honesty* 217–53). In other cases, male authors were motivated by economic competition with women writers and the pressure to conform to the needs of a mass that was also perceived as "engulfing"—the purchasing audience for popular fiction, traditionally cast in feminine terms. F. Scott Fitzgerald tartly ascribed the commercial failure of *The Great Gatsby* to the power of female readers and consumers: "the book contains no important woman character and women control the fiction market at present" (Fitzgerald 203).

While Fitzgerald shared his awareness of the feminization of the 1920s literary marketplace with other cultural commentators of his day, scholarly studies of the modernist cultural moment continue to dismiss popular women writers of the 1920s. Critical analyses such as Michael North's *The Dialect of Modernism* and *Reading 1922: A Return to the Scene of the Modern* and Walter Benn Michaels's *Our America: Nativism, Modernism, Pluralism* provide pivotal examples of modernist scholarship's exclusion of the middlebrow. Such elisions harbor significant consequences for North's and Benn Michaels's analyses: for example, the novels of Edna Ferber, which posit class, ethnic, and racial miscegenation as intrinsic to the creation of the modern American family and nation, call into question Benn Michaels's reading of the racist logic of modernist American fiction. North's vision of the literary marketplace of 1922, metaphorized in an imaginary bookstore, reveals a similar dismissal of the gendered popular:

> I began to imagine myself in a bookstore of the time, browsing among tables containing both *The Waste Land* and Willa Cather's *One of Ours*, or *Babbitt* next to *Jacob's Room*. And though this would have been possible at the time, it is now a little disorienting to think about, because *our way of looking at modern literature so thoroughly insulates such works from one another*. Of course, this conjectural bookstore would also have had newspapers and magazines, not to mention popular novels like Zane Grey's *The Wander of the Wasteland*, which a reader could have taken home along with Eliot to get a different perspective on wandering in the desert (*Reading 1922* v; emphasis added).

North rightly notes how generic and national boundaries have discouraged comparative examination of such authors as Eliot and Cather, Lewis and Woolf; simultaneously, however, he repeats similarly prohibitive hierarchies of culture. The ubiquitous magazines North cites might have contained Wharton's 1922 novel *The Glimpses of the Moon*. Among the popular novels so pervasive as "not to [be] mention[ed]" might have been Edna Ferber's *Gigolo* and Mary Roberts Rinehart's best-selling *The Breaking Point*, Johanna Spyri's *Heidi*, and Frances Hodgson Burnett's *The Head of the House of Coombe*. Fannie Hurst's short story collection *The Vertical City* premiered in 1922, as did Zona Gale's play *Uncle Jimmy*. North's admission of the popular only in the form of best-selling Western author Zane Grey erases the majority of female authors as well as the middle-class female consumers who browsed the bookstores of the early 1920s. As Eric Lofroth notes, "the audience for the best-selling novel [was] predominantly female, and this is indicated also in a study from the 1930s, based on library borrowings, which gives testimony to the fact that contemporary best-selling authors had a much higher proportion of readers—especially housewives—than did the average author" (17). However, canonical modernist scholarship has rarely made use of such lessons, repeating the binaries of high/low and male/female instead.

The middle-class female readers Lofroth identifies found themselves the objects of the burgeoning middlebrow culture industry of the 1920s, which proposed to use literature as a vehicle for self-improvement, to protect literary and cultural values in a moment of enormous cultural flux, and, perhaps most importantly, to sell books in an increasingly fluid literary marketplace. The essays in this anthology follow the direction of Joan Shelley Rubin and Janice Radway's *A Feeling for Books: The Book-of-the-Month Club, Literary Taste, and Middle-Class Desire* (1997) by exploring the nascent culture industry that promoted the cause of the middlebrow author. Rubin begins the work of examining the roles, purposes, and authority of middlebrow culture and its purveyors, emphasizing its roots in the nineteenth-century genteel tradition. Radway delves further into the history of the Book-of-the-Month Club, demonstrating its centrality in the production of middle-class American readers through the racial, gender, and ethnic politics of the works it made available.

This anthology reinforces the important work of such critics as Radway and Rubin but extends it into a productive and very necessary direction by exploring the complexities of a gendered literary field. In so doing, it follows in the direction of the rediscovery of sentimental fiction in the 1970s and 1980s, and the debate over the role of sentimentality in nineteenth-century American culture provides an important scholarly backdrop for many of the essays in this volume. In *The Feminization of American Culture*, Ann Douglas castigated the female sentimental writers of the mid-nineteenth century on for their aesthetic and political conservatism; Jane Tompkins, in *Sensational Designs: The Cultural Work of American Fiction, 1790–1860*, argued that sentimental women's fiction engaged in a general subversion of dominant cultural ideals. In the conclusion of her work, Tompkins responded to the question often posed to scholars of less-canonical texts—"But is it any good?"—by showing the ideological assumptions embedded in aesthetic dismissal of popular women writers. Tompkins usefully moved the debate over female popular literary production beyond New Critical conventions; simultaneously, however, she risked suggesting a subversive power inherent to popular texts, many of which endorse the power of the dominant culture rather than critique it. The authors we explore in this study inhabit a space between the embrace of experimentalism and ambiguity considered characteristic of modernism—and of the New Criticism that elevated it—and the critique of the dominant culture Tompkins locates in the popular. They used their sentimental inheritance not only to appeal to conventional readers but also to "mask the aspiration" their texts "embody to generate a public sphere of opinion and culture making" (Berlant 399). Like the sentimentalists, middlebrow female novelists argued that the personal was indeed political, elevating the feminized culture of feeling as a forum for change over the masculinized sphere of politics. Until recently, however, the liminal status of the works our contributors explore in *Middlebrow Moderns* has forced them into ill-fitting dichotomies and culturally devalued them. Adding them into the critical mix helps us to better understand the full range of literary production and consumption of this period.

It is important to note that despite their popular success—which such highbrow writers as Fitzgerald envied and resented—these women writers simultaneously voiced serious artistic intent. For example, biographer Brooke Kroeger reports that when Fannie Hurst first met Willa Cather, she was as affected by her comments on her stories "as if a buzz saw were cutting me" (35). While all the writers our contributors highlight were best-selling authors—many for decades—a number were awarded Pulitzer Prizes (Ferber for *So Big* and Zona Gale for *Miss Lulu Bett*, among them), attesting to the kind of critical respect they earned. Furthermore, even as these writers assessed the interests of a popular audience, they simultaneously tapped into the most important literary movements in the United States. For example, several experimented with language and vernacular, as in the uneducated but worldly flapperspeak of Anita Loos's Lorelei, the Yidgin of Anzia Yezierska's Lower East Side immigrants, and the Steinian stream of consciousness of much of Fannie Hurst's fiction. Despite their engagement with linguistic experimentation, they remained wary of what Huyssen characterizes as other hallmarks of the modernist aesthetic— "the rejection of all classical systems of representation, the effacement of 'content,' the erasure of subjectivity and authorial voice, the repudiation of likeness and verisimilitude" (54). Although the legacy of modernist studies has been to divorce artistic and popular success, the writers whose work we investigate here often successfully married the two, complicating the modernist cliché of the inverse relationship between artistic quality and popular reception.

These writers did not suffer from an anxiety of influence from the contaminating popular, as high modernists like Eliot and Pound evinced in their dismissive approach to popular culture (see North, *The Dialect of Modernism*); rather, theirs was a confluence of ideas, plots, settings, and themes born of necessity. Sensitive to market demands, popular women writers of the 1920s did not hesitate to capitalize on the success of their more-established counterparts. For example, Anzia Yezierska was often represented as an immigrant author who wrote in a ghetto fiction niche. Yet she was also interviewed by best-selling middlebrow author Gertrude Atherton and portrayed herself as a reader of Fannie Hurst and Edna Ferber. Through these associations, Yezierska attempted to market herself as an author of popular women's fiction rather than one solely limited to ethnic themes and settings. Harlem Renaissance novelist Jessie Fauset, known primarily as a representative of that movement's rear guard, also enjoyed a strategic, although ambivalent relationship with Zona Gale, whose preface to Fauset's 1931 novel *The Chinaberry Tree* mediated Fauset's efforts to portray the black middle class for an Anglo-American literary marketplace.

The essays in *Middlebrow Moderns* situate the popular female authors of the 1920s in a variety of social dimensions. Our contributors show how middlebrow women novelists explored early-twentieth-century national and local politics, touching on such issues as Western expansion, Native American assimilation, and miscegenation; negotiated roles in the exploding mass media cultures of magazines and Hollywood; and articulated gendered concerns over the rising culture of consumption. While the categories provide a means of identifying major trends in middlebrow women's fiction, they are not rigid; the authors our contributors study participated in a wide range of cultural arenas, making efforts at categorization provisional at best. For example, Edna Ferber contributed to the construction of the West as a region in her novel *Cimarron* (1930), responded to the epic narrative of the West provided by 1920s Hollywood, and critiqued the rise of 1920s consumer culture through her heroine, Sabra Cravat. Ferber provides just one example of how middlebrow women writers traversed boundaries of professional situation, genre, ethnicity, and class position. The other authors our volume highlights demonstrate that Ferber was hardly alone in her multiple engagements.

The first part, "Placemaking: Gender, Genre, and Geography," illuminates 1920s middlebrow women authors' concerns with a range of social spaces, from the rural American village at risk of extinction in the age of urbanization, to the mythic notion of the West propagated by masculinist and expansionist thinkers, to a fictional extranational space, Japan. As Thomas Peyser has argued, the late nineteenth and early twentieth century formed an era of globalization much like our own, in which "the unprecedentedly global expansion of Western technological, economic, and imperial systems" called the "very concept of a distinct national identity" into question (4). The spaces middlebrow authors chart are marked by qualities quite similar to those found in the contemporary global arena: conflicts between white expansionists and indigenous people, a rise in immigration, a proliferation of Western commodities, a vogue for tourism, and a passion for the "exotic." Importantly, however, middlebrow novelists located global tensions on home ground as well as abroad, engaging the reader through expected tropes of local color—seen by many scholars as characteristic of the American feminine literary tradition—while simultaneously deconstructing these nostalgic or exotic spaces.

Donna Campbell's "'Written with a Hard and Ruthless Purpose': Rose Wilder Lane, Edna Ferber, and Middlebrow Regional Fiction" explores how these two authors imbued politically charged ideas within what otherwise appear to be nostalgic regionalist texts dedicated to romanticizing the "wild" West. In her Western novels, Lane, Campbell argues, addresses the paradox of "free land" (deflating expectations, perhaps, of the growing back-to-the-land movements, as well as the Depression-era lament of loss and the closing of the frontier) and articulates her own libertarian political philosophy. Ferber's *Cimarron*, often read by contemporary critics as a mediocre attempt at the Western genre, was actually intended as a satire in which the sentimental Prairie Madonna figure, the original Western martyr and mother, is especially parodied.

If the West as imaginary space preoccupies Lane and Ferber, Midwesterner Zona Gale zeros in on the politics of small-town life. Deborah Williams's "The Cosmopolitan Regionalism of Zona Gale's Friendship Village" examines Gale's sensitivity to both racial politics and the literary, linked within an imaginary hamlet called Friendship Village. Gale's version of regionalism, filtered as it is through a progressive political agenda that includes firm commitments to pacifism, feminism, and both social and racial equality, results in a nascent form of cosmopolitanism. "Regionalism," thus configured, is no longer tied to a particular town or country but becomes instead a way of viewing the world as a set of potential neighbors.

This section concludes with Dominika Ferens's "Winnifred Eaton's 'Japanese' Novels as a Field Experiment." Ferens asserts that the mixed-race Chinese-Canadian author, writing under the pseudonym Onoto Watanna, created a fictionalized Japan where she could concoct Mendelian couplings of Asian and white characters. Watanna employed the tropes of exoticist and romance fiction to work out racial and gender conflicts that she experienced in North America but that would bear discussion neither in the realist mode nor in an American setting. In her imaginary Japan, Eaton conducts multiple experiments in sexual selection, creating misceg-enated couples and mixed-race progeny that are unprecedented in U.S. fiction and that allow her to question the rigid boundaries ascribed to racial and cultural identity. Demonstrating the complicity of the romance genre—with its emphasis on forbidden passions—with the scientific rhetoric of race, blood, and heredity that proliferated at the turn of the century, Ferens restores an underappreciated political resonance to Watanna's fiction.

Part II, "The Middlebrow and Magazine Culture," highlights the significance of the mass-market periodical industry to American culture, looking specifically at the relationship between the genre of the woman's magazine and the emergence of the extremely well-paid popular magazine writer. As Ann Douglas points out, innovations in printing technology had occasioned the rise of the woman's magazine as early as the 1850s (*Feminization* 229). Even then, the sales of women's magazines such as *Godey's Lady's Book* far outpaced those of more highbrow publications such as *Harper's* or the *North American Review*. By the 1920s, such women's magazines as *The Delineator, Metropolitan,* and *Good Housekeeping* provided certain women authors with huge salaries and immense reading audiences—incentives that even critically acclaimed novelists had a hard time passing up. While Wharton, for example, chafed at the quick turnaround time magazine publishing required, she happily commanded as much as $40,000 a piece for the serial publication of her 1920s novels (Lewis 473).

Some novelists used periodicals as a route to achieving huge popular success: the editor of *Good Housekeeping*, for example, claimed that Kathleen Norris's name on the cover would sell 50,000 magazines ("Reminiscences"). However, magazine culture emblematized the double bind of commercial success for popular women writers of the 1920s; urged to shape their fiction to fit the demands of a periodical-reading public, they were then accused by critics of "grinding out" or recycling their material (Lewis 484).

Maureen Honey perceives an important blurring of generic boundaries as best-selling novelists were signed by major periodicals to serialize work before it was published. In "Feminist New Woman Fiction in Periodicals of the 1920s," Honey demonstrates that fiction in magazines like the *Ladies' Home Journal* reflected traditional gender ideologies as well as ideas concomitant with the independent New Woman figure.

Janice Radway argues that such middlebrow fare served to placate the middle class in their sterile lives under capitalism; this genre allowed readers to avoid upsetting social and political topics like race relations (13). In an important contrast to Radway, however, Jaime Harker points out that middlebrow advocates, such as Dorothy Canfield Fisher, a Ph.D. in literature and a social reformer as well as a popular novelist, believed that middlebrow institutions and aesthetics had liberatory potential. Harker's essay, "Progressive Middlebrow: Dorothy Canfield, Women's Magazines, and Popular Feminism in the Twenties," documents the political possibilities of women's magazine culture, demonstrating that Canfield's serialized women's fiction articulated a popular feminism distinct from the magazine's consumerist agenda. Harker identifies Canfield, known today primarily for her stewardship of the Book-of-the-Month Club in the 1930s, as an important heir to the pragmatism of William James and John Dewey. In Harker's reading of Canfield's novel *The Brimming Cup*, Canfield reshapes pragmatist thinking to imbue middle-class female daily life—deemed the height of banality by highbrow thinkers—with renewed social relevance.

The material content and layout of mass-market magazines also affect the content of the fiction published in their pages. Sarah Churchwell asserts that popular women's narrative often seems to mirror—even as it may critique or subvert—the strategies of the advertising campaigns upon which its publication depends. In her essay "'Lost Among the Ads': *Gentlemen Prefer Blondes* and the Politics of Imitation," Churchwell identifies a multidirectional flow between the advertising that covered the pages of *Harper's Bazaar*, in which Anita Loos's 1925 novel first appeared, and

Loos's narrative itself, in which narrative and advertising come to resemble each other. Jennifer Wicke and Simone Weil Davis have noted that early-twentieth-century fiction often discloses parallels with advertising through its depiction of commodity culture. As Churchwell repositions Loos's novel in the context of its serial publication, boundaries between novel and ad blur; the ad pages of *Harper's* enhance our attention to Lorelei Lee's compulsive acquisition of commodities.

The third part, "Women behind the Screens," explores the relationship between middlebrow women authors and the Hollywood studios that solicited and bought their work. Hollywood, like the mass-market women's magazine, transformed and translated women's narratives. By now it is almost a cliché that authors maintained ambivalent alliances with this giant of popular culture. However, Hollywood did help keep literary careers alive, and film adaptations were essential to the dissemination of middlebrow narratives that had the potential to complicate standard ideas about American identity. Moreover, Hollywood's success in its classic period was partly due to its growing female audiences, which constituted the majority of ticket buyers by the 1920s.[3] Films of this era often engaged specifically female consumers, inciting their fantasies, and, as historian Nan Enstad comments, generating "new resources for the creation of public identities" (163). A top-ten film list of a survey from 1923 features a number of films originally penned by middlebrow women authors, including Edith Hull's *The Sheik* (1921) and Fannie Hurst's *Humoresque* (1920) (see Koszarski 29). Hollywood adaptations of middlebrow novels often softened or completely altered the radical potential available to original readers; nonetheless, the cross-class appeal of film rendered these narratives even more accessible and garnered greater fame (or sometimes infamy) for their authors.

In "Edna Ferber's *Cimarron*, Cultural Authority, and 1920s Western Historical Narratives," Heidi Kenaga examines how Edna Ferber's Oklahoma novel *Cimarron* and its Academy Award–winning film adaptation can be used to read contemporary debates over authority, authenticity, and the representation of gender in the West. Kenaga shows how Ferber's novel can be viewed as a sophisticated critique of a masculinist tradition of writing about the West, propagated by Theodore Roosevelt, Zane Grey, and Owen Wister, among others. Kenaga explores in particular the effect of Ferber's gender as well as her ethnic and urban affiliations upon the field of Western literary production during the late 1920s and early 1930s, and argues that her work can be understood as a critique of the commemorative process of visual culture.

Through an investigation of the film adaptation of Jewish immigrant author Anzia Yezierska's *Hungry Hearts* by Samuel Goldwyn in 1922, Lisa Botshon parallels the disruptive narrative of the author's ghetto short stories with the process of scripting the film and the final version. Yezierska trafficked in a genre in which setting and "authenticity" were paramount; her narratives, often read as local color, were of particular interest to the Hollywood studio executives. Anxious to sell film via the popularity of an already-known woman author, and wishing to create a product that did not contest the dominant discourse, they neutralized any radicalism found in the writer's published fiction in favor of courting a surer audience.

The final section, "Women and Consumption," explores the role of consumerism in the construction of identity in middlebrow women's narratives. As Elaine Abelson, Rita Felski, and Jennifer Scanlon, among others, have noted, the rise of early-twentieth-century consumer culture—such as the department store—provided women with a measure of access to the public sphere while it concomitantly helped reinforce the idea of women as objects of exchange. For middle-class women of color, however, the pressure to conform to aesthetics of primness in order to avoid the labels of *exotic* or *primitive* mitigated the gratification of consumption. Women's narratives of this era limned the shifting politics and pleasures offered by shopping, both reveling in the possibilities of identity refashioning and cautioning against the futile and powerless role of consumer queen. As Rachel Bowlby notes, the word *consumption* is etymologically linked to the word *consummation* (15), suggesting a displacement of erotic desires in the act of consuming desirable objects. For many popular women writers, consumerism provided a culturally sanctioned means of articulating covert desires for both erotic gratification and economic independence.

In "'An Unwonted Coquetry': The Commercial Seductions of Jessie Fauset's *The Chinaberry Tree*," Susan Tomlinson articulates a nuanced relationship between this African-American writer and the middlebrow. Although conventional critical wisdom has treated Fauset with scorn for her rear-guard position among Harlem Renaissance intellectuals, scholars have recently argued for a more textured understanding of Fauset's literary, editorial, and activist projects. Tomlinson argues against accusations of Fauset's conservatism, showing that her work uniquely lies on a divide between Harlem Renaissance experimentalism and the popular fiction whose forms she appropriates. More specifically, Tomlinson delves into Fauset's depiction of the female consumer as representative of the black middle-class reading audience Fauset hoped to create.

Stephanie Bower's essay, "The Wages of Virtue: Consumerism and

Class Formation in Fannie Hurst's *Back Street*," asks where one might locate a feminist statement within a novel usually considered a melodramatic potboiler. When positioned within early-twentieth-century debates about gender, consumerism, class, and racial identity, Hurst's tale of the fallen woman refuses the usual moralistic condemnation of a woman who translates sexuality into social mobility and offers instead a critique of the sexual economy at the heart of middle-class authority. In *Back Street*, the restraint and self-sacrifice usually celebrated as hallmarks of middle-class authority become a monstrous and ultimately fatal spectacle. Yet Hurst ultimately deflects this critique from class onto race by locating pathological consumption patterns within her Jewish characters. The class transgression often identified with the fallen woman, then, is contained within the biological difference supposedly located within racial categories.

Meredith Goldsmith, in "Shopping to Pass, Passing to Shop: Consumer Self-Fashioning in the Fiction of Nella Larsen," posits that Larsen's fiction compellingly illustrates how black middle-class female identities may be both empowered and jeopardized by acts of consumption. In Larsen's novellas *Quicksand* (1928) and *Passing* (1929), consumerism is linked to the creation of racial identity (in the former) and class identity (in the latter). Goldsmith reads Larsen's poetics of color—especially her descriptions of costume and interior decor—as coding her African-American women characters' desires, and demonstrates how the author challenges the binary of black and white so often ascribed to African-American characters, even while she reminds her readers of the costs of self-fashioning.

While our anthology's exploration of middlebrow culture of the 1920s begins to bridge the gap between the modern and the middlebrow of the early twentieth century, it also illuminates critical understandings of gendered popular culture today. The "culture war" the modernists of the 1920s believed they were waging against the rise of the middlebrow displays some striking parallels with the divisions between high-, low-, and middlebrow culture today. As with the turn into the last century, contemporary technological innovations have fostered the potential democratization of culture, and on the Internet almost any reader may become a critic. Whether posting reviews on Amazon.com, participating in book groups, or developing a web page devoted to his or her own opinions, today's reader of literary fiction possesses an unparalleled opportunity to influence the taste and buying habits of others. The publishing industry has responded to the current proliferation of book clubs by printing reading group guides for literary titles and often attributes the success of midlist books to book club orders (Hall). The Book-of-the-Month Club, believed to have gone the way of "the British royal family and other preposterous pleasures" (Sheed 92) after a series of corporate buyouts and mergers, has been revived with Anna Quindlen, former *New York Times* columnist and author of women's fiction, as one of the judges (Kirkpatrick, "New Judges").

No more trenchant evidence exists of the current war against the middle than in the recent flap between Jonathan Franzen, author of the acclaimed novel *The Corrections*, and cultural impresario Oprah Winfrey. In September 2001, Franzen accepted Winfrey's endorsement of the book for her televised book club (which prompted his publisher, Farrar, Straus, and Giroux, to print half a million additional copies), and taped a two-hour segment and interview. Ultimately, however, Franzen refused to appear on her show, claiming that a spot in the guest chair was inconsistent with his place in the "high art literary tradition" (Kirkpatrick, "'Oprah' Gaffe"). It emerged that Franzen made his decision based on gender as well as class considerations. As he told NPR commentator Terry Gross, he feared that an appearance on *Oprah* would "alienate male readers," and he noted that "it is a source of pain that there are interesting male writers . . . who don't find an audience" because female reader-consumers ostensibly dominate the literary marketplace (Fresh Air, 15 October 2001). Franzen's comments drew a firestorm of discussion from critics on both sides of the cultural divide; Winfrey withdrew her invitation, and the author engaged in a number of defensive apologies. This time, the battle between high and middle-brow culture ended in a stalemate: while many critics supported Winfrey and castigated Franzen in the press (including such otherwise highbrow cultural commentators as Harold Bloom), Franzen won the National Book Award. A few months later, Winfrey retired from the book club business, claiming that it was too difficult to find good books to promote every month (Kirkpatrick, "Oprah to Curtail").

The Franzen-Winfrey tug-of-war reads like an uncanny replay of the culture wars of the 1920s. A modishly bespectacled white male novelist struggles to establish himself as a writer by aligning himself with American male postmodernism in the DeLillo-Pynchon-Gaddis vein. In his effort to appeal to male readers and claim his own place in the "high-art literary tradition," he engages in a compensatory rejection of an African-American female multimillionaire, whose fortune rests largely on her appeal to middle-class women. Ironically, however, the success of *The Corrections* depends largely on that middle-class audience itself—for Franzen's novel, like Vance Weston's *Instead*, "bridges coterie and category" in its ability to engage a wide readership. Experimental, but resisting radical formal innovation, focusing intensely on marriage and family relations, and engaged with pressing social problems, Franzen's novel is full of the stuff that middlebrow fiction—and particularly, women's middlebrow fiction—is made of. Possibly, Franzen's ambivalence toward Winfrey suggests not only the predictable high-cultural defense against the dominance of scribbling, reading, and purchasing women, but the consequences of an attempted masculinist incursion into a gendered middlebrow literary marketplace.

In the failed negotiation between Franzen and Winfrey, one might glimpse the shadow of several gendered high-middle pairs of the 1920s: Mencken and Loos (who submitted the manuscript of *Gentlemen Prefer Blondes* to Mencken's magazine, where it was rejected), Fitzgerald and Ferber (whose success Fitzgerald envied and derided in his correspondence), and Sinclair Lewis and Dorothy Canfield Fisher (whom Lewis called "the worst sort of liar"), among numerous others. Each of these women writers struggled to claim a voice within a largely male, aesthetically exclusive literary establishment; each bridged the chasm of popular and critical acclaim, yet never received the level of respect such an achievement typically commands. These women writers, like the others this volume considers, emerged from the margins of U.S. culture and gravitated toward the middle, using the vehicles of magazine fiction, the Book-of-the-Month Club, and the emergent Hollywood cinema as tools of their mobility. Occupying the gap between middlebrow and modern, they concomitantly called that gap into question. The critical analysis of their work that our collection initiates reveals the centrality of women's writing to the making of American modernist culture.

Notes

1. See Dwight Macdonald's two articles "Masscult and Midcult I" and "Masscult and Midcult II," both published in the *Partisan Review*.
2. The term *middlebrow* also denotes a certain normalcy of "race" and class in that highbrow and lowbrow were metaphorical comparisons between taste and the height of one's eyebrows in the 1880s. *Highbrows* were, of course, privileged whites, while *lowbrows* were the less-tasteful, less-evolved dark others. See the introduction to Rubin's *The Making of Middlebrow Culture*.
3. Richard Koszarski reminds us that we do not have accurate statistics for filmgoing audiences of this era, but he uncovers two telling accounts: "In 1920 Stephen Bush reported in the *New York Times* that 60 percent of film audiences were women, but in 1927 the *Moving Picture World* set the figure as high as 83 percent" (30).

Works Cited

Abelson, Elaine. *When Ladies Go A-Thieving: Middle-Class Shoplifters in the Victorian Department Store*. New York: Oxford University Press, 1989.

Banta, Martha. *Imaging American Women: Idea and Ideals in Cultural History.* New York: Columbia University Press, 1987.

Batker, Carol J. *Reforming Fictions: Native, African, and Jewish American Women's Literature and Journalism in the Progressive Era.* New York: Columbia University Press, 2000.

Bauer, Dale. *Edith Wharton's Brave New Politics.* Madison, Wisc.: University of Wisconsin Press, 1995.

Bayles, Martha. "Imus, Oprah, and the Literacy Elite." *New York Times Book Review,* 29 August 1999.

Berlant, Lauren. "National Brands/National Bodies: *Imitation of Life.*" *Comparative American Identities.* New York: Routledge, 1991.

———. "Pax Americana: The Case of *Show Boat.*" In *Cultural Institutions of the Novel.* Ed. Deirdre Lynch and William B. Warner. Durham, N.C.: Duke University Press, 1996.

Bowlby, Rachel. *Shopping with Freud.* New York: Routledge, 1993.

Butler, Judith. *Gender Trouble: Feminism and the Subversion of Identity.* New York: Routledge, 1999.

Carby, Hazel. *Reconstructing Womanhood: The Emergence of the Afro-American Woman Novelist.* New York: Oxford University Press, 1987.

Clark, Suzanne. *Sentimental Modernism: Women Writers and the Revolution of the Word.* Bloomington: Indiana University Press, 1991.

Cvetkovich, Ann. *Mixed Feelings: Feminism, Mass Culture, and Victorian Sensationalism.* New Brunswick, N.J.: Rutgers University Press, 1992.

Davis, Simone Weil. *Living Up to the Ads: Gender Fictions of the 1920s.* Durham, N.C.: Duke University Press, 2000.

Douglas, Ann. *The Feminization of American Culture.* New York: Doubleday, 1988.

———. *Terrible Honesty: Mongrel Manhattan in the 1920s.* New York: Farrar, Straus & Giroux, 1995.

Eakin, Emily. "Jonathan Franzen's Big Book." *New York Times Sunday Magazine,* 2 September 2001.

Enstad, Nan. *Ladies of Labor, Girls of Adventure: Working Women, Popular Culture, and Labor Politics at the Turn of the Twentieth Century.* New York: Columbia University Press, 1999.

Felski, Rita. *The Gender of Modernity.* Cambridge: Harvard University Press, 1995.

Freedman, Estelle. "The New Woman: Changing Views of Women in the 1920s." *Journal of American History* 61, no. 2 (1974): 372–93.

Hall, Brian. "The Group." *New York Times Book Review,* 6 June 1999.

Hart, James D. *The Popular Book: A History of America's Literary Taste.* Berkeley: University of California Press, 1961.

Hegeman, Susan. "Taking *Blondes* Seriously." *American Literary History* 7, no. 3 (1995): 525–54.

"Helen Thompson Dreyfus: Reminiscences of the James Alden Thompson Family." Interviewed by Carla Ehat and Anne Kent, 2 February 1979. Ed. Marilyn L. Geary. http://countylibrary.marin.org/crm/thompson.pdf.

Heller, Adele, and Lois Rudnick, eds. *1915, The Cultural Moment: The New Politics, the New Woman, the New Psychology, the New Art, and the New Theater in America.* New Brunswick, N.J.: Rutgers University Press, 1991.

Huyssen, Andreas. *After the Great Divide: Modernism, Mass Culture, Postmodernism.* Bloomington: Indiana University Press, 1986.

Hyman, Paula E. *Gender and Assimilation in Modern Jewish History: The Roles and Representation of Women.* Seattle: University of Washington Press, 1995.

Jefferson, Margo. "There Goes the Neighborhood." *New York Times Book Review,* 25 November 2001.

Koszarski, Richard. *An Evening's Entertainment: The Age of the Silent Feature Picture, 1915–1928.* Berkeley: University of California Press, 1990.

Kirkpatrick, David. "New Judges and Niche Marketing Are Part of a Comeback Plan." *New York Times,* 28 June 2001.

———. "'Oprah' Gaffe by Franzen Draws Ire and Sales." *New York Times,* 29 October 2001.

———. "Oprah to Curtail 'Book Club' Picks, and Authors Weep." *New York Times,* 6 April 2002.

Ledger, Sally. *The New Woman: Fiction and Feminism at the Fin de Siècle.* Manchester, U.K.: Manchester University Press, 1997.

Lewis, R. W. B. *Edith Wharton: A Biography.* New York: Fromm, 1985.

Lofroth, Eric. *A World Made Safe: Values in American Best Sellers, 1895–1920.* Stockholm: Uppsala, 1983.

Macdonald, Dwight. "Masscult and Midcult." *Partisan Review* 27, no. 2 (1960): 203–33.

———. "Masscult and Midcult: II." *Partisan Review* 27, no. 4 (1960): 589–631.

Michaels, Walter Benn. *Our America: Nativism, Modernism, and Pluralism.* Durham, N.C.: Duke University Press, 1995.

North, Michael. *The Dialect of Modernism.* New York: Oxford University Press, 1994.

———. *Reading 1922: A Return to the Scene of the Modern.* New York: Oxford University Press, 1999.

Peyser, Thomas. *Utopia and Cosmopolis: Globalization in the Era of American Literary Realism.* Durham, N.C.: Duke University Press, 1998.

Prose, Francine. "A Wasteland of Their Own." *New York Times Magazine,* 13 February 2000.

Radway, Janice. *A Feeling for Books: The Book-of-the-Month Club, Literary Taste, and Middle-Class Desire.* Chapel Hill: University of North Carolina Press, 1997.

Raub, Patricia. *Yesterday's Stories: Popular Women's Novels of the Twenties and Thirties.* Westport, Conn.: Greenwood, 1994.

Rubin, Joan Shelley. *The Making of Middlebrow Culture.* Chapel Hill: University of North Carolina Press, 1992.

Ryan, Mary. "The Projection of a New Womanhood: The Movie Moderns in the 1920s." In *Our American Sisters: Women in American Life and Thought.* Ed. Jean E. Friedman and William G. Shade. Boston: Allyn & Bacon, 1976.

Scanlon, Jennifer, ed. *The Gender and Consumer Culture Reader.* New York: New York University Press, 2000.

Sheed, Wilfred. "There Goes the Judge." *Yale Review* 87, no. 1 (1999): 80–92.

Tompkins, Jane. *Sensational Designs: The Cultural Work of American Fiction, 1790–1860.* New York: Oxford University Press, 1985.

Wall, Cheryl. *Women of the Harlem Renaissance.* Bloomington: Indiana University Press, 1995.

Wicke, Jennifer. *Advertising Fictions: Advertising, Literature, and Social Reading.* New York: Columbia University Press, 1990.

Wong, K. Scott, and Sucheng Chan, eds. *Claiming America: Constructing Chinese American Identities During the Exclusion Era.* Philadelphia: Temple University Press, 1998.

I

PLACEMAKING: GENDER, GENRE, AND GEOGRAPHY

"Written with a Hard and Ruthless Purpose": Rose Wilder Lane, Edna Ferber, and Middlebrow Regional Fiction

DONNA CAMPBELL

When Walter Benn Michaels proposed in *Our America* that "the great American modernist texts of the '20s must be understood as deeply committed to the nativist project of racializing the American" (13), his examination left out popular middlebrow novels such as those by Edna Ferber and Rose Wilder Lane, two writers whose novels both complicate and challenge Michaels's assertions. Close contemporaries Lane (1886–1968) and Ferber (1885–1968) carved out careers in journalism and as professional writers of popular fiction before settling on regional fiction. Starting out as a reporter for the *Milwaukee Journal*, Ferber published her first novel, *Dawn O'Hara*, in 1911, and in the following decade she became famous for several story collections—*Roast Beef, Medium* (1913), *Personality Plus* (1914), and *Emma McChesney and Company* (1915)—that examined issues of labor, urban life, and the "New Woman" through the practical eyes of their heroine, middle-aged clothing saleswoman Emma McChesney. Best known today for her collaborative role in writing the "Little House" series of children's books with her mother, Laura Ingalls Wilder, Rose Wilder Lane was far more celebrated than her mother in the 1910s and 1920s, when she worked as a feature writer for the *San Francisco Bulletin* and published serial fiction, travel sketches, and biographies in *Sunset* and other magazines. When Ferber and Lane turned from journalism and short stories to novels in the 1920s, both received not only popular but critical acclaim for their work. Ferber's *So Big* won the Pulitzer Prize in 1925, and a *New York Times* editorial proposed a Pulitzer nomination for Lane's *Free Land* in 1938. In addition, Lane's short fiction had been included in *The Best Short Stories of 1927*, and her "Innocence" was an O. Henry Award–winning story in 1922 (Holtz 280).

Despite their popularity and relative critical acclaim in the 1920s, Ferber and Lane were stigmatized in later decades as writers whose popular fiction catered to sentimental tastes. Their regional novels share the trajectory of the pioneer chronicle: the family or individual moves to a new land and attempts to tame it or the surrounding community, with mixed results. In her novels, Lane adopted a persona of the quintessential insider, one whose pioneer roots reached back to the 1630s and included successive waves of western migration, the most recent of which had led to her birth in a Dakota claim shanty in 1886. It was a constructed identity that ignored her world travel, her restlessness, and her belief that farming promised little more than being "a slave" to livestock. No less a pioneer through her background as a member of one of the few Jewish families in Appleton, Wisconsin, Ferber constructed for herself a position that held in tension an insider's knowledge and an outsider's perspective. Proud of her research and the native knowledge that assured the authenticity of her scenes, Ferber admitted that scenes such as one set in the Chicago produce market were "written purely out of my imagination" (*A Peculiar Treasure* 277). She carefully wrote outsiders as observers into most of her novels, all the while positing a deep complicity and sense of identification between herself and America, which she saw as "the Jew among the nations. It is resourceful, adaptable, maligned, envied, feared, imposed upon" (*A Peculiar Treasure* 10).

From these artificially constructed yet apparently deeply authentic and compelling personae of insider and outsider, both writers inscribed political truths in a nostalgic regionalist context by interrogating the conventions of the genre in which they wrote. First among these is the figure of the "Prairie Madonna," a popular icon of the times pressed into service as an agent of American identity formation. In addition to taking a more realistic look at this figure, Ferber and Lane critique even as they capitalize on the nostalgic pioneer ideology so prevalent in the twenties—Lane by demonstrating the patent falsehood of the myths of free land and endurance on the Great Plains in *Free Land* and Ferber through her misunderstood satiric portrait of "the sunbonnets" and domestic culture in *Cimarron*. Second, they explore 1920s nativism and racism, which Ferber confronts through the theme of miscegenation recast as exogamy or inter-marriage, a vision that suggests tolerance rather than nativist sentiment and that challenges Michaels's theories. A third convention that Ferber and Lane discredit is the national myth about the acquisition of land and wealth. Finally, the American penchant for collecting objects of material and social culture is revealed for what it is—a project that supports a unify-ing narrative of American history but does so through cultural theft and misunderstanding. In these ways, these novelists' representative works, including Ferber's *Cimarron* (1930) and Lane's *Free Land* (1938), reflect on conventional reconstructions of the past through central issues of the twenties and thirties: the complicated legacy of the pioneer myth, the con-troversy over racism and nativism, the national myth of limitless lands, and the exploitation of objects from other cultures.

First, Ferber and Lane challenged ideas of the conventional Western her-oine. Recast as what Sandra L. Myres and others have called the Prairie Madonna, the "sturdy helpmate and civilizer of the frontier" (Myres 2), this figure, often pictured holding a child and framed by the circular open-ing of the covered wagon, graced such portraits as W. D. H. Koerner's 1921 painting *Madonna of the Prairie*. Writing of these images, Annette Stott has traced a progression from the more passive "True Womanhood" icon of the Prairie Madonna to her more active counterpart of the 1890s and later, the New Woman–inspired "Pioneer Woman." The Pioneer Woman's sun-bonnet bespeaks gentility and civilization even as her active poses, fre-quently holding a gun in one hand and a child in the other, attest to her active participation in the project of westward expansion. According to Stott, representation of these women increased during the 1920s, a period in which cultural awareness of and nostalgia for a usable pioneer past also increased. In writing of this period, Brigitte Georgi-Findlay further con-tends that women's Western novels and narratives "seem to fall into two categories: those that continue to dramatize the story of an eastern woman, most often a young bride, going west, and those that describe growing up female in the Old West. . . . Many of these texts locate themselves in refer-ence to the popular literature of the 'wild' West, drawing on its romantic and nostalgic elements at the same time that they aim to revise stereo-types" (286–87).

In two of her pioneer novels of the 1930s, *Let the Hurricane Roar* (1933) and *Free Land* (1938), Rose Wilder Lane employs and critiques these fig-ures of the Western heroine as she explores the mythology of homestead-ing and land settlement that they exemplify. Drawn from tales told by her mother, *Let the Hurricane Roar* is the conventionally celebratory pioneer tale of Charles and Caroline Ingalls. In it, Lane addresses the paradox that both she and her mother avoid confronting in the "Little House" series: that "free land" is an illusion and that the only way to acquire land is to leave it to seek work and money elsewhere. A more complex revision of this essential plot appears in *Free Land,* Lane's last novel before she abandoned writing fiction for books articulating her libertarian philosophy. Based on the experiences of her parents and of her Ingalls grandparents, this novel was Lane's protest against the devaluation of an American tradition of independence that she felt was being undercut by the New Deal. It is a prototypical piece of Great Plains fiction as Diane Quantic defines the genre in *The Nature of the Place:* "the person who attempts to impose his or her will upon the land is overcome by natural disaster, a blizzard, a prairie fire, or a dust storm, and the person who understands the land's potential reaps bountiful harvests" (4). As in *Let the Hurricane Roar* (1933), in *Free Land* Lane transforms the experiences of her father's life—a life that he said had been "mostly disappointments"—into the familiar pioneer surface narrative of persistence and triumph.[1] The protagonist, David Beaton, marries his childhood sweetheart, Mary, and, full of optimism, moves with her out West to take up a claim. Blizzards, droughts, grasshoppers, heat, thunderstorms, horse-thieves, and other natural and man-made disasters plague them, yet at the end of the novel he decides to stay on his land, an ending congruent with the Great Plains myth.

Beneath this surface, however, lies Lane's bleaker, more pessimistic version of the pioneer myth and the Ingalls family story than that shown in the "Little House" books. Written near the time of Wilder's *By the Shores of Silver Lake* (1939) and *The Long Winter* (1940), *Free Land* incorporates situations from both works, but it tells the darker stories that Wilder felt were unsuitable for the children's series. Dipping from generalized myth into history, Lane exposes the frontier as the site not of limitless opportunity but of inescapable violence over contested territories. The Beatons meet a claim jumper who has killed a man, and they rescue a woman who is nearly dead after giving birth on the trail; after she recovers, she tells them that her husband has been killed and their sheep clubbed to death by cattlemen. Another episode tells of the settlers' lynching of the Bordens, fictional counterparts to the real-life Benders of Kansas, who murdered travelers for their possessions and buried children alive in their always-plowed and never-planted garden plot.[2] The disputes over land gain special resonance in the subplot involving the Peters family, Lane's thinly disguised fictional counterpart for the Ingalls family in Wilder's work. Like the Ingallses, the fictional Peters family has been forced to leave their farm in Indian Territory, a farm that they settled because they had word from Washington that it would be opened for white settlers. They share with the Ingallses a similar family composition and life history, dialogue and set phrases ("there's plenty more down cellar in a teacup," for example), and a desperate honesty conflicting with the struggle to escape an equally desperate poverty. However, the turned dresses, short rations, and optimistic "making-do" spirit of the "Little House" books become here a narrative of outgrown and worn-out clothes, starvation rations, and a family stretched to the breaking point, as exemplified in a tense near-confrontation when David and Mr. Peters, the Pa Ingalls character, both want to steal lumber from an abandoned claim shanty.

In addition to using the traditional man-against-nature themes of the pioneer novel, Lane contrasts the Peters and Beaton families to demonstrate the hardships of prairie life. *Free Land* pits the figure of the Prairie Madonna represented by Mary, David's conventional and literal-minded wife, against the New Western "Pioneer Woman" heroine represented by the half-wild Peters daughter, Nettie. First seen carrying a rifle, Nettie represents the prototype well, with her keen blue eyes, tanned skin, braids "like an Indian woman's," and ambition to work as a teacher so that she can help support her family. Realizing his wife Mary's limitations, David feels drawn to Nettie but realizes that he can do nothing: "'It's different, with you. Nettie, I—It's—You're so—' 'I know,' she said again. . . . 'It's one of the things that don't happen'" (*Free Land* 156). The Peters family also serves as a point of economic contrast to the Beatons, who are initially better off but sink fast in the inhospitable prairie environment. The more obvious signs of the Beatons' increasing poverty, such as limited food and patched clothing, affect David less than more subtle markers of a loss of status, such as the humiliation of having a sod-thatched roof, burning cow chips for fuel, and driving oxen instead of horses: "Even then, and back in York State, only the French drove oxen" (180). In the end, the Beatons can only survive when David's father offers to give the struggling family $2,000 as a gift against David's eventual inheritance. Having demolished popular conceptions of free land, of happy marriage with a woman who is a soul mate as well as housemate, and of self-sufficiency, Lane paints a picture so realistic that David's decision to stay on the farm brought protests from readers and reviewers, one of whom criticized the "false ending" as "the only false note" in the story (Holtz 280).

On the surface, Ferber's novel *Cimarron* also fits the pattern of the pioneer myth of the "eastern woman or young bride going west" that Georgi-Findlay describes; yet its compliance with the outward form of the Western heroine's narrative masks the satire that underlies the novel. Sabra Cravat, the heroine, is a conventionally domestic woman who reluctantly accompanies her romantic scapegrace of a husband, Yancey Cravat, to the Oklahoma Territory in 1889.[3] The novel parallels Sabra's growth from helpless tenderfoot to newspaper editor, clubwoman, and congresswoman with Oklahoma's growth from a wild frontier settlement to an oil-rich and prosperous state. Its central conflict lies in the efforts of what Ferber calls "the redoubtable sunbonnets" (*Cimarron* 248) to make "this new frontier town like the old as speedily as possible," even as Yancey, despite bringing law to the community, "tried to make the new as unlike the old as possible" (*Cimarron* 166). The book's action pivots on this central conflict, Sabra's relentless efforts to "civilize" and impose structure on the disorderly town of Osage, and Yancey's defense of the outcasts, among them the retired madam Dixie Lee and the Osage Indians displaced from the town that bears their name. Sabra defeats Yancey in this battle between civilization and frontier, for, late in the work, the narrative voice announces that "the sunbonnets had triumphed" (376).

Reading *Cimarron* as a conventional celebration of Oklahoma and the pioneering spirit, Ferber's reviewers and fans ignored Ferber's ironic tone and the grim humor with which she saw the triumph of the sunbonnets. Celebrating the region had certainly not been part of her plan. Writing to Mary Austin on 17 November 1931, Ferber protested, "I really know absolutely nothing of the Southwest, and have never traveled in it except to go to Oklahoma, briefly. And Oklahoma I hate and loathe, stern and stem, people and habits, towns and country, up and down, forever and ever" (Letter to Mary Austin). As Ferber pointed out in her first autobiography, *A Peculiar Treasure,* "*Cimarron* had been written with a hard and ruthless purpose. It was, and is, a malevolent picture of what is known as American womanhood and American sentimentality. It contains paragraphs and even chapters of satire, and, I am afraid, bitterness, but I doubt that more than a dozen people ever knew this" (339). Readers instead responded with expectations shaped by the conventions of the pioneer narrative: a civilized woman reluctantly comes to a Western land, remaining to tame it into a domestic territory suitable for statehood. This narrative, a staple in popular works from Bess Streeter Aldrich's *A Lantern in Her Hand* (1928) through Gertrude Finney's *The Plums Hang High* (1955), predisposed audiences to read Sabra's story in the same vein. Admiring Sabra Cravat's strength and understanding it as standard-issue pioneer woman grit, Ferber's audience missed the satire. They failed to recognize that Sabra is also indifferent to art and literature, narrow-minded, racist, and utterly conventional.

In addition to sentimentality, Ferber attacked consumerism and the commercial spirit in the novel, but most readers missed this as well. As Ferber pointed out some years later, "In *Cimarron* I wrote a story whose purpose was to show the triumph of materialism over the spirit in America, and I did show it, but perhaps I was too reticent about it. . . . In *So Big* I used the same theme. . . . Same result. Terrific sales; about nine people knew what I was driving at" (Gilbert 312). Ann Romines points out in *Constructing the Little House: Gender, Culture, and Laura Ingalls Wilder* that learning literacy and consumerism together was part of the acculturation process for many pioneer women. The lessons Sabra learns, however, are inadequate to the task of creating true literacy or culture. Nor is Ferber's satire especially subtle when evaluating Sabra's accomplishments. The "triumph of the sunbonnets" really means that the town of Osage learns to create art by transforming humble kitchen appliances from useful and plain to useless and hideous based on the household hints columns Sabra publishes in the local newspaper: "Women all over the country were covering wire bread toasters with red plush, embroidering sulphurous yellow chenille roses on this, tying the whole with satin ribbons and hanging it on the wall to represent a paper rack. . . . They painted the backsides of frying pans with gold leaf and daisies" (167). Worst of all from the perspective of the food-loving Ferber, the sunbonnets had transformed plain cooking into "sophisticated cookery." As Laura Shapiro notes in *Perfection Salad: Women and Cooking at the Turn of the Century*, "The characteristic sweetness of much American cooking was also established during these years" (Shapiro 193) of the early twentieth century, and the forward-looking Sabra's creation of a pineapple and marshmallow salad, a variation on Fannie Farmer's Los Angeles Fruit Salad (Shapiro 194), provokes her hired girl and future daughter-in-law Ruby Big Elk to derision and Yancey to laughter, despair—"Pineapple and marshmallow salad! 'It is all over with the Republic'" (306)—and a permanent exodus from home. Reading *Cimarron* in the context of the era's "scientific" cookery and women's magazines that published household hints and printed recipes for exactly these kinds of fashionably indigestible dishes, readers failed to see Sabra's household improvement campaigns as parodies.

As a parting shot, Ferber concludes the novel with a scene whose significance should not have escaped the book's original readers. Ten Oklahoma millionaires commission a statue of the Spirit of the Oklahoma Pioneer, a monument for which everyone assumes that Sabra Cravat will be the model. Throughout the novel, however, Yancey has staunchly defended the territory's outcasts, the prostitute Dixie Lee and the Osage, fighting for Indian citizenship and property rights during the debates over statehood: "You white men sold them the piece of arid and barren land on which they now live in squalor and misery. . . . Deprived of their tribal laws . . . herded together in stockades like wild animals, robbed, cheated, kicked, hounded from place to place, give them the protection of the country that has taken their country away from them" (279). When Krbecek, the sculptor, hears these tales from Sabra, he instead creates "an heroic figure of Yancey Cravat . . . [and] touching his shoulder for support, the weary, blanketed figure of an Indian" (381), a statue that despite its paternalism focuses the public gaze on the contested issue of land appropriation rather than simply reinforcing the mythic power of the pioneer woman. To Oklahoma readers and reviewers in 1930, the satiric reference should have been abundantly clear, for in the late 1920s large public statues such as August Leimbach's *Madonna of the Trail* and John Gregory's *Pioneer Woman* (1927) proliferated. Indeed, shortly before Ferber made her first trip to Oklahoma in 1928, businessman Ernest W. Marland had commissioned twelve Pioneer Woman statues by different artists. He exhibited the winning design around the United States before it was "cast in a 19-foot monument for Ponca City, Oklahoma" (Stott 316). In parodying the sculpture competition and rewriting its ending, Ferber sets the record straight about the true pioneer hero—Yancey, the defender of Indian rights—and satirizes the twenties nostalgia that venerates the Prairie Madonna without recognizing, let alone disagreeing with, her rigidly conventional and intolerant attitudes.

Ferber also addresses a second defining concept of twenties thought: nativism, which critic John Higham has defined as an "intense opposition to an internal minority on the grounds of its foreign (i.e. 'un-American') connections" (Higham, quoted in Michaels, *Our America*, 2). According to Marjorie Perloff, for Michaels, nativism is a "commitment to the notion that one's identity is defined by racial difference" (Perloff 99) and that this difference makes "the fear of miscegenation and of the reproductive family . . . become powerful" enough to lead to "the homosexual family and the incestuous family" as mechanisms to prevent mixed-race children (99). In readings of some texts not conventionally modernist in subject and style, Michaels works out his theoretical and historical theses; the latter "describes the emergence of a distinctly modern concept of cultural identity" ("American Modernism and the Poetics of Identity" 121), and the former contends that "questions of race and identity are questions of form and representation" (125) rather than simply of history, an extension of the modernist project of making the work coextensive or identical with the thing. In responding to critics Charles Altieri, Marjorie Perloff, and Robert Von Hallberg, Michaels insists on one point in particular that bears closely on the issues that Lane and Ferber discuss: that "no event in the nativist canon was more frequent than sex with an Indian" (Michaels, "Response," 124), an act attempted so that children could be "as native as their native American parent" even if this connection exists only by association. Ferber confronts the nativism of the 1920s in several regional novels through the theme of miscegenation recast as exogamy or intermarriage. Her heroes, such as Clint Maroon of *Saratoga Trunk* (1941), Pervus DeJong of *So Big* (1924), Jordan Benedict of *Giant* (1952), and even the briefly glimpsed Steve Baker of *Showboat* (1926), who declares himself to be of mixed blood to protect his wife against charges of miscegenation, are blond giants with immense physical strength. Often gamblers and cowboys, they choose women who are not only strong but also strongly racialized: through their looks, like Sabra Cravat of *Cimarron* and Leslie Benedict of *Giant*; through the technique of "doubling" the heroine with another character, as Magnolia Ravenal is linked to Julie Dozier, a late but classic example of the "tragic mulatto" heroine, in *Showboat*; and through their heritage of color, like Clio Dulaine of *Saratoga Trunk*.

In *Cimarron*, despite stereotypical representations of Native- and African-American characters, Ferber employs a broad variety of techniques to critique racial sentiment. Sabra's racially ambiguous black-winged eyebrows and creamy complexion are characteristic of Ferber's heroines, as is the insistence on "old stock" American bloodlines. In *Cimarron* and elsewhere, Ferber satirizes such claims through the names themselves— Sabra[4] is a Venable (suggesting "venerable"), of Wichita—and the ridiculous context in which such snobbery is introduced, as when one of Sabra's neighbors in "that welter of mud, Indians, pine shacks, drought, and semi-barbarism known as Osage, Indian Territory," declares another to be a lady because "Mrs. Nisbett . . . was a Krumpf, of Ouachita, Arkansas."[5] Early in the book when discussing the remorseless Anglo-American outlaw called simply "The Kid," Yancey comments, "Funny thing, I never yet knew a bad man who wasn't light complected, or anyway, blue or gray eyes" (479), a romantic convention of dime novels that takes on racial significance here. Surprisingly for their time, Ferber's novels frequently introduce intermarriage between different ethnic or racial groups (the Steve Baker–Julie Dozier subplot in *Showboat*, Clio Dulaine and Clint Maroon of *Saratoga Trunk*, Jordy and Juana Benedict in *Giant*, among others).

In *Cimarron* intermarriage between whites and other groups is recast as sound eugenics, an infusion of fresh blood to strengthen the pioneer stock.

Michaels suggests that the reason for positing the Indian as ideal citizen is that he is not simply American but a Vanishing American: "It is because the Indian's sun was perceived as setting that he could become . . . a kind of paradigm for increasingly powerful American notions of ethnic identity and eventually for the idea of an ethnicity that could be threatened or defended, repudiated or reclaimed" (38). Indeed, it is the vanishing Osage themselves rather than Yancey who preserve a color barrier (which the novel mentions twice), a racist practice that ironically renders them "pure Americans" and fit partners for white pioneers seeking to legitimate their claim to be Americans as well as for those seeking simply exploitation of the Osage's oil wealth. One example is the story of Sabra's hired girl Arita Red Feather, and her lover, the Cravats' African-American servant, Isaiah. Blinded by her own racism into thinking of Isaiah as a child although he has grown to manhood, Sabra is surprised when Arita bears Isaiah's baby. Although the doctor tells Sabra that the Osage have "kept the tribe pure" except for intermarriage with whites and that discussing the baby could prove dangerous to Arita, Sabra pays little attention since she dichotomizes the issue of color into white/not white, a particularly deadly sort of racism. A few days later, Arita, Isaiah, and the baby turn up missing and meet a terrible fate: Arita and the child are sewn into a bag of uncured rawhide and left to die in the sun, while Isaiah is tied down within striking distance of a rattlesnake.

The other example of cross-racial "hybridity" is the relationship between Yancey and Sabra's son Cim and Ruby Big Elk, an Osage. Their relationship goes beyond Michaels's "sex with an Indian" paradigm to include cross-cultural exchanges such as Cim's participation in the tribe's peyote ceremonies and Yancey's admission that he, too, has taken peyote many times. After the marriage of Cim and Ruby, something largely proscribed or avoided in the nativist/modernist texts Michaels cites, Sabra responds to Yancey's prodding and reluctantly helps herself to the food at the wedding feast, here as in other narratives an act signifying acceptance or the symbolic ingestion of another culture. "This meat—this stuffing—is it chopped or ground through a grinder?" Sabra asks. "'Naw,' [the Osage woman] answered politely. 'Chawed'" (359). Sabra faints, but her acceptance of another culture, however begrudging, sets the stage for her acceptance of her half-Osage grandchildren. As Yancey tells Sabra, from Ruby's strength and Cim's "good stock" will come "such stuff as Americans are made of" (356–57). Whereas the other outsider, Sol Levy, the Jewish peddler, is excluded from the town's emotional life despite the Christlike attributes that show him as simultaneously persecuted and exalted, the offspring of the Native Americans and the flourishing pioneers populate the town, and Cim Cravat's matter-of-fact adoption of Osage ways demonstrates that cultural reciprocity and pride in identity, not assimilation, is the fulfillment of Yancey's dream.

In *Saratoga Trunk*, the racial ambiguity is deliberate as Clio Dulaine manipulates New Orleans's obsession with racial bloodlines to her own advantage. A product of the *plaçage* system of alliances between wealthy New Orleans white men and their light-skinned African-American mistresses—alliances in which "the formality of marriage" (*Saratoga Trunk* 23) played no role—Clio acknowledges both sides of her heritage, the "royal blood of France" of Nicolas Dulaine (26) and the blood of her grandmother Vaudreuil, a "free woman of color." Her actions throughout the novel are performances designed to provoke questions about her identity and to mock the social pretensions she encounters. She shocks the multitudes and thereby leads rather than follows the fashion, whether staring rudely at her half-sister, the legitimate daughter of Nicolas Dulaine, when she goes to the opera in New Orleans, or walking instead of riding to the springs when she arrives in Saratoga. Ignoring the coded systems of racial mixing and segregation followed by generations of her female forebears, she capitalizes on the American infatuation with aristocracy by inventing an entirely new identity. While visiting Saratoga, she pretends to be the widowed Comtesse de Trenaunay de Chanfret and adds an air of authenticity to her disguise by refusing to use her title, telling the hotelier, "I wish to be known only as plain Mrs. De Chanfret" (146). Ferber heightens the sense of artifice through Clio's use of masks. She literally paints herself white to face the world: Her "naturally creamy skin was dead white with the French liquid powder she used. . . . Almost a clown's mask, except for its beauty" (71). Significantly, although many suspect that she is not what she seems, only her lover Clint Maroon, from whom she has no secrets, comments on the unnatural white powder on her face. Her performance in whiteface passes because the transient, ambitious, and insecure denizens of Saratoga are at first too worried about their own social facades to look closely at hers.

Before the masquerade ball that closes the Saratoga season, Clio makes plans to attend as "a French marquise in a powdered wig," the quintessential representation of her false persona. Her costume outrages the gossips and causes them to speculate about her background. One detractor murmurs, "I always thought Creoles were colored people," to which another responds, "New Orleans aristocracy—French and Spanish blood" (31). Knowing their suspicions, she instead adopts a mask caricaturing the other part of her heritage. She paints her face dark brown instead of dead white, transforming herself into a black praline woman, and tosses sweets to the shocked matrons in the concert hall. Like Magnolia Ravenal, she sings powerfully in what Ferber describes as a flawless imitation of black dialect: "She was imitating every wandering New Orleans minstrel and cavorting street band she had ever seen, every caroling berry vendor from the bayous; . . . she was defiance (*sic*) against every convention she so hated" (340). Clio's unplanned and uncontrolled minstrelsy disrupts and mocks the social and cultural aspirations of her Saratoga audience, exposing their pretensions in several ways. By appearing as a caricature of what her audience believes her to be, she uncovers their unspeakable speculations on race and class and drags these ideas into public rather than private discourse. Moreover, rather than simply enjoying what Eric Lott has termed the "spectacle of vulgarity" that was an important feature in early minstrel shows (Lott 138), her audience is alarmed by the vulgarity of a minstrel performance that it does not control. Clio's singing further undermines their high-culture pretensions by spoiling their pleasure in the mundane operatic concert that follows her masquerade. After her blackface turn as the praline woman, Clio dons her whiteface mask once again, returning to the ball dressed as a marquise with white powdered hair and white powdered face as she commands attention and fits easily into the society that she despises. With her power intact, she breaks with convention for good by spurning the wealthy and timid railroad magnate Bart van Steed in favor of Clint Maroon, an adventurer like herself. What she has accomplished through her minstrel's antics, however, is to underscore the volatile nature of performances of race and social class, performances in which all are complicit through the quest for status that brings them to Saratoga.

Through her later heroine, Leslie Lynnton Benedict of *Giant*, which is set in the 1920s, Ferber makes a more direct effort to critique racial performance. Like Sabra, with her dark hair, sallow skin, and dark eyes, the Ohio-born "aristocratic Virginian" Leslie Lynnton is as unconventional in her beauty as in her intellectual pursuits. After a few days' courtship, she marries tall, blond Jordan "Bick" Benedict, the owner of Reata, the largest ranch in Texas, and travels with him to her new home. In a few short years she has borne two children, Jordan, a brunette like herself, and Luz, who is blond like Bick; and gained two admirers: the surly, drunken Jett Rink, whose oil wealth allows him to give free rein to his cruelty and racism; and the seventy-year-old Baldwin "Uncle Bawley" Benedict, who shares with Leslie an appreciation of music and a sympathy for the individual. For the next twenty-five years, Leslie protests in vain against the injustices she sees: the theft of Texas land through early deed swindles and the establishment of the Texas Republic ("And which was aggressor and which defender?" she asks herself when visiting the Alamo [291]); the ranch owners' treatment of migrant workers, their neglect of the workers' deplorable living conditions, and their toleration of parasites like Señor Gomez who profit from the workers' misery; the harsh punishment meted out to illegal aliens; and the appalling lack of health care and basic services in the towns on the ranch.

In many ways, *Giant* is a reworking of *Cimarron* with a more sympathetic heroine and a sharper critique of racism. A pampered Southern belle like Sabra Cravat, Leslie Lynnton marries a powerful man whose ideals she never fully shares and moves to a raw, dusty country where the amenities of civilization and culture are few. Her life includes seeing and eating unfamiliar food that makes her faint and an initial resistance to the land that is now her home. After having a child, she travels to her old home and finds it lacking, a point of decision that both heroines resolve by returning to the harsh new land they left behind. Like Sabra, Leslie sets out to change her environment into something resembling the civilization she left behind, but, more aesthetically gifted than Sabra, Leslie eschews gaudy imitations of Eastern objets d'art and works to integrate the natural colors of the landscape into her home at the ranch, the small stone-and-adobe Main House. Her aim is synthesis of the new and the old, not a duplication of Virginia on the plains of Texas. Her children, like Sabra's, grow up and unsettle her by marrying across racial lines, for despite her more liberal views, Leslie is stunned when her son Jordy marries Juana, the Mexican-American granddaughter of her husband's ranch foreman. Leslie becomes an important figure not because of her matriarchal status but because of her role in shaping the culture of the place, but whereas Sabra leads the way in forcing old cultures over new, Leslie works ceaselessly to remake Texas into an empire more socially just than the oppressively class- and race-bound country to which she came as a bride.

Throughout *Giant*, Ferber insists on the parallels between Reata and Texas as imperial powers set in the middle of a democratic United States, autonomous "countries" with a ruling oligarchy and a caste system based on race and exclusion. Leslie first notices this power structure when she observes gender relations in her new homeland: "[she] began to speculate about the high shrill feminine voices, about the tentativeness, about the vague air of insecurity that touched these women" (168), describing them to her father as "unsure and sort of deferential. Like oriental women" (54).

She also notes that "when the men replied, speaking to the women . . . they changed their tone[;] it was as adults change when they speak to little children, coming down to their mental level" (173). Later, when the men close her out of their discussion with smiles and flattery, she attacks them: "You date back a hundred thousand years. Politics! What's so dirty about your politics that I can't hear it!" (308). Much of the dirty politics involves illegally controlling Mexican Americans, including the corrupt practices of intimidating the ranch hands so that they "vote right . . . like they're told to vote" (310). In the first few chapters, set in the present day after the main action of the novel, Ferber introduces this idea of exclusion by describing Jett Rink's airport and his significantly named Conquistador Hotel, where the lavish, vulgar, spare-no-expense buildings include segregated rest rooms: "One sign read DAMAS. Another, CABALLEROS" (41). Ferber further emphasizes the imperial nature of the "country" of Texas through the device of a pair of minor characters, the deposed king and queen of Sargovia, who accompany the Benedicts to Jett Rink's lavish party and continually compare their own small country with "the seemingly endless reaches of Bick Benedict's empire" (36). In another scene of exclusion that foreshadows one of the novel's major episodes, the king and queen are turned away at the door because of their skin color: "No Mexicans allowed at this party, that's orders and besides none's invited that's sure" (55). Bick rescues the pair, explaining that the doorman has made a mistake, but the closed-door policy that occasioned the incident derives from the same nativist-inspired barriers that Leslie challenges after finding and, with Uncle Bawley's help, hiding a young Mexican boy who has crossed the border illegally.

The most thematically significant episode of racial exclusion occurs near the end of the novel when Leslie, Luz, Juana, and grandson Jordy stop at a roadside diner. Ferber has already established the characters' coloring: Luz, a true Benedict, is blonde, but Leslie, her Mexican-American daughter-in-law Juana, and Juana's son Jordy all have black hair and dark eyes. While Luz parks the car, the rest enter the restaurant and are refused service:

> "We don't serve Mexicans here." . . .
> "You can't be talking to me!" Leslie said.
> "I sure can. I'm talking to all of you. Our rule here is no Mexicans served and I don't want no ruckus. So—out!" . . .
> Luz came blithely in, she stared a moment at the little group on

whose faces was written burning anger; at the openmouthed men and women at the counter and tables.

"Heh, what's going on here!" she said. . . .

Leslie spoke before he could repeat the words. "This man won't serve us. He says he won't serve Mexicans." . . .

"You son of a bitch!" said Miss Luz Benedict. . . . "I'll tell my father! He'll kill you! Do you know who my father is! He's—"

"No! No, Luz. No name. Come."

As they went they heard through the open doorway, the voices of the man and woman raised again in dispute.

"You crazy, Floyd! Only the kid and his ma was cholos,[6] not the others."

"Aw, the old one was, black hair and sallow, you can't fool me." (439–40)

Insulated by a lifetime of race and class privilege from such slights, Leslie at first protests not the "no Mexicans" policy but her inclusion in it ("You can't be talking to me"). Her sense of justice overrides her initial reaction, however, and, now classed as one of the people whose rights she has championed throughout her life, Leslie silently accepts both her complicity in the system she has been powerless to change and the justice of the leveling process she undergoes. The abuses of imperial power have traveled full circle, as she later tells Bick: "You see. It's caught up with you[;] it's caught up with us. It always does" (63). Accustomed to ruling others based on an ideology of ethnic privilege and private property, the Benedicts find themselves judged by the very principles they had preached.

This sense of a just retribution recurs in George Stevens's 1956 film adaptation of the novel. The film makes several changes to the book: for example, an additional daughter is added, so as to pair one daughter with Jett Rink and another with Bob Dietz, the idealistic young progressive farmer; and Ferber's elaborate scheme of blond Benedicts and dark Lynn-tons is not carried out. The greatest shift is in the nature of the decades-long disputes between Leslie and her husband, Bick. In the book version, Leslie continually presses Bick for a greater degree of social justice; the film preserves Leslie's desire for social change, but her confrontations with Bick are instead centered on gender issues and the freedom of the individual. In the film, the theme of gender issues runs parallel to that of racism, but Leslie takes a more passive role in effecting social change. The scene in the diner is staged as a literal fight against prejudice, but Bick acts out of a sense of justice; he is not prodded by Leslie to take a stand. In the film,

Bick protests the shabby treatment of a Mexican family and then starts a fight with the owner of the place as "The Yellow Rose of Texas" plays in the background. After Bick loses the fight, Sarge, the owner, contemptuously tosses a framed sign onto Bick's crumpled body: "We reserve the right to refuse service to anyone"—which, according to the rule of "might makes right" and private property that Bick has upheld all his life, Sarge has a perfect legal if not moral right to do.[7]

In addition to debunking regional conventions, both Ferber and Lane substantially rewrote the national myth of limitless lands. In her early autobiographical novel *Diverging Roads*, which she called "the only book I've ever seriously written" (Holtz 77), Lane directly addresses the question of land ownership. After a career as a telegraph operator, her heroine, Helen Davies, marries and is abandoned by her husband, whereupon she takes over his job as a realtor selling undeveloped farmland in northern California. In this work, Lane somewhat romantically suggests that the question of land ownership rests on a partnership that draws together the elemental forces of farmers and land. As a weary Helen confides in her childhood sweetheart, Paul: "A real-estate salesman hasn't any real reason for existing. . . . We aren't needed a bit. The people would simply take the land if they weren't like horses, too stupid to know their own strength. . . . We're just a lot of parasites living off the land without giving anything in return" (*Diverging Roads* 264–65). By the time of *Free Land*, however, Lane's pessimism about the idea of land ownership and the pioneer dream shows in David Beaton's failure despite heroic efforts. Equally skeptical about the rewards of hard work, Ferber uses similar tropes of unearned wealth gained through oil discoveries or gambling to reject American dream ideology. For example, Sabra Cravat's farm, the only fruitful land around the town of Osage, is found to be so only because the soil lacks the oil deposits that enrich the rest of the town. Her careful husbandry, a staple fiction of the homesteading myth, is dwarfed and rendered irrelevant by the unexpected and unearned wealth of the oil fields. Ferber also speaks more directly to the colonization of nature and culture in the West by linking environmental and cultural destruction as she does in her description of the oil lands of Oklahoma and the despoliation of Cherokee land. As Ferber later wrote, "For centuries the Grabbers had gone their way, unchecked. . . . There it all lay in this fabulous virgin continent, and no one to stop them; no one who cared enough or had courage enough or sufficient foresight to sense the inevitable result of this ravaging" (*A Kind of Magic* 114).

Another familiar theme in these regional novels, the creation of an

American aesthetic through collecting objects of material culture, raises the possibility of a multicultural revision of "Americana" more inclusive than the conservative definition of American editions and artifacts valued by characters such as Percy Gryce in Edith Wharton's *The House of Mirth,* but it does so at the risk of outright theft of another culture. This collection of objects takes at least two forms, the first being the preservation of one's own cultural past through the preservation of significant objects. In a similar way, the culture of Ferber's *Cimarron* relies heavily on classic books, but Sabra values books as objects rather than as texts. When Sabra begins her literary society, the Philomathea Club, for example, she does not bother to read the books she assigns to others. Like the Thanatopsis Club, Sinclair Lewis's satiric version of a book club in *Main Street,* or Edith Wharton's Lunch Club from "Xingu," for "ladies who pursue Culture in bands, as though it were dangerous to meet alone" (Wharton 209), the Philomathea Club values books and reading only as status symbols, and it quickly degenerates into a forum for social competition.

The second form of preservation is the acquisition of objects from another culture, as when Magnolia Ravenal of *Show Boat* sings African-American spirituals to further her career, an appropriation at once tribute and theft.[8] In Ferber's and Lane's work, this acquisition and consumption both of objects and of the collected tales of a romanticized, nostalgic history suggests what Brigitte Georgi-Findlay has described as the 1880s "prehistoric craze and the fascination with antiquity" rooted in ethnology and notions of romantic primitivism (219). In Ferber's work, artifacts such as Selina Peake DeJong's antique Dutch china in *So Big* and Sabra Cravat's handwoven blanket from Mother Bridget exemplify cultural borrowing. Woven by Mother Bridget from strong yarn with an Indian blue dye, the blanket represents a multiply alien culture by evoking the long history of the mission school, its Native-American students, and Roman Catholicism. She gives it to the unheeding Sabra, who carries as a talisman Indian-inspired art into Indian country but fails to see the multiple messages within its beauty.

In Lane's *Free Land,* another act of misguided collection becomes cultural appropriation and outright theft. An educated Easterner and the frontier town's man of science, Dr. Thorne, steals the desiccated, mummified corpse of an Indian baby from an aboveground burial grove. Flushed with excitement at the "sensation" it will cause among scientists, Thorne plans to "send it to the Smithsonian in Washington, D.C." even as David Beaton suggests that "Barnum'd pay you a young fortune for that" (104). In this scene, Lane neatly links two forms of cultural theft; the "scientific" ethnographic observation of the Smithsonian scientists and the tub-thumping commercialism of a P. T. Barnum amount to the same thing: exploitation of the sacred artifacts of Native-American culture for the amusement of the white man. Yet the culture to which such artifacts belong turns out to be neither vanishing nor dead, as Thorne had thought, but very much alive: shortly thereafter, the Indians show up demanding the body, and only the best efforts of the strongest and most respected man in the book can save the situation. Gebbert, a legendary railroad contractor about whom the men compose songs, has all the qualities of a hero: he treats his men fairly, shares their living arrangements, and is not afraid to steal from the institution—the railroad—that steals from him, for "a man that won't steal from a railroad ain't honest" (107).[9] As a hero, he knows enough to respect native culture. A legendary frontiersman, Gebbert speaks with the chiefs respectfully, using "their lingo," and sends David to get the body back within three days, dismissing someone's boast that "any white man can handle six Indians" with "Maybe. Custer's men didn't" (112). The race-to-the-rescue plotting of this episode overshadows but cannot entirely obscure the true tension between the contemporary technological wizardry of telegraph and train used to regain the mummified body and the vanishing but still existent past of confrontations between native peoples and white settlers. Significantly, neither the characters nor the narrative voice mount any kind of defense for this action; indeed, all unite in calling Dr. Thorne a fool.

Despite their status as best-selling regional authors, then, both Ferber and Lane consciously challenged some of the country's favorite myths about itself. As Ferber herself put it when analyzing her books' staying power, "In their very core there lay something more solid, more deeply dimensional than mere entertainment or readability. They had power they had theme they had protest" (*A Kind of Magic* 125). Lane and Ferber wrote popular middlebrow fiction, and both understood the limitations of the forms they had chosen for their writing. Yet in creating middlebrow works that straddle the boundary between high culture and low, in writing novels that both promote and critique regional myths, and in representing race in ways that disrupt the status quo, these two authors change the rules of the genre and, in so doing, reveal their "hard and bitter purpose": to expose and protest the disparity between national promise and regional reality.

Notes

1. See Rose Wilder Lane's interview with Almanzo Wilder prior to writing *Free Land* in *A "Little House" Sampler.*

2. Laura Ingalls Wilder reports the story of the Benders in the *Pioneer Girl* manuscript, the genesis for the "Little House" series. Although John Miller and other Wilder biographers point out that the dates of the Ingalls family's residence in Kansas would have made contact with the Benders improbable, Wilder remembered the horror she felt as a child upon hearing that a little girl her own age had been buried alive.

3. The reluctance she shows is part of the stereotypical representation of the Prairie Madonna, according to Myres and others.

4. In addition to its later meaning of "native of Israel," *sabra* means "prickly pear."

5. Edna Ferber, *Cimarron* (New York: Doubleday, 1930), 172. Subsequent references are cited in the text.

6. S.v. "cholos": "*Disparaging*. A Mexican or Mexican-American," *Webster's Encyclopedic Unabridged Dictionary of the English Language.*

7. For a more extended discussion of this film and Tino Villanueva's *Scene from the Movie "Giant,"* see Rafael Pérez-Torres's "Chicano Ethnicity, Cultural Hybridity, and the Mestizo Voice," *American Literature* 70 (1998): 153–76. Pérez-Torres shows that "In *Giant* mestizaje does not provide an empowered subjectivity, does not offer agency in the epic battle over racial/national redefinitions. The titanic white father stands up for the Mexicans, represented as they are by an ineffectual old man, helpless youngsters, and sobbing women" (160).

8. Magnolia has learned these songs by listening to Julie Dozier, Queenie, and others on the Cotton Blossom. In *Love and Theft*, Lott includes a "self-serving" recollection from the performer Ben Cotton that closely matches Magnolia's experience: "I used to sit with them in front of their cabins, and we would start the banjo twanging, and their voices would ring out in the quiet night air in their weird melodies. They did not quite understand me. I was the first white man they had seen who sang as they did; but we were brothers for the time being and were perfectly happy." Despite the harmful effects of such appropriation, Lott suggests, "in addition to the minor disasters bohemia has perpetrated . . . there is in its activities an implicit tribute to, or at the very least a self-marginalizing mimicry of, black culture's male representatives" (50).

9. In writing *By the Shores of Silver Lake*, Lane questioned the episode in which Uncle Hi in effect steals supplies from the railroad company; Wilder replied that the railroad companies regularly cheated the contractors and that this type of "settling with the company" was common, adding that a common saying was "A man that won't steal from the railroad ain't honest." See Holtz and Romines.

Works Cited

Aldrich, Bess Streeter. *A Lantern in Her Hand.* New York: D. Appleton & Company, 1928.

Altieri, Charles. "Whose America Is Our America: On Walter Benn Michaels's Characterizations of Modernity in America." *Modernism/Modernity* 3, no. 3 (1996): 107–13.

Ferber, Edna. *Cimarron.* New York: Doubleday, 1930.

———. *A Kind of Magic.* Garden City, N.Y.: Doubleday, 1963.

———. Letter to Mary Austin. 17 November 1931. ALS. AU 2372. Mary Austin Collection, Huntington Library, San Marino, Calif.

———. *A Peculiar Treasure*. New York: Doubleday Doran & Co., 1939.

———. *Saratoga Trunk*. Garden City, N.Y.: Doubleday, 1941.

Georgi-Findlay, Brigitte. *The Frontiers of Women's Writing: Women's Narratives and the Rhetoric of Westward Expansion*. Tucson: University of Arizona Press, 1996.

Gilbert, Julie Goldsmith. *Ferber, a Biography*. Garden City, N.Y.: Doubleday, 1978.

Holtz, William V. *The Ghost in the Little House: A Life of Rose Wilder Lane*. Columbia: University of Missouri Press, 1993.

Lane, Rose Wilder. *Diverging Roads*. New York: The Century Company, 1919.

———. *Free Land*. 1938. Lincoln: University of Nebraska Press, 1984.

Lewis, Sinclair. *Main Street*. New York: Harcourt Brace, 1920.

Lott, Eric. *Love and Theft: Blackface Minstrelsy and the American Working Class*. Race and American Culture. New York: Oxford University Press, 1993.

Michaels, Walter Benn. "American Modernism and the Poetics of Identity." *Modernism/Modernity* 1, no. 1 (1994): 38–56.

———. *Our America: Nativism, Modernism, and Pluralism*. Durham, N.C.: Duke University Press, 1995.

———. "Response." *Modernism/Modernity* 3, no. 3 (1996): 121–26.

Myres, Sandra L. *Westering Women and the Frontier Experience, 1800–1915*. Histories of the American Frontier. Albuquerque: University of New Mexico Press, 1982.

Perloff, Marjorie. "Modernism without the Modernists: A Response to Walter Benn Michaels." *Modernism/Modernity* 3, no. 3 (1996): 99–105.

Quantic, Diane Dufva. *The Nature of the Place: A Study of Great Plains Fiction*. Lincoln: University of Nebraska Press, 1995.

Romines, Ann. *Constructing the Little House: Gender, Culture, and Laura Ingalls Wilder*. Amherst: University of Massachusetts Press, 1997.

Shapiro, Laura. *Perfection Salad: Women and Cooking at the Turn of the Century*. 1986; Modern Library Food. New York: Modern Library, 2001.

Stott, Annette. "Prairie Madonnas and Pioneer Women: Images of Emigrant Women in the Art of the Old West." *Prospects: An Annual of American Cultural Studies* 21 (1996): 299–325.

Von Hallberg, Robert. "Literature and History: Neat Fits." *Modernism/Modernity* 3, no. 3 (1996): 115–26.

Wharton, Edith. "Xingu." *The Collected Short Stories of Edith Wharton*. Vol. 2. Ed. R. W. B. Lewis. New York: Scribner, 1968, 209–29.

Wilder, Laura Ingalls, Rose Wilder Lane, and William Anderson. *A Little House Sampler*. New York: Perennial Library, 1989.

The Cosmopolitan Regionalism of Zona Gale's Friendship Village

DEBORAH LINDSAY WILLIAMS

In "What Women Won in Wisconsin," a 1922 essay published in the *Nation*, Zona Gale argued that the rest of the country should follow Wisconsin's example and pass an Equal Rights Amendment to eradicate the discriminatory laws against women that remained on the books even after the passage of the Nineteenth Amendment. The Nineteenth Amendment had granted women only the vote; in every state of the union other than Wisconsin, women still lacked legal equality.[1] The Wisconsin law allowed women freedoms such as serving on a jury, holding civil service jobs, and claiming residency somewhere other than where their husbands lived. Gale presented an earlier version of this brief essay on the floor of the Wisconsin Senate, and it testifies to her equally strong commitments to feminism and regionalism. She uses her local politics to fuel her hopes for national change and emphasizes that what seem to be "women's issues" affect both men and women: "In this matter there is no woman's standpoint and no man's standpoint," she asserts. "There is only the need of our common citizenship to rid our statute books of these vestiges of the old English common law . . . do this for women—yes; and for men; and for the general welfare; and for the children and the children's children." Gale argued that unless other states passed similar laws, the "spiritual genius" belonging to women could not be "liberated into the world." Each state needed to sweep away the "meshes of little circumstances" that prevented women from achieving the "equality of opportunity to express

themselves politically and legally, without discriminations against them"
(185). Her comment illustrates the combination of mysticism and pragmatism that are the hallmarks of her political agenda—"spiritual genius," in
her way of thinking, is a concrete tool for social and political reform. Gale's
reformist energy is further fueled by her unswerving commitment to the
feminist agenda of the early twentieth century and her firm belief that Wisconsin's progressive legal agenda should become a blueprint for the rest
of the country.[2]

When Gale wrote this essay, she was living in her childhood home of
Portage, Wisconsin, which served as the model for all the small towns in
Gale's fiction, sometimes presented as a parochial hamlet that stifled individual freedom and sometimes as an idyllic antidote to big-city life. After
graduating from college Gale left Portage to work as a journalist, first in
Milwaukee and then in New York. After more than a decade in Manhattan,
she returned to Portage, where she lived for the rest of her life. "Sitting
out there in Wisconsin," as one friend described her, Gale was nevertheless involved in a number of liberal movements, including agitating for
racial equality, lobbying for pacifism, and advocating for labor unions.
From Portage, Gale published her critically acclaimed, best-selling novels;
continued to publish nonfiction essays; and wrote a number of plays,
including *Miss Lulu Bett* (1920), which led to her becoming the first
woman to win a Pulitzer prize for drama. Gale's literary successes lent
prestige to the various causes with which she was involved, but her primary focus remained the desire to foster stronger communities in which
people treated one another with fairness and compassion. In all her writing, this focus stays constant, whether she criticizes the United States for
its failure to create egalitarian communities or illustrates how such communities might be created.

Gale's short stories, particularly those about Friendship Village—the
fictional town that made Portage famous—depict her vision of an egalitarian, compassionate community; the small town becomes her lab, a series
of fictional experiments that test her theories about how people interact.
Home of Calliope Marsh, the middle-aged narrator of almost all the
Friendship Village stories, and the ladies of the Friendship Married Ladies
Cemetery Improvement Sodality, the village provided Gale with a way to
present her feminist and progressivist ideas in a nonthreatening and non-
confrontational fashion. The markers of regionalist writing—folksy characters, local dialects, homespun wit—cloak an agenda that many of Gale's
readers would have found shocking, even radical, had she presented her
ideas with the bluntness displayed in "What Women Won in Wisconsin,"

an essay directed at very different readers than those who loved the Friendship Village stories.[3]

Particularly in *Peace in Friendship Village* (1919), Gale uses her village as a model for postwar nationhood, instructing her readers in the importance of resisting xenophobia and racism, while planting the seeds of what might be called a nascent cosmopolitanism. This small Midwestern town, paradoxically, becomes a testing ground for Gale's global vision, which oscillates between an optimistic universalism—all human beings are essentially the same—and a cosmopolitanism that attempts to value rather than fear difference and sees national identity as something learned, not inherited through "blood." Universalism and cosmopolitanism are linked, according to David Hollinger, because "cosmopolitans look beyond a province or nation to the larger sphere of humankind that is the object of universalists." Hollinger points out that an important distinction nevertheless exists between the "universalist will to find common ground" and the "cosmopolitan will to engage human diversity" (84). In *Peace in Friendship Village*, Gale attempts to do both: find common ground between groups and individuals while at the same time recognize and value difference. In moving between these two attitudes, Gale's writing charts the early-twentieth-century intellectual debates about how to wean the world from nationalism and move toward a less divisive set of loyalties. Although Gale never achieves a fully coherent vision of cosmopolitanism, her attempts to do so are nevertheless worthy of note, in large part because—unlike many of her liberal (male) contemporaries—she pegs her hopes of a more peaceful, more neighborly global society on improving the conditions of women: her cosmopolitan village is first and foremost a town in which women are no longer second-class citizens.

Gale's political agenda was largely shaped by the time she spent in New York with such important women as Alice Paul, founder of the National Women's Party, and Carrie Chapman Catt, leader of the National American Woman Suffrage Association (NAWSA), and with the women's organization known as Heterodoxy.[4] She was also a friend and correspondent of Jane Addams, the founder of Hull House in Chicago and one of the leaders of the feminist pacifist movement that was so important to Gale's own world vision. Most important to the development of Gale's progressive politics, however, was her friendship with Robert La Follette and his family, particularly his wife, Belle, and his daughter, Fola, both of whom were active feminists.[5] When La Follette was governor of Wisconsin, his progressive ideas—which included complete overhauls of the tax structure and voting procedures, as well as public investigations into corrupt government officials—coalesced into what became known as the "Wisconsin Idea."[6] According to historian Nancy Unger, La Follette's most recent biographer, La Follette "set out to make the political machinery more directly responsive to the popular will, to promote equal rights over special privilege" (122). In the national imagination, La Follette's Wisconsin existed as a provocative symbol for both progressives and conservatives: for conservatives, the state illustrated the dangers of indulging reformist agendas; progressives used the state as an ideal that they could hold up to the nation. Gale's love of Wisconsin's countryside and its people was bound up with her admiration for La Follette's ideas, which she thought could be the salvation of a country lost in a morass of capitalism, militarism, and inequality.

Gale found further reason to admire La Follette when, as a U.S. senator, he refused to support U.S. military involvement in World War I. Unlike Gale, La Follette was not an absolute pacifist, but he believed that war was more often than not about profit motives masquerading as patriotism. He claimed that "war and rumors are a dreadful diversion for peoples demanding just distribution of wealth. War is the money changer's opportunity, and the social reformer's doom" (Unger 239–40). La Follette's was one of three "no" votes cast when Congress voted to declare war on Germany, a vote that—in combination with his protest of the 1917 Espionage Act—eventually cost him his Senate seat and led to his vilification in the national press: one editorial cartoon in the *New York World* portrayed La Follette receiving the Iron Cross from a gauntleted German hand. Although Wisconsin had originally been proud of its outspoken senator, during the war years, the state decried his pacifist stance and the legislature eventually condemned him for sedition.

Gale worked on behalf of the pacifist cause, serving as the propaganda officer for the newly formed Women's Peace Party (WPP), organized in response to the misogyny of existing peace organizations. In a letter to Jane Addams asking her to chair the new organization, Carrie Chapman Catt wrote that the current national peace societies were "all well endowed . . . very masculine in their point of view. It would seem that they have as little use for women and their points of view as have the militarists" (quoted in Alonso 61). As one of her propaganda efforts, Gale published *Heart's Kindred* (1915), a novel that she dedicated to "Those Who Obey the Sixth Commandment" (thou shalt not kill). The conclusion of the novel takes place in Washington, D.C., at a thinly fictionalized representation of the first WPP meeting, but Gale incorporates actual speeches by Addams and other pacifists, footnoting them in the text so that her readers could see that pacifism was not wild idealism but a thoughtful, measured response to world politics. In the final pages of the novel, Gale articulates a world view that anticipates what Virginia Woolf would write twenty years later in *Three Guineas* (1938): "as a woman, I have no country. As a woman I want no country. As a woman my country is the whole world" (Woolf 109). Gale argues that when pacifism eradicates militarism, "something will come into the world, and it will know nothing of nations. The little loyalties will go. National pride, national 'honor,' patriotism—all the little scaffolds will fall away. . . . the nations are nothing—the people are everything . . . [they] are bound together by ties which nations must cease to break" (218–19). Gale emphasizes the importance of a human identity rather than a national or ethnic identity, suggesting that her readers think of themselves as citizens of the world—as cosmopolitans.

The grand vision of *Heart's Kindred* wraps itself in a regionalist love story that is also a conversion narrative, so that while Gale's readers took in her radical message about world peace, they were lulled by the novel's rather conventional plot line. The novel's hero, Inger, is a violent mountain man from an unnamed Western state who saves the beautiful Lorry Moore from marriage to a man she doesn't love. As he chaperones her on the journey to Washington, D.C., where Lorry hopes to find refuge with relatives, Inger falls in love with her and becomes not only a pacifist but also a feminist. Although this novel is not set in Friendship Village, Inger's thick dialect and his comic encounters with the urban worlds of Chicago and Washington link this novel to those village tales, as does Gale's depiction of the power wielded by women's collective consciousness. Although Inger's transformation seems but another version of nineteenth-century domestic fictions in which a man is changed by a woman's uplifting presence, Gale's novel actually updates mere influence into direct political, public impact. The women in this novel are not working their transformative Christian magic from within the confines of their own homes but have convened at a large public forum in the heart of the nation's capital. The "spiritual genius" of the feminist pacifists causes Inger to realize that "the people are heart's kindred, met here for their world-work, which the nations must cease to interrupt" (*Heart's Kindred* 234). At this point, Gale's pacifist vision roots itself in universalist thought: we are all kindred whose family ties are eroded by the distorting and destructive claims of ethnic or national identities.

Gale campaigned against the war from her parents' house in Portage, giving that small town something to gossip about for the duration of the war—and after.[7] In an effort to ease her disappointment over Portage's hearty endorsement of militarism, Gale threw herself wholeheartedly into La Follette's senatorial reelection campaign in 1922 and his subsequent run for president in 1924. Along with several other prominent women, including Addams and Freda Kirchwey, editor of the *Nation*, Gale campaigned tirelessly on behalf of "Fighting Bob." She wrote a long essay, "Why I Shall Vote for Robert La Follette," which ran in the *New Republic*, and toured the state to raise support for his campaign, pointing out that many of his "radical" ideas were now law. During his presidential bid, Gale redoubled her efforts, giving radio lectures across the country on his behalf. She stressed particularly his support of the Nineteenth Amendment, hoping to galvanize newly enfranchised women to vote for him, linking him to "women's principles": "his progressive policies . . . are politics socialized . . . they regard human life and its right to grow as more important than property rights. The history of these policies in Wisconsin is a history of the fight against special privilege which sought advantage for the few at the expense of the many. This means that an ethical principle has been made into a political faith. Broadly speaking, these are the principles and the faith of most women, outside politics" (quoted in Derleth 153). Her efforts notwithstanding, La Follette carried only one state in the election—Wisconsin, of course—and won only about a seventh of the popular vote. Nevertheless, given his leftist politics and unabashed socialist leanings, historians grant that La Follette's was probably the "most successful leftwing Presidential campaign in American history" (Unger 299).

Gale's own left-wing politics, which so regularly startled the inhabitants of Portage, weave through all her fiction, allowing her to bring to fruition what did not flourish in real life. Her attachment to the Wisconsin countryside and its inhabitants is both geographical and political: regionalism and progressivism, for Gale, shared the same root. If, as Judith Fetterley and Marjorie Pryse assert, "regionalist fiction asserts an essential connection between character and place" (xvii), then it makes sense that the first-person narrator of the Friendship Village stories, Calliope Marsh, often gives voice to Gale's political views. Calliope is Friendship Village's representative of the "Wisconsin idea." Like many of the central female figures in regionalist fiction, Calliope is unmarried and plays several roles in the community: sage, confidante, mediator, goad, and often, social conscience. Similar to the women Pryse discusses in her essay "Reading Regionalism," who might be "conjure women, herbalists, [or] visionaries," Calliope serves a central function: "to critique so as to heal" (51). Calliope directs her sometimes acerbic commentary at small-town versions of the ills that

Gale saw plaguing the rest of the country; what Gale could not fix, Calliope often can.

In *Mothers to Men* (1911), Calliope and the Friendship Village Married Ladies Cemetery Improvement Sodality take on the task of bringing social reforms to the town, usually against the wishes of the town council, which is composed entirely of men (many of whom are married to Sodality members).[8] Often relying on trickery to accomplish their goals, the women manage to institute regular garbage collection, create a small lending library, make store owners keep cleaner shops, and improve the town's capacity for children's health care. Ultimately, however, Calliope realizes that until women have a political voice on the town council, they will always have to rely on roundabout methods, skullduggery, and sheer luck to achieve permanent reforms. Without the vote, women will be able only to "patch up what had been left undone . . . [find] ways of serving that they'd schemed for and stole" (311). The feminist, reformist message of *Mothers to Men* reflects various projects undertaken by La Follette while he was governor, but Calliope is far less threatening than the governor: she is reform in calico, a feminist in the kitchen. Sodality's involvement with community issues mirrors what Gale wrote about in a 1906 report about women's clubs: "The initial steps usually include 'clean-up' days. . . . Next comes constructive work in beautifying [neighborhoods]. . . . This leads *naturally* to work for sanitation . . . medical inspection of school children . . . investigation of . . . child labor, of factory and shop conditions in general—hours, sanitation, wages, and so on, gradually to the whole underlying industrial situation and to the economic conditions which have begotten it" (quoted in Scott 159, emphasis added). There is an organic progression here from cleaning up a neighborhood to cleaning up a country and an economic system; for Gale and other progressives, this link was one of the primary reasons why women everywhere deserved a political voice.[9]

Herself an urbane and well-traveled woman of letters, Gale nevertheless writes as if she were an inhabitant of Friendship Village—which, by virtue of her Portage address, she is.[10] By choosing to live in Portage, Gale rejected the conventional trappings of literary success, a choice that links her with other women regionalists like Sarah Orne Jewett and Kate Chopin. Friendship Village, like Jewett's Dunnet's Landing or Chopin's bayou country, is a village outside the mainstream; it is one of the hallmarks of regionalist fiction that the region being portrayed is off the beaten path, as Sherrie Inness and Diana Royer have argued: "Regional writing allows its practitioners a decentered perspective of the dominant culture's values. This decentered viewpoint lies at the heart of the power regionalist writing has to critique society's values" (2). Inness and Royer claim that "regionalism involves our investment in community, whether that community is a small town or large city and whether it means a group of local residents or people bonded through shared affiliations. Identity, it seems, is deeply entrenched in the conception of regionalism" (7). Gale's attachment to Wisconsin and to communities of women can be found in all her Friendship Village stories, but in the final collection, *Peace in Friendship Village*, her scrutiny sharpens and focuses on questions about identity: What does it mean to be an American? What does it mean to be a community? What do we do about people who are different from us? It is in the answers to these questions that we see Gale formulating her vision of cosmopolitanism.

In the title story of the collection, the Sodality ladies, including Calliope, realize that they have been guilty of discriminating against Friendship Village's immigrant population and resolve to bridge the cultural divide that they have created. The story begins with Sodality putting the finishing touches on their "Peace Pageant," which celebrates the end of the war, while also wondering what they will do now that there is no Red Cross relief work to keep them busy. Mis' Sykes, the unofficial president of Sodality, suggests that because there is "some talking about military preparedness . . . why not us start in and knit for [the next war] *now*?" (22). When the women find a lost child outside the community hall, their plans to start knitting for the next war are put on hold. The child, "the funniest little dud [*sic*] ever I see," according to Calliope, seems to belong to no one in Friendship Village proper, so the women go to the Flats—the outskirts of town where the newly arrived immigrants live, or the "ex-foreigners," as Calliope calls them. The Flats "didn't seem ever to count real regular in Friendship Village doings. For instance, the town was just getting in sewerage, but it wasn't to go in down on the Flats, and no one seemed surprised" (26). Sodality's members only go to the Flats when they need to "see the wash woman, or dicker for a load of wood . . . or get somebody to houseclean" (26); the Flats is the closest thing Friendship Village has to a slum.

As the women go from house to house looking for the little boy's family, at first they see only poverty and dirt—and an opportunity to get manual labor for free. Mis' Sykes suggests that they "get some work out of these folks for the peace meeting to-morrow night," and the other women realize that the immigrants would not "charge anything, being it's for peace . . . we could get the whole thing for free, for patriotism" (28). The women cluck in dismay at the skinny children, the crowded tiny houses, and the scruffy look of the men who are working on the town's new sewer lines. Although Mis' Toplady reminds them that "foreign ain't poison," the other women remain unconvinced. The differences between Sodality's "us" and the Flats' "them" create a seemingly unbridgeable divide, highlighted by Mis' Sykes asking the sheriff to keep a close watch on the Peace Pageant because there might be "lawlessness." The gap between Friendship Village and its immigrant inhabitants is further illustrated by the pageant display, which has two booths: one dedicated to Friendship Village and one designated "Foreign," as a way to celebrate the end of the war in Europe. But the Friendship Village booth is "considerably bigger," and the Foreign booth is "kind of slimpsey . . . we couldn't seem to connect up much of Europe with Friendship Village." Sodality does not—or cannot—see that there are immigrants from all of western and eastern Europe living in the Flats, right under their noses. For the members of Sodality, the abstraction of "Europe" is easier than dealing with the messy reality of "foreigners" living next door.

Sodality's opinions change only after a fire breaks out in the Flats and they see the community spirit that exists among the immigrant families, who rush to help one another in the crisis. The immigrant women talk among themselves about who can take in people who have lost their homes in the fire and listening to them talk makes Calliope feel strange: "always before, in a Friendship Village catastrophe, [Mis' Toplady] and me had been among the planners. But here we were, it seemed, left out" (37). The lesson embedded in being "left out" continues when the lost little boy is reunited with his family, who have lost their house in the blaze. As the family chatters with the lost child in their native language, their neighbors gather around as well, translating for the Sodality women. When they talk, Calliope says, "it seemed so wonderful to see the folks that we had never paid attention to, or thought they knew anything, take those tangled sounds and unravel them for us, easy, into regular, right-down words" (38). The invisible dwellers of the Flats are transformed into knowledgeable people who value the same things that Sodality does: family, home, community. Unlike the inhabitants of Friendship Village, however, who would have asked the police for help with a missing child, the family in the Flats hadn't asked the police for help in finding their little boy because "they knew the law only as something that arrests you" (38).

Once the fire is under control and everyone is safe, the Sodality ladies overcome their "left out" feeling by declaring that the pageant dinner is for the "burned-out folks." Continuing the reversals, it is now Sodality women who wait on the folks from the Flats—and the sheriff is needed, although not to patrol: "he was passing the sugar and cream" (40). The little boy and his mother are ensconced at the center of the Foreign booth, to which other immigrant women have added mementos from home— musical instruments, wedding dresses, children's clothing—so that it seems like "Europe was there in the room." Literally, then, Europe has become a living entity to Friendship Village instead of an abstraction, and as a result, the Sodality women realize that they have found something to do now that the Red Cross no longer needs their efforts. They will use their domestic skills to "teach the women how to feed [their children] better and cost no more . . . take care of them when they're sick" (43). Calliope offers the final gesture of reconciliation between the village and the Flats: "get sewerage down there on the Flats! Don't it belong there just exactly as much as in the residence part?" Up until this point, everyone has simply assumed that the Flats would use the "septic tank" and not benefit from the new technology of waste disposal. It is an unglamorous symbol but important nevertheless: extending "sewerage" to the Flats illustrates Friendship Village's newfound commitment to its immigrant residents, crossing over the line between "us" and "them," making difference less threatening.

According to Stephanie Foote, regionalist writing has always been precisely about the representation of difference because it is a form that "works to preserve local customs, local accents, and local communities" (4), and certainly Gale's Friendship Village stories are no exception. When we think of regionalist writing in this way, it becomes less paradoxical that such a small town could become the site of cosmopolitan imaginings: it is not a big step to move from asserting the importance of small-town communities to asserting the importance of immigrant communities. Staying rooted in the village and preserving its quirks for her readers gives Gale room in which to explore political alternatives. Within the confines of Friendship Village, which were so familiar to her readers, she can suggest, for example, that gypsies, or families named Armachi, or people who speak in "tangled sounds" should be not feared but welcomed. Foote argues further that "regional writing gave strangers with accents literary recognition at exactly the same moment that accented strangers in the form of immigrants were clamoring for recognition and representation in the political arena" (6). Gale's stories give voice to these accented strangers—both the inhabitants of Friendship Village and recent immigrants— and demonstrates that, accents notwithstanding, it is possible for all these groups to create a mutually supportive community.

Other stories in the *Peace in Friendship Village* collection portray similar encounters with ethnic difference, particularly "The Story of Jeffro," one of Gale's most popular tales, first published in *Everybody's Magazine* in 1915.[11] Once again, Calliope becomes Gale's spokeswoman, ridiculing, in this story, the idea that anyone is "purely" American. When Mis' Sykes, the unofficial president of Sodality, warns people to lock their doors because "foreigners" have come to town, Calliope asks her "where were your mother and father born . . . and their folks?" She pursues that line of questioning back three generations, until Mis' Sykes gets to the inevitable "there was three brothers come over together—" and then pounces: "Where'd they come from? And where'd their folks come from? Were they immigrants to America too? Or did they just stay foreigners in England or Germany or Scandinavia or Russia, maybe?" (54). Calliope goes on: "the question was real universal. For all we know, it takes in a dozen nations with their blood flowing, sociable, in yours. It's awful hard for any of us . . . to find a real race to be foreign to. I wouldn't bet I was foreign to no one . . . nor that anyone was foreign, for certain, to me" (54). The Sodality women occasionally chastise Calliope because "she don't draw the line *nowheres*" (208); she refuses to play the game of "us" versus "them." Calliope draws pleasure from knowing people who are not like her and tells Sodality that she wishes she knew someone on Mars (208). Her comments anticipate what Randolph Bourne would write in his famous 1916 essay about cosmopolitanism, "Trans-national America": "We are all foreign-born or the descendants of foreign-born, and if distinctions are to be made between us, they should rightly be on some other ground than indigenous-ness." Calliope's universalism—none of us is *really* foreign to one another—erases the "little scaffolds" of nationalism; she will not partici-pate in the rhetoric about blood purity that was so pervasive in the United States in the early twentieth century. Unlike the universalism of *Heart's Kindred*, however, which was an end in itself, Calliope's universalism leads her to seek what David Hollinger, in *Postethnic America*, has described as the cosmopolitan aim of "voluntary affiliations of wide compass" (81).

Jeffro's arrival forces Calliope to scrutinize not only her neighbors' atti-tudes but also the attitude that the country has toward "foreigners." Her newest neighbor had come to the United States dazzled by the promises he saw in a poster that he shows to Calliope: "It was printed in Yiddish . . . but the picture was plain enough: It showed a mill on one side of the street and a bank on the other. And from the mill a stream of workingmen, with bags of money on their backs, were streaming over toward the bank" (47). Jeffro's faith in this image causes Calliope to wonder "what's America going to do for him?" Then she has a different question: "What's America going to do *to* him" (48, my emphasis). She is aware of both the emptiness of the poster's promise and Jeffro's vulnerability in the face of this promise.

Although the town initially refers to him as "that Jew peddler," Jeffro eventually becomes part of the community, and America seems to be keeping its promises. He is delighted that his son can go to school for free and study free books, astounded when the town's firemen come to put out a fire in his barn for free, speechless when letters from home are brought to his house without his having to pay for delivery. Jeffro's innocent amazement at the benefits of living in the United States makes Calliope feel proud to live in "a Big Land" that does so much for its inhabitants. Eventually, however, this democratic idyll is shattered when Jeffro leaves Friendship Village (entrusting his child to a neighbor and his tiny savings to the town bank) to go work in a mine and earn more money during the winter months. While at the mine, Jeffro joins some of the other miners in a picket line, protesting their low wages. He asks the mine owners why America can give him all sorts of things for free, "but when we want more bread, and we are willing to work for it all day long with our hands, you will not let us have more . . . even when we pay with work" (67). His questions get him shot at by the police who have come to break the strike, and he is thrown in jail. When he finally returns to Friendship Village, Calliope has to tell him that the bank holding his savings has failed and that his money is gone. Jeffro tells her that "I hate America. Being free here, it is a lie!" (70). The promise of the "Big Land" has been revealed as a myth, a revelation that demonstrates Gale's suspicion of capitalist structures and her sympathies with union organizers.

Jeffro never regains his belief in America's promise, and the story ends with his assertion that he will do things "not for America . . . but for you and thes' village. No one else." Friendship Village helps Jeffro, not the "Big Land," and Calliope wonders if "Friendship Village knows things that America hasn't found out yet—but of course that can't be so" (74). Within the confines of the village, despite its failing bank, can be found the "real" democratic ideals that do not distinguish on the basis of wealth, class, ethnicity, or national identity. The town—Gale's model community—does in fact "know things" that the rest of the country seems not yet to have discovered.

Gale's stories reveal a complex relationship to the country outside Friendship Village. Although she fervently believes in the power of democracy and the idea of the United States as the shining city on the hill, she

despises the elevation of profit and power over human lives and communities. She attempts to resolve these complexities by suggesting that the
country simply needs to practice a better, truer form of democracy that
values human rights rather than bottom line totals or abstract concepts
like "patriotism." Through Friendship Village's interactions with the residents of the Flats, Gale sketches out an idea for a community that,
although flawed, does seem to "know things that America hasn't found
out yet." For instance, when Achilles Poulaki is discovered to have stolen
bundles of old clothes to give to his mother, who turns them into rag rugs
that she sells to supplement their tiny income, Mis' Sykes is outraged, in
part because it suggests that the two dollars a week she pays Achilles to do
odd jobs is insufficient. She "wants to make an example of him," but Calliope wonders about the inequities of the system: "first we starve Achilles
on two dollars a week, and then when he steals for his ma, we make an
example of him. Ain't there anything else for him . . . [and why is Mis'
Sykes] willing to make an example of him instead of helping him?" (*Peace*
15).[12]

Instead of allowing Achilles to become a punitive example, however,
Calliope transforms him into an example of democracy's history. In so
doing, she annoys Mis' Sykes and again reveals her own ability to see that
individual differences might strengthen the community. At the end of
Sodality's "Festival of Nations" pageant, as the children—dressed in the
costumes of different countries—file across the stage saying the U.S.
pledge of allegiance, Calliope interrupts and asks Achilles to "say the
words that his Greek grandfather taught him." Achilles instantly recites
"the Athenian boy's creed of citizenship, that Achilles' father had learned
in Greece, and that Achilles' grandfather, that officer in the Greek government, had taught them both" (17). His recital demonstrates to the town
that the so-called American ideals are in fact imported from elsewhere;
they are not indigenous to the United States. At the end of this story, the
young women of the town decide to help the immigrant children learn
English: "We're going to start in with these foreign-born boys and girls . . .
and teach them all the things [they need to know]," says one woman. Calliope adds an important corollary to her statement by pointing out that
"there is a thing or two they can teach us . . . beginning with Achilles"
(19). The women nod at her words, suggesting that Friendship Village will
establish a reciprocal relationship with its new neighbors, thus further
eradicating the boundaries between "us" and "them" and creating a town
that will thrive on, rather than be destroyed by, the cultural differences
of its inhabitants. In their own small way, the inhabitants of the village

demonstrate what Amanda Anderson argues in "Cosmopolitanism, Universalism, and the Divided Legacies of Modernity": cosmopolitanism resists "those parochialisms emanating from extreme allegiances to nation, race, and ethnos . . . [and] aims to foster reciprocal and transformative encounters between strangers variously construed" (*Peace* 268–69).

As Gale describes it, the boundaries of Friendship Village seem infinitely expandable, able to accept anyone into the community. When an African-American family moves into town, however, those expansive boundaries tighten fast against them. Gale was a charter member of both the NAACP and the ACLU and believed that the United States could not flourish until African Americans had equal rights.13 Nevertheless, she sees all too clearly the obstacles standing in the way of racial equality. "Dream" documents Friendship Village's failure—the one failure story in the entire *Peace in Friendship Village* collection.[14]

"Dream" begins with an excited Mis' Sykes carefully watching her new neighbors' possessions being moved in because "folks's individualities is expressed in folks's furniture" (*Peace* 207). But her plans for a reception surprise for the Burton Fernandez family collapse when Calliope informs her that the new residents are "dark," which Mis' Sykes takes initially to mean brunette. Mis' Sykes immediately jettisons her ideas about the quality of her neighbors, sputtering in disgust about "those people" moving in next to her. Calliope extols the family's virtues and cultural accomplishments, telling Mis' Sykes that "Mis' Fernandez is a graduate of a Southern college, and her two children have been to colleges that you and I have never seen the inside of and never will. And her husband is a college professor, up here to study for a degree that I don't even know what the letters stands (*sic*) for" (215). Despite Calliope's insistence that the neighbors are precisely the type of "quality" that Mis' Sykes initially thought they were and despite the fact that their son is a decorated war hero due to return to Friendship Village the next day, Mis' Sykes won't budge. The reasons she gives Calliope about why she will not welcome the Fernandez family into the neighborhood encapsulate the debate going on in the rest of the country about racial difference: "they're different by nature . . . you can't change human nature . . . if the Lord had intended dark-skinned folks to be different from what they are, he'd have seen to it by now . . . [did] the Lord intend them to be educated . . . do they give [medals] to *Negroes?*" (*Peace* 216–17, 221). For Mis' Sykes, race marks an insurmountable difference, while to Calliope, difference is exciting: "I'd always thought that there might be somebody like Mis' Fernandez . . . and here already it was true of some of them. It was like seeing the future come true right in my face" (*Peace* 212).

Mis' Sykes only agrees to host the reception surprise when she realizes what a loss of face it would be for her to concede how wrong she had been about her new neighbors, so the reception goes on as planned. The party is, in fact, a wonderful success, and the Fernandez family is very touched by the town's welcome—until, that is, Calliope wakes from her nap and realizes that the party has happened only in her midday reverie. There will be no reception after all—the ladies of Sodality agree to meet the Fernandez son at the train along with the other returning soldiers, but they will not venture into the Fernandez house. Calliope feels betrayed by the parochial vision of her Sodality cohort, whom she usually can persuade to a broader perspective, and "Dream" ends with her sad comment that "what hadn't happened was for me more real than the things that were true" (*Peace* 231). Friendship Village's treatment of the Fernandez family indicates that the village may not be as separate from the rest of the country as Gale had hoped; Gale's optimistic cosmopolitanism, which has triumphed in these stories over ethnocentrism and misogyny, fails in the face of the harsh reality of racial injustices.

Calliope's willingness to accept the Fernandez family as neighbors and her delight at the family's cultural accomplishments demonstrate the attitude that Ross Posnock characterizes as "cosmopolitan": "Rather than preoccupied with opposition and exclusion, cosmopolitanism regards culture as public property and nurtures the capacity for appropriation as a tool for the excluded to attain access to a social order of democratic equality" (804). In all her fiction, Gale focuses on ways that "democratic equality" could become a reality for everyone rather than for just a privileged few; she clung to the model of Wisconsin progressivism as a manifestation of how that goal might actually be attained, despite her awareness that even left-leaning Wisconsin seemed impervious to the need for racial equality. Because it depends so strongly on Wisconsin politics, Gale's regionalist ethos maps both a geographical and a philosophical space, a dual mapping that allows Friendship Village to become a testing ground for cosmopolitanism.

Gale's cosmopolitanism cannot be separated from her feminism or her pacifism, which create, in her mind, points of connection between people that are deeper and less arbitrary than the "little scaffolds" of nationalism and patriotism. Both men and women will benefit from the shift to a pacifist world, but it is women, "protectors of true civilization and humanity" (*Heart's Kindred* 199), who will actually lead the way toward a world in which war becomes "the out-worn way to settle differences" (*Heart's Kindred* 216). If the model of Friendship Village were to hold true, war would become "out-worn" in part because difference would cease to be a threat; the ability to connect with others despite (or even because of) difference would become a hallmark of a "true civilization."

What Gale called, in 1922, the "spiritual genius" of women was for her a key concept because it was this genius that could, if unleashed, create material improvement in U.S. society—if society would allow it to happen. Calliope Marsh possesses this spiritual genius, which in conjunction with her hard-nosed pragmatism and acerbic wit, help her make Friendship Village a better place in which to live. Calliope and the Ladies Sodality make clear that "women's issues" affect not just women but the entire community. This view, of course, has become something of a critical commonplace among late-twentieth-century political thinkers; once again Gale's ideas are ahead of her time. Although she is now an obscure figure in literary history, her thinking consistently anticipates that of her now more well-known contemporaries—the cosmopolitanism of Randolph Bourne, the reformist energy of Addams, the feminist pacifism of Woolf. Even the speeches of the WPP, which Gale chronicles so carefully in *Heart's Kindred*, accurately forecast the consequences of women getting directly involved in government policy making. It is possible, for example, to trace a direct line from the WPP's first meeting to a dinner for ten foreign ministers hosted by then Secretary of State Madeline Albright in September 1999. An account of this meeting, which ran in the *New York Times*, begins rather oddly, with a description of the dinner—poached quail eggs, mahi-mahi, chocolate soufflé cake—and then says that when it was time to leave, the ministers exchanged hugs and kisses. These affectionate good-byes lead to the article's "twist," buried in the fourth paragraph: all the foreign ministers are women; it's been a sort of high-powered "girls' night out." The ministers met to draft a letter to United Nations Secretary General Kofi Annan, asking that he make the ending of "repulsive trafficking in human beings, predominantly women and children," a central component of foreign affairs (A26). Linking women's issues to foreign affairs is necessary, said Albright, because "unless you make them central to your foreign policy . . . they get kind of shunted aside." In an interview after the dinner, the Finnish foreign minister noted that there were "unexpectedly strong emotions in that gallery at dinner . . . women are always brave initially, saying that they have no special gender problems—until they get to talking with each other and share some unhappy stories." The coy tone of the article notwithstanding, these women wield far more power than even the leaders of the WPP could have hoped for, and although probably none of these ministers would call herself a pacifist, they share a common goal with the WPP: establishing a link between women's issues and global politics. And just as the WPP drew on a diverse and global organization, so too does this group: women from Niger, El Salvador, Luxembourg, Liechtenstein, Madagascar, South Africa, and the Sudan share their stories and emerge with a plan for action. Albright's meeting, like Gale's fiction, illustrates the importance of women coming together across boundaries. The cosmopolitanism of Albright's late-twentieth-century dinner meeting finds its early-twentieth-century counterpart in Gale's Friendship Village, where a cosmopolitan neighborhood flourished within a vision of a peaceful world in which all of us are equal citizens.

Notes

1. Wisconsin was the first state to ratify the Nineteenth Amendment after it was passed in the U.S. Senate, in part due to the efforts of Gale's longtime friend Robert La Follette.
2. I use the term *feminist* rather than *suffragist* here to distinguish between those women who campaigned solely for the right to vote and those who viewed suffrage as but one aspect of a larger effort to redress social wrongs.
3. In *Not in Sisterhood: Edith Wharton, Willa Cather, Zona Gale and the Politics of Female Authorship*, I discuss Gale's two readerships and her corresponding public images in more detail. As an indication of her dual readership, her short fiction appeared in magazines such as *Everybody's Magazine, Woman's Home Companion*, and *Good Housekeeping*; her essays appeared in the *Nation* and the *New Republic*, among others.
4. Heterodoxy was a group of women who met on a monthly basis in New York from before World War I to the beginning of World War II. Founded by Marie Jenny Howe, the group was, in the words of Inez Haynes Irwin, "women who did things openly"—feminists who supported such radical social reforms as birth control, woman suffrage, and equal rights for African Americans. For more about Heterodoxy, see Judith Schwarz's wonderful book, *Radical Feminists of Heterodoxy: Greenwich Village, 1912–1940*.
5. Fola was also a member of Heterodoxy, which she claimed was her only refuge during the tempestuous months following her father's refusal to vote "yes" on Wilson's declaration of war.
6. Charles McCarthy popularized this phrase in his 1912 book of the same name, which helped to spread the progressive agenda across the country.
7. Gale's father was so worried about how her pacifist stance would be perceived that he bought war bonds in Gale's name.
8. The name of this women's club—Gale's gentle spoof on the club movement that gave so many women their first taste of civic involvement in the years before the passage of the Nineteenth Amendment—is a slight misnomer. Not all the women are married, and their activities extend far beyond cemetery beautification.

9. Despite this grand vision, of course, the suffrage movement in the United States was deeply split about whether or not to include African-American women in their pursuit of the vote; ultimately, NAWSA decided against it, lest they lose southern support in Congress. For further discussion of this issue, see, among others, Louise Michele Newman's *White Women's Rights: The Racial Origins of Feminism in the United States.*

10. Fetterley and Pryse argue that one of the hallmarks of regionalism is that, unlike local color, regionalism is written by someone who is a part of the culture being portrayed.

11. "The Story of Jeffro," first published in *Everybody's Magazine* in 1915, is reprinted in *Peace in Friendship Village* with a new preface from Gale, which reads in part: "when I have told this story . . . some one has always said: 'Yes, but there's another side to that. They aren't all Jeffros.' When stories are told of American gentleness, childlike faith, sensitiveness to duty . . . I do not remember to have heard any one rejoin: 'Yes, but Americans are not all like that.' So I wonder why this comment should be made about Jeffro" (45).

12. It is no coincidence that when Mis' Sykes tries on her costume for the Festival of Nations pageant, she wants to wear a crown, even though she is dressed as the United States.

13. Ross Posnock, in "The Dream of Deracination: The Uses of Cosmopolitanism," describes the NAACP and the ACLU (of which Gale was also a charter member) as "cosmopolitan political coalitions" (806).

14. Gale evidently tried to publish this story much earlier in her career, under the title "The Reception Surprise." She sent it to Ellery Sedgwick at the *Atlantic*, who rejected it, and then to the editor of *Everybody's Magazine*, who belied the title of his magazine when he rejected the story, saying that the country wasn't ready for its subject matter. I discuss this story and its publication history in more detail in *Not in Sisterhood.*

Works Cited

Anderson, Amanda. "Cosmopolitanism, Universalism, and the Divided Legacies of Modernity." In *Cosmopolitics: Thinking and Feeling beyond the Nation.* Ed. Pheng Cheah and Bruce Robbins. Minneapolis: University of Minnesota Press, 1998, 265–90.

Bourne, Randolph. "Trans-national America." *Atlantic Monthly*, July 1916.

Crossette, Barbara. "Albright Gathers Top Women to Address Women's Issues." *New York Times*, 26 September 1999, A26.

Derleth, August. *Still, Small Voice: The Biography of Zona Gale.* New York: Appleton-Century, 1940.

Fetterley, Judith, and Marjorie Pryse. *American Women Regionalists.* New York: Norton, 1992.

Foote, Stephanie. *Regional Fictions: Culture and Identity in Nineteenth-Century American Literature.* Madison: University of Wisconsin Press, 2001.

Gale, Zona. *Heart's Kindred.* New York: Macmillan, 1915.

―――. *Mothers to Men*. New York: Macmillan, 1911.

―――. *Peace in Friendship Village*. New York: Macmillan, 1919.

―――. "What Women Won in Wisconsin." *Nation*, 23 August 1922, 184–85.

Hollinger, David. *Postethnic America*. New York: Basic Books, 1995.

Inness, Sherrie, and Diana Royer. *Breaking Boundaries: New Perspectives on Women's Regional Writing*. Iowa City: University of Iowa Press, 1997.

Newman, Louise Michele. *White Women's Rights: The Racial Origins of Feminism in the United States*. New York: Oxford University Press, 1999.

Posnock, Ross. "The Dream of Deracination: The Uses of Cosmopolitanism." *American Literary History* 12, no. 4 (2000): 802–18.

Pryse, Marjorie. "Reading Regionalism: The 'Difference' It Makes." In *Regionalism Reconsidered: New Approaches to the Field*. Ed. David Jordan. New York: Garland Press, 1994, 47–63.

Schwarz, Judith. *Radical Feminists of Heterodoxy: Greenwich Village, 1912–1940*. Norwich, Vt.: New Victoria, 1986.

Scott, Anne Firor. *Natural Allies: Women's Associations in American History*. Chicago: University of Illinois Press, 1991.

Unger, Nancy. *Fighting Bob La Follette: The Righteous Reformer*. Chapel Hill: University of North Carolina Press, 2000.

Williams, Deborah Lindsay. *Not in Sisterhood: Edith Wharton, Willa Cather, Zona Gale, and the Politics of Female Authorship*. New York: Palgrave, 2000.

Woolf, Virginia. *Three Guineas*. New York: Harcourt, Brace, 1938.

Winnifred Eaton's "Japanese" Novels as a Field Experiment

DOMINIKA FERENS

All improbabilities are sheltered behind Japanese witchery,
for—what may not happen in Japan?
—Review of *The Wooing of Wistaria* in the *Critic* (1902)

I n the 1850s, an Austrian monk named Gregor Mendel conducted a
series of botanical experiments on pink and white sweet peas in a
monastery garden. We remember him today as a scientist who was
ignored by his contemporaries but whose article on pea hybridization was
simultaneously rediscovered in 1900 by three far-seeing researchers, giving rise to modern genetics. Yet recent studies have shown that scientists
at the turn of the century would not have responded as enthusiastically to
Mendel had they not already been invested in developing a theory of biological inheritance, a project that had acquired great urgency within their
lifetimes (Bowler 110–12, Darden 40). Before the geopolitical upheavals of
the late nineteenth century, before the colonial race, before the mass
movements of peoples between continents, and before the tremendous
class upheavals in the West caused by the Industrial Revolution, Mendel's
sweet peas were just that: sweet peas in an agricultural experiment. The
rhetoric of "dominance" versus "balance" of "dark and light population
types" did not acquire its special resonance for several decades. By 1900,
however, Mendel's sweet peas were found to hold the answer to the genetic
transmission of "unit characters," dominant and recessive traits that determined the number of grains in an ear of corn but also, supposedly, the
color of a child's skin, physical and intellectual "fitness," and even criminal
tendencies.[1]

In turn-of-the-century Western thought, "race" was understood to

account for differences in behavior, cultural practices and beliefs, and technological advancement of different peoples. In other words, the terms *race*
and *culture* overlapped to a much greater extent than they do now. The
word *culture* was used in the singular, interchangeably with *civilization*,
until Franz Boas introduced the plural usage around 1900. Boaz also
argued for the transforming influence of the environment on heredity, but
decades would pass before this idea, popularized by his students, would
gain wide acceptance.[2]

In the author Winnifred Eaton's formative years, popular discourse was
straining in the opposite direction. The volume of writings that invested
race with meaning rapidly increased as the vernacular absorbed such scientific concepts as hybridity, natural and sexual selection, and "superior"
and "inferior races." Herbert Spencer and Thomas Huxley had given a
new impetus to the nature versus nurture debate, but though popular sentiment at the turn of the century had tipped in favor of nature, the debate
was far from settled and Eaton needed no encouragement to join it.
Because of the social disadvantage imposed on her by the "half-caste" designation, Eaton had reason to question racial determinism. She also had
ample counterevidence gathered from personal experience and observation of her Chinese mother and biracial siblings—evidence she marshaled
in the genre of ethnographic romance. In representing successful "couplings" across race and in showing culture to be a product of nurture
rather than nature, Eaton attempted to assuage white fears of "coupling"
with nonwhites.

Winnifred Eaton's investment in this project was certainly understandable. As a half-Chinese/half-English Canadian who rose to fame as the
self-invented Japanese author Onoto Watanna at the end of the nineteenth
and beginning of the twentieth centuries, she began to conduct her own
genetic experiments using a fictional Japan as her field. Her complex
racial, class, and gender positioning drove her to seek new perspectives
that would account for her own biracial female subjectivity. Mendel-like,
she created characters of different races, made their paths cross, moni-
tored the environmental factors, introduced control groups, and kept
records. Several of her early works suggest that race is something of a
cipher and that culture is not genetically transmitted. Ten years into the
new century, however, Eaton came out with the novel *Tama*, which rein-
states the position of race as essence. In the language of genetics, the biracial heroine's Caucasian "characters" are aligned with the traits that allow
the "light population" to dominate the "dark." As the white half of Tama's
genetic makeup dominates her looks, so must the white man—a scien-

tist—subdue the hostile Japanese in order to win her. He does so as an individual (by overcoming an armed samurai with his bare hands) but also as a metonym for Western civilization, secure in the knowledge that he is "a citizen of a mightier country than this" (*Tama* 146).

Criticism of Winnifred Eaton's work does not account for this shift toward a more conservative mainstream view of race during the first decade of her career. Until recently, Eaton's "Japanese" novels had been discussed as formulaic romances set in exotic locales, or as exercises in literary tricksterism by a writer resistant to racial categorization. Lately, critics have been reading Eaton's work in new and productive ways to explore such themes as "cultural liminality" (Noreen Groover Lape) and the bonding of women across racial lines (Samina Najmi). I propose to read several of the novels through the trope of controlled field experiment. I argue that Eaton combined "romance" and "Japan" to create a fictional space where almost anything could happen; in that space she could work out racial and gender conflicts that she experienced in North America but that would not bear discussion in the realistic mode and in American settings. While I agree with my predecessors that to a certain extent Eaton succeeded in uncoupling race from culture, I want to caution against reductionist efforts to claim Eaton as the unrecognized practitioner of race theory as we know it today. By doing so we may repeat the error of Mendel's rediscoverers, who, as Peter Bowler argues, "read a great deal into his paper" in order to claim him as the precursor of their young discipline (103).

Yuko Matsukawa's essay "Cross-Dressing and Cross-Naming: Decoding Onoto Watanna" (1994) marks a change in the scholarly attitudes toward Eaton from a guarded curiosity to an almost unqualified enthusiasm for her subversive strategies. Noreen Groover Lape sets out to recuperate Winnifred Eaton from the status of Edith Eaton's errant younger sister by pointing to the former's successful representations of the "fluidity of cultural identity" (252). For Carol Vivian Spaulding, Eaton is an inspiring example of radical racial indeterminacy and a creator of characters who elude all efforts at racial categorization. Similarly, introducing her discussion of Eaton's *The Heart of Hyacinth*, Samina Najmi suggests that "Onoto Watanna is far ahead of her time in breaking free of the notion of biological race to show how a fluid identity can empower women" (129). Going furthest in vindicating Eaton, Najmi claims, "Watanna advances a concept that has only recently been termed [by Jonathan Okumura] 'situational ethnicity'" (144). I want to complicate these recent interpretations of Eaton's race theory by juxtaposing three of her earlier novels, *Miss Numè of Japan*

(1899), *The Heart of Hyacinth* (1903), and *A Japanese Blossom* (1906) with *Tama*, the 1910 "Japanese" novel that broke a four-year hiatus. To get a clearer sense of Eaton's ideas on race, we need to ask whether she saw culture as independent of race, how her views evolved over time, who in her fiction had access to "cultural fluidity," and how her works reinscribed racial determinism.

In the first years of her career, from about 1898 to 1904, Eaton wrote a number of well-researched ethnographic articles on topics such as "Japanese Girls and Women," "New Year's Day in Japan," and "Everyday Life in Japan." Judging by the contents of contemporary magazines, demand for such reading matter was high, and editors welcomed contributions from "native informants." Her first novel, *Miss Numè*, was brought out by Rand McNally, a publishing house that specialized in maps, guidebooks, and missionary tracts.[3] The first edition was illustrated with studio photographs of Japanese women, much like those in countless travel narratives in the heyday of *Japonisme*. Evidently the publishers felt *Miss Numè*'s ethnographic content would appeal to one or both of their target audiences: tourists and missionaries. Yet Eaton was less of an ethnographer concerned with the particulars of Japanese culture than an armchair ethnologist trying to understand the nature of race—the source of her own exotic difference in the eyes of mainstream society. Using ethnographic information collected by travel writers, in one novel after another she probed the relation between race and culture, and tested the possibility of interracial love.

That first novel, written two years before Eaton herself was married, studies the role played by race in courtship or love, which social science had come to call *sexual selection*. Marriage, the crowning moment of traditional romantic fiction, together with the process of selection leading up to it, acquired a new significance in the last decades of the nineteenth century when evolutionary theory began to take hold of the popular imagination. In Gillian Beer's words, "Darwin . . . emphasized not only natural—that is unwilled—selection, but also sexual selection. Both the individual will and the internalized values of a community play their part in the process of sexual selection. . . . It began to be asked what emotions, values, and reflex actions help the individual and the race to survive" (210). To write about love and marriage in turn-of-the-century America was to engage such highly charged discourses, whether one was Edith Wharton observing the courtship rituals of high society, or Winnifred Eaton contemplating the marriage options (or lack thereof) for a Eurasian working girl. Scholars such as Xiao-Huang Yin and Noreen Groover Lape have looked closely at the theme of marriage in the fiction of the Eaton sisters, but they have done so with little reference to turn-of-the-century race theory and the stakes surrounding racial intermarriage in Eaton's lifetime.[4] My interest lies in the ways in which Eaton used the genre of ethnographic romance to express her ideas on race and culture.

The children of Grace and Edward Eaton surely did not doubt that interracial love exists; they were themselves a product of it and experienced love for non-Eurasians. The question was not *whether* but *where* interracial love could exist. Place is therefore central to the "sexual selection" debate. Racial taboos regulating sexual selection posed problems for any literary treatment of miscegenation on American soil. Here white workers demanded the exclusion of Asians to protect what few privileges they had against "unfair competition," while eugenicists argued for the protection of middle- and upper-class whiteness from contamination through intermarriage with the "unfit"—those morally, physically, intellectually, and racially "inferior." Winnifred Eaton's sister Edith, who in 1909 would write, "I believe some day a great part of the world will be Eurasian" ("Leaves" 224), avoided the subject of miscegenation for the first fifteen years of her career. A single newspaper article, "Half-Chinese Children" (1895), and a short story, "Sweet Sin" (1898), are the sole exceptions. In both cases, the lives of the people concerned are deeply troubled, and "Sweet Sin" ends with the protagonist's suicide. Evidently, neither the real America nor a fictional "America" offered an acceptable setting for interracial love and marriage.

Japan, on the other hand, was outside the purview of American labor unionists, nativists, and eugenicists alike, and since miscegenated unions were not uncommon in the history of Western imperialism, the idea of interracial love in an exotic land was perfectly acceptable to late-Victorian readers. As Amy Ling writes, "though laws against miscegenation were on the books in many states during this time, Onoto Watanna's interracial romances seemed acceptable as long as they took place in Japan" (51). Cases such as those in Eaton's fiction involved a handful of Western tourists abroad and were no cause for concern. She planted them in a society stratified by gender and class but not race, where she could either invert the value of whiteness and color or create situations where white people were so few and had entered "Japan" so recently that the meaning of their whiteness was still negotiable. In her stories, Westerners enter communities that already have preconceived notions of whiteness, but they are given a chance to prove their individual worth. Upper-class Japanese are often portrayed as paradigms of tolerance and intellectual curiosity, while middle- and working-class Japanese take on some of the characteristics of North American nativists.

Although Amy Ling (49) and others have argued that Eaton's "Japanese" fiction follows old formulas, and even the narrator of Eaton's autobiographical novel *Me* confesses, "My success was founded upon a cheap and popular device" (153–54), there is a startling novelty about her miscegenation plots. For how conventional is the story of a young white American woman who seduces a Japanese student on his way home from the United States, while her fiancé woos and weds the Japanese student's betrothed (*Miss Numè*)? Where else do we encounter a "formulaic" tale of transculturation in which a white female infant is left to the care of a Japanese woman and develops a fierce attachment to Japan, while her surrogate mother's half-English son is bred to become an Englishman (*The Heart of Hyacinth*)? Can we really categorize as "formulaic" a romance that begins with the marriage of a widowed Japanese businessman to a young American widow (*A Japanese Blossom*)?[5] Each of these plots is a skeleton straight out of the American closet. Each plays on age-old racist narratives of white women despoiled by brown men, of white children snatched by gypsies, of the Oriental despot who holds a white slave in his harem. What allows Eaton to bring these skeletons out of the closet is her willingness to accommodate some reader expectations while defying others. The drapery around the skeletons *is* conventional, as is the creaky machinery of "mistaken identity" and "changing places" she used so often. Yet the machinery that made Eaton's novels stagy and therefore nonthreatening allowed her to sidestep the Asian equivalent of the "tragic mulatto" narrative—that of Madame Butterfly. Although this narrative evolved in times of slavery to reify the boundary between the proprietor class and human property, the racism that doomed white-Asian unions and their offspring was an extension of that which created the "tragic mulatto." Only with distant "Japan" as a setting was Eaton able to conceive and publish miscegenation stories with happy endings.

If we read Eaton's "Japan" as a field experiment, her plotting is better understood as controlled rather than contrived. Plot and character diagrams of *Miss Numè, The Heart of Hyacinth,* and *A Japanese Blossom* are deliberately symmetrical. In Mendelian experiments the scientist plants a "dark" and a "light population" of the same flowers on opposite sides of a field, then manually cross-pollinates them, and in the following season assesses whether one color has come to "dominate" or the "population types" balance each other. Similarly, Eaton's novels throw together two "population types" and follow the outcome. The cross-pollination occurs on either a cultural or a biological level, or simultaneously on both. Of course because of the social/cultural dimension, the symmetry can never be perfect: the stories are enacted on "Japanese" soil where whites are a minority. Gender-specific conventions in Japan and in the West create another asymmetry, and the unequal power of Japan and the United States in the international arena further distorts the picture. Nonetheless, in novels like *Miss Numè* and *Hyacinth*, Eaton attempts to match every interracial encounter with one in which the race and gender are reversed. For every successful experiment in cultural assimilation, there is usually a control group of characters who for various reasons resist the influence of the other culture. Finally, since Eaton's "Japan" functions like a photographic negative of North America, American racist assumptions have their Japanese equivalents.[6]

To produce *Miss Numè* Eaton rewrote an existing novel, John Long's *Miss Cherry-Blossom of Tokyo* (1895), partly redressing the race and gender imbalance of the earlier text and making alterations to disguise the borrowed elements. The borrowings have, as far as I know, gone undetected. Long is better known as the author of a collection of short stories that includes "Madame Butterfly" (1898), itself a rewrite of Pierre Loti's *Madame Chrysanthème* (1893). Eaton had already once critically engaged Long in her short story "A Half-Caste" (1899), which exposes the racist underpinning of the "Madame Butterfly" narrative. Interestingly, like Eaton, Long never visited Japan; according to the *Dictionary of American Biography*, all his Japanese writings are "based on the observations of his sister, Mrs. Irwin Correll, wife of a missionary." Thus Eaton's "Japan" is thrice removed from reality: observed by a missionary's wife and transformed into a fantasy by her brother. Drawing selectively on Long, Eaton absorbed some of his racist stereotypes. Yet the changes she made were substantial enough to alter the meaning of the story, so a comparison of the two texts is in order.

Long set *Miss Cherry-Blossom* in Tokyo's diplomatic milieu. His characters are a mix of Western consular staff, white men and women of leisure, and a handful of their Japanese counterparts. Eaton maintains Long's cast of major and minor characters, including a Japanese girl and an American diplomat, a scheming married woman and an abandoned fiancée, but she inserts several figures that alter the balance of power in the story. Eaton's Japanese girl, Miss Numè (Plum Blossom), and the white diplomat, Arthur Sinclair, are both betrothed to other people. Arthur's fiancée Cleo and Numè's childhood sweetheart Takashima meet on shipboard on the way to Japan, and it is Cleo rather than Takashima who initiates their love affair. The text constructs the Japanese man as a desirable partner for Cleo (and several other white women on board), though one rendered "impossible" by the miscegenation taboo. A sympathetically drawn busybody, Mrs. Davis, introduces Arthur to her friend Numè to cure him of his prejudice against Japanese women. But when Arthur comes to like one Japanese woman too much for Mrs. Davis's liking, she does all in her power to prevent miscegenation. Arthur and Numè succeed in getting together in spite of Mrs. Davis, but the Western taboo that keeps white women from marrying men of color is as deeply imprinted on Cleo's mind as on the author's, so that the former continues to deny her love for Takashima and drives him to suicide.

Unlike Eaton, Long makes no pretense at balancing his "population types." His interest lies in the effects of the interracial encounter on his white characters. Cherry-Blossom acts as a foil. Her simple if not simple-minded chatter throws their sophistication into relief. The white characters fill the book with high-society banter that Cherry-Blossom cannot follow, let alone contribute to, yet they insist on her symbolic presence in their midst. As one worldly matron puts it, "Miss Cherry-Blossom, you must come with us to give the necessary local color to the affair" (84). By contrast, Eaton's Numè, a reincarnation of Cherry-Blossom, is allowed as much space to think and speak as the three other lovers. Though she, like Cherry-Blossom, is infantilized and stereotyped, we are made to understand from the attention other characters pay her that her words and thoughts are as engrossing as those of Cleo or Arthur. One of Long's minor male Japanese characters, the disloyal secretary, splits into two men in *Miss Numè*: another minor but less odious secretary, and Takashima, one of the two romantic leads. However stereotypical these characterizations of the Japanese, we need to see them in light of Eaton's effort to balance the ratio of Asian to white characters and redistribute agency as well as charisma among them.

In her stylized "Japan," Eaton conducts a double experiment in sexual selection. To a contemporary reader, the novel may seem to do little more than reinforce nineteenth-century racist assumptions that while white men may possess women of color, any union between a man of color and a white woman is unnatural and punishable by death. Eaton had, to some degree, internalized this belief since of the four lovers it is Takashima who has to die. Nonetheless, to have cast an Asian male as a romantic hero to whom several white women are attracted, and whose behavior toward Cleo is impeccable by Victorian standards, was an unprecedented step in American fiction. It is not the inappropriateness of Takashima's declaration of love but Cleo's cowardly rejection of it that the reader is asked to condemn. The union between Arthur and Numè *is* happily consummated once Arthur overcomes his "unreasoning prejudice" toward Japanese women (83).

In *Miss Numè*, Eaton gives us a fictional study of various grades of cultural assimilation in progress, from the elderly characters of both races who are too set in their ways to accept difference, through newcomers to Japan who insist on imported foods and heavy Western furniture, to Arthur Sinclair who very nearly "goes native." Admittedly the transculturation is not quite symmetrical, for the text assumes the Japanese have more to learn from the Westerners than the reverse. Though Numè has never left Japan, she has picked up many Western ideas and a little English by interacting with her father's American neighbors. She studies Western ways throughout the novel. Takashima has been following the same track when we first meet him: after eight years in American schools he has undergone the greatest transformation of any of the characters. He is so changed, in fact, that he can no longer fit into the prescribed role of a Japanese son.

However, many racial "traits" thought to define "Americanness" and "Japaneseness" are in flux throughout the novel, and if not all attributes typically assigned to one or the other of the races are disputed, a good many are shown to be present in both. White Americans, caught up in a linear notion of civilization, claimed the apex on the grounds of intellectual development, aesthetic sensibility, and capacity for deep emotion. In nineteenth-century Western thought, a "highly developed" aesthetic sense was not just a function of being smarter than someone with "simpler" tastes. A person capable of appreciating the beauty of rugged Alpine peaks was understood to be a fundamentally better, more spiritual being. Matthew Arnold's *Culture and Anarchy* and Herbert Spencer's essays "Personal Beauty" and "Progress: Its Law and Cause" talk about aesthetics in a moral and developmental framework. To question the racial hierarchy, Eaton foregrounds the emotional and artistic sensibilities of her Japanese characters. We often see Takashima, who "like the rest of his countrymen . . . was a passionate lover of nature," quietly contemplating the beauty of a sunset at sea or Mount Fuji. An articulate aesthete, Takashima holds his own in conversations with Westerners. Numè, in turn, carries the story's emotional burden. She is a hyperfeminine bundle of passions—love, fear, pain, confusion, and despair—rather than the emotionless doll some of the white characters believe her to be. Several Americans stoop to base tricks and evasions, while their Japanese counterparts exhibit a strong sense of dignity and responsibility. Thus the text denies that "American- ness" is any guarantee of integrity or moral superiority.

Eaton's first three novels, *Miss Numè*, *A Japanese Nightingale*, and *The Wooing of Wistaria*, all tackle the problem of race from the point of view of young adults who must work around preexisting prejudices, taboos, and laws in order for sexual selection to take its "natural" course. The next two novels I discuss here, *The Heart of Hyacinth* and *A Japanese Blossom*, center on the socialization of children, particularly on the ways in which certain culture-specific predispositions commonly thought to be hereditary are, in fact, learned. Of Eaton's novels, *The Heart of Hyacinth* probably works hardest against Western assumptions of cultural superiority.

The action of *Hyacinth* covers seventeen years, from the day of Hya- cinth's birth to her marriage. Hyacinth is born in Madame Aoi's house, to a dying white woman who seeks refuge there from a faithless white hus- band, Richard Lorrimer. Hyacinth's development is paralleled by that of Koma, eight years her senior, son of Aoi and a wealthy Englishman who is now dead. The goal of this controlled experiment is to see the effect of a Japanese environment on a genetically white child and the effect of an English education on a Japanese-English boy raised in isolation from his Japanese peers. The narrator studies the children's relationship to their environment and to each other at four critical stages in their lives, reveal- ing the subtle changes that have taken place in the interim. At each point we are asked to gauge the degree to which they have grown into or away from Japanese culture. The age and gender asymmetry between the chil- dren complicates the comparison. It makes for interesting interactions and adds variety to the otherwise predictable plot.

Madame Aoi has converted to Christianity and English is spoken in her home, though she retains Japanese dress. She keeps her son away from Japanese children so as to raise him as his father's heir. Two sets of cul- tural influences tug at Aoi and her children. Each side is represented by a handful of character-types, few of them endearing. The villagers, the schoolteacher, and the Yamashiro family whose son wants to marry Hya- cinth, stand for traditional Japan. Two English missionaries, an American lawyer and a diplomat, and eventually Hyacinth's father with his second wife, descend on the Aoi household in an attempt to draw the resistant Hyacinth westward.

At the time of Hyacinth's birth, Koma is a withdrawn, lonesome child; the narrative then skips about seven years during which foster brother and sister are inseparable. The story resumes when Koma is a youth of sixteen devouring Western literature. Hyacinth has become a naughty tomboy with no inkling of the troubles ahead. The author captures the family in a symbolic tableau, looking at their own dim reflections in the well: "'See,' said little Hyacinth. 'There's big cherry tree in well, and little girl under it also.' Aoi looked at the reflection, lingered pensively at the three faces in the water, then drew away. 'Come,' she said. 'Listen; those temple bells already are beginning to ring'" (48). In this private moment they are still just a family, not defined by anyone else. Hyacinth, a child deliberately raised without mirrors, does not even recognize herself at the bottom of the well. No outsider—not even the narrator—comments on the incongruity of their small group. No one, as yet, has a stake in claiming the children's racial allegiance. But the bells interrupt their private moment, calling them to church, and on this Western holiday the two ministers will advise Aoi to send Koma to England, in accordance with his father's will.

When the West claims Koma, Hyacinth rebels against the authority of the church and turns to the Japanese community. After a time she so thoroughly identifies with it that she "would shout strange names whenever the gaunt figure of the white missionary appeared. 'Foreign debbil! Clistian!'—such were the names this little Caucasian girl bestowed on the representatives of her race" (66). Koma claims his English roots offstage, apparently without impediments. When four years later he returns, Hyacinth shuns him too, until he changes out of his dark suit into a kimono. At twelve, Hyacinth learns from Koma that she herself is white, but the knowledge does not affect her love for Aoi and for Japan. She wears the kimono as camouflage and is not interested in trying on her mother's American dress that Aoi has kept as an heirloom. At seventeen, she accepts a marriage proposal from a strictly traditional Japanese family. The news of her father's arrival from America makes her run for the hills, and when she finally has to face him, she acts the role of a demure Japanese maiden for protection:

With drooping head, Hyacinth softly entered the room. At first glance she seemed no different from any other Japanese girl, save that she was somewhat taller. She was dressed in kimono and obi, her hair freshly arranged in its smooth butterfly mode. Her face was bent to the floor, so that they could scarcely see more than its outline.

She hesitated a moment before them; then, as though unaware of the impetuous motion towards her of the man she knew was her father, she subsided to the mats and bowed her head at his feet. (232)

Readers who have come to know Hyacinth as a vivacious, willful young woman can now see in close detail each of the elements of her Japanese persona: the clothing, hairdo, demeanor, and exaggerated performance of the ceremonial bow. In fact the motif of dressing and undressing repeatedly draws attention to the constructedness of racial difference. Scenes of Aoi and Hyacinth coaxing their hair into appropriate styles, of Aoi, Hyacinth, and Koma practicing their English on each other, of Koma changing into and out of Western clothes, of strangers reading contradictory meanings into Hyacinth's features depending on what they believe to be her "true" race—all reinforce the narrative's message that heredity does not determine a subject's cultural identity. The novel's climactic moments are those in which Hyacinth and Koma make decisions concerning family and national allegiance. Paradoxically, the white Hyacinth asserts her Japaneseness by breaking the long-standing Japanese tradition of filial piety and acting in defiance of her white father. The biracial Koma, in turn, chooses to remain in Japan in order to marry Hyacinth, and thus places love for his family over the allure of life in the West.

The wearing off of cultural difference through intimacy is the theme of *A Japanese Blossom*, a fictional study of Japanese and American children brought together by chance in one household. As in *Hyacinth*, Eaton is interested in children's reactions and adjustment to another culture depending on their age and gender. Instead of tracking two children through childhood and adolescence, here she introduces characters ranging from infancy to seventeen, and compresses the action into the two years immediately before and during the Russo-Japanese war of 1904–5. While Eaton continues to question racial determinism, she also exploits the American public's fascination with Japanese military prowess and, in effect, comes close to making it a national trait. Consequently, *A Japanese Blossom* can be viewed as a transitional novel between her antideterminist early fiction and the later *Tama*, which bears traces of eugenicism.

A Japanese Blossom focuses on children's changing responses to miscegenation, cultural conflict, and war, presenting a model for resolving racial prejudice within the family. Yet even as the novel condemns brutality, the war provides a glamorous, titillating backdrop. In effect, we are left with an ambivalent text that upholds pacifism but is itself energized by war. Much has been said about the impossibility of effectively contesting a phenomenon without representing and thus reinscribing it. *A Japanese Blossom* is a peculiar case in point because it invokes Japan's victory over Russia as evidence that invalidates once and for all the claim that Asians are an "inferior" race.

Although the story of *A Japanese Blossom* was neither more nor less far-fetched than Eaton's earlier plots, it failed to enchant in the way *Wistaria* and *Hyacinth* had—perhaps because the author misjudged the mood of the times. When she began writing, Japan's popularity had reached a high point on the East Coast, but by the time the book came out voices alarmed at Japan's expansionism had begun to dominate. Eaton had also lost sight of her intended audience: though the text dealt with adult themes, its comic elements and focus on children placed the book in the juvenile fiction category.

By this time, Eaton, too, was tiring of japonica and resented that publishers pressed her into this niche. In 1906, she wrote *The Diary of Delia* in Irish brogue and published no more novels until 1910. When she resumed her career after the break, it was with another "Japanese" novel, *Tama*, a text very different from the three discussed above in terms of historical setting and characterization, as well as attitudes toward heredity and race. In sharp contrast to *Blossom*, *Tama*'s action goes back to the end of the feudal era and the emperor's restoration in 1871, with references to the 1850s. There are also significant differences between the characters of *Tama* and its predecessors. In the earlier novels, the white and Japanese protagonists were ordinary rather than heroic: Arthur, Cleo, Takashima, and Numè were nice enough people but were burdened with a generous share of weakness.

Hyacinth's and Koma's exceptionality lay in their peculiar social positioning, not in any innate qualities, and the Kurukawa children were quite ordinary. Each of these fictional experiments in transculturation seemed to offer hope that, in time, racial intolerance can be overcome since history is responsible for behavioral differences commonly attributed to race. In *Tama*, that hope begins to crack. The white American teacher, O-Tojin-san, who comes to the town of Fukui to set up a college is a hero not just of exceptional intellect and moral character but also of Herculean proportions. The heroine, Tama, is a Puck-like imp, singular in every way. Child of a Japanese priestess and an Englishman, she is blond, blue-eyed, *blind*, and lives in the wild, hounded by her mother's people who believe her to be a fox-woman—an evil spirit in human flesh. Tojin's mission in *Tama* is not to learn a new way of life but to reeducate the Japanese and save Tama from them. Tama's role is to allow herself to be tamed and saved.[7] Next to Tojin and Tama, the other characters in the novel are dwarfed, reduced to a faceless mob of "foreign-haters," or displayed for comic relief.

Interestingly, Tojin's character is based on a combination of two historical figures: William Griffis and Lafcadio Hearn. Griffis worked in Japan in the years 1870–74, including a year in Fukui, under circumstances similar to those described in *Tama*. Hearn came to Japan two decades later, married a Japanese woman, and stayed permanently. Both were teachers. Whereas Hearn's face had been disfigured by an eye injury, the fictional Tojin's is marked by smallpox. Both men are extremely self-conscious about their looks: Hearn always posed for photographs with the disfigured side of his face away from the camera, while Tojin is afraid to let Tama see him at all, for fear she might reject him. The myth of the fox-woman is most likely a borrowing from Hearn, who introduced American readers to this and other legends.

Instead of doing a close reading of the novel, which has already been astutely analyzed by Rachel Lee, I focus on the shift in Eaton's literary approach to race and culture that led her to idealize whiteness and embrace exceptionalism. In my analysis of the three earlier texts I have attempted to point out the (imperfect) symmetries that make for awkward plots but preserve some semblance of balance between the races. *Tama*, on the other hand, is remarkable for the imbalance between the male and female protagonist; between the heroic American and the cowardly, superstitious Japanese; between the enlightened West and the as-yet-unredeemed East. Although the novel condemns racism, bigotry, and mob violence, it firmly links these transgressions to the Japanese. Thus it rationalizes any racial prejudices white readers bring to the text.

Whereas the earlier novels downplayed the notion of "blood" or racial affinity, *Tama* makes it crucial once more. It is because Tojin recognizes in Tama "his own skin and blood" (107), because of "her unbound hair of gold, her bosom and face of snow" (171), that his curiosity about her turns into a sense of responsibility for her well-being. Tojin and Tama seek one another obsessively, through great obstacles, because each has heard of the other's whiteness. The sight of Tama's blond tresses sparks in Tojin a "revolution, mad, irresistible passion of the primitive man" (172). In declaring to Tama, "You are not Japanese" (123), Tojin assumes that since Tama has inherited her father's physical characteristics, she is also somehow culturally white. The more time and passion Tojin invests in pursuing Tama, the less interest he takes in his students until he abandons them altogether. Thus to elevate whiteness the novel must devalue the Japanese. It is tempting to say that, whether consciously or not, Eaton managed to circumvent her publishers' injunction to "stick to [her] last" ("You Can't Run Away From Yourself" 5)—japonica—by writing a "Japanese" romance about white people.

Except for the portrayal of a handful of Tojin's favorite students, the text repeatedly tropes the Japanese as animals, scuttling "like panic-stricken rats" or "snarling" and "growling" like "whipped dogs." Why might such negative images of the Japanese have worked their way into *Tama?* Why are Tojin and Tama inscribed in a messianic discourse, he promising to lead her "out of the wilderness," she asserting, "You are the light"? Why the "aureole" around her head? Why the need to reassure readers in 1910 of white superiority?

As I suggest above, public sentiment toward Japan did start to turn after 1905. According to historian Roger Daniels, the effects began to be felt most strongly on the West Coast, starting with the move in California to segregate Japanese schoolchildren in 1906 and to prevent "aliens ineligible for citizenship" from purchasing land. One by one, states began to extend the "Mongolian" category in pre-1902 antimiscegenation statutes to include the Japanese, and after 1909, seven states passed new legislation prohibiting Japanese from marrying whites (Sollors 402–7). On the national level, Congress passed a bill to ban Japanese immigration via Hawaii, Mexico, and Canada in 1907, and early in 1908 the Gentlemen's Agreement was negotiated with Japan, whereby the Japanese government would not issue passports to laborers bound for the United States (Daniels 38–45). The growing mistrust of Japan can best be measured by the preparations initiated by the U.S. Navy for defense in case of a Japanese attack on the Philippines or the West Coast.[8] William Griffis, champion of the Japanese since the 1870s, was surely responding to these alarming signals when he wrote *The Japanese Nation in Evolution* (1907) offering proof that the Japanese are racially white. Griffis claims that since the Japanese are descended from the Aryan Ainu tribes, "to-day the white man's blood is in the Japanese, for the better working of his own brain, the improvement of his own potencies, and the beautifying of his own physiognomy. The Aryan features in the Japanese body and mind are plainly discernible, and in thousands of typical instances they are striking" (26). Although he concedes that the Japanese have an admixture of Malay and Mongol blood, he states emphatically that they are unlike the Chinese in physiology, language, and customs, and must therefore be treated on par with other Caucasians. When Americans designated the Japanese the "new Yellow Peril," Griffis made them white.

Compounded with the deteriorating image of the Japanese was the growing preoccupation with the concept of race in America. If the number and type of entries in the *Reader's Guide to Periodical Literature* is any indication, between 1905 and 1910 there was an explosion of popular writings on race and heredity. *Reader's Guide* for the decade of 1890–99 contains just seven references to articles on "race" and ten on "eugenics." In the next volume covering 1900–1904 there are six articles listed under "race" and two under "eugenics." However, from 1905 to 1909, there are twenty-seven entries on "eugenics," sixteen on "race," forty-four on "race problems," twenty-five on "race riots" (against African Americans, Japanese, and Chinese), over a dozen on "race suicide," as well as references to such listings as "Caste; Immigration; also Chinese; Jews; Negroes; also names of countries, subheads Native races."

Although the number of published articles may not necessarily be correlated with a sudden deterioration of race relations in America, for those had been turbulent for centuries, it does mean that Americans were reading more than ever into race, and writing about whiteness with astonishing passion. "Sexual selection," wrote Havelock Ellis in the *Eclectic Magazine* (which also published Eaton's and her husband's work), "even when left to random influences, is still not left to chance; it follows ascertainable laws. . . . People do not tend to fall in love with those who are in racial respects a contrast to themselves; they do not tend to fall in love with foreigners" (19). Once the very notion of sexual selection between races is eradicated, one can concentrate on the "eugenic ideal," which will allow the races at a "high stage of civilization" to compensate for their dwindling numbers: "If the ideal of quantity is lost to us, why not seek the ideal of quality? . . . are we now not free to seek that our children, though few, should be at all events fit, the finest, alike in physical and psychical constitution, that the world has ever seen?" (15). It is worth considering what those powerful discourses may have meant to Eaton, a professional writer immersed in the popular culture of the day.

Keeping the arguments of Ellis and Griffis in mind, we should give Eaton full credit for using her fiction to explore racial intermarriage and the possibility of Asians assimilating Western cultural values and vice versa. It does become apparent, however, that her fictional experiments with "decoupling" culture from race were contingent on the approval of her reading public. In times when the general public wanted to believe that "like is attracted to like" (Ellis 19) and that elite Western culture is a synonym for Culture, it would have been difficult to write about sexual selection across all races and to hold up cultural fluidity as an ideal even if Eaton were strongly invested in the cause. Cultural fluidity in Eaton's novels is available to biracial characters whose features are ambiguous, and to the refined, educated Japanese and Caucasians. Working-class characters of both races, like the Irish nanny Nora in *Blossom*, or Tojin's servants in *Tama*, seem frozen in their ethnic ways. Neither is cultural fluidity available to the black Jamaicans in *Me* (1915) or to the Chinese men in *Cattle* (1924) and *His Royal Nibs* (1925). Finally, cultural fluidity in Eaton's fiction means, with a few exceptions, the freedom to choose Western ways and, in the case of the biracial protagonists, to marry a white person.

To point out the contradictions in Eaton's understanding of race is not to discount the value of her texts in their own right or their value as unique historical records. On the contrary, her novels give us a rare insight into the complexities of turn-of-the-century mainstream ideology of race inflected by the agile, inquisitive mind of a biracial writer. It was the concept of race that absorbed Eaton in the early years of her career rather than the pursuit of systematic knowledge of Japanese culture. As I argued above, Eaton found in the genre of ethnographic fiction a suitable platform from which to interrogate race and redefine miscegenation. Her choice of "Japan" as a fictional space for exploring such controversial subjects was motivated precisely by its geographical and cultural distance from the United States, and by its positive image. The American press had, for some time, been styling Japan as a sort of anti-China—a more energetic, tractable, and progressive Asian nation. Consequently, the Japanese were felt to be less alien than any other nonwhite people. Had Eaton been interested in ethnography as such, she might have chosen a more easily accessible group and engaged in her own participant observation. Had she felt the need to identify with a nonwhite community, her life might have followed a course similar to that of her sister Edith (who eventually joined a Chinese immigrant community). Instead, like the nineteenth- and early-twentieth-century anthropologists, Eaton based her writing on solid ethnographic homework. When in the wake of the Russo-Japanese war Japan's exotic aura began to wane, Eaton sought difference elsewhere: inside the home where lines of class divide the kitchen from the parlor, on the closing Western frontier, and in the dance halls of San Francisco's Barbary Coast.

Notes

A longer version of this paper is included in *Edith and Winnifred Eaton: Chinatown Missions and Japanese Romances* (Urbana: University of Illinois Press, 2002).

1. The idea of reading Eaton's "Japanese" novels through the rhetoric of Mendelian genetics occurred to me at a joint talk by biologist Banu Subramian and rhetorician Michael Whitmore, "Tropes in the Field: A Rhetoric of Science in Action," given at UCLA in May 1998. In a subtle, self-reflexive way the speakers explored the intersection of the humanities and the sciences to make language visible in scientific description and to probe the ideological entanglements of rhetorical

studies. Examining Subramian's dissertation on the hybridization of morning glories, Whitmore pointed out the continuing indebtedness of Mendelian genetics to the discourse of struggle, balance, and domination, as well as to the evolutionary discourse of race. This paper reverses Subramian's and Whitmore's strategy in that it borrows scientific terms to elucidate literary texts.

2. See Stocking, *Race, Culture, and Evolution*, 46–49, 61–76; Clifford, *Predicament of Culture*, 92–93; and Carl Degler, *In Search of Human Nature*, 139–211.

3. I thank Jean Lee Cole for this insightful piece of information.

4. Subsequent to writing this paper I became aware of Pat Shea's article "Winnifred Eaton and the Politics of Miscegenation in Popular Fiction," which covers some of the same ground as "Japan as a Field Experiment." Although I also examine the impact of sexual and racial environment on Eaton's fiction, I reach different conclusions.

5. Writing against the Madame Butterfly paradigm, according to which Asian women inevitably fall for white blackguards, David Henry Hwang in his play *M. Butterfly* tries to make his audience imagine the reverse: "Consider it this way: what would you say if a blonde homecoming queen fell in love with a short Japanese businessman?" It is remarkable that Eaton tackled the same racist stereotype as far back as 1906.

6. It is not my intention to deny that the Japanese harbored prejudices against Westerners. Akira Iriye's study *Mutual Perceptions* makes it clear that in their encounters with Americans the Japanese were often guided by racist assumptions. Also Benedict Anderson suggests that Japan's transformation into a nation-state after 1854 was, in part, facilitated by racist sentiment. I merely suggest that Eaton's rendition of Japanese prejudices was not based on firsthand knowledge but rather reflected the situation in America where a stronger majority exercised its power over a disenfranchised minority.

7. Rachel Lee interprets the symbolic aspect of Tama's blindness: if Tama stands for a Japan infused with Western ideas but still resistant to them, Tojin's power to bring to Fukui a white surgeon who removes the cataracts from Tama's eyes parallels his own role as civilizing agent to the Japanese.

8. Daniels as well as Tupper and McReynolds show that diplomatic considerations led President Taft and Congress to temper the rampant racism of California legislators and labor unionists. Certainly not all Americans were swayed by the Yellow Peril rhetoric, but as Daniels demonstrates, even the East Coast was rocked by war scares in 1907 and 1912–13.

Works Cited

Beer, Gillian. *Darwin's Plot: Evolutionary Narrative in Darwin, George Eliot, and Nineteenth-Century Fiction*. London: Routledge, 1983.

Bowler, Peter. *The Mendelian Revolution: The Emergence of Hereditarian Concepts in Modern Science and Society*. Baltimore: Johns Hopkins University Press, 1989.

Clifford, James. *The Predicament of Culture: Twentieth-Century Ethnography, Literature, and Art*. Cambridge, Mass.: Harvard University Press, 1988.

Daniels, Roger. *The Politics of Prejudice: The Anti-Japanese Movement in California and the Struggle for Japanese Exclusion.* New York: Athenaeum, 1974.

Darden, Lindley. *Theory Change in Science: Strategies from Mendelian Genetics.* New York: Oxford University Press, 1991.

Degler, Carl. *In Search of Human Nature: The Decline and Revival of Darwinism in American Social Thought.* New York: Oxford University Press, 1991.

Eaton, Winnifred [Onoto Watanna]. *The Diary of Delia: Being a Veracious Chronicle of the Kitchen with Some Side-Lights on the Parlour.* New York: Doubleday, 1907.

———. *The Heart of Hyacinth.* New York: Harper, 1902.

———. *A Japanese Blossom.* New York: Harper, 1906.

———. *Miss Numè of Japan: A Japanese-American Romance.* Chicago: Rand McNally, 1899.

———. *Tama.* New York: Harper, 1910.

———. *The Wooing of Wistaria.* New York: Harper, 1903.

———. "You Can't Run Away From Yourself" (typescript, n.d., 192?). Winnifred Reeve Papers, University of Calgary Library, Special Collections.

Ellis, Havelock. "Eugenics and St. Valentine." *Eclectic Magazine* 147, no. 1 (1906): 14–20.

Griffis, William Elliot. *The Japanese Nation in Evolution.* London: Harrap, 1907.

———. *The Mikado's Empire.* New York: Harper, 1877.

Huxley, Thomas H. *Evidence of Man's Place in Nature.* New York: Appleton, 1886.

———. *Evolution and Ethics and Other Essays.* New York: Appleton, 1894.

Hwang, David Henry. *M. Butterfly.* New York: Plume, 1988.

Iriye, Akira. "Japan as Competitor, 1895–1917." In *Mutual Images: Essays in American-Japanese Relations.* Ed. Akira Iriye. Cambridge, Mass.: Harvard University Press, 1975, 73–99.

Lape, Noreen Groover. "West of the Border: Cultural Liminality in the Literature of the Western American Frontiers." Ph.D. diss., Temple University, 1996.

Lee, Rachel. "Journalistic Representations of Asian Americans and Literary Responses, 1910–1920." In *Interethnic Companion to Asian American Literature.* Ed. King-Kok Cheung. Cambridge: Cambridge University Press, 1997.

Ling, Amy. *Between Worlds: Women Writers of Chinese Ancestry.* New York: Pergamon Press, 1990.

Long, John Luther. *Miss Cherry-Blossom.* Philadelphia: Lippincott, 1895.

Matsukawa, Yuko. "Cross-Dressing and Cross-Naming: Decoding Onoto Watanna." In *Tricksterism in Turn-of-the-Century American Literature: A Multicultural Perspective.* Ed. Elizabeth Ammons and Annette White-Parks. Hanover, N.H.: University Press of New England, 1994, 106–25.

Najmi, Samina. "Representations of White Women in Works by Selected African American and Asian American Authors." Ph.D. diss., Tufts University, 1997.

Shea, Pat. "Winnifred Eaton and the Politics of Miscegenation in Popular Fiction (Popular Literature and Film)." *MELUS* 22, no. 2 (1997): 19–35.

Sollors, Werner. *Neither Black Nor White: Explorations in Interracial Literature.* Cambridge, Mass.: Harvard University Press, 1997.

Spaulding, Carol Vivian. "Blue-Eyed Asians: Eurasianism in the Work of Edith Eaton/ Sui Sin Far, Winnifred Eaton/Onoto Watanna, and Diana Chang." Ph.D. diss., University of Iowa, 1996.

Spencer, Herbert. *Progress: Its Law and Cause*. New York: J. Fitzgerald, 1881.

Stocking, George W. Jr. *Race, Culture, and Evolution: Essays in the History of Anthropology*. New York: Macmillan, 1968.

Tupper, Eleanor, and George E. McReynolds. *Japan in American Public Opinion*. New York: Macmillan, 1937.

Yin, Xiao-Huang. "Between the East and West: Sui Sin Far—the First Chinese-American Woman Writer." *Arizona Quarterly* 47, no. 4 (1991): 49–84.

II

THE MIDDLEBROW
AND
MAGAZINE
CULTURE

Feminist New Woman Fiction in Periodicals of the 1920s

MAUREEN HONEY

It is becoming increasingly clear that American writers of the early twentieth century were drawn to the subject of woman's proper place as a site of dynamic change and redefinition of the self. Magazine fiction reflected this cultural preoccupation, and it is this medium that most spoke to masses of women locating themselves within the new century. Whether we look at the passing narratives published in the *Crisis* of Harlem Renaissance writer Jessie Fauset, the critiques of colonialist patriarchy in stories of the *Century* by Mexican-American Maria Cristina Mena, the biracial Japanese romances of Winnifred Eaton (Onoto Watanna) published in *Harper's Weekly*, or the modern love stories of Zona Gale, Edith Barnard Delano, or Elinor Glyn published in mainstream women's magazines, we find a common concern with women's autonomy as free agents. In addition, such writers framed many of their romances with an interrogation of male authority figures who try to control their female employees, wives, sweethearts, or daughters. High culture artists addressed these issues as well, but the middlebrow writer publishing in a mass medium operated in a narrative landscape of archetypal characters representing old and new ways of being, as well as traditional and modern conceptions of woman's place in the developing industrial order. They were thus able to draw more clearly the battlelines in a gender war over how women were to fit into the modern world of new technologies, educational opportunities, and changing cultural values.

I maintain that one of the central aspects of this modernist literary wave, dating from about 1914 through 1930, was the appearance of a protofeminist popular heroine whose career aspirations are reconciled with her need for a nurturing personal life that supports her modern ambitions and talents. A New Woman character similar to this figure had appeared in American fiction at least by the 1890s, but prewar magazine stories largely concluded in romantic failure or serious compromise of her desire to live in the world on her own terms.[1] The aspiring professional, writer, actress, painter, or singer left the parental home (usually in a Midwestern small town) for adventure in the great metropolis (usually New York) with high hopes but returned, a chastened and disillusioned prodigal daughter, to a lifestyle uncomfortably similar to that of her traditional mother. Alternatively, she stuck with her career goals but was unable to form a satisfying personal life and endured much emotional deprivation or even death.[2] In contrast, after World War I began—apart from the occasional "angel of the hearth" or flapper who loses out to a more modest rival—the thrust of romance fiction was toward a positive resolution of the heroine's conflict between autonomy and love. She was often able to have it all—financial success, creative work, and a supportive intimate relationship. Even when she was unable to make a good love match, her vocational rewards tended to balance her romantic losses. Indeed, the definition of modern marriage in these tales, for good or ill, is that a wife does not automatically quit wage work to devote her life to the home, and she expects her mate to be a comrade rather than a breadwinner.

Heroines of this period are frequently described as "restless," eager to do something "useful" in the world, and anxious to flee the circumscribed orbit of parental authority in order to make their way in an urban environment bustling with change and possibility. They are in geographical as well as other kinds of movement, frequently abandoning small-town communities for metropolitan areas. In doing so, they reject settled, family-oriented life on the margins in favor of open-ended, individual effort within the heart of modern technological society. Blanche Gelfant has identified this journey as the heroine's existential voyage toward self-definition: "Freedom seems to [the heroine] inherent in a fluid if disorganized urban society, one that by its disorder and indifference has released her from the roles assigned to women by history and myth" (45).[3] Big city anonymity gives the heroine a chance to remake herself into a New Woman in harmony with the dawning new age of individual opportunity.

The New Woman heroine's flight from a small town, where her mother endures a selfless, unstimulating existence, signals the shattering of an old consensus about the nature of women and progress. Many early feminists maintained that women rightly occupied a unique space, separate from the world created by men. The complaint was that men's sphere had grown too powerful, and they insisted on strengthening women's domesticating influence. Both Rosalind Rosenberg and Nancy F. Cott argue that the distinguishing feature of *modern* feminism, that defined in the 1920s, was the assertion of an essential sameness between women and men and the ensuing demand that women have equal access to the public marketplace of ideas and commerce. This core tenet of modern feminist thinking is fictionally represented in women's magazines by the small town—a dying vestige of woman's past isolation from civilization's inner workings—and the beckoning urban center, alive with possibility. The New Woman heroine leaves behind whatever power she had in the familial community because it is on the periphery of life; its separation from the public workings of society makes her vulnerable to a deathlike passivity that comes from being irrelevant in the modern world.

This literary discussion of expanded female roles was arguably at its most intense and optimistic pitch in the middlebrow fiction produced by and aimed at women in the World War I era and its aftermath, but it has received little attention from scholars. Largely unread, keeping silent vigil in libraries, this literature is testament to an era when the market for magazine fiction was huge. Conservative estimates place the number of periodicals in the United States by 1923 somewhere in the neighborhood of 3,000, with a combined per-issue circulation of 128,621,000 (Peterson 58–59). To put these figures in perspective, the population at this time numbered around 114 million; only 60,000 homes possessed radios in 1922, yet as early as 1905 there was an average of four magazines to every household—a figure that increased dramatically over the ensuing twenty years.[4] The mass-market magazine industry took root before the advent of talking pictures in 1927, the dominance of radio in the 1930s, and the explosion of high-quality, low-cost paperback books just prior to World War II, but these media, by all accounts, did not curtail readership, which continued to grow until the 1950s.

Magazines aimed at women were the circulation leaders of the early twentieth century and by the middle 1920s were the type most likely to amass circulations of one million or more. Three of the five top leaders in advertising revenue in 1920, for instance, were the *Ladies' Home Journal*, *Woman's Home Companion*, and the *Pictorial Review* (Peterson 63, 84). It was the decision in the early teens to include a large amount of fiction that propelled the circulation of these and other industry giants into the millions and that constituted their core marketing strategy throughout the postwar period. The case of *Cosmopolitan* is instructive. Beginning as a journalistic magazine emphasizing world and civic affairs, *Cosmopolitan* increased its circulation by 70 percent through serializing Robert W. Chambers's 1912 romance *The Common Law*, illustrated by well-known artist Charles Dana Gibson. Thereafter, the magazine included two serials and five or six short stories per issue, achieving a circulation of one million by 1915. Editor Ray Long was hired in 1918 because of his reputation for recognizing mass appeal fiction, and by 1931 *Cosmopolitan* enjoyed a circulation of 1.7 million, with each issue including four serials and a dozen short stories (Mott 4:491–503).

Periodicals originally designed as fashion or household service magazines in the late nineteenth century shifted their emphasis, gradually including more fiction and hiring top book illustrators as well as best-selling authors. *Good Housekeeping*, for example, initially saw itself as a household management magazine aimed at the homemaker, but by 1904 it was beginning to include fiction by popular writers such as Margaret Deland and Mary Heaton Vorse. With the advent of fiction editor William Frederick Bigelow in 1913, *Good Housekeeping*'s identity was largely shaped by regularly featured middlebrow novelists such as Mary Roberts Rinehart and Kathleen Norris, and circulation grew from 200,000 in 1908 to over a million in the 1920s. Similarly, *Woman's Home Companion* blossomed under the thirty-year editorship of newspaperwoman Gertrude Battles Lane, who began in 1911 to include two serials and four or five stories per issue. Offering as much as $85,000 in the 1920s for the serial rights to a novel by Sophie Kerr, Dorothy Canfield Fisher, or Edna Ferber, the *Companion* reached a circulation of two million by 1927 (Mott 5:133–36). So lucrative was the magazine market for writers that even those now included in the literary canon published in mass periodicals. Edith Wharton, for example, received an $18,000 advance from the *Pictorial Review* for serialization rights to *The Age of Innocence* in 1920, and she published most of her fiction in periodical venues (Wolff 1111).[5] Willa Cather's *The Professor's House* was published by *Collier's* in 1925 and *My Mortal Enemy* by *McCall's* in 1926. Indeed, it was the practice of editors to negotiate serialization rights with famous authors before their novels or memoirs were published in book form.

For ideological as well as practical reasons, this wealth of literary material for the cultural historian barely has been tapped. The sheer volume of stories in the twenty- to thirty-year period when magazines published large amounts of fiction is staggering. My own research, for example, which took place over nine years, covered only seven magazines from 1910 to 1930, and I read an average of only one story per issue every other month.[6] The time it took me to read a single story or serial installment ranged from thirty to forty-five minutes, so anyone interested in analyzing the narrative patterns of mass periodical fiction during its heyday has difficulty merely ploughing through the material in a systematic way.

Even more inhibiting, however, is the disdain with which many contemporary literary critics have regarded middlebrow women's fiction. As Richard Ohmann and others remind us, the distinction between low and high culture was not as pronounced in the nineteenth and early twentieth centuries as it later became and magazines participated in a "discourse of high culture," but the image of women's magazines as purveyors of substandard fiction has been hard to displace (Ohmann, *Selling*, 236). These magazines did largely rely, it is true, on formula stories, most of them romances, with archetypal characters, conventional plots, and unrealistic endings. Many of them were hastily and poorly written. The hallmarks of mass-market fiction writers are speed, volume, and predictability, none of which aids in composing great literature. Analysts of popular culture have made inroads into how we view middlebrow or formula literature, however, and their work has paved the way for the volume in which this essay appears.[7] Because such fiction was mass marketed, we can use it as a barometer of sorts for public attitudes toward major issues of the day, such as women's roles in American culture.[8] We can also examine the extent to which middlebrow writers participated in the construction of a distinctly modern literature with new kinds of characters, plots, and rhetorical patterns. This essay describes some of the protofeminist qualities of a new kind of literary heroine in fiction of the modernist period created by women writers publishing in this market.

A key to the modern New Woman's success is her vitality, a quality that appears in fictional heroines after the Civil War and that distinguishes them from the nineteenth-century sentimental heroine, whose purity is marked by physical frailty and vulnerability.[9] Fragility, fainting, illness, and death were signs of the sentimental heroine's spiritual superiority and fine feelings; she was too pure for this corrupt world with its mercenary rules of commerce, cynical political machines, and brutal male power. Her realm was the home, the influence of which she hoped to extend to civilization at large. In contrast, the New Woman of the early-twentieth-century era relished action and strenuous physical activity. She was athletic, healthy, eager to take on challenges in the nondomestic world.[10]

By the 1910s, the woman of action had made great headway in replacing the delicate ideal of sentimental fiction and was becoming central to a new fantasy of competence in the roughest circumstances. This character not only developed beyond tomboy status to mature womanhood, she was able to combine her love of adventure with romance. A good example of this emergent protofeminist ideal is "The Sob-Lady" by Elizabeth Frazer, published in September of 1915 by *Good Housekeeping*.[11] Susanne Brown is a new kind of romantic heroine in American popular fiction—a mate, a comrade—not an ethereal woman on a pedestal parodied via her rival, Angela Lake, whose name symbolizes the other-worldliness and placidity of a former era. Angela wears, appropriately enough, angelic gowns of soft lace and misty pastels, whereas the down-to-earth Susanne Brown prefers suits with "mannish" hats. The contrast between these characters is mirrored in their approaches to writing: Susanne is in a constant rush to cover her beat as a New York City newspaper reporter, whereas Angela sequesters herself to write "Literature." Angela's dreamy conception of writing is far removed from the hardheaded, no-frills approach taken by Susanne, who compares her newspaper stories to the fire engines she often chases, "racing into action, horses straining, driver cursing, siren screaming, smoke belching, sparks trailing—no time to look back and see what sort of fancy track they're leaving" (316).

Angela's representation of the old sentimental ideal, though modernized by her dedication to art, is further emphasized by her blond hair and blue eyes, while Susanne is dark-haired, a reversal of earlier fictional phenotypes casting active brunettes in negative roles of egocentric rebellion. (Susanne's girlhood companion, in fact, is a dog named Rebel.) Susanne's lack of delicate femininity is the story's true subject, which makes repeated reference to her sweating body, disheveled appearance, and practical clothing. The plot centers on her romance with an old childhood friend, which is disrupted by his temporary infatuation with the ethereal Angela. Compounding her heartache is the fact that Susanne loses her job by reporting too truthfully on an assignment. Forced to rely on her grit for survival, Susanne ultimately wins both the man and a new job through believing in herself, despite what the world seems to say about women of action.

The pitting of old against new gender ideals is at the core of a later story, "Bird Girl," by Vivien Bretherton, also published in *Good Housekeeping* (March 1929). The woman of action in this piece is a pilot, Vandy Cameron, who knows as much about airplanes as does her father, the owner of an aircraft company. Our first glimpse of Vandy, as she emerges from her plane after performing dangerous aerial maneuvers before the admiring eyes of "the world's most famous pilot," Brian Scott, is of a "straight, boyish" figure with short dark hair. Shocked that the daredevil pilot is a woman, Brian is further taken aback by Vandy's forthright handshake and bold self-introduction. All of these qualities place Vandy in dramatic contrast to her high-school friend, Narcissa Elliot, whose feigned helplessness and cosmetized glamour appeal to Brian's regressive side, overshadowing his attraction to Vandy. The story ultimately favors Vandy's version of womanhood, however, when she and Brian are forced to parachute out of her burning plane and Vandy takes charge of the situation. Having been pulled to safety by the heroic Vandy, who resets his dislocated arm, Brian realizes that he needs an amazon rather than a delicate clinging vine in his world of speed, adventure, and flight.

The narrative pairing of these heroines near symbols of American technological might—the urban fire truck and the airplane—symbolizes the New Woman's integration into a gender-marked sphere of male control, the modern American city, and its marketplace of developing technology. To become comfortable with machinery was one way a heroine could challenge restrictions placed on her as a woman and move closer to the center of an emerging industrial landscape. Vandy Cameron's technological expertise and Susanne Brown's ability to write like and report on fire engines mark them as inhabitants of a twentieth-century world in which noise, speed, power, and invention are no longer the exclusive province of men. Women too could operate the levers of technology and, just as importantly, be accepted as comrades and intimate companions by modern men.

Similarly, large numbers of New Woman heroines are artists. Whether she be painter, singer, dancer, actress, or writer, the artist heroine's desire to dedicate her life to art alienates her from the traditional woman's world of selfless devotion to family. For one thing, the artist works alone and claims private space, whereas women's family role entails rather constant interaction with others. In addition, the artist engages in work that lasts, as opposed to the unceasing, ephemeral nature of housework. Dedication to art also identified this character as a modern person, for the artist represented the twentieth-century ideal of individual freedom and self-expression. The privileging of art over commerce, individual opportunity over ethnic or class origins, feeling over rationality, creativity over plodding practicality became a hallmark of the postwar Jazz Age. The Progressive Era bohemian, who chose ideals and poverty over material success, became a mainstream character in popular magazine fiction after the war largely in the shape of an artist. This character could be either male or female, but the emergence of the professional woman heralded larger opportunities for women of all kinds.

Rachel Blau Du Plessis illuminates the transitional utility of the artist heroine for this era when she argues that the *kunstlerromane* pioneered by women writers in the late nineteenth century encoded conflict between the empowered woman and the cultural barriers to her achievement. Using a romantic image of the unconventional genius, writers could legitimate the artist heroine's rejection of a traditional, gender-bound role.[12] The artist embodied many traits associated with women's supposedly special qualities—heightened emotionality, keen intuition, love of beauty, attraction to harmony, superior sentiment or fine feeling, and wider latitude of self-expression. At the same time, she was a symbol of change and modernity, for the artist demonstrated her talents in a bold and public way, calling attention to her achievements and seeking validation for them. She also often appropriated for herself the label of artistic genius, a term which had been coded as masculine. The artist heroine, then, formed a bridge between private and public realms, female and male spheres.

As Du Plessis points out, most late-nineteenth-century *kunstlerromanes* by women pose an unresolved conflict between the artist's happiness as a woman and realization of her vocational ambitions. Love, in a word, is incompatible with creative work. This pattern held in women's magazine fiction until the middle of the second decade, when artist heroines found sympathetic men who admired and supported their art. In "The Lotus Eater" by Grace Sartwell Mason, published in the January 1918 *Good Housekeeping*, we first see the heroine, Mary, through the eyes of a woman friend, who admires her as Mary strolls down Fifth Avenue carrying a huge portfolio under her arm. This opening establishes Mary as an urban woman who wears sensible casual attire, walks with a self-assured stride, and ignores the commercial wares in shop windows as her gaze focuses on a more lofty aesthetic goal. The triangle in this story involves two men who court Mary, one of whom is a self-absorbed painter, a narcissistic dilettante who ignores her needs, and the other a mature businessman, who adjusts his busy schedule to hers in order not to impose on Mary's "precious time" and burgeoning career. His successful automobile concern does not keep him from appreciating the quality of her painting; indeed he has "a feeling for Mary's talent that was next . . . to reverence" (33). It is the businessman who wins Mary's love, and the impending marriage of auto dealer and artist symbolizes the successful merger of modern American business and female artistic ambition.

In these stories the artist heroine is committed to feeling and aesthetics in a society that values efficiency, logic, and profit. Her career in the arts underscores the New Woman's attempt to live by humanistic values and rise above the materialistic competitiveness she finds in the city. The idea that such values were endangered by the metropolis and could be preserved by dedication to art had already appeared in turn-of-the-century American novels, when female artist characters similarly migrated to urban centers. In his study of the period, for instance, Carl S. Smith argues that in these novels art is connected to freedom, imagination, love, and a humane moral order, with women largely representing that configuration (7–9). Unlike the stories of this earlier era, however, when artistic powers are often not enough to create a humane environment, the woman artist of the 1920s generally comes to feel at home in the cityscape.

These ideas are animated in a modernist fictional landscape in "The Girl Who Slept in Bryant Park" by Scammon Lockwood, published in the February 1920 *Ladies' Home Journal*.[13] Opening with the heroine seated on a park bench in New York City, desolate and impoverished, we learn that she has fled the Midwest and a fiancé to become a painter. Her parents and beau strongly disapprove; they all believe Bella should give up her work to become a homemaker in Toledo, Ohio. After eight months of vain attempts to sell her paintings, however, Bella is lonely, homesick, broke, and ready to give up, until she creates a masterpiece as a result of her homeless sojourn in the park. It is only when she gives away her last two dollars to a homeless man and sells her engagement ring that she is able to paint the city as her subconscious mind sees it rather than in a way that she thinks will sell. Finally believing in her artistic imagination, Bella's painting opens up doors of art galleries as well as her loved ones' hearts. Captivated by her vision of the urban landscape, Bella's fiancé moves his Toledo drop-forge company to New York so that he can support his future wife's career: "Compared to what you have done, my factory isn't worth a fig" (52).

Similarly, "The Tyrant" by Sophie Kerr, published in the July 1926 *Woman's Home Companion*, for which Kerr was managing editor, centers on the heroine's artistic transformation of urban commerce into something with which she can have a human relationship.[14] The contrast between an earlier generation steeped in male supremacy and ill equipped for the modern world and the new is drawn from the story's outset as the heroine shoulders financial responsibility for her ineffectual, helpless, recently widowed mother. Barely out of high school, the androgynously named Avery quickly finds her first job in a factory to be "nauseating drudgery" and decides to focus on her art class as a point of self-definition and meaning. Determined to make a living without sacrificing her deepest needs, Avery's wall murals created for wealthy clients lead her to be hired by a New York architectural firm to decorate commercial buildings. Metaphorically, she puts her creative stamp on the urban world of commerce by adding color and warmth to its architecture, as her employer envisions. When faced with an attractive suitor who insists that she give up her work to be his wife, Avery articulates the new feminist idea that gender should not result in distinct roles: "In my world there's only one rule, one law, and that is, if you have any gift, you must not cheat it or play with it . . . talent has no sex" (7). She resists "the tyrant" of patriarchal dominance in favor of a professional relationship with an employer who believes women and men should be equal partners in creating an artistic commercial landscape.

This belief in the harmonious merger of public and private, art and business, male and female lies at the heart of New Woman modernist fiction. Male engineers, architects, and managers are featured consistently, for instance, as symbols of the new American order. Significantly, they often view positively the heroine's commitment to work outside the home and consider her a comrade rather than a helpmeet. Though occasionally the suitor's old-fashioned views prove intractable, as in "The Tyrant," the usual course of events leads from conflict over the heroine's career to final harmony and mutual dedication to work. Men who can overcome a false sense of pride at being the breadwinner find their wives and sweethearts eager to make them happy, as long as the women feel free to develop their talents, and these are the relationships that succeed.

In "Henry's Divorce" by Edith Barnard Delano, published in the June 1929 *Ladies' Home Journal*, for instance, a modern marriage runs into trouble when the husband suddenly decides he wants an old-fashioned wife who stays home and cooks, cleans, and tends to his needs. His wife is a highly successful department store display designer who runs their New York apartment with wonderful efficiency, but the protagonist becomes disgruntled over not being the sole object of her attention; when he contracts the flu, he runs home to mother for sympathy. He also begins flirting with a former girlfriend who believes wives should dedicate themselves to their husbands' comfort, but both escape routes quickly close themselves off. The old flame turns out to be a bore next to his wife's youthful vigor, good humor, and superior understanding of his needs, while his mother's constant attention smothers him; her lack of interest in current events is an intense annoyance. It is his working wife who makes him happy—a woman who has kept her maiden name, who smokes in a comradely fashion with her male colleagues, and who knows what is going on in the world. Their modern marriage in an urban apartment, with ready-made meals and other technological conveniences, thrives on the equal participation of both partners in the work arena.

The theme of New Women embarking on modern relationships with men supportive of their commitment to a career is accordant with studies of the 1920s done by Nancy F. Cott, Rosalind Rosenberg, and Paula Fass indicating that hierarchical conceptions of marriage were being supplanted with a model of companionate union among young women. Male intellectuals as well, Rosenberg tells us, were alienated by many aspects of Victorianism, including the notion that men and women should inhabit separate spheres. Rosenberg describes the support these men gave to women graduate students challenging the doctrine of female uniqueness (xvii). This moderation of nineteenth-century views and its popularity is reflected in the fact that male writers for these magazines also created New Woman heroines who convert men to egalitarian ideas; in the popular fiction that portrays modern marriage as a partnership women are allowed to play multiple roles, as long as they are loving and supportive mates.

Scholars have established that the movement from separate spheres to a model of companionship with men resulted in losses as well as gains for middle-class women. One loss was, in the words of Carroll Smith-Rosenberg, "the female world of love and ritual," which reached its zenith in the nineteenth century and fostered strong affectional ties between women. Some have argued that women cut themselves off from a vital political base in penetrating male spheres of American life. Eschewing a gender-based culture of female influence, they lost the sense of identity and support that had propelled demands for women's rights. Paradoxically, feminists' modern vision of gender equality in the postwar decade helped lead to the disappearance of feminism as an effective political movement. Simultaneously, homophobic attacks on unmarried women in bonded relationships during the 1920s made problematic the "romantic friendships," in Lillian Faderman's words, that were common among single female professionals at the turn of the century.[15]

These losses are also reflected in middlebrow magazine fiction. Heroines embarking on their journey toward self-actualization tend to be cut off from other women, especially the mother, who often dies at the beginning of the heroine's quest. Similarly, heroines who have bonded with another woman in personal and professional ways become romantically attached to male intruders who disrupt the relationship. In the *Delineator's* July 1927 "The Tornado" by Sarah Addington, for instance, the protagonist, Annabelle Parkinson, is a Latin teacher in her forties who has come to New York from Indiana and enjoys a fifteen-year very close friendship with sister teacher Anne Posey. She and Anne are close enough that they are planning a vacation to Europe and have spent many weekends together visiting Anne's mother. They are close enough, indeed, that Annabelle is tormented by guilt over a secret budding romance with a former suitor that threatens her bond with Anne. She is ambivalent about dating him, flattered by the attention but happy with her life and "uncomfortable" at the thought of what a marriage would do to the friendship with Anne. Divining that Annabelle is being courted by a man who intends to take her away, Anne introduces her to a brother, whom Annabelle likes because he has Anne's "sweetness, spirit, and sturdiness." Nonetheless, Anne's brother alarms Annabelle with his whirlwind energy and desire to take care of her—hence the story's title, which suggests the ruinous destructive impact of a man on this close friendship. She feels smothered by his ardent courting, strangled by his embrace. Despite her obvious revulsion, Annabelle marries Anne's fraternal double as it is the only way her friend believes they can stay together (he will not insist that Annabelle quit working or move away).

The facile substitution of a brother for what is obviously the heroine's primary relationship to a woman in this story rings false and disturbs with its heterosexist implications, but it tells us something about the transitional quality of the modernist era. Committed to leaving hearth and home behind while looking for a relationship of equality, New Woman characters are situated in contexts that make relationships with men look much like the same-sex friendships of the previous generation. They can find love without being condemned as lesbians, hold to an independent course, and enjoy the companionship of women too. The specter of the lonely career-oriented pilgrim, childless and unwed, that stalks fictional pioneers into the new century is shown to be an outmoded stereotype. On the negative side, however, bonding between unmarried women, a source of strength to suffragists and female professionals, is framed as a relic of the last century, unhealthy, and undesirable as an alternative to modern marriage.

Whereas romantic friendships between women appear in magazine fiction throughout the 1920s, sometimes in positive terms, women of color are noticeably absent except in stereotyped roles. Racism pervaded mainstream magazines both in content and in the exclusion of nonwhite writers, with the important exceptions of Eurasian Winnifred Eaton (Onoto Watanna), who published in the *Ladies' Home Journal, Good Housekeeping*, and other venues prior to 1920, and Mexican-born Maria Cristina Mena, who published in *Cosmopolitan* and *Household Magazine*.[16] Narrative subjugation of ethnic minority women into subordinate roles occurred regularly and relied on stereotypes of the Indian maiden, exotic Oriental, comic domestic, or tragic mulatta. The whiteness of New Woman stories reflects the racist practices of white editors, their exclusionary view of their audience, and the failure of the suffrage movement to make race a priority in the struggle for women's rights. The social debate over gender had been framed for years by racist arguments, acceptance of segregation, and reference to white middle-class models of feminism, and mainstream periodicals mirror this reality.[17]

It is important to recognize the racist exclusion of nonwhite characters and writers from New Woman middlebrow fiction of dominant culture magazines and to seek out feminist narratives in period venues like the *Crisis, American Indian Magazine*, and presses that published nonwhite authors. For instance, in the multifaceted movement to end slavery and then during Jim Crow, African-American women writers often used elements of New Woman plots in tune with white middlebrow writers. Harlem Renaissance editor and writer Jessie Fauset best illustrates this narrative convergence. Published in three installments of the NAACP's 1920 *Crisis*, Fauset's story "The Sleeper Wakes" is typical of her treatment. It features a mulatta heroine passing for white who shares some major characteristics of the modernist New Woman character. Amy Kildare has left a traditionally run home in Trenton, New Jersey, to make a career for herself in New York City. Finding employment in a Greenwich Village bakery, Amy is befriended by a divorced painter who lives off alimony payments and advises Amy to marry a wealthy man in order to pursue her own interest in art. Her ensuing marriage to an older man, a retired broker, disrupts Amy's career plans; however, in brave New Woman fashion, she divorces him, then returns his alimony payments after becoming a success in the fashion business. Amy has not found the enlightened marriage she had hoped for, in part because she allowed herself to be an economic dependent, but she finds fulfillment and self-esteem as a big city designer.

Fauset's narrative is as concerned with race, however, as the standard New Woman plot ignores it. Amy's passing for white leads to personal disaster when she marries a white Southerner, a racist who insults his black servants and forces Amy to live in Richmond, Virginia. His racist language and abuse of the staff repulse Amy and move her to "come out" as an African American, which is the catalyst for her divorce. Already feeling hemmed in by her role as homemaker and genteel wife, Amy's act of racial solidarity with the servants in her household causes her to question the white patriarchal images of beauty and success she has absorbed from the Hollywood movies she loved so much as a child. Amy comes to realize that her desire to be beautiful and successful through passing has made her weak and that she has been blinded to the ugly reality behind romantic screen images she has uncritically accepted.

Amy's growing rejection of the dominant culture's white beauty ideal is central to her ultimate rejection of traditional marriage, as is her realization that she must reject the fantasy of living as a pampered princess. The slave-like economic dependence of wives and people of color on a patriarchal racist like her husband becomes the story's focal point as Amy wakes from her false dream of finding happiness by playing the role of wealthy white wife. Fauset drives this point home by featuring colors prominently in the narrative while disparaging white things. Amy prefers colored jewels to diamonds or pearls, for instance, because the white stones appear to her "hard," "cold," and "dead." Her favorite room in the house is the drawing room because it is "a wonderful study in browns." When she goes into dress designing, Amy uses mannequins of many hues and shapes so that she can design for nonwhite women, who come in a variety of colors and sizes.

Likewise, Fauset's novel *Plum Bun* (1928) follows the usual narrative lines of the artist-heroine story. Angela Murray is an aspiring painter who leaves her parents' traditional Philadelphia home to make a living in New York, where she joyfully immerses herself in a vibrant community of artists, intellectuals, and workers. She enters the city with characteristic New Woman exuberance, buoyed by her dreams of artistic accomplishment, an inheritance from her deceased mother, and a sense of exhilarating autonomy provided by the city's anonymous throngs. The price for this new world is high, however, since to enter it Angela must pass for white. She quickly finds that her white bohemian friends and wealthy fiancé fuel an alienation and loneliness that her exciting lifestyle cannot assuage. She feels painfully cut off from the African-American students in her art class, for example, and the guests at the Greenwich Village parties she attends strike her as superficial, especially compared to the "fuller, richer" black people she encounters in Harlem. Moreover, her fiancé reveals himself to be a racist overbearing chauvinist, and Angela ultimately leaves him, disgusted with the subordination of her artistic ideals and self-respect the relationship exacts.

A wedding of the commercial (male) center with artistic (female) ideals does not occur in this novel as it tends to in middlebrow fiction produced by white writers. Although Angela's white fiancé is a mining engineer—a typical occupation for artist-heroine suitors—she rejects him in favor of an African-American artist, a man who proudly claims his racial heritage. Significantly, Angela rejects the commercial (white) center to live in the city of art, Paris, and is joined there by her artist-comrade, who supports her work as a portrait painter. Together they embark on an egalitarian relationship centered around the uncorrupted values of pure artistic production and African-American life.

The white New Woman heroine overcomes prejudice against her gender within a system that is portrayed as basically open to any person with talent, fortitude, and ambition. Her dedication to work is ennobling, making it possible for her to improve the modern scene even as she enters it. The profoundly skeptical treatment of success in Jessie Fauset's fiction highlights the race privilege behind challenges to sexism in women's periodicals and indicates the accommodationist framework in which they were posed. Fauset shows that modern America is racist, and her heroines fatally compromise their integrity in order to enter it. The lure of gender equality blinds them to the penalties they face as nonwhite women until their critique of the modern world's whiteness opens a new path of empowerment as modern black women.

Chinese-English writer Winnifred Eaton, writing under the pseudonym Onoto Watanna, similarly complicated her romances with references to racial prejudice, in her case against Asians. Sprinkling her narratives with New Woman figures, who often serve as protectors for her Eurasian or Japanese protagonists, Eaton centered a number of tales on heroines whose unspecified ethnicity marginalizes them in tales animated by interrogation of race as well as gender restrictions. An example of Eaton's double focus is *Marion: The Story of an Artist's Model*, serialized in *Hearst's Magazine* May–November 1916. It concentrates on an aspiring Canadian artist who is beset by a number of setbacks as she moves from Montreal to Boston to New York in her quest for a career in painting. More hardhitting than fiction run in women's magazines, the story features a heroine who encounters degrading propositions from married men, fends off sexual harassment from employers, suffers a severe battering by an artist who tries to rape her, and is reduced to posing in the nude for an art class. Through it all, Marion refuses to give up her dream of becoming an artist and ultimately finds creative work, a lover who respects her art, and success in New York City. She travels the New Woman path of overcoming obstacles faced by single women in urban environments, dedication to artistic ideals, and combining career success with an egalitarian marriage.[18]

At the same time, there is a subtext in *Marion* alluding to the heroine's subaltern status as a member of an outcast ethnic group. Although the narrative never specifies her race, Marion describes herself as "dark" and "foreign-looking," so exotic that she becomes a model for Orientalist painting, much in vogue at the time. The novel opens, in fact, with Marion's painful account of overhearing as a ten-year-old in Montreal (where Eaton was born and raised) a neighborhood shopkeeper describing her family as "foreign." Confessing that she "hates" her exotic looks, as a child Marion longs for blond hair and blue eyes so that she can feel beautiful. Throughout the story, she is propositioned by white men who make it clear that she is not the kind of woman one marries, and, at one point, a famous artist who employs her says she resembles an illegitimate half-white / half-native girl he knows. It is only when Marion meets a progressive Greenwich Village painter, who believes in her artistic gifts and respects her, that the painful self-consciousness Marion has suffered all her life dissipates. Although not nearly as direct in its interrogation of racism as Jessie Fauset's narratives, *Marion* makes it clear that the protagonist must overcome a greater degree of prejudice than is produced by gender bias alone.

Winnifred Eaton's contestation of race boundaries is more pronounced in her Japanese novels, which are set in Japan and feature Japanese or Eurasian heroines. Passing as a Japanese writer through her pseudonym, Onoto Watanna, Eaton produced several romances in the prewar years that fall outside the time parameters of this essay, but they are worth discussing for the ways in which Eaton wrote within the New Woman of color pattern. Although they anticipate rather than participate in the postwar middlebrow feminist movement, I think the nine Japanese novels Eaton published between 1899 and 1912 illustrate well the ways race complicated gender issues for feminist writers of color in the modern period. Typical of her work is Eaton's most famous novel, *A Japanese Nightingale* (1901), written in part to counter the wildly popular archetype of Asian female subservience created in John Luther Long's novella, *Madame Butterfly* (1898), and the subsequent play produced by David Belasco (1900).[19] Eaton's half-white, half-Japanese protagonist, Yuki, is a freelance geisha dancer performing at teahouses in Tokyo to support her widowed Japanese mother and Eurasian brother studying at Harvard. Although she lives as an outcast from Japanese society because of her biracial ancestry, Yuki's dances are considered transcendent works of art for their ability to transport (male) audiences to a heightened realm of emotional experience.

The romance centers on Yuki's unconventional marriage to an American heir to a shipping fortune, Jack Bigelow, who falls deeply in love with her Eurasian beauty, delightful personality, and enticing mystery. Although Yuki is financially dependent on Jack, she maintains an autonomous agency by secretly funneling the money to her mother and brother, disappearing for days at a time, and refusing to take Jack to her mother's home or even tell him what her true family origins are. Ultimately, Yuki leaves her husband for two years as she travels on an American theater agent's ship touring Asia to search for talent to put on the U.S. vaudeville stage. Meanwhile, Jack searches vainly for her all over Japan. Reversing the *Madame Butterfly* myth, in which a heartbroken geisha waits futilely for the return of her American lieutenant husband, *A Japanese Nightingale* follows the deserted American husband in his sorrowful search for the talented Eurasian wife who has awakened in him a love too profound to forget. When Yuki returns to her faithful lover, she makes it clear that Japan is her home, and there they will reside in mutual respect, trust, and harmony on the outskirts of Tokyo.

As in this novel, Eaton's Japanese romances most often unite irresistible Japanese or half-caste women with Western men who fall in love with their extraordinary beauty, resilience, independence, and warmth. Although these heroines do not follow precisely the New Woman modern path of urban career, Eaton positions them as New Women of an Asian sort, descendants of noble families within an ancient culture of equal stature with the West and well equipped for modern international marriages. They possess business acumen, artistic training, and/or detailed knowledge of Japanese history and mythology. They are perfectly capable of surviving on their own, and frequently do, but they are also open to the modern Western idea of romantic love, rejecting traditional arranged marriages with men chosen by their families or exploitative relationships with disrespectful male chauvinists. Setting her novels in Japan allowed Eaton, moreover, to link her heroines with a country emerging from feudal isolation in the Meiji Era, when Japanese political leaders, businessmen, and educators forged ties with the industrial West to modernize their society. This backdrop of Japanese modernization combined with a distinct feminist validation of women characters' strength marks Eaton's Japanese tales as early New Woman stories that interrogate stereotypes of Asian subservience, preindustrial backwardness, and inferiority to the West. Significantly, however, virtually all of her biracial romances occur in Japan, where American readers were less likely to protest such unions. Her heroines are often schooled by American women in the arts of modern courtship and inspired by Western feminism, but they do not enter American society itself.

For white women, the modernist era was a time of optimism and excitement, perhaps generated by the heady experience of women's enlarged participation in the work world in World War I, passage of the suffrage amendment, rebellion against Victorian prudery, or a combination of these. Many mass-circulation magazine stories that they read and wrote contain characters who overcome prejudice against their sex to create new more-fulfilling lives at the heart of metropolitan America. These heroines can triumph because the modern context is portrayed as one that values individual talent and relegates narrow views to the provinces. Progress in these tales is social as well as material, artistic as well as commercial, female as well as male.

Women of color, on the other hand, found a radically different America, both in their imaginations and in reality. Asians were bombarded with exclusion laws and battled dispossession from California farm land. Native Americans were reeling from a genocidal war and traumatic uprooting. Chicanas suffered from backbreaking migrant work and marginalization of their mestiza heritage. African Americans faced segregation, poverty, and lynch mobs. Integration into white-dominated America could be illusory at best and, at worst, a dangerous journey into hostile, alien territory. At the same time, nonwhite women writers like Jessie Fauset and Winnifred Eaton could and did create a new kind of heroine who demanded both meaningful work and equality in love, and freedom from gender and race prejudice, the harmonious merger of divided worlds. The Harlem Renaissance posited a "New Negro" who entered modernizing America as an equal largely through artistic accomplishment and values, just as dominant culture women's fiction imagined a New Woman able to participate in the public sphere while not sacrificing love. Likewise, the *Japonisme* era of turn-of-the-century America provided Winnifred Eaton with an opportunity to create sympathetic Eurasian characters who believed in a new world where love across racial lines could blossom.

Both models of New Women, white and nonwhite, portrayed the twentieth-century urban center as a site of dramatic empowering change for women, but the issue of racism in modern America profoundly divided these two groups of women writers. White writers and readers could imagine autonomous heroines carving futures wherein love did not need to be sacrificed to creative work. Women of color, on the other hand, saw gender and race prejudice as inextricably entwined and having to be tackled at the same time.[20] Both groups portrayed widening opportunities for women in the dawning new century, but the sense of how easily barriers could be made to drop varied considerably. White characters merged more readily into America's burgeoning urban centers, able to find meaningful work and supportive intimate relationships, while nonwhite heroines faced a rockier trajectory, often locating themselves in safer environments outside cityscapes dominated by white male power structures. Life on the margins of American corporate activity seemed more compatible with their efforts to transcend race and gender prejudice.

There are lessons to be learned from recovering this moment in women's literary history, so long elided by scholarly attention to experimental modernist fiction. Some of these lessons are negative: a heritage of racism within the struggle for women's rights and marginalization of lesbians. On the positive side, however, we can see that contemporary feminist issues were around before the second wave of feminism. The existence of early popular literature with feminist overtones suggests widespread interest in new ways of thinking about women, an openness to female autonomy that can inspire our own visions of change. Furthermore, the voices of modernism were more diverse than we have recognized. These writers were pioneers, and the stories they created animate egalitarian ideals that are yet to be fully realized.

This backward glance at fiction considered marginal to the literary canon strengthens our assessment of the movements for gender and race equality in the early twentieth century. The notion that women of the 1920s turned their backs on those who fought to expand their options can be balanced by reference to the continuing presence of work-centered egalitarian romances in women's periodicals throughout the period. As Elaine Showalter cautions in her study of this era, the decade after suffrage represents, at worst, a political postponement and, at best, a triumph of enlarged aspirations for feminists. In addition, scholars such as Houston Baker Jr. are highlighting the participation in the modernist literary movement of nonwhite writers, many of whom were women.[21] New Woman stories are evidence of that continuing interest, shared broadly across ethnic groups, and they affirm that 1920s women were modern individuals with needs for creative work, progressive intimate relationships of equality, and an appetite for changing the world on their own terms.

Notes

1. The stories I read from 1910 to 1914 support this view, as do scholarly studies such as Carl S. Smith's *Chicago and the American Literary Imagination, 1880–1920*.

2. Well-known examples of novels with failed New Woman heroines include Elizabeth Stuart Phelps's *The Story of Avis* (1879), Ellen Glasgow's *Phases of an Inferior Planet* (1898), *The Awakening* by Kate Chopin (1899), and Edith Wharton's *The House of Mirth* (1905).

3. Edith Wharton satirizes this character in the figure of Undine Spragg of *The Custom of the Country* (1913), serialized in *Scribner's*. Here, the small-town female migrant devours everyone in her path with her voracious appetite for material success in the world's great cities.

4. Richard Ohmann addresses this in "Where Did Mass Culture Come From: The Case of Magazines."

5. Most of Wharton's novels were serialized in periodicals, including such masterpieces as *The House of Mirth* (*Scribner's* 1905), *The Custom of the Country* (*Scribner's* 1913), and *Summer* (*McClure's* 1917). She published extensively in women's magazines such as the *Ladies' Home Journal*, the *Delineator*, and *Woman's Home Companion*.

6. The magazines were the *Ladies' Home Journal*, *Good Housekeeping*, *McCall's*, *Woman's Home Companion*, *Cosmopolitan*, the *Pictorial Review*, and the *Delineator*. My total story sample was 924 short stories and serials.

7. Among the most influential critics reframing our understanding of women's popular fiction are Janice Radway, Tania Modleski, and Jacqueline Bobo.

8. For more on how early magazines can be analyzed in terms of their role in gender construction, see Ellen Gruber Garvey and Helen Damon-Moore.

9. Authors who provide overviews of this ideal include Barbara Welter, Herbert Ross Brown, and Nina Baym.

10. It should be noted that a revival of the fragile feminine ideal competed with the robust New Woman at the turn of the century, when a cult of the invalid took hold in fin-de-siècle culture. For a description of this cult, see Bram Dijkstra and Elisabeth Bronfen.

11. This piece and some others discussed here are reprinted in my anthology *Breaking the Ties That Bind: Popular Stories of the New Woman, 1915–1930*. Elizabeth Frazer published primarily in *Good Housekeeping* and the *Saturday Evening Post*. She served as an ambulance service nurse and then as a war correspondent in France during World War I.

12. Other useful studies on this subject are by Linda Huf, Susan Gubar, and Suzanne W. Jones.

13. Male as well as female writers created New Woman romances for women's magazines of this era.

14. Sophie Kerr was an immensely popular writer in the early twentieth century, specializing in romances about successful career women. Although she married in 1904, she published under her maiden name and in many ways resembled the heroines she created. Born in Denton, Maryland, in 1880, Sophie Kerr took up journalism in Pittsburgh and then became a fiction writer in New York City, where she resided most of her adult life. She earned a master's degree in 1901 (from the University of Vermont) and a Ph.D. in literature in 1942 (from Washington College). She and her husband had no children.

15. Also see Estelle Freedman's study of the culture of women in the early part of the twentieth century.

16. Native American Zitkala-Sa published autobiographical stories in the *Atlantic Monthly* in the early 1900s. These are reprinted in *American Indian Stories* (Lincoln: University of Nebraska Press, 1985), originally published in 1921. Maria Cristina Mena's fiction is reprinted in *The Collected Stories of Maria Cristina Mena*, ed. Amy Doherty (Houston: Arte Publico Press, 1997). A selection of Winnifred Eaton's magazine fiction is being reprinted by University of Illinois Press (ed. Elizabeth Rooney).

17. See, for example, studies by Rosalyn Terborg-Penn, Erlene Stetson, and Paula Giddings.

18. *Marion: The Story of an Artist's Model* was also published in book form (New York: W. J. Watt, 1916). The story was purportedly the author's true memoir and was published anonymously (although by then many readers knew the author to be "Onoto Watanna"), which is perhaps why its frank treatment of nudity and violence could be tolerated. On the other hand, the memoir reads like a novel and has all the hallmarks of romantic fiction.

19. An analysis of these two narratives frames a paired reprinting of both texts in *"Madame Butterfly" by John Luther Long and "A Japanese Nightingale" by Onoto Watanna (Winnifred Eaton): Two Orientalist Texts*, ed. Maureen Honey and Jean Lee Cole (New Brunswick, N.J.: Rutgers University Press, 2002).

20. I discuss this duality at greater length in "'So Far Away From Home': Minority Women Writers and the New Woman."

21. See also Cheryl Wall.

Works Cited

Baker, Houston A. Jr. *Modernism and the Harlem Renaissance*. Chicago: University of Chicago Press, 1987.

Baym, Nina. *Women's Fiction: A Guide to Novels by and about Women in America, 1820–1870*. Ithaca, N.Y.: Cornell University Press, 1978.

Bobo, Jacqueline. *Black Women as Cultural Readers*. New York: Columbia University Press, 1995.

Bronfen, Elisabeth. *Over Her Dead Body: Configurations of Femininity, Death and the Aesthetic*. New York: Routledge, 1992.

Brown, Herbert Ross. *The Sentimental Novel in America, 1789–1860*. New York: Octagon Books, 1975.

Cott, Nancy F. *The Grounding of Modern Feminism*. New Haven, Conn.: Yale University Press, 1987.

Damon-Moore, Helen. *Magazines for the Millions: Gender and Commerce in the "Ladies' Home Journal" and the "Saturday Evening Post," 1880–1910*. Albany, N.Y.: SUNY Press, 1994.

Dijkstra, Bram. *Idols of Perversity: Fantasies of Feminine Evil in Fin-de-Siecle Culture*. New York: Oxford University Press, 1986.

Du Plessis, Rachel Blau. *Writing Beyond the Ending: Narrative Strategies of Twentieth Century Women Writers*. Bloomington: Indiana University Press, 1985.

Faderman, Lillian. *Surpassing the Love of Men: Romantic Friendship and Love Between Women from the Renaissance to the Present*. New York: William Morrow and Co., 1981.

Fass, Paula. *The Damned and the Beautiful: American Youth in the 1920's*. New York: Oxford University Press, 1977.

Freedman, Estelle. "Separatism as Strategy: Female Institution Building and American Feminism, 1870–1930." *Feminist Studies* 5 (Fall 1979): 512–29.

Garvey, Ellen Gruber. *The Adman in the Parlor: Magazines and the Gendering of Consumer Culture, 1880s–1910s*. New York: Oxford University Press, 1996.

Gelfant, Blanche H. "Sister to Faust: The City's 'Hungry' Woman as Heroine." In *Women Writers and the City: Essays in Feminist Literary Criticism*. Ed. Susan Merrill Squier. Knoxville: University of Tennessee Press, 1984.

Giddings, Paula. *When and Where I Enter: The Impact of Black Women on Race and Sex in America*. New York: Bantam Books, 1984.

Gubar, Susan. "The Birth of the Artist as Heroine: (Re)production, the *Kunstlerroman* Tradition, and the Fiction of Katherine Mansfield." In *The Representation of Women in Fiction*. Ed. Carolyn Heilbrun and Margaret Higonnet. Baltimore: Johns Hopkins University Press, 1983.

Honey, Maureen, ed. *Breaking the Ties That Bind: Popular Stories of the New Woman, 1915–1930*. Norman: University of Oklahoma Press, 1992.

———. "'So Far Away From Home': Minority Women Writers and the New Woman." *Women's Studies International Forum* 15 (1992): 473–85.

Huf, Linda. *A Portrait of the Artist as a Young Woman: The Writer as Heroine in American Literature*. New York: Frederick Ungar, 1983.

Jones, Suzanne W., ed. *Writing the Woman Artist: Essays on Poetics, Politics, and Portraiture*. Philadelphia: University of Pennsylvania Press, 1991.

Modleski, Tania. *Loving with a Vengeance: Mass Produced Fantasies for Women*. Hamden, Conn.: Shoestring Press, 1982.

Mott, Frank Luther. *A History of American Magazines, 1885–1905*. Vol. 4. Cambridge, Mass.: Harvard University Press, 1957.

———. *A History of American Magazines, 1905–1930*. Vol. 5. Cambridge, Mass.: Harvard University Press, 1968.

Ohmann, Richard. *Selling Culture: Magazines, Markets, and Class at the Turn of the Century*. New York: Verso, 1998.

———. "Where Did Mass Culture Come From: The Case of Magazines." *Berkshire Review* 16 (1981): 85–101.

Peterson, Theodore. *Magazines in the Twentieth Century*. Urbana: University of Illinois Press, 1964.

Radway, Janice. *Reading the Romance: Women, Patriarchy and Popular Literature*. Chapel Hill: University of North Carolina Press, 1984.

Rosenberg, Rosalind. *Beyond Separate Spheres: The Intellectual Roots of Modern Feminism*. New Haven, Conn.: Yale University Press, 1982.

Showalter, Elaine. *These Modern Women: Autobiographical Essays from the Twenties*. New York: Feminist Press, 1978.

Smith, Carl S. *Chicago and the American Literary Imagination, 1880–1920*. Chicago: University of Chicago Press, 1984.

Smith-Rosenberg, Carroll. "The Female World of Love and Ritual: Relations Between Women in Nineteenth Century America." *Signs* 1 (Autumn 1975): 1–29.

Stetson, Erlene. "Black Feminism in Indiana, 1893–1933." *Phylon* 44 (December 1983): 292–98.

Terborg-Penn, Rosalyn. "Discrimination Against Afro-American Women in the Women's Movement, 1830–1920." In *The Afro-American Woman: Struggles and Images.* Ed. Sharon Harley and Rosalyn Terbor-Penn. New York: Kennikat Press, 1978.

Wall, Cheryl. *Women of the Harlem Renaissance.* Bloomington: Indiana University Press, 1995.

Welter, Barbara. "The Cult of True Womanhood, 1820–1860." *American Quarterly* 18 (Summer 1966): 151–74.

Wolff, Cynthia Griffin, ed. *Edith Wharton: Novellas and Other Writings.* New York: Library of America, 1990.

Progressive Middlebrow: Dorothy Canfield, Women's Magazines, and Popular Feminism in the Twenties

JAIME HARKER

To understand what is at stake in the public support of popular women's literature today, one need only pay attention to the heated debates about literary value and market forces that surrounded Oprah Winfrey's televised book club and her advocacy of books. Most disheartening about such debates was the assumption that Oprah's cultural intervention was unprecedented. The precursors to Oprah's Book Club have been largely forgotten, for the modernist literary canon of the twenties has erased the many institutions and authors who served as a key link from the sentimental writers of the nineteenth century to second-wave feminism and the popular women's writing that Oprah championed. To find these exemplars of popular feminism in the twenties, however, one must go beyond modernist manifestos, little magazines, and narrow modernist histories and excavate middle-class culture in its sources: in book clubs, women's magazines, and the larger middle-class currents of humanism, pragmatism, and liberalism. Women's magazines, in particular, provided a lucrative forum for popular women writers. One of the most influential and interesting was the popular novelist and educator Dorothy Canfield, who exemplifies a middle-class liberal activism and literary ethos that I term "progressive middlebrow." By investigating Canfield's writing career, and especially her key cultural interventions through novels like

The Brimming Cup (1921), I make the case for a larger excavation of middle-class women's writing in the twenties.

New England Legacy and Pragmatist Influence

At first glance, Dorothy Canfield would seem to belong to the conservative middle class against which literary modernism, as Gordon Hutner claims, defined itself. Dorothy Canfield wrote in the twenties and thirties for women's magazines, which Helen Damon-Moore has argued were profoundly conservative publications meant to keep women in traditional, and powerless, roles (197). The only other commonly known facts seem equally damning: Canfield was the only contemporary novelist lauded by the conservative New Humanists in 1930, and she served as a judge for the Book-of-the-Month Club committee that both selected Richard Wright's *Native Son* and required Wright to edit his work.[1] For most critics, these facts condemn Canfield to the ranks of the narrow-minded genteels against whom high modernists had to struggle.

A closer look at Dorothy Canfield's career, particularly her relationship to progressivism and women's magazines, shows a more complicated and interesting story. Dorothy Canfield, as one of the most prominent voices of middle-class liberalism in the twenties and thirties, was the secular, modern heir of sentimental activist-writers like Harriet Beecher Stowe and Lydia Maria Child. The great-granddaughter of abolitionists, with Vermont roots that predated the Revolutionary War, Canfield came from a New England tradition of middle-class uplift that was to come under gleeful attack by modernists and Americanists in the twentieth century.

Canfield's immediate family history, however, belies simple dismissals of Canfield as a producer of antimodern sentimentality. Canfield grew up in the Midwest—Ohio, Kansas, and Nebraska (where she began her long friendship with Willa Cather)—with her father, a university professor, and her mother, a would-be artist who led her daughter on extended stays in Paris and Spain (Washington 16). Her father was an outspoken advocate of racial and gender equality who scandalized polite society by inviting Booker T. Washington to his home while at Ohio State University. At the turn of the century, her father became the librarian at Columbia University, and Canfield enrolled as a graduate student, earning her doctorate in 1903. Immersed in the muckraking, impassioned, nonconformist atmosphere of Manhattan, Canfield refused to wear a corset and hotly debated free love, atheism, women's rights, racial equality, labor laws, political corruption, economic monopolies, and public education (Yates 70). Before the youth rebellion of the twenties, Canfield lived in the tumult of "modern" ideas, where varied political and social causes dominated both literature and public life.

At the crux of progressive ideas was pragmatist philosophy, most publicly articulated by William James and John Dewey, a professor at Columbia during Canfield's tenure there. Pragmatism replaced Christian piety as the grounding for societal reform. What justified political and social intervention was neither God's will nor an abstract notion of truth or reality, but as William James termed it, the "cash-value" of ideas—their pragmatic results in a world where absolute truth is unknowable. James's *Pragmatism*, the movement's most accessible manifesto, reveals a deep concern with what contemporary critics would term "the postmodern condition." James explains, "For pluralistic pragmatism, truth grows up inside of all the finite experiences. They lean on each other, but the whole of them, if such a whole there be, leans on nothing. . . . To rationalists this describes a tramp and vagrant world, adrift in space . . . without even a centre of gravity to pull against" (260–61). Within such a "tramp and vagrant world," pragmatists rejected the establishment of an all-inclusive metanarrative and instead insisted on experimentation, experience, and contingent values to determine personal behavior and larger societal reform.

Pragmatism has particular implications for the practice of writing. For pragmatists, literature creates vicarious experiences that construct "truth" and so can be a key tool for progressive causes. As George Hutchinson argues in *The Harlem Renaissance in Black and White*, pragmatists believed that the experience of reading could overcome regional, cultural, and class differences (47); Dewey conjectured that reading may "institute a more intimate association between human beings separated thousands of miles from each other than exists between dwellers under the same roof" (*Democracy and Education* 5). *Art as Experience*, Dewey's most comprehensive elaboration of the relationship between community and art, identifies the separation of art from common cultural experience as a uniquely Western phenomenon that shows the stratified and deleterious nature of industrial society. Art is simply an experience "in which the whole creature is alive and in which he possesses his living through enjoyment" (27), distinct in its properties but not essentially different from other sensual experiences of people, which, too, are aesthetic in their way. What makes art an especially valuable experience is the access it provides to other cultures and people. "Civilization," Dewey explains, "is uncivil because human beings are divided up into non-communicating sects, races, nations, classes and cliques" (336). Art, however, has the ability to bridge such differences because it creates "a community and continuity that do not exist physically" (336). Art is "pure experience," creating an "imagined community" that may provide the basis for an egalitarian, just society by creating community and affirming common humanity. Pragmatists identified racial inequality as one key rift that art could heal, an idea that influenced W. E. B. DuBois and Alain Locke, who studied with William James. Pragmatist aesthetics sought to heal increasing social, economic, and racial stratification.

Pragmatism—particularly its focus on education, insistence on contingent truth and pragmatic results, and conception of art as vicarious experience—had an enormous impact on Canfield's subsequent career as a popular novelist and a public intellectual. Though trained as an academic, she turned down a professorship in French to direct her talents and energies, through fiction, toward society at large. Her activism was based not on Christian orthodoxy, like that of the sentimentalists, but on a pragmatic use of commonly held beliefs for her liberal vision. On her writing desk, she kept a quotation from John Dewey: "New vision does not arise out of nothing—old things in new relations serve a new end" (Yates 90). Canfield built on traditional beliefs and even traditional prejudice to lead her readers toward more progressive views on gender and race. For her, writing was a form of public service, different from her forebears' abolitionist activism only in its medium.

The means to fulfill the aims of pragmatist aesthetics seemed increasingly possible with the evolution of print technology at the turn of the century. Advertising and publishing magnates like Munsey and McClure made magazines cheaper and more available than ever before; paperbacks had a similar effect on the book market; public libraries made the question of economic status and access to print moot (at least for those in large urban centers) (Tebbel 179). The costs of books and "serious" magazines like the *Atlantic Monthly* had made the idea of a national audience in the nineteenth century little more than metaphoric. Now, a truly national audience seemed both possible and necessary in the liberal public sphere Progressives were imagining. Some thought that the revolution in print technology was an inherently democratic innovation that would create a public to which serious writers could address themselves in financial security. The newly evolving literary marketplace was, at best, equivocal in the pressures it put on writers to be marketable. Whatever the economic realities, however, the possibilities were exhilarating.

Dorothy Canfield began her writing career during the heightened expectations of the Progressive era, which prepared her for popular success in the twenties and thirties. After successfully placing some of her own short stories, Canfield was represented by Paul R. Reynolds, the first literary agent in the United States and a formidable expert on the literary marketplace.[2] Reynolds's acumen allowed Canfield to depend on a regular income from her writing.[3]

As the Progressive era drew to a close, Canfield had all the crucial conditions for literary success—leisure to write, sympathetic and well-paying periodicals, a skilled and aggressive agent, and a prestigious and financially solvent publishing house. It was her public relationship to World War I, however, that vaulted her to true fame. With personal and academic connections to France (her Ph.D. was in medieval French, and she studied at the Sorbonne), Canfield took the side of the Allies and went to France before the United States entered the war. She wrote for American popular magazines, neither praising nor protesting the war, but instead focusing on its effect on ordinary people—doctors, farmers, pharmacists, teachers. If her writing embedded German atrocity stories and served as propaganda for the virtuous, victimized French allies, it also refused to recognize war and violence as the most important thing and kept its focus on people and their suffering. Canfield became a celebrity when the United States entered the war. After the Allied victory, she returned home, proud with other Progressives of Wilson's war for democracy and hopeful that this conflict would lead to a progressive, lasting peace. She could hardly have foreseen the collapse of the Versailles treaty, her own disillusionment with it, and the subsequent backlash against liberalism that would greatly influence American society in the twenties.

Women's Magazines and Progressive Middlebrow in the Twenties

In the 1920s postwar disillusionment led larger "culture wars" that pitted moderns against genteels and demonized middle-class culture as the cause of World War I. Janice Radway explains that the new term *middlebrow* emerged in the twenties as a reaction to the "developments, fears, and concerns" surrounding immigration and the rise of mass culture (*A Feeling for Books* 208). Specifically, critics attacked book clubs like the Book-of-the-Month Club as middlebrow bastardizations that led to the standardization of American culture and the demise of intellectual individualism and the public sphere. "Middlebrow critics," Radway explains, "were represented not merely as 'popularizers' but as dictators, policemen, and enforcers of conveyor-belt culture" (208). The middlebrow became a symbol of the commercial corruption of the public sphere, which, antimiddlebrow critics claimed, was egalitarian, free, and rational. With book club judges selecting the "best" books of the month, however, American readers were suddenly in bondage to a uniform authority. From its first usage, the middlebrow was already deeply implicated in consumerism and, consequently, low aesthetic standards. In the minds of these critics, it was popularizers like the Book-of-the-Month Club judges who dictated literary authority. The term *middlebrow* was devised to condemn the attempts of educators and writers to democratize culture.

Writers associated with what would later be termed modernism further attacked the middlebrow for attempting to bridge the gap between "art" and "life"; Radway argues that the middlebrow was an example of "cultural miscegenation." In 1941, for example, Virginia Woolf called the middlebrow "betwixt and between" (180): it is "a mixture of geniality and sentiment stuck together with a sticky slime of calf's-foot jelly" (182). These two terms, *geniality* and *sentiment*, are key to the devaluation of the middlebrow. Highbrows and lowbrows, Woolf claims, are naturally in alliance with their respective focus on art and life itself. "The true battle," she continues, "lies not between highbrow and lowbrow, but between highbrows and lowbrows joined together in blood brotherhood against the bloodless and pernicious pest who comes between" (184). That "bloodless and pernicious pest" is, of course, the middle class. Woolf concludes her half-facetious tirade: "If any human being, man, woman, dog, cat or half-crushed worm dares call me 'middlebrow' I will take my pen and stab him, dead" (186). The emergent modernist aesthetic insists that life and art are separate spheres and must, for the purity of both, remain so. The soon-to-be-defined academic field of modernism would rigidify this distinction as the key to integrity, beauty, and truth. Woolf's implicit aesthetic becomes the only valid definition for art; it continues to control and dominate most definitions of the "literary," making all other aesthetics look cheap and tawdry in comparison.

Amid these highbrow proclamations of doom, however, were ardent supporters of newly emergent middlebrow institutions epitomized by the Book-of-the-Month Club—advocates who saw in such institutions the fulfillment of pragmatist aesthetics' utopian aims for art. Dorothy Canfield articulated her support in terms of American democracy. In her 1927 book on adult education, *Why Stop Learning?*, Canfield argued that highbrows "feel the same intimate distaste for the idea of education open to every one which their grandfathers felt for the idea of the alphabet open to every one. They feel it the same sort of penetrating blow struck at their superiority. And they are right. It is" (16). She grants that conservatives may be right who claim that if "attention is paid to the taste of the general public . . . the ruling taste will become bad" (70), but she prefers "the faithful lovers and friends of ordinary people who have a mystic faith in their possibilities as the best hope for us all. . . . [They] are fighting for the privilege of flinging open to all the world the doors of the storehouse of civilization's experience and aspirations" (77). To reach the "general public," Canfield argued that one must take a "middle course" and neither "give the public what it wants" nor "try to force it to take what you think it ought to have" (148):

> [You] must give up some of the fine flowers and bloom of culture you think people ought to have but apparently do not want; you must patiently consider ways and means to emphasize what is good in what they already want; above all, you must invent means to bring out their unguessed latent desire for better things. This is not a base compromise with ugly reality; it is only common sense applied to education. It is not base, because all normal, unperverted, reasonably healthy human beings do honestly desire something better than what they have. All they need from a teacher is to be reminded of that desire, to be shown how to try to attain it instead of stifling or mutilating or caricaturing this instinctive human reach upwards. (148)

In this "middle course," Canfield felt that flexibility in aesthetic approach and in the emerging middlebrow literary institutions was key.

The Book-of-the-Month Club is the most famous middlebrow institution, but there were others, many of which Joan Shelley Rubin detailed in her 1992 book *The Making of Middlebrow Culture*. Middlebrow institutions included book clubs, radio programs, correspondence courses, and women's magazines. For white, middle-class women, women's magazines were an increasingly important and surprisingly substantive institution. In the twenties, women's magazines purchased women's writing at unheard-of prices. *Everybody's Magazine* paid $3,000 for the serialization rights to *The Squirrel Cage* in 1910; *McClure's*, outbidding the *Woman's Home Companion*, paid $15,000 sight unseen for *The Brimming Cup* in 1920, a price that Canfield, writing confidentially to her agent Paul Reynolds, thought "a perfectly sinfully whopping price" (Letter to Paul Reynolds, 12 February 1920). And the prices would go up throughout the twenties and early thirties. Gertrude Lane regularly serialized Canfield's novels in the *Woman's*

Home Companion for $20,000 and in 1933, at the height of the Depression, paid $30,000 for the serialization rights to *Bonfire*. Women's magazines brought equally outrageous circulations. Elizabeth Wyckoff, in 1931, estimated that 2.6 million people purchased the women's magazines Dorothy Canfield wrote for, and three to five times as many people actually read them (43). Only pulp magazines and newspapers could claim a wider readership.

Women's magazines were not simply a lucrative source of income, however; they also contained political possibilities. Mass-circulation magazines had, since the 1890s, used fiction to obtain readers for the advertisements that funded them (Garvey 4). Whatever the motivation for including fiction and feature articles, however, their presence in women's magazines cannot be reduced to commercial consumption only. After the passage of the Nineteenth Amendment in 1920, many women's magazines shifted part of their focus to educating women for more active participation in political and public life. The *Woman's Home Companion*, for example, had a regular column for "new voters" and published articles that encouraged women to run for office and organize for liberal causes like school funding. Some of the leading political writers of the day contributed articles and brief biographies to women's magazines, and presidential candidates frequently took out full-page advertisements, as did the Republican Warren G. Harding in a 1924 issue of *McCall's*. The *Woman's Home Companion* proudly detailed its commitment to women in politics in a preelection editorial in 1924 and had long supported women's suffrage, even as the *Ladies' Home Journal*, edited by Edward Bok, opposed suffrage. Women's magazines in the twenties and thirties contained considerable content from a range of political positions. They updated nineteenth-century republican motherhood for a changed social scene that permitted direct political involvement rather than "influence." Many women's magazines may have justified women's political involvement through their noble influence as mothers, but they were, nevertheless, encouraging political expression.

The question of women's magazines remains very complicated, and they are certainly not unambiguous means to political and cultural equality. Helen Damon-Moore, in her study of the *Ladies' Home Journal*, characterized the common male editor's attitude toward women magazine readers as condescending; editors viewed their female readers as unthinking, apolitical provincials (197). Perhaps the difference for Canfield in the 1920s and 1930s is that she worked with female editors (like Gertrude Lane of the *Woman's Home Companion*) who considered their readers as thinking, intelligent individuals and who were interested in changing the possibilities for women's magazines. It is no accident that Canfield's biography was written sympathetically by Elizabeth Yates, a women's magazine editor. Refusing to disdain the readers of women's magazines, Canfield was able to influence an enormous audience on political and cultural issues. Though moderns sneered at women's magazines, they represented an influential middlebrow "culture of letters" in the twenties and thirties.

The middlebrow suggested not only literary institutions but a certain kind of literary aesthetic focused on the aesthetic experience of the reader rather than the formal skill of the writer—an aesthetic strikingly similar to the pragmatist ideal. Middle-class readers, Radway argues, value books not for linguistic innovation but "because they are seeking a model for contemporary living and even practical advice about appropriate behavior in a changing world" ("The Book-of-the-Month Club" 535). Ultimately, as Radway elaborates in *A Feeling for Books*, middlebrow reading is about sentiment—it causes the reader to feel intensely, to identify passionately, to respond personally. Middlebrow institutions like the Book-of-the-Month Club, Radway argues, provide for their middle-class readers a "sentimental education" (*A Feeling for Books* 17).

Radway has deep reservations about the political results of this sentimental education. The intense emotion awakened by the middlebrow, she argues, served only to placate the middle class in their sterile lives under capitalism; it created for the middle class a kind of "dream world," which avoided potentially upsetting or challenging topics like race. "Too often," she concludes, the solution to "serious social problems" was the "moral, ethical, and spiritual rehabilitation of the individual subject alone" (13). For a group of progressive middlebrow writers like Dorothy Canfield, however, middlebrow institutions and aesthetics provided a forum for literary liberalism and pragmatist aesthetics in the twenties and thirties. What I term "progressive middlebrow" kept a highbrow concern with serious issues while satisfying both the lowbrow's demand for accessibility and entertainment and its fundamentally ethical judgment of the artistic. It attempted to establish a middle ground in which literature heals, creates community, and saves the nation.

Such sentiments have been thoroughly critiqued in postmodern theory, and it is difficult to imagine anyone making such humanist claims for literature today without at least a wink. It is a mistake, however, to assume that such humanist rhetoric is nothing more than a hypocritical mask for bigotry. Progressive middlebrows adhered to their liberal faith as devotedly, though perhaps less dogmatically, as nineteenth-century sentimentalists. That faith had certain consequences, both enabling and limiting. To understand the complexities and nuances of American culture and literature, it is better to explore the strengths and limitations of humanist aesthetics like progressive middlebrow than to dismiss its relevance before ever reading a line.

The political possibilities of middlebrow's "sentimental education" were irresistible to many popular women writers of the 1920s. Encouraging identification with cultural others, progressive middlebrow writers like Dorothy Canfield worked to persuade all Americans to question gender roles, abhor race prejudice, accept cultural others, and condemn class hierarchies—and they did so within the ostensibly reactionary confines of middle-class literary institutions.

"The Other Side of Main Street": *The Brimming Cup*

The publication history of *The Brimming Cup*, serialized in 1920 and published in book form in 1921, provides a striking example of Canfield's political interventions through women's magazines. The official beginning of the bohemian twenties is often marked by the publication of a novel that became a runaway best seller and the topic of spirited discussion and debate: Sinclair Lewis's *Main Street*. Known as the novel that "shattered one of the most sacred American myths, that of the friendly village" (Hutchisson 9), *Main Street* sparked a "national debate" about American materialism, hypocrisy, conservatism, class hierarchy, and indifference to art and beauty. The novel details Carol Kennicott's hopeless attempt to combat the mind-numbing banality of America's small town. Her failure to transform or even resist the relentless mediocrity of small-town America, traditionally seen as the bulwark of democracy, exposes the insidious bankruptcy of American civilization and justifies the modern revolt against cultural mores and traditions. As James Hutchisson explains the larger cultural effect of Lewis's novel, "Editorials debated its veracity, a popular song entitled 'Main Street' appeared, and parodies of the story followed" (43). The term "Main Street" became part of the vernacular (as "Babbitt" would later). The publication of *Main Street* issued a challenge to middle-class propriety, and with it, modern American youth culture began its assault on what it termed "genteel" culture.

A concomitant cultural trend in Lewis's novel, one much less noted in scholarship, is its rejection of political activism. *Main Street* is as much a critique of the reform tradition as a "revolt from the village." Lewis satirizes Carol Kennicott's efforts to reform the town as relentlessly as he does

the boors and Babbitts of Gopher Prairie. Carol's romantic desire to transform the prairie town into a place of beauty and grace is shamelessly
manipulated by the prosaic Dr. Kennicott. The middle class—hostile to
culture, refinement, and beauty—vehemently opposes redemption and
resists Carol actively and passively. Carol is sickened by her own self-righ-
teousness, which mirrors that of the town, and can't help but wonder if
she is transforming herself into a priggish small-minded Gopher Prairie
woman through her desire for change. Reform would make her little more
than a carbon copy of the high-school teacher, to whose provincial mind
Gopher Prairie is advanced civilization. For Lewis, the reform cure is as
debilitating as the sickness of American mediocrity and hypocrisy. *Main
Street* is a political novel that attacks the very relevance of politics. This
rejection of reform, of course, maintains the status quo as surely as middle-class philanthropy, but for the moderns, reformers were the enemy.

Canfield quickly recognized this postwar reaction against reform on her
return from France in 1919, and her impatience with it, in part, motivated
The Brimming Cup. *McCall's*, a new women's magazine, capitalized on her
war writing fame to pay her, sight unseen, for a serialized novel. Bessie
Beatty, the editor, wanted a novel that dealt with all the turmoil of the day,
including the role of marriage. Interested in getting past the "fashion" of
much of the modern revolt, Beatty intended the book as a study of what
this new philosophy might actually mean for women.

McCall's serialization of *The Brimming Cup* was just the beginning of
the novel's success. *Main Street* and *The Brimming Cup* were, respectively,
the number one and number two best-selling novels of the year in 1921.
Most critics on both sides of the great debate saw the novel as a direct
answer to Sinclair Lewis's attack on American life; in *Collier's Weekly* in
1921, William Allen White termed *The Brimming Cup* "the other side of
Main Street." Alfred Harcourt wrote that Canfield's novel was helped by
all the publicity *Main Street* received (57). Exact figures are difficult to
obtain, but the book went through at least four printings of perhaps
20,000 copies each, and in 1922 Harcourt, Brace, and Company produced
a cheap edition of 50,000. *Main Street* and *The Brimming Cup* were widely
read and hotly debated; together the considerable cultural capital of the two
novels provides a complex, nuanced reading of the "modern" revolt of the
twenties. In the public debate between modern and genteel, *The Brimming
Cup* and *Main Street* functioned as symbolic antagonists.[4]

Canfield argued that cities were thoroughly standardized, mechanized,
anonymous, and commercial; small towns (like those in Vermont) with
their own indigenous traditions had the natural beauty and quiet needed

for the rich inner life that Carol in *Main Street* so longs for. Focusing on a middle-aged married woman who, dissatisfied with her marriage, considers an affair, *The Brimming Cup* transforms a small Vermont town into complicated and transformed American cultural terrain.

Formally, *The Brimming Cup* tells its story in a third-person narrative that resists an omniscient authorial presence and describes each character's thoughts and motivations from his or her own perspective. Even though the main focus of the story is on Marise Crittendon, Canfield doesn't tell the story from Marise's perspective, for the point of all her fiction is to turn her middle-class readers from their apolitical "personalism" to a larger communal engagement. By writing from the perspectives of many characters, Canfield fulfills the pragmatist literary credo—literature provides pure experience of many different kinds of people, and brings understanding and community.

The Brimming Cup tells the story of a classic love triangle. Marise Crittendon, married to Neale and living with three small children in a small Vermont town, has grown dissatisfied with the monotony of her life. The New York millionaire Vincent Marsh comes to spend the summer, and his arrival coincides with Marise's awakening to her discontent. The main drama of the plot centers around Marise's attraction to Vincent and her temptation to leave the solid, prosaic Neale for a life of glamour, passion, and ease.

Supporting characters include Eugenia Mills, Marise's wealthy, self-indulgent, and trivial childhood friend whose obsession with Neale provides an overlapping love triangle to that of Marise, Neale, and Vincent; Nelly and Gene Powers, a mismatched couple who are part of another (perceived) love triangle; Aunt Hetty; Marise's three children, constant symbols of her discontent and her purpose; and Mr. Welles, a retired businessman (for Vincent Marsh's company) who sees his retreat to Vermont as a defeat and who gradually discovers new strength and purpose. These characters' experiences and choices profoundly affect Marise's own, both in her temptation and her resolution. No decision, the narrative demonstrates, is ever entirely personal; community choices affect even one's decisions about marriage.

Marise's choice between Vincent and Neale isn't simply about passion and personal preference but involves larger cultural issues, including the role of labor and the increasing stratification between classes of drudgery and leisure, and the definition of culture and its meaning and importance in a democracy. By skillfully interweaving all of these issues within a conventional love story, Canfield transforms the story of a marriage saved into a progressive promise of a nation healed and redeemed through art, activism, and republican motherhood.

Canfield, through Marise, explores alternatives to class-bound, highbrow culture. Marise loves Beethoven, quotes Goethe, and otherwise has the trappings of high culture; this is what first drew Vincent to her. But she doesn't have the same fetish for culture that the moderns have—the insistence on (and dependence upon) distinction from the masses. Dismissing a Jamesian Europhilia, Marise explains, "It may be obtuseness on my part, but I never could see that people who lived in the Basses-Pyrénées are any more cultivated or had any broader horizons than people who live in the Green Mountains. My own experience is that when you actually live with people day after day, year after year, you find about the same range of possibilities in any group of them" (45). "Culture," for Marise, isn't separate, sanctified, and European; it exists wherever people do. Culture depends upon people's ability to have aesthetic experiences, and those experiences may be found in unusual places.

One of the most striking commonplace aesthetic experiences in *The Brimming Cup* is the blooming of the cereus, a "crabbed, ungainly plant-creature," which blooms one day each year into "a wonderful exotic flower of extreme beauty" (80). Everyone in the town, "tired from their day's struggle with the earth," goes to see the cereus bloom. Canfield uses this as a metaphor of the role a pragmatist aesthetic can play in the lives of ordinary people. Her description of the flower's bloom is especially lyric:

> One big, shining petal was slowly, slowly, but quite visibly uncurling at the tip. From that moment on, she saw nothing, felt nothing but the opening flower, lived only in the incredibly leisurely, masterful motion with which the grotesquely shaped protecting petals curled themselves back from the centre. Their motion was so slow that the mind was lost in dreaminess in following it. Had that last one moved? No, it stood, still, poised breathlessly . . . and yet, there before them, revealed, exultant, the starry heart of the great flower shimmered in the lamplight. (82)

Marise is as moved by the blooming of the flower as she is by Beethoven or Goethe—perhaps more so because this experience is valued by and available to everyone in the town, not just the favored few. Vincent, of course, dismisses the significance of this "rite of the worship of beauty," insisting that these "dull, insensitive, primitive beings would infinitely prefer a two-headed calf or a bearded woman to your flower" (84). Rhetorically, however, Canfield doesn't allow Vincent's questioning to erase the sublime significance of the flower; Marise must learn to fight modern questioning and affirm the reality of what she experiences.

Once Marise has decided to stay in her marriage, she discovers an aesthetic fulfillment unknown to the highbrow Vincent and Eugenia by sharing a democratized culture with the laborers in Ashley. Directing the men's chorus, she guides them to embrace the music and feels the joy of a shared communion.

> For a moment there hung before her eyes the powerful, roughly clad bodies of those vigorous men, their weatherbeaten faces, their granite impassivity, under which her eye had caught the triumph of the moment, warming them as it did her, with the purest of joys this side of heaven, the consciousness of having made music worthily. The whole valley seemed to be filled to its brim with that shout of exultation. It had taken all of her patience, and will-power, and knowledge of her art and of these people to achieve that moment. But it had lifted her high, high above the smallness of life, up to a rich realm of security and joy. (316)

Marise bridges the chasm between high and low culture to participate in a Deweyan experiential art that binds the community together, and in that creation of art, she finds a basis for faith.

Another basis for faith is activism, which needs desperately to be revitalized in the aftermath of World War I. Marise has lost faith in the ability of reform to change anything. The Versailles treaty was "a hideous bad joke on all the world that fought for the Allies and for the holy principles they claimed" (101). She feels "terribly fooled with our idealistic hopes about the war" (103), and this makes her wonder whether "we are being fooled again when we try for the higher planes of life" (103). "Perhaps," she concludes, "those people are right who say that to grab for the pleasure of the senses is the best" (103), for her humanism is badly shaken by the war. This postwar despair, of Marise and the moderns, was seen by many as the end of Progressivism.

Marise had her ideals dashed by the war; Mr. Welles, the retired businessman, had whatever idealism he might have held crushed years before in the amoral universe of American industrialism. He "detested the sort of 'life' he'd experienced in business" (28) because "the only reality in the world of men" is that "if you didn't cut the other fellow's throat first he would cut yours" (132). He had seen his retirement as a final defeat. However, Mr. Welles rouses his will and his enthusiasm through what most people in Ashley, Marise included, dismiss as the "Negro problem." A letter from his niece about the indignities suffered by African Americans in the South enrages him, and he agonizes about it until it becomes not a "problem" but a personal and American responsibility, for "Americans that happen to be coloured people ought to have every bit of the same chance to amount to their best that any Americans have. . . . That wrong feeling about coloured people, not wanting them to be respected as much as any American, is . . . a tree that's got to come down" (175–77). Mr. Welles invokes American idealism to support his condemnation of racism; he finds, at the end of his life and beneath all his disappointments, a belief that can sustain him. Canfield doesn't use the trope of America as predominantly in this novel as she does in others, but her ideal of exemplary nationhood is central in the embedded rejection of racism and Mr. Welles's exemplary decision to go South. As a citizen, Mr. Welles feels compelled to make injustice in another part of the country his personal responsibility, and his decision affects Marise profoundly in her own struggle of conscience over her marriage. She is outraged by what seems to her a masochistic pleasure in sacrifice: "He's going to do harm, in all probability, mix up a situation already complicated beyond solution, and why is he? So that he can indulge himself in the perverse pleasure of the rasp of a hair-shirt" (224). Vincent, pressuring Marise to leave her husband and children, makes the analogy between Mr. Welles's pointless self-sacrifice and Marise's sense of duty.

The narrative of *The Brimming Cup* recuperates activism not only for what it can achieve in the world but for what it provides the activist. Nowhere is this more clear than at the end of the novel, once Marise has decided to stay in her marriage. She receives two letters—one from her modern friend, Eugenia, who has rejected self-sacrifice, and one from Mr. Welles, who has embraced what his Vermont neighbors see as martyrdom. Eugenia, with the whole world at her disposal, is consumed by ennui and bemoans, "There is no corner of the modern world which is not vulgar and common. Democracy has done its horrible leveling down with a vengeance" (317–18). Mr. Welles, by contrast, finds fulfillment in his embrace of humanism and reform: "I'm just swept back into youth again. It makes me very much mortified when I think what a corking good time I am having and what sanctimonious martyr's airs I put on about coming down here. . . . Working as I am, nobody feels about me the laid-on-the-shelf compassion which everybody (and me too) was feeling before. I *am* somebody here" (318). Activism, action, and impersonal commitment bring what riches and sophistication cannot, and they bring contingent and human rewards.

Activism and experiential art become fused, for Marise, in the role the moderns most deride and condemn: motherhood. Sentimental culture was transfixed by the sublimity of motherhood, and as Ann Douglas elaborates in *Terrible Honesty: Mongrel Manhattan in the 1920s*, the Victorian matriarch both appalled and transfixed the moderns, who desperately attacked her to break her spell. Vincent, as the spokesperson for the moderns in *The Brimming Cup*, consistently attacks motherhood as a dangerous, unnecessary, outmoded concept. He compares motherhood to drug addiction: "two different ways of getting away from reality" (99).

Victor criticizes the masochistic self-sacrifice of motherhood for the stranglehold it places on heterosexuality as well as for its unsavory connection to working-class labor. Canfield demonstrates that housewives, especially housewives like Marise living in small towns, exist as a sort of amalgam of upper and lower classes because they have husbands whose prosperity frees them from outside work yet spend the majority of their time in physical labor and recurrent, often thankless, tasks. When early in the novel Marise dismisses Vincent's reference to the "big world" and asserts that "[his] world everywhere is about as big as [he is]," Vincent's response outlines the fundamental class difference upon which his sense of self and privilege depends—and shows what Marise's life lacks: "Mr. Marsh eyed her hard, and shook his head, with a little scornful downward thrust of the corners of his mouth, as though he were an augur who refused to lend himself to the traditional necessity to keep up the appearance of believing in an exploded religion. '*You* know where the big world is,' he said firmly. 'It's where there are only people who don't have to work, who have plenty of money and brains and beautiful possessions and gracious ways of living, and few moral scruples'" (47–48). In rejecting Marise's life as a housewife, Vincent condemns not only her "moral scruples" in remaining in a passionless marriage but her everyday immersion in menial, trivial details—the antithesis of "culture." Marise, it seems, must choose between them to find fulfillment and freedom.

Canfield extricates Marise from this moral quandary by revising the terms of the debate. The sexual liberation of the moderns, in her rhetorical universe, is anything but liberating for women; motherhood, reimagined and expanded, is an exemplary model of how to heal industrialism's breach between labor and intellect, poor and rich. While Freud, Nietzsche, and other moderns seem to free women from traditional responsibilities and allow them sexual desire and pleasure, they really imprison women in the most traditional of roles. New women, Canfield argues, are really not new at all; as usual, women are valued only for their ability to inflame and gratify male desire. Modern ideas about the primacy of passion enslave women to the same subordinate, childish position of the genteels, only with different justifications.

Marise's decision not to leave her husband comes through a new awareness that part of her discontentment and her longing for passion is related to the beginnings of aging. As Vincent thinks, "Was it not the worst of calamities for all women to grow old? What was there left for a woman when she grew old?" (258). To find meaning and value only through one's ability to be "plucked" (as Marise imagines it) means that women must resign themselves to identities as passive sexual objects.

Neale, whom Vincent perceives as an unimaginative and boorish husband, understands that women are more than their ability to engender desire, and he respects Marise's integrity and autonomy in a way that the passionate lover Vincent never does. Canfield embeds her critique of modern sexuality in Neale's interior monologues. He critiques the problem of this modern overemphasis on passion when he overhears a conversation between Vincent, Marise, and Eugenia: "That notion, solemnly accepted by the would-be sophisticated moderns, for instance, that a woman of beauty and intelligence was being wasted unless she was engaged in being the 'emotional inspiration' of some man's life: which meant in plain English, stimulating his sexual desire to that fever-heat which they called impassioned living. As if there were not a thousand other forms of deep fulfillment in life" (158). In fact, Canfield shows that Vincent's desire for Marise is really a desire for possession; sexual desire is implicated in a patriarchal desire to dominate, to possess, to subdue. Vincent, finding an indication of Marise's discontent and pliability, responds in triumph: "The deep, fundamental, inalienable need for possession stretched itself, titanic and mighty" (157). He wants her to yield, to tremble, to be plucked; the verbs show the inequity inherent in the passion. Marise must choose not between duty and passion but between autonomy and submission—and her greater autonomy comes through marriage, not through Vincent's illusory freedom.

Certainly, Canfield is stacking the deck in favor of marriage. Freda Kirchwey accused her of dodging the issues in a contemporary review in the *Nation* (117), and there is a certain amount of pandering to married women by suggesting that their self-sacrifice actually allows for greater freedom than sexually liberated flappers could enjoy. By validating Marise's commitment to her marriage and celebrating reproductive roles as central to women's lives, Canfield is appealing to her readers' conservative inclinations. Canfield always seemed to choose self-sacrifice over personal fulfillment, in her novels as well as in her life, and that impulse curtailed how radically she challenged cultural norms.

On the other hand, Canfield's critique of the limitations of "free love" for women resonates throughout feminist criticism, particularly for second-wave feminism reacting to the continued misogyny of free-love radicals in the 1960s. Even more importantly for Canfield's pragmatist aesthetics, her acceptance of traditional reproductive roles for women allows her to transform a previously conservative institution into one more communal and progressive, and because she affirms the central role of marriage in women's lives, she can transform and expand it as she could not if she assaulted the entire institution. Within the limitations she sets for herself, she is able to argue for a serious liberalization of republican motherhood.

Through Marise's reconceptualized, communal motherhood, she finds the most autonomy and fulfillment, just as the constraints of fatherhood provide the most happiness for Neale. Canfield's modernized republican motherhood insists that men should become more like women, traditionally conceived as communal, nurturing, and responsible, rather than women "modernizing" themselves to become more like men, traditionally conceived as selfish, promiscuous, and irresponsible.

Housewives, in fact, have a closer connection to "reality" because they work with their hands. Initially, Marise is attracted to Vincent because he promises to save her from labor: "There had been many parts to this: her revolt from the mere physical drudgery of her life, from giving so much of her strength to the dull, unsavoury, material things. This summer, a thousand times in a thousand ways, there had been brought home to her by Vincent, by Eugenia, the fact that there were lives so arranged that other people did all the drudgery, and left one free to perceive nothing but the beauty and delicacy of existence" (265). This division of labor, emblematic of industrial society's stratification, is what *The Brimming Cup* explicitly rejects. For Marise ultimately concludes that their "freedom from drudgery" does not "give them a keener sense of the beauty and delicacy of existence" (265). Their separation from the lot of common humanity makes them less satisfied, more addicted to despair as a stimulant that obscures the ennui of their lives. Marise concludes that all should share in the world's drudgery and do their part so that no one person must do it all. There is something ennobling in this work, something that connects one to the real—that is, to working-class reality and to what enables the more "elevated" experiences.

> The existence in the world of so much drudgery and unlovely slavery to material processes was an insoluble mystery; but a life in which her part of it would be taken by other people and added to their own burdens . . . no, she had grown into something which could not endure that!
>
> Perhaps this was one of the hard, unwelcome lessons that the war had brought to her. . . . The bitterness of those days had shocked her imagination alive to the shame of sharing and enjoying what she had not helped to pay for, to the disharmony of having more than your share while other people have less than theirs. (265)

Marise's life as a mother is her way of "taking her share," of working to heal the industrial breach in America. Her seemingly self-interested, narrow life can be one way out of the quandary.

The Brimming Cup, then, rewrites republican motherhood for the secular demands of modernity. Self-sacrifice and impersonal commitment are the best things for Marise but not because women are by nature more spiritual and selfless than men. Rather, Marise's development from desiring personal gratification to accepting larger self-sacrifice represents her growth into maturity, her claiming of adult responsibilities and adult autonomy. Even more importantly, Marise's reconceptualized motherhood transforms her private responsibilities into a public trust and provides the model for activist, involved citizenship. While making her decision to stay with her husband, she transcends a self-individualism in the name of a civic collectivism, rooted not in otherworldly faith but in progressive ideals: "Her heart swelled and opened wide to a conception of something greater and deeper in motherhood than she had had; but which she could have if she could deserve it; something so wide and sun-flooded that the old selfish, possessive, never-satisfied ache which had called itself love withered away, its power to hurt and poison her gone" (269). Marise finds herself able to embrace Mr. Welles's quixotic quest to the South, and cares for Ralph Powers, whose parents tragically died, because "any child who needed a mother so much was *her own child*" (307). Through her embrace of civic collectivism, Marise "had at last stepped outside the narrow circle of personal desire, and found all the world open to her" (289). Marise's affirmation guides *The Brimming Cup*'s readers to their own liberal vision of communal responsibility.

Canfield, however, skillfully constructs this communal vision using the rhetorical persuasions of individualism. Marise must look to herself and her own experience as the only valid authority and realizes that for her, life with Neale will allow her to be who she is most completely. She must constantly rid herself of all outside voices but especially those of the new, clamorous Greenwich Village crowd, whose radical prescriptions seem most designed to keep her from hearing her own voice. The new trendy catchphrases become simply another prescriptive model to prevent women from choosing their own lives. None of this glib labeling, however, necessarily has anything to do with her. Conventional considerations— including the effect of divorce on the children—cannot prevail; all that matters, as Neale tells Marise, is "what is best for you." The truth remains only within Marise, and that truth leads her outside of herself. Canfield thus recuperates American individualism for middle-class women and uses American pragmatism to connect the middle-class mother to the larger ideals of American democracy. With a middle-class woman as a model, Canfield can have it both ways; she uses individualism to claim collectivism.

Dorothy Canfield finds new justification for old principles of responsibility, sacrifice, and commitment. In her secular recuperation of Christian duty, he that will lose his life will find it, not in some dimly promised heavenly glory but here and now, in this world. Canfield restores, in a world of shifting values, some things that are eternal—integrity, courage, and perhaps ultimately, justice.

Popular Feminism and Modern Cultural Critique

Dorothy Canfield's embrace of her middle-class readers and her faith in their essential goodness made her critically suspect in her own day and almost entirely forgotten now. The modern critical mode defined its "terrible honesty" against the pernicious cancer it found everywhere beneath the hypocritical platitudes of the middle class. H. L. Mencken caricatured that enemy as an insidious "mushy multitude,"

> that huge body of honest and right-thinking folk which constitute the heart, lungs and bowels of this great republic—that sturdy multitude which believes in newspapers, equinoctial storms, trust-busting, the Declaration of Independence, teleology, the direct primary, the uplift, trial by jury, monogamy, the Weather Bureau, Congress and the

moral order of the world—that innumerable caravan of middling, dollar-grubbing, lodge-joining, quack-ridden folk which the Socialists sneer at loftily as the *bourgeoisie*, the politicians slobber over as the bulwark of our liberties. (Nolte 167)

"The essence," Mencken continues, of best sellers aimed toward such an audience, "is sentiment, and the essence of that sentiment is hope. Its aim is to fill the breast with soothing and optimistic emotions—to make the fat woman forget that she is fat . . . to prove that this dreary old world, as botched and bad as it is, might yet be a darn sight worse" (167). Unrealistic, stupid, "middling," the American middle-class public was beneath notice and contempt. Sinclair Lewis transformed this deep-rooted suspicion of the American masses into his vision of American fascism, *It Can't Happen Here*. The horror of the American mainstream, hypocritical on its surface and capable of violent repression, lynching, and brutality underneath, is perhaps the modern critical mode's most permanent legacy. That American culture never fails to provide new evidence of its banalities and its violence only lends credence to the pessimism of the moderns.

What American literary and cultural criticism has lost, perhaps, is the passionate devotion to America's possibilities, the fascination paired with revulsion that characterizes the best writing of moderns. When Sinclair Lewis affirms writers' "determination to give . . . to an America that is as strange as Russia and as complex as China, a literature worthy of her vastness" ("American Fear"), he betrayed a faith in American culture that middle-class writers like Dorothy Canfield spent their careers fostering, manipulating, and professing. Canfield's popular feminism and pragmatist aesthetics comprised a progressively evangelical engagement with American culture—an engagement to which contemporary cultural critics often aspire but which their revulsion often makes difficult. Serious investigation into the equivocations, failures, and triumphs of progressive middlebrow writers like Dorothy Canfield may liberate modern literary criticism from the burden of its own mythological equivocations.

Notes

1. See Malcolm Cowley, *After the Genteel Tradition: American Writers, 1910–1930*; Sinclair Lewis, "The American Fear of Literature"; Hazel Rowley, *Richard Wright: His Life and Times*.
2. For a discussion of Reynolds's career, see his memoir *The Middle Man: The Adventures of a Literary Agent*.

3. Through Reynolds, Dorothy Canfield placed her writing in the leading muckraking magazines of the day. *Everybody's Magazine* serialized two of her novels: *The Squirrel Cage* in 1910 and *The Bent Twig* in 1914. *The Squirrel-Cage* critiques the damaging effects of rapid industrialization and the rigid gender codes that condemn men to alienated labor and women to sterile trivialities. Her next novel, *The Bent Twig*, took up the leading questions of the Progressives, including labor, the evils of capitalism, social work, hereditary disease, and the role of women. However, its primary focus is Deweyan, investigating the function of progressive education in constructing independent, public-minded citizens. Both novels are guided by a liberal emphasis on public service and the eradication of class divisions.

4. Canfield did not read *Main Street* until after she had completed *The Brimming Cup* and thus did not write her novel as a direct refutation, but she disagreed with much of Lewis's perspective. While praising Lewis for writing a "mighty good novel," she wrote in a letter to Alfred Harcourt that "Mr. Lewis takes a rather superficial view of human problems. . . . It is fine to see that a book seriously, honestly, written in an attempt at accuracy and understanding of American life, gets attention and success although there is not a meretricious note in it, nor an insincere one. I don't believe the American public is such a blatant idiot as it is made out" (Letter to Alfred Harcourt, 10 November 1920). Lewis, for his part, dismissed *The Brimming Cup*. Soon after the publication of both novels, Lewis was introduced to Canfield by Alfred Harcourt; he reputedly told her, "You're the biggest kind of liar" (Yates 150). Canfield was in general much more sympathetic to Lewis than he was to her; she read *Babbitt* "with the greatest approval" and praised the "real honest pathos and tragedy" of the novel (Letter to Alfred Harcourt, 9 October 1922).

Works Cited

Baym, Nina. *Woman's Fiction: A Guide to Novels by and About Women in America, 1820–1870*. Urbana: University of Illinois Press, 1993.

Canfield Fisher, Dorothy. *The Bent Twig*. New York: Henry Holt and Company, 1915.

———. *The Brimming Cup*. 1921. New York: Virago, 1986.

———. "Book Clubs." In *Dorothy Canfield Fisher: In Memoriam*. New York: Book-of-the-Month Club, 1958.

———. Letter to Pearl Buck, 20 June 1942. Dorothy Canfield Fisher Collection, University of Vermont Library.

———. Letter to Alfred Harcourt, 10 November 1920. Dorothy Canfield Fisher Collection, University of Vermont Library.

———. Letter to Alfred Harcourt, 9 October 1922. Dorothy Canfield Fisher Collection, University of Vermont Library.

———. Letter to Paul Reynolds, 6 February 1920. Paul Reynolds Collection, Columbia University Library.

———. Letter to Paul Reynolds, 12 February 1920. Paul Reynolds Collection, Columbia University Library.

————. Letter to Paul Reynolds, 17 February 1920. Paul Reynolds Collection, Columbia University Library.

————. *The Squirrel-Cage*. New York: Henry Holt and Company, 1912.

————. *Why Stop Learning?* New York: Harcourt, Brace and Co., 1927.

Cowley, Malcolm. *After the Genteel Tradition: American Writers, 1910–1930*. Carbondale: Southern Illinois University Press, 1964.

Damon-Moore, Helen. *Magazines for the Millions: Gender and Commerce in the "Ladies' Home Journal" and the "Saturday Evening Post," 1880–1910*. Albany, N.Y.: SUNY Press, 1994.

Dewey, John. *Art as Experience*. New York: Minton, Balch & Company, 1930.

————. *Democracy and Education: An Introduction to the Philosophy of Education*. New York: Macmillan, 1916.

Douglas, Ann. *Terrible Honesty: Mongrel Manhattan in the 1920s*. New York: Farrar, Straus and Giroux, 1995.

Fetterley, Judith. *The Resisting Reader: A Feminist Approach to American Fiction*. Bloomington: Indiana University Press, 1989.

Garvey, Ellen. *The Adman in the Parlor: Magazines and the Gendering of Consumer Culture, 1880s–1910s*. New York: Oxford University Press, 1996.

Harris, Susan. *Nineteenth Century American Women's Novels: Interpretive Strategies*. Cambridge: Cambridge University Press, 1990.

Hedrick, Joan. *Harriet Beecher Stowe: A Life*. New York: Oxford University Press, 1994.

Hofstadter, Richard. *The Age of Reform: From Bryan to F.D.R.* New York: Vintage, 1955.

Hutchinson, George. *The Harlem Renaissance in Black and White*. Cambridge, Mass.: The Belknap Press of Harvard University Press, 1995.

Hutchisson, James. *The Rise of Sinclair Lewis, 1920–1930*. University Park: Pennsylvania State University Press, 1996.

Hutner, Gordon. "Imperialism and the Middle Class in Modern American Fiction." Unpublished conference paper. American Studies Association Conference. Detroit, Mich. 12 October 2000.

James, William. *Pragmatism: A New Name for Some Old Ways of Thinking; Popular Lectures on Philosophy*. New York: Longsman, Green and Co., 1907.

Karcher, Carolyn. "Reconceiving Nineteenth-Century American Literature: The Challenge of Women Writers." *American Literature: A Journal of Literary History, Criticism, and Bibliography* 66, no. 4 (1994): 781–93.

Kirchwey, Freda. "Victory Before Battle." *Nation*, 7 December 1921: 113.

Lewis, Sinclair. "The American Fear of Literature." In *A Sinclair Lewis Reader: The Man from Main Street, Selected Essays and Other Writings: 1904–1950*. Ed. Harry E. Maule and Melville H. Cane. New York: Pocket Books, 1953.

————. "Foreword." In *Henry Ward Beecher: An American Portrait*. Ed. Paxton Hibben. New York: The Press of the Readers Club, 1942.

————. *Main Street*. 1920. New York: New American Library, 1980.

Nolte, William H., ed. *H. L. Mencken's Smart Set Criticism*. Ithaca, N.Y.: Cornell University Press, 1968.

Radway, Janice. "The Book-of-the-Month Club and the General Reader: On the Uses of 'Serious' Fiction." *Critical Inquiry* 14 (1988): 516–38.

————. *A Feeling for Books: The Book-of-the-Month Club, Literary Taste, and Middle-Class Desire*. Chapel Hill: University of North Carolina Press, 1997.

————. "On the Gender of the Middlebrow Consumer." *Southern Atlantic Quarterly* 93, no. 4 (1994): 820–45.

————. "The Scandal of the Middlebrow: The Book-of-the-Month Club, Class Fracture, and Cultural Authority." *South Atlantic Quarterly* 93, no. 4 (1994): 871–94.

Reynolds, Paul Revere. *The Middle Man: The Adventures of a Literary Agent.* New York: Morrow, 1972.

Rowley, Hazel. *Richard Wright: His Life and Times.* New York: Henry Holt and Company, 2001.

Rubin, Joan Shelley. *The Making of Middlebrow Culture.* Chapel Hill: University of North Carolina Press, 1992.

Tebbel, John. *Between Covers: The Rise and Transformation of American Book Publishing.* New York: Oxford University Press, 1987.

Tompkins, Jane. *Sensational Designs: The Cultural Work of American Fiction, 1790–1860.* Oxford: Oxford University Press, 1985.

Washington, Ida H. *Dorothy Canfield Fisher: A Biography.* Shelbourne, Vt.: The New England Press, 1982.

Williams, Deborah Lindsay. *Not in Sisterhood: Edith Wharton, Willa Cather, Zona Gale, and the Politics of Female Authorship.* New York: St. Martin's, 2001.

Wilson, Christopher P. *The Labor of Words: Literary Professionalism in the Progressive Era.* Athens: University of Georgia Press, 1985.

Woolf, Virginia. "Middlebrow." *The Death of the Moth.* New York: Harcourt, Brace, and Co., 1942, 180–86.

Wycoff, Elizabeth. "A Neglected Bestseller." *Bookman* 74 (September 1931): 40–44.

Yates, Elizabeth. *Pebble in a Pool: The Widening Circles of Dorothy Canfield Fisher's Life.* New York: E. P. Dutton & Company, 1958.

"Lost Among the Ads": Gentlemen Prefer Blondes *and the Politics of Imitation*

SARAH CHURCHWELL

Peggy: "No, I never read advertisements."
Irene: "Well, I know one you had better read."
(Listerine used as a mouth wash quickly overcomes halitosis [unpleasant breath])
—Listerine Ad, *Harper's Bazar* (September 1925)

By the time Anita Loos's *Gentlemen Prefer Blondes* became a 1953 musical film starring Marilyn Monroe, it had already enjoyed a remarkably (re)productive career as a stage musical (1949), a silent film (1928), a stage play (1926), and a best-selling novel (1925). *Gentlemen Prefer Blondes* did not begin life as a novel, as is usually claimed: it developed out of serialization, appearing from March to August 1925 in the ladies' magazine *Harper's Bazar*.[1] What little critical attention *Blondes* has received has focused exclusively on its two most discrete (and academically established) forms: novel and Hollywood musical. The original form that *Blondes* took, however, was not self-contained but indefinite. Furthermore, although most readers, then and now, have focused on the story's sexual politics, *Blondes* is also pervaded by contemporary anxieties about cultural capital, advertisement, imitation, and the middlebrow.[2] Reproducing itself monthly for each new installment, *Blondes* both replicated and mocked the cultural politics of the magazine in which it appeared. Uneasiness about commercialism and publicity pervades the history of *Blondes* from inception to reception. With ever-expanding boundaries, *Blondes* is characterized by "indiscreteness" as indiscretion, and by growth through replication, as the magazine format materially disallows the presumptive "centrality" of fiction and "marginality" of advertisement.

Loos emphasizes the specific context of the pages of *Harper's Bazar*, largely disregarded by the scholarship on *Blondes*, in her repeated "biographies" of the book, which accentuate both the conditions under which *Blondes* was produced and the "Bazaar" where it was eventually sold. Loos recounted the origins of *Blondes* in at least four different memoirs; the story has usually been treated by critics, if at all, as an ironic anecdote.[3] Yet this story reveals a great deal, albeit perhaps unwittingly, about professional and sexual competition in the American literary marketplace in the 1920s.[4] According to Loos's accounts, *Blondes* was never conceived as a full-length work but rather began life as a sketch and developed extempore. Its evolution was thus affected—even determined—by the magazine that printed it: "as Lorelei appeared one month in *Harper's Bazar*, Anita was frantically writing the next month's installment" (Snow, quoted in "Biography" xli).[5] Loos was already a well-known and well-paid professional writer at the time *Blondes* appeared, writing prolifically in Hollywood and also publishing in commercial magazines like *Vanity Fair*. However, she maintained that at every stage of its development, *Blondes* was marked by a lack of professional seriousness, although the book version scrupulously revised the magazine version.[6]

Loos first composed *Blondes* on a train en route from New York to Hollywood for an audience of one, a man upon whom the unhappily married Loos said she had a crush, a man who also happened to be a magazine editor and "the most famous and most influential writer" of his day, compared by contemporary newspaper editors to Dr. Johnson and Voltaire: H. L. Mencken (Hobson 251). That the sketch was to court favor with, even "seduce," Mencken seems clear, but whether the seduction was to be sexual, intellectual, professional, or all of the above remains an open question. Loos wrote the sketch, she said, in order to belittle a "witless blonde" whom Mencken preferred over her; Loos was herself a beautiful brunette and, she declared, unquestionably "the smarter" of the two women (*Cast* 73–74). In every version of her tale, Loos maintains that it was Mencken, not she, who insisted that the sketch be published. Protesting that it was too subversive for his influential satirical magazine *American Mercury*, Mencken told Loos, she claims, to send the sketch to *Harper's Bazar*, "where it would be read by a frivolous public and, lost among the ads, wouldn't offend anybody" (*Girl* 267).

The "frivolous public" who would be reading a fashion magazine was, of course, female. Loos's repeated insistence that *Blondes* was not written seriously conforms to the conventional derogation of the commercial female magazine writer (and reader). In her accounts, Loos defines "real novelists" as male writers and compares herself to a series of them, published and endorsed by Mencken, to differentiate and deprecate ure text she produced. "Any real novelist such as Sherwood Anderson, Dreiser, Faulkner, or Hemingway" would have "curdled his readers' blood" with the same story, and F. Scott Fitzgerald not only would have, "but indeed . . . did" tell the same story in a tragic vein (presumably in *The Great Gatsby*) ("Biography" xxxix).[7] Characterizing the difference between the "real" novelist and the "fake" as one of tone, Loos reiterates that she approached *Blondes* from a feminized, "infantile," "childish" comic perspective, rather than from a serious, tragic one.[8] If Loos is not like these "real" male novelists, then it follows that *Blondes* is not a "real novel" but a counterfeit. And counterfeit authorship is precisely what Loos satirizes Lorelei Lee for attempting, in the form of an illiterate diary, the most conventionally feminine and least professional written form and the only one Loos herself explicitly repudiated.[9] Lorelei is the negative to Loos's positive in almost every respect: blond where Loos is brunette, dumb where Loos is smart, amateur where Loos is professional, prostituted where Loos is virtuous, vulgar where Loos is cultured, and ignorant where Loos is a *cérébrale*. Loos displaces her anxieties about being a self-made, self-supporting, "professional woman" onto Lorelei.[10]

Despite Loos's reiteration of the accidental nature of *Blondes*'s publication, there is good reason to ask whether she might have submitted the sketch professionally to Mencken and been turned down; surely it is no coincidence that *American Mercury* satirized precisely the same targets that Loos would attack in *Blondes*.[11] If it was indeed a professional submission to one of the most highly regarded magazines of the day, then the rebuff was a serious one. America's foremost masculinist critic had consigned her sketch to a "frivolous" ladies' magazine. Loos's repeated references to *Blondes* as a "little sketch," a "little critique," and a "little book" produced as a "vanity edition" by "a friend" at Boni & Liveright may well be defensive camouflage in response to Mencken's prior belittlement ("Biography" xl–xlii).

Instead of being "lost among the ads" in *Harper's*, however, *Blondes*'s subsequent popularity with an enormous commercial audience of both sexes was powerful enough to alter the ads—and audience—of *Harper's* itself, bringing male readers to the magazine for the first time. A feedback loop was created in which the magazine's readers elicited an extension of the story that itself extended and affected the readership of the magazine. Publishing not just in, but for, a magazine problematizes conventional assumptions about the distinction between text and context: in unnatural cultural selection, the environment adapted to the object rather than the other way around. Mencken's joke that a text might be "lost among the ads" is an anxious one, revealing the fear that the literary may be eradicated by its contact with commerce. *Gentlemen Prefer Blondes* ultimately reflects a world in which economic capital, cultural capital, social capital, and sexual capital are promiscuously exchanged, a system in which art participates with its eyes averted.

Gentlemen Prefer Blondes first appeared in the March 1925 issue of *Harper's Bazar* and ran for five further monthly installments before ending in August, fittingly emerging in the precise middle of the decade it would come to exemplify. The 1920s were characterized by unprecedented commercial expansion, during which the total volume of national advertising rose by 50 percent between 1919 and 1929.[12] Warren I. Susman has argued that by the 1920s, "advertising became not only a new economic force . . . but also a vision of the way the culture worked: the products of the culture became advertisements of the culture itself" (xxiv). Reading *Blondes* in the context of the advertisements that appended it reveals the ways in which *Blondes* itself comments on this culture of advertisement. Accounts like Susman's can occlude the ambivalent reaction of professional writers to advertisement; the triumphalism of advertising in the 1920s is firmly allied with middle-class capitalist values, but those who conceived of themselves as artists also identified with "high culture" and intellectual elitism. American writers at this time were negotiating two mutually exclusive ideologies: a European, aristocratic discourse of taste as "high class," and an American, middle-class, democratic egalitarianism. Professional writers found themselves trapped between the need to sell and the need to be what Lorelei would call "refined"—that is, "artistic." *Blondes* both enacts and mocks these imperatives.

Sex and gender are never far from questions about the symbolic authority of the author, or from the masculinized professional ethos of business. The commercialism of advertisement and of magazine writing (a medium always already "contaminated" by advertisements) is figured as prostitution throughout the American literary discourse of this decade.[13] As Andreas Huyssen has famously argued, modernism associates itself with the masculine in part because art itself is increasingly feminized—and classed—by its association with "refinement." However, the analogy between books and prostitution may also derive from the endless reproducibility of the commodity; in an age of copyright, the book—like sex—in theory at least may be infinitely fungible, and magazines exemplify the anxiety about reproduction and circulation as debased copy rather than

auratic original.[14] For the commercial female writer, the anxiety about
prostitution is considerably less metaphorical than for the male writer;
feminine gentility was incompatible with commerce, circulation, and the
public sphere. In the 1920s a professional woman writer still risked being
perceived as unnatural or deviant for writing, and feminine labor and self-
advertisement more generally had always to brave association with the pro-
miscuity and commerce of prostitution. Loos negotiates this landmine in
two ways: she deprecates *Blondes* as conventionally feminine, infantile,
childish, frivolous, private, and little, and she represents writing as not
being work. Although she did not always disparage the result, Loos habitu-
ally downplayed the *labor* of writing.[15]

The anxiety about prostitution is also linked with anxieties about imitation and circulation. That which is willing to sell itself is intrinsically less
valuable than that which secedes disinterestedly from the marketplace:
"the real thing" transcends commodification, and the commodity is a mere
reproduced imitation of real value. These binaries are decidedly classed:
the poles of art/commerce (*qua* literature/advertisement, novel/magazine)
always invoke high/low; they are, in addition, variously troped as aristo-
cratic/bourgeois, male/female, pure/prostituted, author/reader, valuable/
worthless, original/imitative, unique/reproduced, disinterested/inter-
ested. In the 1920s these anxieties coalesced around the category of the
middlebrow, as critics like Joan Shelley Rubin and Janice Radway have
recently shown.[16] The "middlebrow" resulted when literature and advertisement combined forces to sell the commodified markers and discourses
of "high culture" to the aspiring middle classes. The middlebrow was
defined as the mass produced, the mass advertised; Virginia Woolf defined
the middlebrow by what it bought: "Queen Anne Furniture (faked, but
none the less expensive)" (Woolf 183).

The boom economy of the 1920s guaranteed sufficient money and leisure for more people to aspire to "self-improvement" than ever before; that
self-improvement was often, though not exclusively, related to books. The
1920s saw volumes like Will Durant's *The Story of Philosophy* and Emily
Post's *Etiquette* become best sellers, the Book-of-the-Month Club and its
imitators were launched, John Erskine began his "great books" curriculum
at Columbia, and Boni & Liveright sold a "modern library" of uniformly
bound "required reading."[17] As a result of what F. Scott Fitzgerald[18]
referred to as "the recent American strain for 'culture,'" books themselves
became a mode of self-advertisement: "Ownership of books, which had
traditionally bestowed a certain elite cultural credential, meant less and
less per se as unprecedented numbers of Americans began to buy books

for a host of reasons, including explicitly for their iconographic powers" (Benton 270). Books were becoming fetishized, brand names in a consumer society formed by the beginnings of modern mass marketing and advertising.

It is for being middlebrow in all these ways that Loos satirizes Lorelei Lee, the antiheroine of *Gentlemen Prefer Blondes*. Lorelei is not just a prostitute but also an artistically and socially pretentious aspiring parvenue: she is illiterate, imitative, and self-advertising, using men, diamonds, and books indiscriminately as accessories. *Blondes* takes the form of Lorelei's diary, which is not merely for private consumption; Lorelei writes it to advertise herself to the men whom she hopes will give her money and social capital ("I am taking special pains with my diary from now on as I am really writing it for Gerry," she explains in the first installment. "I mean he and I are going to read it together some evening in front of the fireplace" [*Blondes* 12]). Judging books by their covers, Lorelei doesn't read Conrad but likes his books because "a girl never really looks as well as she does on board a steamship, or even a yacht." So she asks her maid, Lulu, to "let all of the housework go and spend the day reading a book entitled 'Lord Jim' and then tell me all about it, so that I would improve my mind while Gerry is away" (*Blondes* 8, 13). That is, Lorelei only needs to appear to have improved her mind; appearance is reality when it functions as a credential. Self-improvement by Lorelei's definition comes from external social and economic capital rather than internal change. While both Hegeman and Blom have pointed out that Lorelei is a commodity fetish, hoping to trade sex for economic and social power, one might more comprehensively note that she is at once consumer par excellence, commodity, advertisement, broker, merchant, and owner—a veritable personification of idealized consumer capitalism, complete with the absence of labor.[19] What Lorelei is selling is less sex than it is desire through advertisement; her economy is that of the tease. In fact, Lorelei is the ideal reader of the magazine in which she made her debut.

Reading the numbers of *Harper's* in which *Blondes* appeared, one discovers that, materially speaking, Mencken's prediction was quite literally correct: the story of *Blondes* is visually "lost among the ads" in the magazine. So overwhelming seems the cumulative force of these ads that it is unsurprising that what began as a sketch parodying Lorelei's literary pretensions rapidly became a satire of consumerism. There was no table of contents in *Harper's Bazar* until 1926, and before then the first 80 pages or so of each 120-page issue consist entirely of advertisements. When a table of contents was introduced, part of its function was to feature—that is, advertise—the fiction that could be found in the issue.[20] The symbiotic economic relationship between advertising and mass-market magazines is clear. Magazines depended upon advertisers to keep circulation costs down, and advertisers found in mass-market magazines an unprecedentedly direct mode of reaching (and creating) potential consumers. However, the reciprocity of this relationship was not merely financial. As magazines created stylized, individual looks that would enable and enhance audience loyalty, editorial content and advertising context were deliberately rendered visually similar as well. The resemblance between content and advertising in *Harper's* is so strong that it is not always immediately apparent where the advertisements end and the fiction begins. The similarity is particularly marked during the first half of the twenties, when advertisements and fiction alike were illustrated with pen and ink drawings. By 1927, along with other magazines of the period, *Harper's* more frequently used photographs in fashion layouts as new technology made them cheaper to reproduce, a practice that began to differentiate visually between editorial and advertising pages.

In *Advertising Fictions: Advertising, Literature, and Social Reading*, Jennifer Wicke has argued that reciprocity is a disavowed—and constitutive—characteristic of both fiction and advertising in general, and that they are so interdependent we cannot read one without the other. The equivalence of advertisement and editorial content creates a version of what Wicke calls the "tautological threshold," the "uncanny space produced by advertising, stealing its procedures from literary self-commentary and from the theatricality of words on display—as display," in which publicity becomes "a labyrinthine discourse, a textual infinite regress, where every item of publicity worked to create new items, and every ad or performance was given value not for its content, but for its role in an exploding series" (63). There was a similar decision, deliberately gendered, in the development of women's magazines, as others have suggested:

> Editors [of women's magazines in the 1920s] moved advertisements toward the fronts of their publications, out of the advertising ghetto in the back; next they began placing ads in close proximity to editorial material on the same subject . . . women's magazine publishers led in the development of market research studies, probing the lives and preferences of readers and aiding advertisers in their investigations of ways to most effectively promote to women. By seeking out advertisers and describing readers in terms of their potential as consumers, women's journals also played a crucial part in developing what

Edward Kirkland has called "the feminization of American purchasing," reinforcing women's role as consumer. (Zuckerman 60)

Like Wicke's "tautological threshold," *Gentlemen Prefer Blondes* was an "exploding series" of stories that engendered an exploding series of advertisements in which the story sold the magazine and the magazine sold the story, creating an "infinite regress" of reproduction, imitation, and simulation, all based on "the theatricality of words on display—as display." For all that she claimed *Harper's* to be an accidental venue for her story, Loos's satire became remarkably attuned to the pages of *Harper's*, and the object of her satire is the *Harper's* reader. Visually and thematically, the text of *Blondes* and the context of *Harper's* reproduce each other.

With *Vogue*, *Harper's* formed "a special subset of the women's magazine market" known as the "class fashion periodicals" that was "aimed at an elite segment of American women" (Zuckerman 19). First appearing in November 1867, *Harper's* was subtitled "A Repository of Fashion, Pleasure and Instruction"; by the 1920s, "instruction" in social sophistication and affectation pervades the pages of *Harper's*. Hardly an advertisement or a feature does not make some reference to the *haut monde*, variously imagined. Each issue opened with that month's New York "social calendar"; studio portraits of American and European aristocracy were scattered throughout the pages; fashion layouts were highly stylized drawings designed around "where you winter" and what to wear on shipboard going to Paris for *haute couture*. The advertisements relentlessly marked their products as aristocratic. Vici kid shoes were worn by "the foot aristocratic"; Morny bath and toilet luxuries are "used by seven royal courts." In May 1925 a "little English felt cloche" is the "sensation of the year. The list of smart English women who are wearing it reads like Burke's peerage."

Harper's was actually selling itself as an instruction manual in middlebrow social pretension, offering the fetish objects of cultural capital to arrivistes who were waiting to arrive and advertising that cultural capital could be bought and sold. The advertisements and features in *Harper's* indiscriminately mix aristocratic with demotic signs. Peggy Hoyt has a common Irish name, but she advertises her shop as "milliners and dressmakers to the American Aristocracy" and places at the bottom of her ad two faux heraldic shields. Turning the page, one encounters a full-page ad for Campbell's soup at "12 cents a can," which features a manorial hall, complete with suit of armor; the copy explains that even in "homes of prominence" the soup has been "left in the hands of Campbell's French chefs." Consumerism breaks down class distinctions in this social fantasy of mass-produced high culture that is equally available—and desirable—to everyone.

In the January 1925 *Harper's*, an advertisement for Macy's department store offers "authentic reproductions of the most desirable" Colonial antiques at prices "which make them available to families of moderate incomes." Not so much paradox as tautology, the "authentic reproduction" was understood as the mark of the middlebrow, who could purchase the signs of "high culture" thanks to the technology of mechanical reproduction. Thus Bonwit Teller advertises not Paris gowns but "replicas" of Paris gowns that could be purchased through mail order. The magazine's emphasis on economizing is decidedly middle class: "That awful hole just above your smart pump," laments one running ad campaign. "Can you afford to throw away a stocking so new? . . . At the price you expected a lot of wear from that pair of stockings."

"Smartness" is ubiquitous in these advertisements, always imminent but out of reach.[21] As the ultimate (and, Loos claims, original) dumb blond, Lorelei needs exactly what *Harper's* is selling: smartness.[22] It is precisely around the question of her smartness that Loos's text will divagate. Although Lorelei has been described as "a low brow admirer of bourgeois culture," she is in fact a middlebrow aspirant to "high society"; the confusion is telling and derives from the double-edged disparagement of the middlebrow as tasteless and the bourgeois as debased (Matthews 208). Lorelei indiscriminately displays all the markers of cultural and economic capital she can find, but ineptly: when she can't determine how to wear a diamond tiara with bobbed hair, she ties it on—backwards. Like the reader of *Harper's*, Lorelei, too, makes the middlebrow error of thinking that "smartness" can be found in the accoutrements of culture.

Reading *Blondes* in the context of *Harper's*, one finds satire and its target literally side by side, as Loos mocks Lorelei for buying what the reader of *Harper's* is told to fantasize about. The reader of *Harper's* is instructed in what to wear on shipboard sailing for Europe; Lorelei sets sail. The reader is informed that "The Small Sports Hat is Particularly Smart on Board Ship" and advised, "for shopping in Paris and for travel abroad, always choose the small hat"; Lorelei goes to the children's department with Fanny Ward to buy small hats. Lorelei arrives in Paris and breathlessly sees something "historical" at last: "at the corner of a place called the Place Vendome, if you turn your back on a monument they have in the middle and look up, you can see none other than Coty's sign . . . where Mr. Coty makes all the perfume" (*Blondes* 52–53). In the same issue are ads for "Le Poudre de Coty" and for "the charming salon of Bourjois," located in the

144

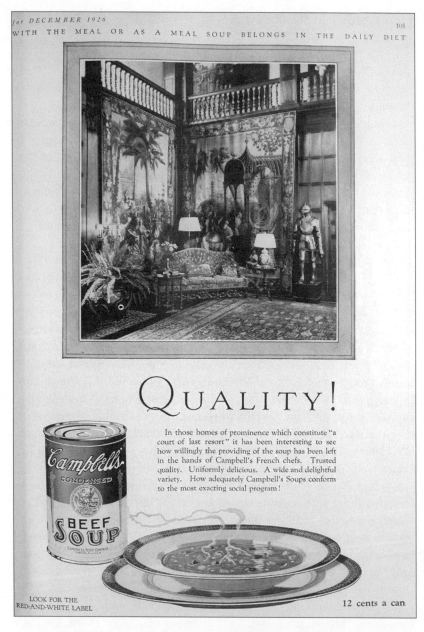

QUALITY!

In those homes of prominence which constitute "a court of last resort" it has been interesting to see how willingly the providing of the soup has been left in the hands of Campbell's French chefs. Trusted quality. Uniformly delicious. A wide and delightful variety. How adequately Campbell's Soups conform to the most exacting social program!

LOOK FOR THE
RED-AND-WHITE LABEL

12 cents a can

Harper's Bazar *sold the signs of cultural pretension to middle-class readers as this December 1926 advertisement for Campbell's Soup shows; although only "12 cents a can," it is still to be found in "those homes of prominence" (decorated with suits of armor) that "willingly" have left the soup "in the hands of Campbell's French chefs."*

Place Vendôme.[23] The deep cogitation that the magazine insists fashion should require elicits many of Loos's jokes. A feature in August 1925, headlined with the copy "Paris now contemplates the new hat," is immediately followed by the title of Loos's final installment, "Brains are Really Everything." Certainly Ralph Barton's illustrations of Lorelei and Dorothy for the magazine visually emphasize the equivalence between text and context: Lorelei and Dorothy contemplate Paris while wearing hats that strikingly resemble the ones "Paris contemplates."

Blondes ruthlessly punctures the social pretensions of both Lorelei and the middlebrow Harper's reader. The April 1925 issue, in which Lorelei and Dorothy sail for Europe, also ran a short story called "The Savage: A Beguiling Story of Americans in France that Will Surprise You." "The Savage" features a hero called Dolf, who gets a "little thrill" from calling the Countess de Flournay by her first name: "It was an innocent snobbishness, that thrill, and he was honestly prouder of the fact that it had taken five years to arrive at it than of the privilege itself. . . . 'We should have been slapping each other on the back in a couple of weeks, probably, in America!' he mused." Dolf's "innocent snobbishness" is an illusion of democratic aristocracy in which Harper's believes, but Loos does not. The democratic aristocrat is precisely the fantasy of the middlebrow, like the advertisement that pretends that people on Fifth Avenue eat Campbell's Soup, too. The magazine repeatedly stages encounters between the "innocently snobbish" American and the corruptly snobbish European; Loos equably satirizes all social pretension. In May Lorelei and Dorothy arrive in London, where they encounter aristocrats, some of whom, Loos has Lorelei artlessly explain, are "Ladies." "And some who are not Ladies are honorable. But quite a few are not Ladies or honorable either, but are just like us" (Blondes 35). In the next paragraph, Lorelei and Dorothy meet a countess of their own, who seems Loos's answer to Dolf's "innocent snobbishness" at imagining himself slapping the Countess de Flournay on the back. Pretentious Lorelei complains at the countess's behavior (the spelling errors are, of course, Lorelei's): "But I do not think the Countess acted like a Countess ought to act because she laughed very, very loud and she said that Dorothy was really priceless and she grabed Dorothy and kissed her and held her arm around her all the time. I mean I really think that a Countess should not encouradge Dorothy or else she is just as unrefined as Dorothy seems to be" (Blondes 36). If the countess is "unrefined" for encouraging Dorothy's "familiarity," then Loos is including Dolf—and thus the magazine's readers—in her mockery. Loos's satire consistently reveals the disjunction between an older definition of culture as character

"If you turn your back on a statue and look up you can see none other than Coty's sign." Harper's Bazar, June 1925. Ralph Barton's illustrations for Gentlemen Prefer Blondes strongly resemble the visual style of the magazine in which it appeared.

"Paris Now Contemplates the New Hat." Here, readers of Harper's Bazar in June 1925 are urged to contemplate the new hat along with Paris, while Lorelei, wearing the new hat, contemplates Paris.

and a modern evacuation of culture into mere theatrical display that can be affected by anyone—and that makes everyone equally "unrefined" (one thinks of Fitzgerald's famous definition of personality in *The Great Gatsby* as "an unbroken series of successful gestures" [6]). If socially democratic, Loos is culturally elitist, reproducing an ideology of taste, but one that does not respect class boundaries: as Lorelei repeatedly notes when she encounters vulgar aristocrats, "I mean there seems to be something common between us" (*Blondes* 72). Loos's humor resides in the duality of a social language of refinement in which words do not say what they mean, punning on the gap between social and literal meanings.

The plot of *Gentlemen Prefer Blondes* turns on a series of impostures, as Loos burlesques an entire social economy based on emulation: Lorelei is not aberrant but exemplary. Lorelei travels in company with her witty, outspoken, and "unrefined" friend Dorothy from New York to London to Paris to Vienna, at each stage of their picaresque journey encountering opportunists even greater than themselves, whom they consistently outmaneuver. Lorelei and Dorothy triumph in part because they always succeed in replacing the real thing with imitations. The first and funniest of the book's constitutive swindles is an elaborate double-cross in which, after wheedling a diamond tiara out of Sir Francis Beekman, Lorelei and Dorothy proceed to dupe the French lawyers his wife sends after it, one of whom Lorelei, spelling phonetically, calls "Robber." Yet Lorelei is much better (or worse) than a mere thief: she dangles a fake tiara in front of the lawyers, sells it to them, steals it back, and then resells it—all while keeping the real tiara locked safely away. By the end she has reduced the lawyers to tears. Although Hegeman has noted the implicit critique of sexual economics as commodity fetishism in this episode (541), its emphasis on simulation as deception also links the episode thematically to Loos's central preoccupation with intellectual and social pretension.

Moreover, the impostures are not only on the level of plot; Loos represents Lorelei's language—which is to say the language of *Blondes* itself—as the ultimate counterfeit. Lorelei attempts to increase her social and sexual value by trading a series of commodities, which she sees as infinitely fungible, but the very first commodity is the status of the literary itself, as Lorelei begins the diary that will become *Blondes*. Kept by Gus Eisman, "the button king," Lorelei considers becoming an "authoress" and marrying Gerald Lamson, a famous author. "It would be strange if I turn out to be an authoress," muses Lorelei after remarking with surprise on finding herself "writing a book instead of reading one" (*Blondes* 3–4). Soon "depressed" by Gerald's seriousness ("I mean he never seems to get tired of talking and he does not seem to even want to go to shows or dance or do anything else but talk, and if I don't really have something definite to put my mind on soon I will scream" [*Blondes* 17]), Lorelei allows herself to be persuaded to trade up. Gus Eisman will send her to Europe to "broaden out and improve [her] writing," thus effectively outmaneuvering his rival (*Blondes* 17).

As the story begins, Lorelei explains that Gus Eisman is "educating" her (*Blondes* 4). Loos patently derides the sexual politics that turn Lorelei into yet another commodity for "the button king" to purchase, politics that certainly also constitute the central theme of Loos's "biographies" ("back in 1926 [Lorelei] was considered . . . as such hot stuff that she would smirch my reputation" [*Girl* 270]). With her short skirts, bared legs, and bobbed hair, Lorelei is very much a stereotypical flapper, sexually but not economically emancipated. Hegeman points out that "if Lorelei is a professional 'kept woman,' then, we may say, sex is her business. More generally, however, this connection of sex and labor may be related to an ideological transformation in the '20s in which sex was, in essence, being redefined as women's work" (534). Although much of Hegeman's persuasive reading aims to uncover "the subtextual nature of sexuality in *Gentlemen Prefer Blondes*" (539), her emphasis on the "subtext" of sex effaces Loos's more overt, textual emphasis on the bonds among social, artistic, and linguistic pretension as self-advertisement, and the relationship between advertisement and value. Hegeman argues reductively and tendentiously that for Lorelei "*education* is a code word for sex" and that *brains* is "a similarly coded reference to sex appeal" (540). *Education* and *brains* are not arbitrarily chosen codes, and they by no means always refer to sex. By defining *education* as an exclusively sexual euphemism, Hegeman herself conflates sex and economics. Lorelei's use of the words *education* and *brains* do not function solely as what Hegeman terms "coded references to sex appeal" (540); rather, they enable Loos to reveal and deride the interpenetration of cultural and sexual politics.

Lorelei far more often uses "educate" to mean "pay for" or "financially support" ("Mr. Eisman spends quite a lot of money educating a girl" [*Blondes* 5]) than she does to mean "have sex with." That support is implicitly in exchange for sex, but Lorelei tirelessly keeps up the pretense, as when she explains why she "gave up" trying to be an actress when Mr. Eisman began supporting her: "when a gentleman takes such a friendly interest in educating a girl as Mr. Eisman does, you like to show you appreciate it, and he is against a girl being in the cinema" (*Blondes* 5–6).

One of the reasons for keeping up the pretense is, of course, that the diary has been written to be read aloud "in front of the fire": it is part of Lorelei's accessorizing. Yet Lorelei uses "educational" to denote anything potentially valuable, which could, but need not, include sex. "Educational" does indeed mean "self-improving" for Lorelei; it is simply that she doesn't define self-improvement as interior development but rather as upward social mobility—which, for her, can entail sex. When Lorelei finds London unappealing, she observes: "Everything is much better in New York, because the boat comes right up to New York and I am really beginning to think that London is not so educational after all. . . . Mr. Eisman really sent me to London to get educated so I would hate to tell him that London is a failure because we know more in New York" (*Blondes* 33). Clearly "educate" cannot here mean "have sex with." "Education" and "improving her mind" are the same as "worthwhile"; in Lorelei's (indubitably sexualized) work ethic they are all the opposite of "wasting time": "I am not going to waste my time going around with gentlemen because if I did nothing but go around I would not finish my diary or read good books which I am always reading to improve my mind. But Dorothy really does not care about her mind and I always scold her because she does nothing but waste her time by going around with gentlemen who do not have anything" (*Blondes* 19). Lorelei is trying to increase her value, and in the beginning of the story Gus Eisman endorses Lorelei's program of self-improvement as value-added: "Mr. Eisman always likes me to have literary people in and out of the apartment. I mean he is quite anxious for a girl to improve her mind and his greatest interest in me is because I always seem to want to improve my mind and not waste any time" (*Blondes* 5–6). Although Hegeman has argued that Lorelei "scrupulously euphemizes anything even vaguely related to sex" (534), "education" is just one of many of Lorelei's constitutive euphemisms, and sex is not the only thing she uses language to conceal. The object of Loos's satire is not only sex, in other words, but also euphemism itself.

For all her tendency to use language as a means of concealment, Lorelei equally and simultaneously employs euphemism as a means of display. Lorelei's diction is at the heart of the book's satire in a way that has not been sufficiently appreciated. John T. Matthews dismisses Lorelei's "misspellings, malapropisms, and monumental ignorance" as the "low-level humor" of *Blondes* as an example of "mass culture" (213). Conversely, Hegeman raises Lorelei's errors to the "height" of Gertrude Stein's modernist experimentations with vernacular in *Three Lives* (527). Both arguments, however, overlook the obvious with a vengeance. Lorelei is an artist *man-*

qué; surely we are not to take her errors seriously as art but rather seriously as errors. Lorelei's mistakes play a crucial role in the story's thematics of simulation. Her language helplessly reveals itself as a fake; she tries pretentiously to sound more "educated" than she is, as when she repeatedly describes herself as "a refined girl like I." Pretension, unlike pretense, fails to convince—it is betrayed by its very excess. Lorelei attempts to deploy what John Guillory calls "linguistic capital," which she wears like a diamond necklace, but with her misusages, Lorelei is, in effect, flaunting a necklace recognizably made out of paste. Language (like "smartness") becomes just one more commodity for the middlebrow to purchase.

Lorelei's relationship to language is implicitly political: she achieves power by successfully manipulating or simulating the language of "refinement." Lorelei's locutions emphasize the importance of knowing "the name of word(s)" as if this will help distinguish the valuable from the counterfeit, but the joke is that these euphemistic locutions are themselves patently counterfeit. Lorelei is shocked the first time she sees a diamond necklace made out of paste, "which is the name of a word which means imitations" (*Blondes* 53). Dorothy remarks that "'paste' is the name of the word a girl ought to do to a gentleman that handed her one." The repetition of the phrase "name of a word" and the punning, infinitely tautological definitions and translations reveal the eternal possibility of fraudulent representation, of language unmoored from meaning. Even Lorelei, superlative con artist that she is, deems this state of affairs "depressing," as it reveals that her weapons could also be used against her. In the version that appeared in *Harper's*, Lorelei at first concludes, "So it really makes a girl feel depressed to think a girl could not tell." In the book version of *Blondes*, Loos added, "that it was nothing but an imitation. I mean, a gentleman could deceive a girl" (*Blondes* 53–54). Loos's joke is, of course, that Lorelei is perfectly willing to be deceived by the gentleman in the Victorian, sexual sense but distressed at the possibility of being commercially defrauded, and she considers this state of affairs objectionable primarily because she is herself an imitation out to deceive the gentleman, both sexually and economically. Eventually, however, Lorelei perceives the ways in which she could use imitation jewels to her own advantage and comes back around to the value of replicas: "I got to thinking things over and I really got to thinking that an imitation of a diamond tiara was quite a good thing to have after all" because she can use it to get the real thing, which she does. That joke encapsulates Lorelei's practice: she is perfectly happy to use replicas in order to get what she wants, but what she wants is the real thing.

The ability to distinguish the real from the counterfeit—and to achieve the real—is the basis of power in Lorelei's world.

Lorelei's faith in simulation is inextricable from her faith in dissimulation. She almost always withholds her honest opinions, even—or especially—from her diary, given that it, too, is a commodity in Lorelei's economy, in which everything is potentially for sale. This is not to say that Lorelei has no privacy, however, or no interiority. On the contrary, she ruthlessly suppresses anything that might lower her value. Language is power, both positively as display and negatively as silence. The language of refinement provides Lorelei with an excuse for never saying what she thinks and for always speaking in code. Lorelei guards her tongue around everyone except Dorothy, who is the only person to whom Lorelei says what she means. These unguarded exchanges provide some of the story's funniest moments as the veil of euphemistic "refinement" is partially lifted, and Lorelei betrays her truly mercenary motives. When Dorothy shows up at the Paris Ritz with a "veecount," she calls Lorelei to come downstairs and join them, as Lorelei reports: "So I said How did a Frenchman get into the Ritz. So Dorothy said he came in to get out of the rain and he has not noticed that it is stopped. So I said I suppose you have picked up something without taxi fare as usual. Why did you not get an American gentleman, who always have money. So Dorothy said she thought a French gentleman had ought to know Paris better. So I said he does not even know it is not raining" (*Blondes* 51). One of the jokes of *Blondes*, in other words, is the way that Lorelei's language simultaneously betrays her ignorance and her shrewdness: she knows much less than she thinks and much more than she says. Lorelei finds platitudes particularly helpful in concealing her true grasp of every situation behind a mask of "self controle" that is at once ostensibly genteel and deeply guileful: "Henry said that when he looked at all of those large size diamonds he really felt that they did not have any sentiment, so he was going to give me his class ring from Amherst College instead. So then I looked at him and looked at him, but I am to full of self controle to say anything at this stage of the game, so I said it was really very sweet of him to be so full of nothing but sentiment" (*Blondes* 101). Lorelei is in fact "to full of self controle" to say anything at any stage of the game; self-restraint is her hallmark, and euphemism her calling card.

Lorelei's habitual policy of concealment derives at least partly from her suppression of a disreputable past, including a trial for shooting her former boss and lover for "deceiving" her ("so when I found out that girls like that paid calls on Mr. Jennings I had quite a bad case of histerics and my mind was really a blank and when I came out of it, it seems that I had a revolver in my hand and it seems that the revolver had shot Mr. Jennings" [*Blondes* 25]). Lorelei only reveals her questionable past when forced to, and even then continues to hide it behind euphemism and strategic silences. When she accidentally encounters the district attorney from her trial, for example, Lorelei aggrievedly notes that "he called me names that I would not even put in my diary"—presumably because she might end up reading it in front of the fire with whatever man she is currently trying to dupe (*Blondes* 25). The layers of Loos's joke start to reveal themselves. Lorelei's policy of gentility means that she "must" hide her own dubious past, but the existence of such lacunae in themselves reveal precisely what they are meant to disguise.

As if to deflect attention away from the fact that she never says what she means, Lorelei obsessively says "I mean," which, along with "it seems," are her favorite locutions. Any given page is scattered with these phrases, often in the same sentence: "I mean it seems that Gerry is madly in love with me"; "I mean some of the girls in London seem to be Ladies which seems to be the opposite of a Lord"; "I mean the more I travel and the more I seem to see other gentlemen the more I seem to think of American gentlemen" (*Blondes* 14, 35, 76). Euphemism and simulation put Lorelei in a recurrent state of requiring translation: she must always explain what she means, and when she does she reveals more than she intends, as when she helpfully defines "delightful": "Major Falcon is really quite a delightful gentleman for an Englishman. I mean he really spends quite a lot of money" (*Blondes* 22). The joke of translation becomes compounded when Lorelei moves into foreign languages and must negotiate the "resemblance" between different words: "I mean French is really very easy, for instance the French use the word 'sheik' for everything, while we only seem to use it for gentlemen when they seem to resemble Rudolf Valentino" (*Blondes* 69). Lorelei's repetition of "it seems" and "I mean," along with her emphasis upon resemblance, suggests not only her innocence and self-consciousness but also the degree to which her story is a performance designed to impress her audience and the way in which language is, for Lorelei, almost—but not quite—meaningless, an accessory constantly on display.

If Lorelei's words are contingent upon the audience to whom she displays them, Dorothy is Lorelei's complementary opposite. As direct as Lorelei is indirect, Dorothy always says what she thinks regardless of her audience. Although Hegeman reads Dorothy as the book's touchstone, "the voice of liberated, unhypocritical moral authority" (529), Dorothy at least colludes with and often actively contributes to all of Lorelei's scams, and she is perfectly willing to be supported by men (including allowing Mr. Eisman to pay her way across Europe as Lorelei's extremely nominal "chaperone"). Dorothy tells the truth not because she's more moral but because she's more forthright. Lorelei continually "quarrels" with Dorothy over her failure to pay lip service to social structures, as when she refuses to share Lorelei's assumed "reverance" for patriarchy: "So then Dorothy and I had quite a little quarrel because every time that Dorothy mentions the subject of Mr. Eisman she calls Mr. Eisman by his first name, and she does not seem to realize that when a gentleman who is as important as Mr. Eisman, spends quite a lot of money educating a girl, it really does not show reverance to call a gentleman by his first name. I mean I never even think of calling Mr. Eisman by his first name, but if I want to call him anything at all, I call him 'Daddy' and I do not even call him 'Daddy' if a place seems to be public" (*Blondes* 5). Dorothy may not be the voice of morality, but she is the voice of unpretentious egalitarianism, refusing the social hierarchies that Lorelei embraces.[24] When Lorelei and Dorothy land in London, they meet impoverished Lady Shelton, who tries to sell them some flowers made out of seashells. Dorothy recognizes this ruse and calls a spade a spade: "in America we use shells the same way only we put a dry pea under one of them and we call it a game" (*Blondes* 36). Lorelei's response is, "I mean, I am really going to have quite a hard time in London with Dorothy because she really should not say to an English lady what she said" (*Blondes* 35–36). Lorelei objects not to Dorothy's shrewd recognition of the con games in which everyone in her world (including Dorothy) engages, but to her lack of "self controle" in "saying" so "to an English lady." Lorelei is concerned that Dorothy's "low" speech will lower her value on more than one occasion: "I really wonder if I did right to bring her with me. . . . I mean she really gives gentlemen a bad impression as she talks quite a lot of slang" (*Blondes* 22). Plain speaking becomes the mark of the democrat, while double-talk is the hallmark both of the aristocrat and of the swindler.

Lorelei considers Dorothy's democratic directness "unrefined" because it is literally "worthless"; it is her favorite way of denoting Dorothy's general failure to take sufficient advantage: "So Dorothy and I had quite a little quarrel. . . . I told her I was not so unrefined that I would waste my time with any gentleman who was only a ballroom dancer when he had a job. So Dorothy said Gerald was a gentleman because he wrote her a note and it had a crest. So I told her to try and eat it" (*Blondes* 46). For Lorelei, if "refinement" is the language of realpolitik, to be "unrefined" is to be improvident, impractical, and neglect chances for self-improvement: "I told [reporters] I was nothing but a society girl from Little Rock, Arkansas.

So then I became quite angry with Dorothy because one of the reporters asked Dorothy when I made my debut in society at Little Rock and Dorothy said I made my debut at the Elks annual street fair and carnival at the age of 15. I mean Dorothy never overlooks any chance to be unrefined, even when she is talking to literary gentlemen like reporters" (*Blondes* 100). "Refinement" is finally, for Loos, simply an act, a middlebrow performance. Lorelei and the world around her are all acting, but Dorothy the democrat follows her feelings and refuses to dissemble: "Dorothy is always getting to like somebody and she will never learn how to act. I mean I always seem to think that when a girl really enjoys being with a gentleman, it puts her to quite a disadvantage and no real good can come of it" (*Blondes* 42). "Refinement," in other words, is Lorelei's euphemism for euphemism, in which her language marks itself as at once imitation and lie.

After *Blondes* had ended, in order to publicize *Brunettes*, Loos began appearing in the pages of *Harper's* in a series of self-advertisements that promoted and simultaneously disavowed her resemblance to her characters. The first, which appeared in the April 1926 issue, shows a cartoon drawn by Ralph Barton, which announces: "This is Anita Loos." Ralph Barton's illustrations for *Blondes* were highly stylized and strikingly resemble the pen and ink drawings that accompany the fashion layouts. When Loos appears as a cartoon drawn by Barton in an ad for *Brunettes*, she thus becomes both advertisement and part of her own text as the copy of the ad shows. The ad is selling fiction as imminent imitation, an origin invented to be imitated. In repeating that Loos is "trying to think up another one," *Harper's* is promising not only that *Brunettes* will imitate *Blondes* (which it both did and didn't) but also that Loos will successfully imitate herself, so that she will in turn be imitated at "the next dinner party." Furthermore, what Loos is trying to think up is printed as an advertising slogan, complete with randomly capitalized nouns. But in creating an imitation, the ad is also creating a rivalry: Loos must vie with her own past performance in hopes (perhaps vain—she is "trying") not of surpassing herself but merely of coming up with "another one as good." Simulation becomes rivalry, and Loos is set in professional competition against herself—and against her characters.

A month later, when *Brunettes* premiered in May 1926, it was flanked by two studio portraits: first came a cartoon pen-and-ink "studio portrait" of Lorelei and Dorothy, which was followed by a photographed studio portrait of Loos. The text reads:

This is Anita Loos. Why Do Gentlemen Prefer Blondes? That is the question that seems to be agitating dinner table conversation these days. And what do the ladies prefer? And will Anita Loos repeat her

THIS is ANITA LOOS thinking of *more* funny things for Every-body who is Anybody to read (in the May issue of Harper's Bazar) and quote at the next dinner party.

ANITA LOOS, as you all know, is the author of GENTLEMEN PREFER BLONDES, "the most amusing book of the year," whose classics *always appear first* in Harper's Bazar.

This soulful portrait of ANITA LOOS was drawn on the back of a menu card at the Ritz; it represents The Most Talked of Authoress in one of her thoughtful moods. She is here trying to think up another one as good as *"A Kiss on the Wrist Makes You Feel Good but a Diamond Bracelet Lasts Forever."*

REMEMBER!
THE MAY NUMBER
of

Harper's Bazar

"This is Anita Loos . . ." Harper's Bazar, April 1926. The advertisement for the fiction resembles the fiction itself, as text and context blur. Drawn in imitation of her characters, Anita Loos is also solicited by the magazine's copy to imitate herself in the pages of the magazine.

success with her announced second book on the same lively topic. . . . Second successes are as rare as rare, but you will see that we are right. Seconds are usually rewrites, but not this one. The first chapters that appear in this issue of *Harper's Bazar* are, it is true, a review of the old ground and the taking in of new, though familiar, territory. But after that! Well, we have read it, and we are here to tell you that Anita Loos isn't asking any one to please remember her past successes. She steps right out in front and does another one.

The anxiety about repetition, imitation, and circulation is manifest; *Harper's* admits that "seconds are usually rewrites" but assures its readers of originality while it promises "another one" that is both "new, though familiar." The effect of comparing the two declarations ("this is Anita Loos"), one below a cartoon and one below a photograph, both of which mimic the text and context of *Blondes*, is to turn the author into an advertisement for her fiction and her fiction into an advertisement for herself, as she moves from character toward the "reality" of photography. The layouts produce a functional equivalence between reader, author, and character. Cartoons of the author are exchanged for mock "photographs" of the characters, placed outside the boundaries of the fictional context. Photographs of the author, contrarily, bear exactly the same caption as the cartoon: "This is Anita Loos." The author enters the story as the characters escape it, and the story begins to infiltrate its context, just as its context has already helped define it.

The success of *Blondes* meant that it permeated fiction, advertising, and publicity outside of its own borders in the magazine: one ad declared that "Blondes prefer Henning's" shoes, and "so do their discriminating sisters—*Brunettes*." The text's success was measured by the advertisements it elicited and produced. That advertisements for men's products began to "pour" into the magazine in response to the popularity of *Blondes* meant that the readership of the magazine had changed. The "frivolous public" Mencken felt was the only appropriate audience for Loos's insufficiently "serious" story revealed itself to be male as much as (if not more than) female. The advertisements and features that addressed themselves to male readers were characteristically domesticated. As Loos reports: "gentlemen themselves had taken to reading *Harper's Bazaar* [*sic*]; ads for men's apparel, cars, and sporting goods were pouring into the office" (*Girl* 270). In fact, ads for cars appeared in issues prior to the publication of *Blondes*; the majority of post-*Blondes* ads for men's consumer goods seem to be for apparel. If the presumption was that men were reading *Blondes* because it was considered sexually provocative, many of the "male" ads and features position the men in conventionally feminized spaces or attitudes. An ad for Oshkosh trunks places a man in shirtsleeves, tying his tie in front of a mirror, a conventionally "feminine" pose. Men are encouraged to think about jacket-length: "the greatest change in this season's sack suits," explains a feature in November 1926, "is the decreased length of the jacket." The article opens by reassuring men that thinking about clothes will not compromise their masculinity: "Many men have the mistaken idea that to be well groomed is to be considered foppish." "Foppish" was, of course, a code word both for "effeminate" and for "aristocratic" and thus by mutual association (through femininity and through degeneracy) implied homosexuality. This anxiety may have arisen from features such as the one that had appeared in February 1926 explaining what the "modern man" seeks from the "modern house," and depicting a man standing in a decidedly "foppish" pose, with foot delicately pointed, inside a room with walls "entirely lacquered in tête de nègre" and lit "by a large gilded dome in the center," looking out. As Lorelei and Dorothy traveled boldly out into the world, men were revealed at home, reading about their exploits while thinking about decor and "contemplating" the hats, shirts, and suits they might buy. The gendering of the literary marketplace revealed itself, too, as a reciprocal relationship, as the definitional literary relationship of male authors and female readers "exchanged" places. As men began reading this story by a commercial female writer, they began to resemble the female reader—if not to imitate her.

Imitation began to spiral into a *mise-en-abîme* of resemblance, simulation, and reproduction, as other texts rushed to capitalize upon the success of *Blondes*. In November 1926, *Harper's* ran a story called "Tooth-Paste." Visually, the first page of "Tooth-Paste" resembles an advertisement, but it is instead fiction about advertisement and commodification:

> When Lorelei Bocock discovered her resemblance to the girl brushing her teeth with "Lorelei Superlative Enamel," she was so incensed that it became logically a question of more pearls from Dad to calm her.
>
> "It was bad enough to have named the old thing for me, Dad. It's worse to be teased about it."
>
> . . .
>
> The advertisements for "Lorelei Superlative Enamel" were strikingly suggestive. People believed the face of the manufacturer's daughter looked out from the sheets of the magazines. They said Lorelei was "a peach" to immolate her good looks in order to roll up the family millions.

Lorelei Bocock, who resembles the model for Lorelei Superlative Enamel, is a clear imitation of Lorelei Lee; she is herself replicated by toothpaste, which in turn is advertised (and replicated) by her photograph, which replicates (but is not) her. Lorelei Bocock is "incensed" by her resemblance to the girl in the photograph, which in turn suggests her resemblance to toothpaste—and may suggest her resemblance to Lorelei Lee. As comical as this sounds, Marie Van Vorst, the author of "Tooth-Paste," seems to have intended a serious exploration of commodity culture.[25] Simulation is indistinguishable from commodification, which in turn is indistinguishable from advertisement: Lorelei Bocock is not only an advertisement for toothpaste, toothpaste is an advertisement for her. And "Tooth-Paste," whether wittingly or no, becomes an advertisement for *Gentlemen Prefer Blondes*, as publicity exponentially multiplies through "allusion"—and through replication.

Gentlemen Prefer Blondes was published as a book by Boni & Liveright at the end of 1925; although Loos claims it was a "little" "vanity edition," it was also the second–best-selling novel in America of 1926. Once *Blondes* was a book, it circulated promiscuously. *Blondes* not only sold well, however, it was admired by much of the literary and intellectual elite of its day. James Joyce, whose eyesight was failing and who therefore had to curtail his reading, wrote in a letter that he had been "reclining on a sofa and reading *Gentlemen Prefer Blondes* for three whole days" (*Letters* I:246). Carl Van Vechten said it was "a work of art," and William Empson wrote Loos a love poem (*Fate* 63). William Faulkner wrote Loos a fan letter, which concluded: "I am still rather Victorian in my prejudices regarding the intelligence of women, despite Elinor Wylie and Willa Cather and all the balance of them. But I wish I had thought of Dorothy first" (*Fate* 63–64). Aldous Huxley wrote Loos to say that he "was enraptured by the book," had "hugely enjoyed the play," and though he would only be in the States for a few days hoped to arrange a meeting with her, asking that she "please forgive [his] impatience and accept the sincere admiration which is its cause and justification" (*Fate* 166). George Santayana even proffered *Blondes* as his vote for the greatest work of philosophy by an American. It would be tendentious to argue that Joyce, Van Vechten, Faulkner, Empson, Huxley, and Santayana all had their tongues in their cheeks (though Santayana almost certainly did) and that because they were writers of "high art" they must ipso facto have been contemptuous of "commercial" fiction. The admiration of Edith Wharton, for one, was no doubt sincere. She "unhesitatingly pronounce[d] [*Blondes*] the greatest novel since *Manon Lescaut*" and sent a postcard to the editor of *Vanity Fair*, which said "[I am] now reading *the* great American novel (at last!) and I want to know if there are—or will be—others and if you know the young woman, who must be a genius" (Carey 109). Even Bertrand Russell and Oliver Wendell Holmes are both reported to have read and enjoyed it.

The blurring of these supposedly historical categories is precisely the point: Is *Blondes* properly understood as low, middle, or high? Is cultural capital produced by the status of the text, its characters, its author, or its readers? "Tooth-Paste" resembles not only *Blondes* but also Edith Wharton's *The Custom of the Country*, which *Blondes* itself resembles. Why is *The Custom of the Country* high and *Blondes* middle or low (and why don't we know which it is, if these categories are self-evident, or even useful)? The difference between the reputation of Loos and that of Wharton shows that gender is not the answer, nor is commercialism per se, for at her peak Wharton too was a best seller. While tone, form, length, and intention are certainly factors, the difference may also, however, have something to do with replication as equivalence. Wharton maintains an ironic fastidious distance from her mercenary antiheroine Undine Spragg, but Loos fully inhabits the vulgar voice of Lorelei Lee. Nor did Loos ever disparage, as did Wharton, the commercialism of magazine, film, or best seller, implicitly refusing to bite the hand that fed her. Instead, she willingly participated in self-advertisement and reveled in the success of her book.[26]

As Rubin notes, the "middleness" of middlebrow culture is not merely its vertical middleness between "high" and "low" but also "its capacity to preserve aspects of gentility while reinforcing the priorities of a modern 'business civilization'" ("Between" 165). Thus, for example, when Wyndham Lewis denounced *Blondes* in his essay "Time-Children," he lambasted it for being "unvirtuous and mercenary," for its "illiteracy, hypocrisy, and business instinct" (74). Loos attempted to tread this line between gentility and mercantilism in a commercialized aesthetic context. Rubin argues that because of current scholastic practices of either blindly endorsing the "canon" or "constructing an alternative pantheon out of the materials of popular culture," the middlebrow continues to be "slighted" (*Making* 165). Because of the erasure of the middlebrow, Rubin contends, "today students of American literature are more likely to become acquainted with Hemingway and Fitzgerald" than with the "middlebrow activities" of critics like Alexander Woollcott and Dorothy Fisher. For all her laudable concern to return the "middle" ground to the conversation, Rubin nonetheless reaffirms the definitional "height" of Hemingway and Fitzgerald, erasing the fact that they were publishing in precisely the same venues as the "middlebrow" writer neglected by literary history. For instance, Fitzgerald and Loos wrote for the same magazines (and worked on the same films), while Hemingway and Loos both published their first novels with the same publishers (Boni & Liveright) and in the same year.[27] Rubin tries to recuperate the middlebrow while keeping the distinctions alive, but the distinction itself is in some ways specious. Ironically, all of these professional writers ambivalently participated in art's history of repudiation of the marketplace in order to sell their art more successfully as art. Admitting the commercial into artistic consideration might well be the only mark of the middlebrow writer. Understood this way, Loos, Mencken, and, for that matter, Wharton, Fitzgerald, and Hemingway are all properly recognized as "middlebrow": they were part of a new professional managerial class that was self-supporting and "businesslike" and yet also conceived of itself as or aspired to be tasteful, refined, cultured. Given that the middlebrow aspires to high culture, however, the middlebrow by definition never recognizes him- or herself as such. Like the "masses," the middlebrow is always someone else.

Notes

1. The magazine was spelled *Harper's Bazar* until 1929, when it was changed to its current spelling of *Bazaar*.
2. Throughout this article, I rely on Pierre Bourdieu's notion of symbolic or cultural capital as the power accrued by access to legitimate knowledge and education, and social capital as status, prestige, and social honor. See Bourdieu, *Distinction*.
3. See Hegeman, for example, who remarks that *Blondes* was written to "entertain one of the most vociferous critics of American middle-class life" and repeats that the "joke was on Mencken himself, whose sexual fascination for young blonde flappers seemed comically antithetical to his disgust for the shallow tastes and mores of America's 'booboisie.'"
4. What follows is an abbreviated version of the textual and publication history of *Blondes*; I have analyzed Loos's memoirs and this context in more detail elsewhere.
5. "The Biography of a Book" is Loos's preface to *Gentlemen Prefer Blondes* and *But Gentlemen Marry Brunettes* in the Penguin edition. It is cited parenthetically in the text as "Biography."
6. These revisions are occasional but careful. For the convenience of the reader, my page references will be to the Penguin paperback edition of *Blondes*; unless indicated, the text is the same as in the magazine.
7. Hegeman and Preston, among others, note the similarity between *Blondes* and *The Great Gatsby*.
8. Partly this insistence is due to Loos's penchant for pretending that she was in her early twenties when *Blondes* appeared, when in fact she was in her late thirties.
9. Loos opens her memoir *Kiss Hollywood Good-by* by divorcing herself from Lorelei

and, implicitly, from other female diary keepers: "In my youth," the memoir begins, "I never kept a diary, feeling that a girl who could sell her words for money had other fish to fry" (*Kiss* 9). From the beginning Loos marks herself as a professional writer and the diary as constitutively a private, amateur form. That Lorelei writes in the only form Loos marked as not for sale suggests the degree to which Loos defines her mode of authorship against Lorelei's.

10. In her introduction to the Penguin *Blondes*, Regina Barreca summarizes Loos's stance toward her professionalism: "Loos was never comfortable with her success, as hard as she worked for it. . . . Told by her husband and illustrator—and in myriad ways by the culture at large—that women could not write and still be truly feminine, that women's writing was therefore by definition unnatural, even aberrant, Loos yielded to this cultural straitjacket and so considered herself monstrous" (xxiii–xxiv). As Hegeman notes: "for Loos and many other 'professional ladies' of the '20s, the inescapable subtext of their lives in the public sphere was, broadly speaking, sex. This subtext, in turn, frequently became the ideological basis by which their labor was devalued, obscured, or credited to the benefit of men" (539).

11. In *A Girl Like I*, Loos describes Mencken's response to her "private joke" as follows: "Were he still editing *The Smart Set*, he said, he would gladly use it, but he didn't think it was right for *The American Mercury*, the more serious publication he now edited. He frankly told me he felt my heroine would be an affront to most readers. But Menck suggested that I send my sketch to *Harper's Bazaar* [sic]" (*Girl* 267). In *Kiss Hollywood Good-by*, Loos makes the even stronger claim that Mencken lacked the courage to publish the piece, telling her "I'd publish this in *American Mercury*, but I don't dare to affront my readers" (*Kiss* 194). Despite Loos's insistence on Mencken's failure of nerve, that anyone in 1920s America could have believed that Mencken feared "offend[ing]" his readers strains credulity. As Schrader points out, Mencken's comment, if he indeed said it, was "lame and uncharacteristic" (5). Both Schrader and Singleton treat Loos's offering the piece to Mencken as a case of professional submission and rejection.

12. Reed notes that advertising rose over the decade from $2,282 million to $3,426 million (152).

13. Fitzgerald famously wrote Hemingway of his rising fees for the *Saturday Evening Post*: "the *Post* now pay the old whore $4000 a screw" (Bruccoli 169). A similar anxiety about commercialism as prostitution pervades Hemingway's career, as seen in *The Sun Also Rises*, "The Snows of Kilimanjaro," and *A Movable Feast*, among others.

14. In other words, not everyone agreed with Walter Benjamin, who argued in "The Work of Art in the Age of Mechanical Reproduction" that the "aura" of the original work of art was lost in reproduction and that the democratic potential of such a loss was cause for celebration.

15. For example, Loos declares airily, "I never learned to type, having always found it more cosy to loll on a chaise longue and write on a clipboard" (*Cast* 73). However, Carey reads such comments as part of Loos's minimizing of her own labor. She was customarily up every morning at four and writing by six, and editors and publishers "were impressed by the labor and patience that went into that breezy, seemingly tossed-off style characteristic of Anita at her best" (304, 279). Argua-

bly, Loos chose to represent herself "lolling" about on a "chaise longue" because such an image links femininity with a "gentility" that could substitute for the "high art" with which it was so closely associated.

16. See Rubin, *The Making of Middlebrow Culture*, and Radway, *A Feeling for Books: The Book-of-the-Month Club, Literary Taste, and Middle-Class Desire.*

17. Loos satirized the Book-of-the-Month Club, which was launched in 1926, in the first episode of *Brunettes*: Lorelei writes, "And so I gave Henry a supscription [*sic*] to the Book of the Month Club that tells you the book you have to read every month to make your individuality stand out. And it really is remarkable, because it makes over 50,000 people read the same book every month" (*Blondes* 135). The early humor in *Brunettes*, like that of *Blondes*, centers (perhaps anxiously, given that it is a sequel) on the question of originality and imitation.

18. Fitzgerald attempted to cash in on this phenomenon, proposing to Charles Scribner that he create a version of Liveright's "Modern Library," experiments that, Fitzgerald explained, "have been made possible, I believe, by the recent American strain for 'culture' which expresses itself in such things as uniformity of bindings to make a library" (Bruccoli 57). Although Fitzgerald here seems scornful of the superficiality of "uniformity of bindings," he also insisted to his editor, Max Perkins, that his bindings always be published uniformly.

19. See Hegeman (532–46) and Blom.

20. In February 1926, while *Harper's* was running Loos's story "Why Girls Go South," which appeared in the magazine between *Blondes* and *Brunettes*, it ran an advertisement on page 24: "Speaking of serious endeavors," it said, "leads us to HARPER'S NEW FICTION PROGRAM. It includes *more* Fiction in each issue and the very best fiction that can be had (and Harper's Bazar is the only smart fashion magazine that publishes fiction at all). Note the eight illustrious names in this issue— Irvin S. Cobb, Hugh Walpole, Robert Hichens, E. Barrington, Anita Loos, Sir Philip Gibbs, Arthur Somers Roche, and Marie, Queen of Roumania—and let them speak for the new plan of emphasizing Fiction in Harper's Bazar. Fashions, of course, will retain their preëminence."

21. In just a few examples, we are told that Peggy Hoyt sells "Smartness beyond Comparison." Bandettes and girdles are "what the smart world wears beneath the straight slim gowns of today." "Smart costume has become standardized," "knickers and make-up" are the "two requisites of the modern smart woman," and "no shoe is smarter than that which sports the mottled leather known as lizardskin." The Coxwell Chair company explains that "to lounge smartly is an art" and promises that their chair "strikes the keynote of smartness with comfort."

22. The magazine that launched Mencken's national reputation was *The Smart Set*. The *OED* offers "the smart set" as one of its examples of the meaning of *smart* that denotes elegant and aristocratic: "13. Fashionable, elegant, esp. in a very high degree. (Common in recent use, from c1882.)" The *OED* comments that "the reappearance of the word in this sense was the subject of much comment and criticism in newspapers, etc., from about 1885, and the phrases smart people, smart society, the smart set, etc., have been commonly used as a general designation for the extremely fashionable portion of society (sometimes with implication of being a little 'fast')."

23. Some of the copy in *Harper's* is so fatuous as to seem a parody of itself: "When in Egypt, dress as the Parisienne does" is an absurdity worthy of Lorelei at her best, as is *Harper's* assurance that "Jane Régny has solved the problem of what to wear when you ride a mile on a camel."

24. Dorothy is hardly sexually emancipated, however. For a discussion of her tendency to be duped by men, see Hegeman and Barreca.

25. Lorelei Bocock (like Wharton's Undine Spragg) misguidedly marries a European, Fernando, who comes from a successful merchant family but is himself a failed artist. By the end of the story, Fernando's paintings "reek of tooth-paste," but they are selling, and Fernando's uncle thinks to himself: "His nephew had become a merchant, like his family, a producer of marketable goods" (132). Fernando and Lorelei's Italian son squeezes a tube of paint, and "the crimson color flowed from the tube like the tooth-paste" (132).

26. For all her deprecation of her "little" book, Loos carefully catalogues its successes: "the first edition sold out on the day it reached the bookshops and, although the second edition was of sixty thousand copies, it was exhausted almost as quickly. I believe the book ran into forty-five editions before the early demand had ceased. Naturally there have been a number of soft cover editions through the years. But I feel that Lorelei's accomplishments reached a peak when she became one of the few contemporary authors to be represented in the *Oxford Book of Quotations*. Following its American publication, *Gentlemen Prefer Blondes* became a best-seller in thirteen languages (Note to Krushchev: Where are my royalties, Tova-rich?)" ("Biography," xlii). In the later *A Girl Like I*, Loos is even less self-effacing: "In 1950 Lorelei came to be included in the new edition of *The Oxford Dictionary of English Quotations*, making me, as her instigator, one of the extremely few living writers to attain those august pages" (*Girl* 273). For all the comic "humility" of ascribing authorship to Lorelei, Loos is standing up and taking her place in literary history—and in a volume, moreover, that did not include Henry Louis Mencken.

27. In addition to *Blondes*, in 1925 alone, Horace Liveright also published Hemingway's *In Our Time*, William Faulkner, Eugene O'Neill, Theodore Dreiser, Sherwood Anderson, Robinson Jeffers, Hart Crane, Ezra Pound, e.e. cummings, Dorothy Parker, Jean Toomer, Nella Larsen, S. J. Perelman, Nathanael West, and Ben Hecht. Of Liveright and his editors, Lillian Hellman remarked, "they were not truly serious men, I guess, nor men of the caliber of Max Perkins [Fitzgerald's editor at Scribner's], but they had respect for serious writing" (quoted in Fine 25). Loos's biographer Gary Carey asserts that Liveright's reputation was one of the reasons that Loos chose them, along with the fact that editor Tommy Smith was a friend of hers (95).

Works Cited

Benjamin, Walter. "The Work of Art in the Age of Mechanical Reproduction." In *Illuminations*. Trans. Harry Zohn. New York: Harcourt Brace Jovanovich, 1968.

Benton, Megan. "'Too Many Books': Book Ownership and Cultural Identity in the 1920s." *American Quarterly* 49, no. 2 (1997): 268–97.

Blom, T. E. "Anita Loos and Sexual Economics: 'Gentlemen Prefer Blondes.'" *Canadian Review of American Studies* 7, no. 1 (1976): 39–47.

Bourdieu, Pierre. *Distinction*. Trans. Richard Nice. London: Routledge and Kegan Paul, 1984.

Bruccoli, Matthew, ed. *F. Scott Fitzgerald: A Life in Letters*. New York: Penguin, 1995.

Carey, Gary. *Anita Loos: A Biography*. London: Bloomsbury, 1988.

Fine, Richard. *West of Eden: Writers in Hollywood, 1928–1940*. Washington, D.C.: Smithsonian Institution Press, 1993.

Hegeman, Susan. "Taking *Blondes* Seriously." *American Literary History* 17, no. 3 (1995): 525–54.

Hegeman, Susan, and Claire Preston. "Ladies Prefer Bonds: Edith Wharton, Theodore Dreiser, and the Money Novel." In *Soft Canons: American Women Writers and Masculine Tradition*. Ed. Karen L. Kilcup. Iowa City: University of Iowa Press, 1999, 184–201.

Hobson, Fred. *Mencken: A Life*. Baltimore: Johns Hopkins University Press, 1995.

Huyssen, Andreas. *After the Great Divide: Modernism, Mass Culture, Postmodernism*. Bloomington: Indiana University Press, 1986.

Joyce, James. *Letters of James Joyce*. Ed. Stuart Gilbert. London: Faber and Faber, 1957.

Lewis, Wyndham. *Time and Western Man*. London: Chatto and Windus, 1927.

Loos, Anita. *Cast of Thousands*. New York: Grosset & Dunlap, 1977.

———. *Fate Keeps on Happening: Adventures of Lorelei Lee and Other Writings*. Ed. Ray Pierre Corsini. London: Harrap, 1984.

———. *Gentlemen Prefer Blondes* and *But Gentlemen Marry Brunettes*. Introd. Regina Barreca. New York: Penguin, 1963.

———. *A Girl Like I*. New York: Viking, 1966.

———. *Kiss Hollywood Good-by*. New York: Viking, 1974.

Matthews, John T. "Gentlemen Defer Blondes: Faulkner, Anita Loos, and Mass Culture." In *Faulkner, His Contemporaries, and His Posterity*. Ed. Waldemar Zacharasiewicz. Tübingen: Francke, 1993, 207–21.

Radway, Janice. *A Feeling for Books: The Book-of-the-Month Club, Literary Taste, and Middle-Class Desire*. Chapel Hill: University of North Carolina Press, 1997.

Reed, David. *The Popular Magazine in Britain and the United States, 1880–1960*. London: British Library, 1997.

Rubin, Joan Shelley. "Between Culture and Consumption: The Mediations of the Middlebrow." In *The Power of Culture: Critical Essays in American History*. Ed. Richard Wightman Fox and T. J. Jackson Lears. Chicago: University of Chicago Press, 1993.

———. *The Making of Middlebrow Culture*. Chapel Hill: University of North Carolina Press, 1992.

Schrader, Richard. "'But Gentlemen Marry Brunettes': Anita Loos and H. L. Mencken." *Menckeniana* 98 (1986): 1–7.

Singleton, M. K. *H. L. Mencken and the "American Mercury" Experiment*. (Durham, N.C.: Duke University Press, 1962.

Susman, Warren I. *Culture as History: The Transformation of American Society in the Twentieth Century*. New York: Pantheon Books, 1973 (rev. 1984).

Woolf, Virginia. *The Death of the Moth and Other Essays*. New York: Harcourt Brace, 1942.

Zuckerman, Mary Ellen. *A History of Popular Women's Magazines in the United States, 1792–1995*. Westport, Conn.: Greenwood Press, 1998.

III

WOMEN BEHIND THE SCREENS

Edna Ferber's Cimarron, Cultural Authority, and 1920s Western Historical Narratives

HEIDI KENAGA

The first film version of Edna Ferber's 1930 novel *Cimarron*, released by the newly formed corporation Radio-Keith-Orpheum (RKO) in 1931, was critically well received and was the only Western during the classical studio period to win an Academy Award for Best Picture.[1] If the Western is, following André Bazin, the American film par excellence, it seldom has reached the pinnacle of what the industry has constructed as the most valuable critical recognition—securing an Oscar.[2] This is due, in part, to the lingering connotation of Western fiction as "lowbrow" and formulaic. Yet *Cimarron* occupies a different stratum on the hierarchy of cultural production, in part because of Ferber's status as a Pulitzer prize–winning author, the novel's broad success as commercial fiction, and the narrative's scope as historical spectacle. Genre studies most often address *Cimarron* in terms of its relationship to Ferber's novel, which is described as a regional historical epic focusing on the impact of the opening of the Cherokee strip upon the Oklahoma territory or as a historical romance with a "strong" female lead character, implicitly assumed to derive from Ferber's authorship.[3] Literary and cultural historians have commonly focused on this last feature, noting feminists' neglect of Ferber's novels, which often feature such atypical characters.[4] The analysis that follows addresses issues of authorship and adaptation to some extent, particularly the effect of Ferber's gender and ethnicity upon the field of Western literary production. Clearly the set of interpretive strategies that might be applied to the cinematic text include authorship and adaptation, and in the analysis that follows I will address both to some extent, particularly the effect of Ferber's gender upon the field of Western literary production. However, my primary goal is to situate the production and consumption of *Cimarron* within an emergent cycle of middlebrow Western metanarratives that transformed the pulp novel subject into a document of national historical commemoration, illuminating the complex foundations of Ferber's critique of a masculinized "pioneer culture." My discussion positions *Cimarron* at the nexus of these formations, showing how the reception of the book and film participates in contemporary debates over who could legitimately represent the experiences of women and men in the West. Ultimately, my examination uncovers a central paradox in both middlebrow literary production and Hollywood filmmaking practice during the rise of nativism in the 1920s: to promote the public perception of Americanness and an appreciation for a "white" historical legacy, RKO executives chose a work by Ferber—a Jewish, cosmopolitan writer associated with cultural elites—as their source material.

Cimarron is considered the last of what are commonly called "epic Westerns," a group of movies spurred by the phenomenal success of Famous Players–Lasky's *The Covered Wagon* in the early 1920s. The most important films of this cycle include Fox's *The Iron Horse* (1924), Paramount's *The Vanishing American* (1925), and United Artists' contribution in 1926, *The Winning of Barbara Worth*. Of course, Western fiction had long been a mainstay of first pulp and later "slick" mass-market magazines, and this was replicated in the serial and B-Western productions of the silent era. However, after *The Covered Wagon*, the cinematic depiction of Western historical figures and visualization of episodes from the expansionist metanarrative became not just financially remunerative but also culturally legitimated. American film studios—especially Paramount and Fox— became adept at exploiting the cultural sanctioning of the genre, revising the meanings associated with attending a Western.[5]

The studios adopted such strategies, in part, because during the postwar era the increasing influence of movies in American life threatened the economic and social power of traditional elites. Influential individuals who resented the industry's control by "nonnatives" attacked studio ownership, the Federal Trade Commission began antitrust investigations into Paramount's alleged restraint of trade activities, and public-interest groups initiated federal censorship measures to regulate transgressive movie content. These multiple challenges were often conflated as the film industry became a crucial site of struggle for political and social factions sup-

porting racial nativism in American domestic policies.[6] In response, the
industry established a trade association, the Motion Picture Producers and
Distributors of America (MPPDA) in 1922, to deflect the array of challenges to its hegemony. Its mandate, "to establish and maintain the highest possible moral and artistic standards of motion picture production, by
developing the educational as well as the entertainment value and the general usefulness of the motion picture," was designed with public relations
in mind (Moley 226).[7] Under the aegis of Will Hays, the association initiated and established formal links with national civic, educational, and
patriotic organizations with a vested interest in the "improvement" of
motion pictures, such as the General Federation of Women's Clubs, the
Boy and Girl Scouts of America, the National Education Association, the
American Library Association, and the Daughters of the American Revolution.[8]

Westerns had seldom sparked much controversy and were viewed as an
innately American form, so it is not surprising that during this unstable
period the studios developed strategies to market the frontier past, appro-
priating its cultural power in order to best serve economic ends. Their cultivation of "authentic" Western prestige features had financial motivations;
by repackaging a children's genre into something that might interest adult
patrons as well, the producers could exploit a new production trend. However, such films were also the result of the MPPDA's ongoing public relations tactic to reconstruct the business as less a commercial enterprise
than an authoritative and socially responsive cultural institution. Further,
since the industry was subject to nativist attacks, it pursued material that
could be readily marketed as more than simple entertainment. Such
"national documents" offered the movie patron triumphal visualizations
of the frontier experience that demonstrated the significance of the Western expansion to the country's present economic power. Neither the "high-
art" masterworks of European cinemas nor the "lowbrow" product of the
studios' standardized practices, the "epic" Western can be viewed as the
cinematic artifact of "middlebrow" culture in the 1920s. As Janice Radway
has argued, the term *middlebrow* "ought to be understood as a figuration
of that middle ground produced by new social mediation, the developing
relationship between the huge mass audience on the one hand and an
entirely new cultural elite on the other, immigrant entrepreneurs . . . who
were building cultural empires that were also enormously successful busi-
nesses" ("Scandal" 726).[9] Thus, those "cultural entrepreneurs" who had
established the American film industry became engaged in the cultivation
of selective cinematic document rather than mass-market product, as they

labored under pressure to develop movies whose consumption could be viewed as prosocial.

Correspondingly, the studios distributed these prestige Western features carefully, with special marketing strategies designed to refigure spectatorship as an edifying, educational, even patriotic act. Such tactics included invitation-only premieres at top ticket prices, an opening-night audience comprised of often nationally known political, social, and business leaders, and elaborate publicity campaigns. Sometimes these films were given an extended roadshow tour, a way of further connoting the exclusivity and singularity of the feature via select bookings at legitimate theaters, complete with traveling orchestra and special score. In part, this effort at legitimation relied on the studios' appropriation of a discourse on authenticity emergent in the early twentieth century—a discursive formation constructing positions of authority from which individuals could speak about the "real West," that is, disseminate historical knowledge about frontier culture and experience.[10] Multiple social and cultural institutions as well as political contexts helped maintain this discourse, which was highly (if not solely) vested in male artists. Best known of these were writers, journalists, and popular historians such as Theodore Roosevelt, Owen Wister, and Zane Grey. These Western chroniclers commonly legitimized their claim to speak authoritatively about the West by drawing upon racial and nativist ideologies or constructing personal histories dependent upon formative, epiphanic experiences in the West. These men were "motivated to 'westernize' themselves . . . by their individual dissatisfactions with their eastern heritage," constructing a frontier myth that emphasized the fundamental "virtues of hardihood and manliness" to American life.[11]

While Theodore Roosevelt and Zane Grey are the best known of the early-twentieth-century male authors on the West, popular writer Emerson Hough achieved a similar position.[12] From 1897 to 1923 Hough published thirty-four books about the frontier, but it was through his twenty-year association with the *Saturday Evening Post* that Hough achieved fame as an authoritative chronicler of the pioneer experience. *Post* editor George Horace Lorimer cultivated a cadre of writers, Hough among them, whom his readers would come to view as "legitimate" authorities with a national reputation.[13] As with Grey and Roosevelt, the writer's autobiographical narrative reified his ostensibly authentic, experiential links to the West. Born and raised in Iowa in 1857 as a "pioneer boy," Hough acquired "a passion for the open prairies, the woods, and the streams." But he was not physically strong and was plagued by several illnesses throughout his childhood. Like Roosevelt, Hough combatted this perceived weakness by actively pursuing a "strenuous life" of school athletics and intellectual rigor, becoming a voracious reader. Like Grey, as a youth Hough was most influenced in his views of the West by his exposure to literature, specifically historical fiction such as Henry Howe's *Historical Recollections of the Great West.*[14] As Chicago editor of *Forest and Stream,* Hough traveled to remote areas of the West and the Plains states on journalistic assignments, always alert to the publication possibilities of his observations. In 1897 he wrote "The Story of the Cowboy," which received critical acclaim from well-known Western writers, including Roosevelt. This nonfiction work was soon considered the authoritative text on the cattle industry, contributing to the growing perception that Hough not only witnessed but participated in the events he wrote about. The reviewer in the *Chicago Tribune,* for example, claimed that his "account of the rude and stirring life of other days spent upon the plains . . . has all the graphic vigor of an eye-witness and expert cow puncher." Yet as Hough biographer Carole McCool Johnson points out, "most of his hours in the saddle had been spent in the pursuit of sport and not cattle."[15]

Influenced by the rise of racial nativism in the United States during the teens and war years, Hough became overtly xenophobic. These views were coupled with an increasingly nostalgic belief that the frontier heritage and its racial and gender ideologies were now dangerously imperiled in the new century. These views emerged with particular force in his postwar writing, especially a series of sketches for the *Post* about "Traveling the Old Trails." These articles, which acclaim the "purity" of the Anglo-Saxon men and women who endured the Western trek in years past, combine historical chronicle, colorful description, authorial commentary, and political polemic. "The true flag of America is the flag of the frontier," he concludes.[16] Such an aphorism summarizes Hough's agenda to construct a national myth of origin that reverses the social and cultural transformations of modern life, especially those deriving from immigration, urbanization, and a consumption economy. The tutorial value of the frontier experience for contemporary women was the writer's special concern in his popular 1918 history, *The Passing of the Frontier: A Chronicle of the Old West.*[17] Here Hough paid tribute to the role of the "pioneer woman" by invoking a revisionist rhetoric:

The chief figure of the American West, the figure of the ages, is not the long-haired, fringed-legging man riding a raw-boned pony, but the gaunt and sad-faced woman sitting on the front seat of the wagon, following her lord where he might lead, her face hidden in the same ragged sunbonnet which had crossed the Appalachians and the Missouri long before. That was America, my brethren! There was the seed of America's wealth. There was the great romance of all America—the woman in the sunbonnet; and not, after all, the hero with the rifle across his saddle horn. Who has written her story? Who has painted her picture?[18]

The questions at the conclusion of the passage, posed as a challenge to male Western historians putatively responsible for the neglect of the pioneer woman, emphasize the importance of her historiographic inscription and her commemoration through visual culture. At Lorimer's urging, Hough soon took up the task himself in his most popular novel, *The Covered Wagon* (1922).[19] This work, as well as the film adaptation produced by Paramount in 1923, merit close examination if we are to fully understand the cultural work performed by the historical Western text during the 1920s.

Elaborating on the ideological concerns of its two key precursors, the "Traveling the Old Trails" series and *The Passing of the Frontier, The Covered Wagon* depicts the course and fate of a large wagon train leaving Westport Landing (what is now Kansas City) in 1848 for the northwest, following the Oregon Trail. The plot centers around a romantic triangle, involving the daughter of one of the wagon train leaders (Molly Wingate), the villain who desires her (Woodhull), and an upstanding former Army officer (Banion) who harbors an "undeserved stain" on his reputation that Woodhull uses to convince Molly to marry him instead. On the way to Oregon, the travelers endure a number of perilous events, from prairie fire to Indian attack to river fordings. The fierce elements and constant struggle to keep alive, combined with news of gold found on the West Coast, results in internal strife over whether the train should continue to Oregon or divert to California. The train actually splits, with one party going northwest to their original destination while the other, under Banion's leadership, goes west. Later, after a failed ambush, Banion kills Woodhull at a prospecting camp in the Sierras and, since his name has been cleared through the assistance of friends, returns to Oregon and Molly.[20]

Reviewers usually described the novel as a genuine, albeit artless document of the frontier experience, praising its historical value and nativist sentiments rather than its aesthetic innovation.[21] Several writers specifically applauded the focus on the pioneer woman; in Molly Wingate, one noted: "[Hough] has drawn a type of the pioneer girl and woman of which we may well be proud. On the paper cover of this book the opening of the prairie schooner has been well chosen by the artist as a halo to frame her head and the radiating lines of the canvas wagon back well suggest angel wings, epitomizing the protection, service, and sacrifice of the American woman of that pioneer period."[22] The illustration is W. H. D. Koerner's *Madonna of the Prairie*, which also appeared on the cover of the first *Post* issue in which the story appeared. Sitting alone on the buckboard of a covered wagon, her head framed not by the customary sunbonnet but rather the "halo" of the canvas cover, this image of the pioneer woman was endlessly circulated during Paramount's prerelease advertising and marketing program. In the finished film, a cinematic rendering of the Koerner image introduces the main female character, Molly Wingate. Largely as a result of the huge popularity of the *Covered Wagon* narrative, successful in three venues (magazine serial, book, and motion picture) from 1922 through 1925,[23] statements extolling the transcontinental move under "covered wagons" as a shared event of national origin appear throughout public discourse.[24] The "Molly" iconography signifies the ideal female American progenitor. Seldom initiators of action unless paired with a male figure who makes the decisions, such passive but hardy women were figured as the "precious cargo" to be brought West or, as in Hough's view, as "the seed of America's wealth." The painting also recasts Molly as Madonna, a maternal Christian figure who represented a return to what historian Barbara Welter has called the "cardinal virtues [of] the Cult of True Womanhood" in the nineteenth century: piety, purity, submissiveness, and domesticity.[25] Into the late twenties, the pioneer woman was a ubiquitous and multivalent historical sign, suggesting the inevitable westward march of American progress under the stewardship of this forthright figure, while at the same time critiquing modernity, particularly the era's "New Woman," who was more interested in consumer goods, leisure-time activities, and pursuits independent of the home.

This commemorative process emerged throughout visual culture. The dedication of a public memorial to the "Pioneer Woman" near the Cherokee strip in 1930 is particularly salient in this context because *Cimarron* (both novel and film) ends with a similar event.[26] In late 1925, Edward C. Marland, president of an Oklahoma oil company, invited a number of nationally known sculptors to submit bronze models in competition for a monument called the "Pioneer Woman of the West." Within public discourse, his initiative was styled as both philanthropic venture and noble civic duty. Donating 2,000 acres and $300,000 to the project, Marland claimed—as if taking his lead from Emerson Hough—that such recognition was overdue: "Looking about our Western country in the last few years

W. H. D. Koerner's painting Madonna of the Prairie, *the cover illustration for the 1922* Saturday Evening Post *issue in which* The Covered Wagon *originally appeared. Reprinted by permission of the Buffalo Bill Historical Center, Cody, Wyoming; gift of the artist's heirs, W. H. D. Koerner III and Ruth Koerner Oliver; 25.77.*

I saw monuments to Buffalo Bill, Kit Carson, and a dozen other pioneers. Great men, every one of them, and a fine thing to honor their deeds. But what about the pioneer woman?"[27] Cultural historian Kirk Savage has argued that sponsors of such monuments "worked hard to sustain the fiction that they were merely agents of a more universal collective whose shared memory the project embodied. . . . They had to summon the symbolic . . . participation of a 'public' that the monument would represent."[28]

In subsequent years, such symbolic participation was still deemed crucial in securing the legitimacy of such public memorials. Early in 1927, Marland sent twelve three-foot models on a national tour, starting in New York, with subsequent exhibitions in Boston, Chicago, Washington, Kansas City, Oklahoma City, and other major cities. Marland noted that he sought "the opinion of the public as well as that of prominent art critics, publishers and directors of art museums" in making his decision. Thus, gallery visitors in all of the tour's locations were asked to vote for the best statue. At first, Marland told the sculptors that there were two requisite elements of the figure: a sunbonnet as headgear and an accompanying child, since the pioneer woman had carried "the seed of America's wealth" to the frontier. Later, the artists were given a freer hand; nonetheless, all but two of the models have sunbonnets, and only one does not depict a child. The eventual winner was Bryant Baker's statue of a sunbonneted woman, striding across the prairie, holding a male child by the hand and clutching a small bag and a Bible. Described as "pretty" and a "pleasant enough commercial piece," this figure is more idealized than the "gaunt and sad-faced" figure in a "ragged sunbonnet" described by Hough in *The Passing of the Frontier.* The inclusion of the Bible, as opposed to the gun or ax carried by five other figures, implies the significance of the pioneer woman in bearing Christianity and the codified knowledge associated with the East out to the West.[29]

In order to encourage Oklahomans' participation in the Pioneer Woman dedication, Governor W. J. Holloway declared 22 April 1930 a statewide holiday. More importantly, "symbolic participation" by the American nation was fostered via an invention of the industrial age, radio, when NBC decided to broadcast the proceedings. As Savage notes, "the more widely the monument campaign appealed, the more enthusiasm it seemed to generate, the more convincingly its public would come to resemble the democratic vision of one people united by one memory."[30] The radio audience heard speeches from Ponca City by Marland, Bryant Baker, Will Rogers, and Governor Holloway, and from Washington by President Herbert Hoover and Secretary of War Patrick Hurley (described as a "product of the pioneer woman of Oklahoma"). In his address, President Hoover noted that pioneer women "carried the refinement, the moral character and spiritual force into the West," while Secretary Hurley overtly acknowledged the tutorial uses of such monuments for the present day: "In the erection of this monument we pledge a reverence to the woman who has laid the foundation of the character of our community, State and nation. . . . Every citizen who passes this way and looks upon this memorial will be strengthened in the conviction that this State shall be kept worthy of the woman whom this bronze statue commemorates."[31] Editorial response in the *New York Times* suggests that the sponsor of the Pioneer Woman monument had successfully devised a commemorative event with both national scope and unifying power: "The woman as pictured in this statue belongs not to Oklahoma alone. The rest of the country will see in her the form and features of the woman of every frontier from Maine to California."[32]

Echoing Emerson Hough's lament about the historiographic neglect of the pioneer woman, Secretary Hurley concluded that this was "probably due to the fact that most of the pages of history are written by men about men."[33] He did not, however, go so far as to suggest that more women should engage in the production of such pages. Given these specific historical and cultural contexts, Edna Ferber's address of the frontier heritage, particularly the pioneer woman, in *Cimarron* can be understood as an engagement with an existing tradition that until that time was almost entirely the province of male writers. Not surprisingly, Ferber's authorship of the Oklahoma story came under scrutiny. The film industry had found episodes in Western history not just lucrative but fungible properties as well, bartering the artifacts of national culture for social legitimacy and sanction. However, Ferber was not perceived in public discourse as an authoritative source for the dissemination of historical knowledge about the West—neither by birthright (she was female and Jewish) nor by personal history or experience (she was born in the Midwest). In addition, although Ferber was often described as a regional writer, she was much identified with New York life, particularly its literary and theatrical elites. In her autobiography, Ferber herself foregrounded this apparent incongruity in her account of the novel's origin. After a tour of Oklahoma, her longtime friend and journalist William Allen White regaled her with stories about the state's oil rush history. He urged her to write about it, but Ferber refused, recalling the "tough job" that writing *Show Boat* had been: "No, the story of Oklahoma is a man's job. . . . No more big open spaces for me. Let somebody else do the American-background stuff. Too hard work" (*Treasure* 325–26).[34] Comparing this account of *Cimarron*'s genesis with the origin of *The Covered Wagon* reveals Ferber's liminal position within the field of Western literary production. An influential editor encourages the writer to pursue the topic, yet assumptions about gender and "authenticity" of authorship inform the exchange. White introduces Ferber to the "masculine West" (although having experienced the frontier as a tourist), and she replies in kind, as if the "gendered spaces" of the West require a male chronicler.

Ferber's personal correspondence suggests she may have had other qualms about the material than that offered in her autobiographical narrative.[35] In May 1928, she decided to "have a tourist's look at this Oklahoma" herself, interviewing local inhabitants in smaller towns, doing research in Oklahoma City, and visiting the state's oil capital, Tulsa. In letters to her family, Ferber wrote of her despair in finding any "freshness" in the subject matter: "There's enough stuff, God knows, for a ten-volume novel. But some of it has been done, much of it is bad man, Indian, pioneer stuff that is an old story," particularly in the movies. Ferber found the Oklahoma historical materials like "an old fashioned western—the kind of thing I'd walk out on if they were doing it at the Harper or Rivoli." However, Ferber hammered out a final draft within a year, and in late 1929 the first chapters appeared in *Woman's Home Companion*, a popular periodical with a predominantly female readership.[36]

As popular Western fiction, *Cimarron* is a compelling case study to the extent that it appears to be the only successful epic Western written by a woman. Yet given the cultural context within which it was produced and circulated, it can also be read as a rather skillful critique of the relationship between gender and the dissemination of "authentic" historical knowledge about the West. A careful analysis of *Cimarron* indicates Ferber's implicit characterization of the male Western writer as historical fabulist. What she described as the improbable, "movie-like" quality of her research into Oklahoma's historical legacy resulted in a foregrounding of the imbrication of fact and fiction in the historical work, particularly in terms of the divergent and competing ways that men and women's experiences often figure in such a process. The foreword to the novel contains the following declaration:

Only the more fantastic and improbable events contained in this book are true. There is no attempt to set down a literal history of Oklahoma. All the characters, the towns, and many of the happenings contained herein are imaginary. . . . In many cases material entirely true was discarded as unfit for use because it was so melodramatic, so absurd as to be too strange for the realm of fiction. . . . There was no Yancey Cravat—he is a blending of a number of dashing Oklahoma figures of a past and present day. There is no Sabra Cravat, but she exists in a score of bright-eyed, white-haired, intensely interesting women of sixty-five or thereabouts who told me many strange things as we talked and rocked on an Oklahoma front porch.[37]

Ferber inverts the hierarchy between actual events and fiction so that the invented becomes acceptable as historical truth. Similarly, she inverts the hierarchy of gender in relation to the origins of the narrative. Yancey is clearly more abstract, distant, mythified, whereas Ferber more directly locates Sabra's origin in real Oklahoman women who witnessed the historical episodes detailed in the novel. We know that she interviewed men of the same age, but she chooses to acknowledge these women's contribution by citing their oral history as the dominant source. In the first two chapters, Ferber sets up Yancey Cravat as something like a historiographic straw man, "a bizarre, glamorous, slightly mythical figure. No room seemed big enough for his gigantic frame; no chair but dwindled beneath the breadth of his shoulders. . . . Rumor, romantic, unsavory, fantastic, shifting and changing like clouds on a mountain peak, floated about the head of Yancey Cravat" (7, 9). His chief appeal lies in his oratorical style and incommensurate skills as a raconteur. Thus, the 1889 Oklahoma land rush that begins the novel is not narrated directly but rather presented via Yancey's recollection of its events for the benefit of Sabra's antebellum relatives, the aristocratic Venables from Mississippi now living in Wichita. He describes the panoramic rush for this rapt audience in a highly cinematic way: "Whole scenes, as he talked, seemed to be happening before his listeners' eyes" (11). Although Yancey himself is enthralled with the recounting of such scenes, his actual participation in nearly all such episodes in *Cimarron*—including the two land rushes, the shootout with the Kid and his gang, and the Spanish-American War—are never directly described but rather are related secondhand. Thus, from the start of the novel, Ferber foregrounds the importance of storytelling and mythmaking to the institutions of pioneer culture, overtly positioning male control of the narrative while women (or the feminized Venable men) form an enthralled but passive audience.

In these early chapters of the novel, Ferber also interrogates the cultural function of the "pioneer woman" ideal from the popular frontier fiction and films of the period. Yancey tells Sabra's family that he admired the many hardy women he met during the land rush, but he has to defend their uncouth appearance against the Venables' disdain. Once, as he waited in a line for a vital drink of water, he noticed that

the one behind me in the line was a woman of forty—or looked it—in a calico dress and sunbonnet. She had driven across the prairies all the way from the north of Arkansas in a springless wagon. She was like the women who crossed the continent to California in '49. A gaunt woman, with a weatherbeaten face, the terribly neglected skin . . . that means alkali water and sun and dust and wind. Rough hair, and unlovely hands, and boots with mud caked on them. It's women like her who've made this country what it is. You can't read the history of the United States (all this he used later in an Oklahoma Fourth of July speech when they tried to make him Governor) without learning the great story of thousands of unnamed women . . . good women, with a terrible and rigid goodness that comes with work and self-denial. Nothing picturesque or romantic about them . . . no, their story's never been told. And if it's ever told straight you'll know it's the sunbonnet and not the sombrero that has settled this country. (15–16)[38]

Yancey is so moved by her forlorn appearance that he ends up giving her his cup of water, the last in the bucket. While there are clear allusions here to Hough's discourse on the neglect of the pioneer woman in historical accounts, Ferber deflates their "picturesque or romantic" presentation in *The Covered Wagon*'s "Molly" image by (re)visualizing their bodies as much trammeled by the inhospitable terrain. Further, her careful insertion of the parenthetical remark about the political value of Yancey's rant links this discourse to the nationalist rhetoric implicit in historical chronicle. In this way, Ferber skillfully recirculates the myth of the pioneer woman while also revealing the ideological function of its puritan sentiments during the contemporary era. Throughout *Cimarron*, she subverts idealizations of this figure that may conveniently be used to critique their more indulgent modern granddaughters. When Sabra's mother vehemently objects to Yancey's plan to take Sabra and son Cim back to the Oklahoma territory, her father counters that their daughter "favors those pioneer women . . . the woman in sunbonnet and calico to whom Yancey had given his cup of water; she was the women jolting endless miles in covered wagons, spinning in log cabins, cooking over crude fires; she was all women who have traveled American prairie and desert and mountain and plain" (27–28). When her mother refuses to relent, Sabra later takes her leave from a more suitable maternal figure, aptly named "Mother Bridget," who remembers "the wild and woolly days of Kansas." She gives Sabra a wool blanket she wove with her own hands for the wagon trip west, echoing Yancey's claim that "here in this land, Sabra, my girl, the women, they've been the real hewers of wood and drawers of water" (36). Thus, Sabra is refigured as Mother Bridget's de facto descendant: she dons the sunbonnet that one of the Venables had "jokingly given her at parting," learns how to deal with the constant jolting of the wagon by learning to "sway with it," and finds a measure of happiness and "delightful detachment" in their journey through the wilderness (50–52).

At the same time, Sabra cannot leave the accoutrements of civilized, Eastern life behind. When they finally arrive at Osage, Yancey is elated at the frontier appearance of their "future home." All Sabra can see is "something that looked like a wallow of mud dotted with crazy shanties and tents," and she can think only of those sartorial "elegancies" she brought from Wichita, "the green nun's veiling trimmed with ruchings of pink which lay so carefully folded, with its modish sleeves all stuffed out with soft paper, in the trunk under the canver of the wagon" (62). She feels herself an "onlooker" (69) in Osage, with nothing in common with those women in sunbonnets she sees. For Sabra, "here in this Oklahoma country life had been set back according to the frontier standards of half a century earlier" (82). Soon she devotes herself to building a home for her family and establishing a newspaper, the *Oklahoma Wigwam*, a venue by which she can build a "social order" in the community (130–31). Concurrently, Ferber links the emergence of this order with descriptions of the women's great yearning for Eastern "elegancies" in their rough frontier homes, completely overwhelming those Osage inhabitants (such as Yancey) determined to keep it "wild and virgin land." For example, Sabra's home quickly becomes a "social center" when it is discovered that she receives *Harper's Bazaar*, and she dutifully prints the latest innovations in the domestic arts in the paper (133–36).

In this way, Ferber targets the Oklahoma commemoration of the stoic Pioneer Woman as an idealized progenitor who had "a terrible and rigid goodness that comes with work and self-denial." Rather, it is the "indomitable materialism" and particularly genteel values of those sunbonneted women of Osage that form the foundation of a burgeoning consumer culture. The range of consumables soon extends beyond items of home decor to encompass the objects of intellectual capital as well. As the newspaper begins to flourish, Sabra founds the Philomathean Club, which as she tells Yancey will "take up literature . . . maybe early American history . . . also current events." Later this club, together with an array of hereditary societies, comprise a women's club movement in Osage (138–39, 220–21). These groups "began to go in for Civic Betterment, and no Osage merchant or professional man was safe from cajoling and unattractive females in shirtwaists and skirts and eyeglasses demanding his name signed to this or that petition" (240).

Yancey eventually abandons the family and business in Osage to satisfy his wanderlust, and Sabra's power and prestige come to surpass his. Her stewardship of the *Wigwam* makes her a force in the territory, and she uses the club movement as a platform for enacting a program of "civic virtue." The enormously successful town madam, Dixie Lee, and "the saloons that still lined Pawhuska Avenue, the gambling houses, all the paraphernalia of vice, were anathema lumped together in the minds of the redoubtable sunbonnets." When the local population finds the clubs' temperance campaign intolerable, Dixie's establishment is next in line to be "routed by the spiritual broomsticks and sunbonnets of the purity squad" (199–200). Yancey's sudden fortuitous return to Osage results in Dixie Lee's acquittal on the charge of disorderly conduct, but the crusade for "Civic Betterment" undertaken by Osage's "purity squad" continues. Here again, Ferber uses historical fiction to enact contemporary skirmishes over cultural power. Historian Alison Parker has shown how the interests of the Women's Christian Temperance Union (WCTU) went beyond promoting abstinence from alcohol, seeking to disseminate a "pure" culture in opposition to the "degraded" forms of popular media increasingly available to the public. During early decades of the century movies had "eclipsed all other cultural forms as the most attractive, potent, and dangerous,"[39] but the founding of the MPPDA in 1922 had not resulted in the level of self-censorship desired by those groups who had agitated for its establishment. Parker details the peak of the WCTU's campaign for federal intervention during 1925–33, "when the great popularity of movies and their increasingly sexualized content led to a broad pro–movie censorship movement led by Christian organizations."[40] Such efforts resulted in the film industry's stricter enforcement in 1934 of the Production Code, a document that "enunciated the moral principles underlying screen entertainment."[41] While Ferber does not explicitly incorporate the growing phenomenon of motion pictures into *Cimarron*, the association of "sunbonnets" with the "purity squad" in a narrative conceived and produced during 1928–31, largely in response to the contemporary appropriation of frontier imagery in an attempt to construct a "usable past," is not coincidental. Her metonymic description of the members of the women's clubs as "sunbonnets" deliberately challenges the benevolent, spiritual connotation of such headgear mobilized by a masculinized pioneer culture and expressed by such artifacts of visual culture as public monuments and motion pictures. At the same time, Ferber critiques those women's activist groups that seek to "regulate society's morals" as well as the "content of American culture."[42] By the 1920s, such organizations garnered sufficient cultural power to foster a nascent middlebrow culture, fertile ground for the emergence of the "epic" Western cycle during this period.

Although *Cimarron* was widely interpreted as "a colorful romantic Western American novel," Ferber wrote that it was actually a bitter satire designed to present "a malevolent picture of what is known as American womanhood and American sentimentality" (*Treasure* 339).[43] Although the novel was generally well reviewed, at least one group of contemporary readers agreed with what Ferber called its "malevolent" aspect. Upon publication of the novel in 1930, Oklahoma newspapers bristled with criticism of its depiction of their state's history. The *Cimarron News* reported that "panning Edna Ferber's novel 'Cimarron' is just now a diversion of Oklahoma publications" and cited in particular an editorial in the capital's main newspaper, the *Daily Oklahoman*, which condemned Ferber as a "rank outsider" interested only in the "lurid phases" of the state's development.[44] The writer herself claimed that she received a "flood of letters, [ranging] from remonstrance to vilification" about the book.[45] The controversy primarily concerned the legitimacy of Ferber's authorship—whether her chronicle of Oklahoma frontier origins could be understood as "authentic," given her gender, urbanity, and ethnicity. Ferber's brief sojourn in the state (thirteen days) and status as an "outsider" had made the issue of the novel's historical verisimilitude all the more pressing. Even if the writer herself was not attacked, regional publications often detailed the factual errors found in *Cimarron*. For example, *Harlow's Weekly* chided Ferber for the novel's "mistakes" and "anachronisms," and positioned the review next to a brief requiem ("Passing of a Pioneer") written by a local woman to a well-known regional figure, as if Ferber's account needed to be offset by an "authentic" folk tribute.[46] While some newspapers in the region, especially those in Kansas, came to her defense (probably the result of William Allen White's influence in that state), others, such as the *Dallas Morning News*, perceived a dissonance between writer and subject. One reviewer, Stanley Vestal, identified as the author of "Kit Carson," "'Dobie Walls, and So Forth" and an inhabitant of Oklahoma for a "long period of years," commented:

> Miss Ferber doubtless received a great deal of authentic incident from her informants during her brief stay in Oklahoma, but she was so completely ignorant of the spirit of the frontier days that she spoiled most of her materials in shaping them for fiction. . . . Her contact

with Western life . . . was too brief and too deliberate for much com-
prehension of its motives, its deep-seated conservatism, its reverence
for racial standards . . . in short, Miss Ferber writes of Oklahoma as I
might write of China a generation ago after spending a week in Hong-
kong.[47]

Even if Oklahomans understood that she was neither a popular nor academic historian, her apparent lack of interest in extensive research was
taken as evidence of her inability to discern the basis of "legitimate" Western historical fiction. Literary tributes to the pioneer by Theodore Roosevelt, Zane Grey, and Emerson Hough were properly motivated by civic
duty and produced in the interests of historical veracity, never by personal
gain or aggrandizement. Vestal's comments about Ferber's "deliberateness" suggest she intended to capitalize upon the contemporary popularity
of frontier imagery, sentiments echoed by another writer who suggested
she came to Oklahoma just to "get copy"—the most exploitable material—
rather than the facts and oral history.[48] Conflated with such criticism is
nativist bias and anti-Semitism, implied by the last line of Vestal's comment. Constructed as a "nonnative" and racial Other, Ferber approaches
Oklahoma's history as if it were a foreign country.

Such sentiments were occasionally expressed outright, as in an editorial
to which Ferber refers in her autobiography: "This Ferber woman is the
most unpleasant personality that has ever come into Oklahoma. . . . Why
doesn't she stay in the ghetto where she came from?"[49] Probably the most
notable example is found in a *Bartlesville News* piece, which recalls the
impression the writer made upon her visit to the city in 1928: "Edna Ferber is remembered in Bartlesville as an extremely offensive personality
garnished with a profusion of hair dye and egotism." When during Ferber's visit a local "gentleman of education and culture" volunteered his
knowledge of the state's history, she dismissed the offer, commenting she
wasn't "interested in the facts":

> "Say, Big Boy," she blatted in that tone children in the Ghetto are apt
> to use after about the third shot of Oklahoma corn, "I know my busi-
> ness. Folks will be reading my books ten thousand years after they
> have forgotten how to spell your name. I'll find some dumb publisher
> who will know as little about the state as I do and he will take my story
> all right . . ."
>
> Her attempt to tell the story of the "run" into Oklahoma is laugh-
> able and idiotic and the book is filled with such falsification of dates,

places and historical events that it never can pass for anything like a historical novel. . . . [But] it probably achieved its purpose, which could have been nothing more highly inspired than the desire to keep the kosher-meat grinder working until she could bring together another collection of misinformation and another dumb publisher.[50]

This account constructs material acquisition as well as the accumulation of personal power as Ferber's primary motivations. Her putative racial allegiances as a Jewish American were viewed as incongruent and in fact inimical to the appropriate origin of the "authentic" Western chronicle. While Ferber may have been a suspect voice within the discourse on authenticity because of her ethnicity and urbanity, what the *Bartlesville News* piece articulates most clearly is anxiety about power and how authorial control over this historical legacy was a site of struggle during the 1920s. Ferber's established success as a writer would secure a national audience for *Cimarron* and thus a broad measure of cultural authority; in this way, her work posed a threat to the guardians of pioneer culture.

However, the construction of "authority" within the sphere of cultural production is neither fixed nor univocal but rather negotiated and historically contingent. In those quarters where Ferber's frontier narrative received some endorsement, the challenge posed by her intervention was defused by a strategy of appropriation rather than disavowal and censure. For example, several columnists applauded Ferber, "an internationally known writer," for "leading Oklahoma into literature," because "her writing skill insures the permanency of the record. There is nowhere in history or fiction a duplication of the Oklahoma experience."[51] Perhaps Ferber would be "good copy" for the state and its history, as opposed to the other way around. Such appropriation is most evident, however, in how Ferber was handled during the Pioneer Woman dedication in April 1930, soon after *Cimarron* was published in book form. E. W. Marland cautiously invited the writer to be his houseguest for the occasion of the unveiling of the Pioneer Woman statue. "I am sure you will like the monument, in which you will surely see some of the spirit of your Sabra Cravat," he wrote to her.[52] Marland may have grasped the irony of the situation: in a ceremony dedicated to the pioneer woman, all the participants on the dais were men. No doubt aware of her unpopularity with the state's elites, Marland was unable to invite her to make a speech. Further, Ferber had targeted just such sculptural commemorations at the end of her novel. Late in Sabra's career, long after Yancey has disappeared and she has achieved her greatest success as a congresswoman, "ten of Osage's most unctuous millionaires contributed fifty thousand dollars each for a five-hundred-thousand-dollar statue that should embody the Oklahoma Pioneer." The sculptor wanted to interview Sabra Cravat. Osage wondered: "Do you suppose he'll do her as a pioneer woman in a sunbonnet? Holding little Cim by the hand, huh? Or maybe in the covered wagon." At the end of their conversation, the artist is very moved by Sabra's account of her life in Oklahoma with Yancey, "the outlaws, the early years of the paper, the Indians, oil" (304). Yet when the "Spirit of the Oklahoma Pioneer was unveiled a year later, with terrific ceremonies," it depicts not Sabra but the "heroic figure of Yancey Cravat stepping forward with that light graceful stride in the high-heeled Texas star boots . . . one beautiful hand resting lightly on the weapon in his two-gun holster. Behind him, one hand just touching his shoulder for support, stumbled the weary, blanketed figure of an Indian" (306). This satire of the ideological strictures implicit in historical commemoration may well have been Ferber's response to the Marland campaign for the memorial during the late 1920s. Although the actual statue in Ponca City depicts a pioneer woman, its genesis as well as the selection of speakers for the dedication—Marland, Bryant Baker, native son and nationally known Oklahoman Will Rogers, and particularly Herbert Hoover's radio address as civic paterfamilias—illustrates the cogency of her commentary. The constitution of the panel also demonstrates Ferber's liminal position in terms of not just gender but also ethnic identity within the discourse on authenticity on the West. Not surprisingly, it appears that Ferber refused E. W. Marland's offer to attend the dedication.

It was only after the film adaptation of *Cimarron* premiered in early 1931 and began to achieve critical success that Oklahomans' resentment of the book abated, in part because the literary text was increasingly conflated with the cinematic one. During the 1920s, Paramount and Fox had translated the appropriate handling of the Western prestige property into big profits, but in the early sound era none of the "covered wagon west" stories, such as *The Big Trail*, had done that well, suggesting that perhaps the cycle had run its course.[53] However, epic Westerns had not yet exhausted their public relations value as prestigious "documents" of national culture. This was partly because under the aegis of the MPPDA the studios used such Western historical features to deflect "questions of oligopoly control and trade practice" toward concerns over movie content, which "were of greater public interest, and could be resolved at less economic risk to the majors." Yet these two domains are interdependent; as Richard Maltby has argued, discourses on censorship during this period were less about eliminating offensive words than about delineating "the cultural function of entertainment and the possession of cultural power."[54]

As a relatively new player in this arena, the RKO corporation opted for a Western story that could help legitimize its emergent status in the American film industry, particularly as a "pioneer" in technological innovation. Founded in late 1928 to exploit a new sound-recording system, RKO soon positioned itself on the vanguard of the modern age's mass communication networks. One advertisement for the company's films heralded "Radio's Pageant of the Titans and the Thundering Dawn of Electrical Entertainment!"[55] Such movies were forward-looking, perhaps even prophetic, to be distinguished from the nostalgic silent-era wares favored by the older studios. Correspondingly, a narrative that depicted frontier origins as well as their transformation into the contemporary industrial age would have seemed most appropriate to RKO management.[56] *Cimarron* fit the bill: its temporal scope differed somewhat from previous epics, covering the period 1889 to the present day (1929) and detailing what happened *after* the transcontinental trek had been made—what occurred after the "seed of America" had, as it were, been planted. The screenplay stayed fairly close to the novel's general structure, focusing on Sabra, particularly her stewardship of the newspaper and championing of social causes. In this way, RKO could promote itself as the "forward-thinking" studio by acknowledging the growing influence of American women in political and civic life during the postwar era. At the same time, the adaptation subtly effaced Ferber's critique of male Western writers' historical fictions by softening the more unpleasant aspects of Yancey's irresponsibility, inefficacy, and later decline. This strategy reshaped the potentially subversive features of the novel into a more acceptable form for mass consumption; it confirmed patriarchal control of the historical narrative—the reign of "Titans"—while creating an acceptable space for women's supporting role in the industrial age. This corporate vision is well reflected in RKO's two-sheet poster for *Cimarron*. The heavily masculinized depiction of Yancey, with ripped shirt and exposed muscled chest as he forges his way through Oklahoma, will brook no feminine challenge, in terms of either authorship or textual feature. Not only does he dwarf Ferber's name above the title, his body almost entirely obscures Sabra's frightened face, as she watches, horrified by his violence and power. This iconography not only resolutely situates the story, "as terrific as all creation," as the province of male action and authority but also positions the new movie company, RKO, as the originator of a historically commemorative episode of near-Biblical proportions.[57]

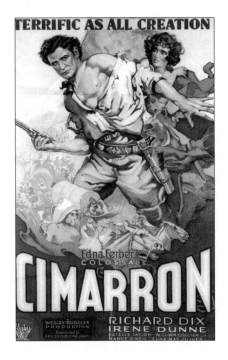

RKO's two-sheet poster for Cimarron, *1931, which foregrounds Richard Dix as Yancey Cravat. Reprinted by permission of the Wisconsin Center for Film and Theater Research, Madison, Wisconsin.*

In other respects, however, the film version of *Cimarron* preserves one of the novel's most distinctive features. The Americanism of previous "epic" Westerns had been designed to help combat criticism about the putative nonnative or "alien" ownership of the studios, so the inclusion of immigrant, ethnic characters in such narrative may have been viewed as counterproductive. Halfway through the novel, Ferber introduces a Jewish character, notions peddler Sol Levy, as an Eastern immigrant to Osage:

> He belonged in crowded places, in populous places, in the color and glow and swift drama of the bazaars. God knows how he had found his way into this vast wilderness. Perhaps in Chicago, or in Kansas City, or Omaha he had heard of this new country and the rush of thousands for its land. And he had bummed his way on foot. He had started to peddle with an oil-cloth-covered pack on his back. Through the little hot Western towns in the summer. Through the bitter cold Western towns in the winter. They turned the dogs on him. (145–46)

Despite the townspeople's anti-Semitic attitudes, Sol prospers in Osage, eventually founding the Levy Mercantile Company, booster of and frequent advertiser in the *Wigwam*. Finding herself and the paper in financial trouble during one of Yancey's absences, Sabra's "economic survival was made possible only through [Sol's] almost shamefaced generosity" (146–48). He becomes her primary confidant, especially in business matters. When in later years Sol decides to run for mayor of Osage, he wins the *Wigwam*'s editorial support as well as Yancey's active campaigning on his behalf. But the town considers this a lost cause, since the consensus was that only a "real American" could hold that post (188–90, 227–29).[58]

The RKO version of *Cimarron* includes many of these incidents, foregrounding Sol as a figure worthy of compassion and respect. Unlike in the novel, in the film the character is introduced quickly, the day after Yancey and Sabra arrive in Osage. Soon afterward, the villainy of town outlaw Lon Yountis is demonstrated when he baits Sol in the street, forcing him to drink liquor and shooting at his feet. Visualizing a description from the novel, the movie features a striking shot of Sol falling backwards onto a large feed scale, his arms spread out across the top horizontal bars in an approximation of the crucifixion pose (148–49). Yancey comes to his rescue, just as he helps fallen women, Native Americans, and other "defenseless" characters. From this point on, Sol is productively linked with Yancey's integrity as an embodiment of the frontier ideal, as well as with Sabra's entrepreneurial success in building the *Wigwam*. The film thus maintains Ferber's critique of the earlier epics' racial nativism, counterpointing the Molly-as-Madonna iconography so prevalent in *The Covered Wagon* with her own vision of the Western progenitor—Jewish immigrant Sol cast upon the cross in a dusty frontier street. When in a later scene Sol tells Sabra that Yancey (who has abandoned her and the newspaper again) will inevitably be "part of the history of the great Southwest," that "it's men like him who build the world," clearly an ironic revisionist impulse is at work.

Challenging the status quo in the American film industry during the early sound era was at the forefront of RKO's marketing strategy for *Cimarron*. This movie would demonstrate how the studio's use of technological innovation distinguished it from the now-passing silent period, or even from the most recent sound films by other producers. Upon its release, RKO claimed in trade publications that "The Talkies are Born Today"— even further, the "Motion Picture [is] Reborn in Drama Terrific as All Creation."[59] Yet RKO applied the same tactics developed by Paramount and Fox to encourage the desired response to *Cimarron* as a national document of historical value: the extensive publicity and advertising campaign months prior to the opening and selective distribution and exhibition strategies. There were the requisite invitation-only screenings with President Hoover at the White House and a set of gala openings in New York, Chicago, Los Angeles, and, of course, Tulsa and Oklahoma City. In each location, the studio provided city officials, local politicians, society figures, and civic commissioners (usually of the school system) with tickets. After the premiere in New York, *Cimarron* was shown twice a day with reserved seating only. Via this careful promotion and circulation of their banner talkie film for 1931, RKO sought to refigure the consumption context as a kind of public space for the commemoration of national achievement, with the studio as the de facto beneficiary.[60]

It appears that most of *Cimarron*'s reviewers "took the bait" extended by RKO's exploitation apparatus, positioning the film as something much more than the standard B-Western fare and, moreover, as something of promise from the sound studio RKO. Writers described the film as "authentic," even "educational," and a "valid historical document . . . of a little publicized and exciting phase of U.S. expansion."[61] Although she is frequently mentioned as the author of the original novel, few commentators credited Ferber as the source of the film's historical veracity. Typical was the *New Yorker*'s assessment: *Cimarron* sought to "instill in its spectators an interest in the gradual growth of that great tract of land which from sheer wilderness becomes eventually the State of Oklahoma," but since it was based, after all, on an Edna Ferber novel, its true educational value lay in the expert "historical detail" and thrilling reconstruction of the land rush offered by the film producers. As one New York daily claimed, *Cimarron* was "easily the best and most important screen venture that has as yet emerged from the Radio-Keith-Orpheum studio"; according to trade magazine *Photoplay*, the film was "by far the finest thing Radio Pictures and Richard Dix have ever done." Going even further, *Literary Digest* acclaimed *Cimarron* not just "the best of all Western talkies [but] one of the talking screen's outstanding achievements." After his laudatory, morning-after notice in the *New York Times*, Mordaunt Hall wrote in a subsequent Sunday-edition review that *Cimarron* was "original" and offered spectators much more than just a recycling of an "episode from a silent film" with sound added.[62] Such comments reflect RKO's own promotional claims that their epic film represented "motion pictures reborn." The available reception material indicates that RKO was able to garner from the corps of trade and professional reviewers the traditional benefits of innovative authorship—albeit through deft marketing, what the trade paper *Variety* called "that prize Radio campaigning."[63] This does not mean, of course, that *Cimarron*'s status as a best seller by one of the nation's most popular writers did not represent a marketable aspect of the production. Ferber's name constituted a presold audience for the film and thus almost always appeared in RKO's advertisements. Following standard industry practice of attaining the author's reaction for publicity purposes, producer William LeBaron arranged a preview screening for Ferber in New York a few weeks before the opening.[64] However, other than one brief newspaper comment that Ferber "liked" the movie, I was unable to find a more detailed account in RKO promotional materials.[65] In her autobiography, Ferber remarked that although the film version of *Cimarron* was the "finest motion picture that has ever been made of any book of mine," she was still "bitterly disappointed" because she felt that the novel's satirical intent had not survived. Ironically, she noted, the movie's critical success prompted Oklahoma officials and state elites to "relent" in their views of her, realizing it was "good publicity" for the region. "I was invited to be a guest of honor (whatever that implies) at statue unveilings, banquets, old-home weeks," she wrote. "Oklahoma senators and congressmen in Washington telegraphed me to come to the capital for the opening of the motion picture. I did not take advantage of these hospitable offers."[66] Ferber's charitable response ten years later should be countered with an archival trace of her reaction at the time. The solicitation to attend the Washington premiere of *Cimarron*, described as "Edna Ferber's romantic adventurous epic of a new empire—Oklahoma," can be found in her papers, an elegant invitation very neatly ripped in two.[67]

In addition to being well received in critical venues, *Cimarron* eventually won three Oscars at the Academy of Motion Pictures Arts and Sciences' awards ceremony in November 1931. In the late 1920s, the industry had established this institutional mechanism to "enhance the public's perception of the social and aesthetic value of Hollywood's products," so RKO management was probably satisfied that their marketing strategies for the film had helped them achieve a new status. Yet *Cimarron*'s poor box-office return failed to meet the studio's expectations, not even recovering its negative cost.[68] The deepening Depression may have curtailed the moviegoing habits of the American public, or perhaps the cycle of "epics" had run its course by 1931. However, a more significant factor may have been RKO's inability to fully exploit Ferber's authorship of the Western historical epic as "authentic" or "legitimate." Given her gender, urban, or ethnic allegiances, she was perceived as having no intuitive connection to the frontier legacy. Unlike *The Covered Wagon* and similar prestige features of the 1920s, *Cimarron*'s tutorial value as a document of the nation's Western heritage was undermined by contradictory views about its origin.

One contemporary account constructed Ferber as a kind of dilettante whose interest in the panoramic historical subject stemmed from the economic motivations of the publishing and film industries. Corey Ford's parodic sketch collection, *In the Worst Possible Taste*, lampooned the writer as "a leader of the Panoramic School of Fiction. . . . It was apparently the practice of [these] historical novelists to find a period in American history which had a lot of local color, then to go out and roll in it till the facts stuck like burrs to their fur." Ford describes Ferber as a literary Yancey Cravat, eagerly awaiting the land rush for hot new properties with "thousands and thousands of [other] hungry novelists, milling around the border like novelists in Hollywood, studying our histories, worrying over maps, thumbing our volumes of research eagerly. We were riding on the crest of a new public vogue, and there was a wild light in our eyes. Facts were at a premium. If you didn't have a date, you borrowed one from your neighbor. I finally bought the History of Oklahoma for a dollar, after standing in line three hours, from a woman just ahead of me." At the close of this sketch, Ferber heads out in her covered wagon, "horses harnessed and waiting. . . . My contracts for serial-rights and movie-rights are all sewed up."[69] Ford's satire shows a sophisticated understanding of both the commercial demands of the literary marketplace and the cultural currency of frontier topics in the late 1920s. Yet it is within the sites of visual culture that we find the most cogent interrogation of Ferber's contested position within the discourse on authenticity during this period.

Miguel Covarrubias, "one of America's most penetrating and ruthless caricaturists,"[70] often illustrated Ford's parodies. His paintings, drawings, and cartoons of figures in the New York art and literary world appeared in national magazines such as *Life*, the *New Yorker*, and the *Nation* as well as in newspapers across the country. Covarrubias's *Vanity Fair* illustrations, accompanied by Ford's "saber-tongued" captions, were especially popular. His drawing of Ferber for *In the Worst Possible Taste* has the legend:

Seated on the front of her Covered Wagon and cracking her blacksnake whip over the trusty steeds which have already carried her several times across the continent, from New York to Hollywood, our Pioneering Edna ("Sue Big") Ferber sets out once more to explore the famous Bad Lands between Fact and Fiction: the empire of the Pseudo-Historians, the Panorama-Painters and the Scope-Seekers of literature. "If the truth were really known, my friends" (Edna had said all this before, and doubtless would again) "it is the sunbonnet and not the sombrero that started this racket."[71]

Miguel Covarrubias's caricature of Edna Ferber, ca. 1930. Reprinted by permission of the Art Collection, Harry Ransom Humanities Research Center, University of Texas at Austin.

Revising Koerner's *Madonna of the Prairie,* Covarrubias presents a modernist version of Molly-as-Ferber, a vigorous, independent female pioneer, whip in hand, grim visage offset only by the single stylish strand of pearls at her neck. The ubiquitous sunbonnet frames an angular face with a strong chin and a prominent nose, counterpointing the idealized Anglo-Saxon physiognomy of Koerner's painting with a stereotypical representation of ethnic features. Covarrubias's caricature suggests the disturbing, potentially subversive aspect of Ferber's expedition into the "empire of the Pseudo-Historians, the Panorama-Painters." A wealthy, cosmopolitan, urbane Jewish-American woman, who never married or had children, takes charge of the covered wagon seat, as both the "seed of America's wealth" and dissembler of this very fiction. Yet by targeting her masquerade as the pioneer woman, the illustration exposes precisely what was at stake—cultural power, the acquisition of an "authoritative" position from which to speak about the nation's frontier heritage—when the publishing and motion picture industry mined the Western historical metanarrative for commodifiable events and figures. When situated within these discursive formations, Edna Ferber's *Cimarron* offers a complex analysis of pioneer culture in the 1920s, revealing how the epic texts of Western fiction and film operated to legitimize these industries' claims to historical knowledge and thus secure cultural power.

Notes

This article expands upon a short paper I presented at the 1997 MLA convention in Toronto, Canada. I would like to thank editors Meredith Goldsmith and Lisa Botshon for their helpful feedback on an earlier version of the manuscript.

1. Crafton 554–55. *Cimarron* was nominated for seven Academy Awards, including Best Picture, Best Actor (Richard Dix), Best Actress (Irene Dunne), Best Director (Wesley Ruggles), Best Cinematography (Edward Cronjager), Best Adaptation (Howard Estabrook), and Best Set Decoration (Max Ree). It won the first and the last two categories. It also won the most votes in the trade paper *Film Daily*'s yearly "Best Pictures" nationwide poll of trade, magazine, and newspaper critics, and made the National Board of Review's list of Ten Best American Films for 1931 (*1932 Film Daily Yearbook* 23, 63). There was another adaptation of Ferber's novel released by MGM in 1960, a Cinemascope version directed by Anthony Mann, with Glenn Ford as Yancey Cravat and Maria Schell as Sabra, which is usually considered inferior to the first version.

2. Bazin 140–48. Unlike other writers of the time, Bazin foregrounds the gender dynamics of the genre: "[In the western], women, all up and down the social scale, are in every case worthy of love or at least of esteem or pity. The least little prostitute is redeemed by love and death. . . . The myth of the western illustrates, and both initiates and confirms woman in her role as vestal of the social virtues, of which this chaotic world is so greatly in need. Within her is concealed the physical future" (145). Such a view well describes the array of female characters in *Cimarron* (Sabra, Dixie Lee, Mrs. Wyatt), although Ferber's treatment of these figures in American frontier narratives is satiric.

3. See, for example, Everson's comment that *Cimarron* was "commercially the 'safest' [of the early sound epics] in that it was based on a best-selling novel by Edna Ferber. . . . [*Cimarron*] tended to be bogged down in character studies and had the structural flaw of presenting its highlight—the massive Cherokee Strip landrush sequence—at the beginning of the picture. Thereafter, the typically sprawling Ferber canvas depicted the growth and development of Oklahoma as an oil-rich state over the years more in terms of emotion and heartbreak than in visual excitement" (113–14). The *BFI Companion to the Western*'s entry on *Cimarron* is similar: "It is far more interested in being a family saga and a pageant of American history than it is in being a Western . . . the film is perhaps best considered as a woman's picture out West" (255). The *Overlook Film Encyclopedia: The Western* focuses on the historical origin of the story, the "spectacular land rush

sequences," and describes Sabra Cravat as an "entrepreneur" who finishes what her husband cannot when his "wanderlust reclaims him" (29).

4. For discussion of Ferber's position in the literary canon and analysis of the female characters in *Cimarron* (the novel), see Mulrooney (chaps. 1 and 5), Chappel (chap. 6), and Shaughnessy (chap. 8).

5. For an extended analysis of the cultural, historical, and industrial contexts of this production trend, particularly as they relate to the silent Paramount films, see my doctoral dissertation, "'The West Before the Cinema Invaded It.'" For a brief discussion of the early sound epics, see Slotkin 253–56, and Fenin and Everson 173–78. Both suggest that this trend was profitable, but in fact both *The Big Trail* and *Cimarron*, despite the latter's strong critical reception, lost money (Crafton 552).

6. *Variety*'s weekly column "Inside Stuff—Pictures" described Henry Ford's series about the motion picture industry in his newspaper, the *Dearborn Independent*: "Ford's weekly is currently carrying a series of articles 'showing up' the Paramount franchise system. Without specifying any particular race, as [is] the weekly's policy, it features Adolph Zukor and other members of the Jewish race as the controllers of the picture industry that dictates to the exhibitors" (41).

7. This history of the MPPDA generated by the organization itself describes Will Hays as "'the one hundred percent American,' as the human counterpart to Middletown" (39), which also suggests the importance of Hays's perceived WASP identity and "lack" of ethnic signifiers to his appointment as film industry ombudsman.

8. Moley, chap. 12.

9. Radway, "Scandal," 726. See also Radway's *A Feeling for Books*, especially 247–53.

10. For a fuller discussion of the discourse on authenticity, see Kenaga, "'The West Before the Cinema Invaded It,'" chap. 1.

11. White 52, 106, 108, 147, 185; see also Slotkin, chap. 1.

12. My discussion of Emerson Hough's life and career is derived from three secondary sources: Wylder, Johnson, and Cohn.

13. Cohn 146; Johnson 113–15.

14. Johnson 12–15.

15. Wylder 5; the quote is from Johnson 57.

16. Hough, "The Road to Oregon," 165.

17. Hough, *Passing*, vol. 26 in the Chronicles of America Series. The idea for this series originated in March 1916 amid the Americanization movement and anxieties about the patriotism of "hyphenates" in an ethnically heterogeneous population. According to *The New Historians: A Booklet About the Authors of the Chronicles of America*, the "officers of Yale University Press saw from the outset vast educational possibilities and opportunity for distinct service to the country" (3–5). The Chronicles were soon made into a series of educational shorts by Pathé; see "Yale's Movie Version of American History" in *Literary Digest*.

18. Hough, *Passing*, 93–94.

19. The original story appeared in the *Saturday Evening Post* in eight installments during the late spring of 1922. Lorimer also helped determine the final form of the story; Hough rewrote it twice at his request (Cohn 147; Bigelow 23; Tebbel 75–76). However, since these last two works are hagiographic accounts of Lorimer

and the magazine, the story about the origin of the *Covered Wagon* narrative may well be a publicity narrative.

20. As a subsidiary of the Curtis Publishing Company, Grosset & Dunlap specialized in producing "movie editions" of popular books. These hardcover texts were illustrated with stills from the film adaptation.

21. The review by Louise Maunsell Field in the *New York Times* is representative: "the events the novel describes are of such great interest and importance, and the value of placing them in that fictional form which will, no doubt, cause them to reach so many more readers than would any other is so decided, that one does not feel inclined to find fault with the book because of its deficiencies . . . for to all real Americans the theme of the making of America must necessarily be one of pride and of enthralling interest" (26).

22. Furlong 3.

23. Koerner was "one of America's best-known magazine and book illustrators of the Twenties and Thirties." Starting with his illustrations for the "Traveling the Old Trail" series, Koerner began a collaboration with Hough that would have continued had the writer not died suddenly in 1923. Hough was notoriously hard to please, but he loved Koerner's work and found his visualization of Molly exactly what he had in mind. After the tremendous success of *The Covered Wagon* (book and film), Koerner specialized in Western themes, providing illustrations for most of the important Western writers of this period, including Zane Grey, Hal G. Evarts, Oliver LaFarge, and Conrad Richter (Grover 1–14; Hutchinson 19–22).

24. According to Hutchinson, the serial caused the *Saturday Evening Post*'s circulation to jump from about 2 million to 2,264,000; this does not account for additional readers beyond the original purchaser, which the editors of the *Post* calculated as three per issue (21). The film adaptation of *The Covered Wagon* was one of the most financially successful movies of the silent era. It ran for 59 weeks at the Criterion in New York, breaking the previous record held by *The Birth of a Nation*, and for months in Los Angeles, Boston, and Chicago. Hough's death in 1923, just after the roadshow release of *The Covered Wagon*, heightened the nostalgic tone in print discourse toward the "vanishing" frontier legacy. See, for example, "A True Romancer of the West" 832; "Emerson Hough's Dying Message" 25–26; Malloch, "A Comrade Rides Ahead," 225.

25. Welter 152.

26. For contemporary commentary on the "Pioneer Woman" monument competition and the models submitted, see "Marland Praises Women Pioneers" 32; Young, "Pioneer Women," 98–100; "Woman with a Sunbonnet" 26–27; "Art: Pioneer" 20–21, 28. For photographs of the twelve models, see the rotogravure section of the *New York Times*, 27 February 1927, 4. For contemporary coverage of and commentary on the unveiling of the Bryant Baker statue in Ponca City, see articles in the *New York Times*, "To Honor Pioneer Women," 17 April 1930, 5; "The Pioneer Woman Praised by Hoover," 23 April 1930, 4; "The Pioneer Woman" [editorial], 29 April 1930, 26.

27. "Woman With a Sunbonnet" 27.

28. Savage 6.

29. There was disagreement over the artistic and historical merit of many of the models, most clearly expressed by Stark Young in the *New Republic* and indicated by

the different balloting results reported in various areas of the country. The photographs in the *New York Times* reveal the wide array of aesthetic traditions chosen, from Greek classicism to Maurice Sterne's "Byzantine cowgirl." Several commentators noted the sway of popular culture imagery on the figures: in *Time*, the statue by Jo Davidson "shows the influence of 'The Covered Wagon' motif . . . his tall spare woman leans forward as she scrutinizes the prairie horizon for her Dan'l, who is probably delayed during a storm at Faro Pete's Saloon" (21). The Baker model was the favorite of New York exhibition attendees, which may well have affected Marland's decision.

30. Savage 6.

31. "The Pioneer Woman Praised by Hoover" 4.

32. "The Pioneer Woman" 26.

33. "The Pioneer Woman Praised by Hoover" 4.

34. Ferber, *Treasure*, 325–26. Julie Goldsmith Gilbert's biography of her great-aunt, *Ferber: A Biography*, repeats this account of the origin of *Cimarron* (359–60). In describing the origin of *Cimarron* in White's stories about his trip, Ferber noted in her autobiography that she had to "make a shamefaced confession. I knew literally nothing of Oklahoma until that evening. It was a State in the Union. . . . I didn't know when the Indian Territory had become a state; I had never heard of the land rush of 1889."

35. Letter to the "Foxes and the Ferbers," 15 May 1928; letter, 19 May 1928, from Pawhuska; letter, May 1928, Edna Ferber Papers [U.S. Mss. 98AN], State Historical Society of Wisconsin, Box 1, Folder 1. The writer also discusses her Oklahoma itinerary in *Treasure* (329–30).

36. Ferber, *Treasure*, 330–34. During the summer of 1929, she stayed with writer Louis Bromfield and his family in their secluded home in the Basque region of France, where "the writing of Cimarron went steadily on in this gay and secluded environment. Nothing could have been farther from Oklahoma, not only geographically but also in spirit, background and feeling. That was good, that was what I liked." Perhaps this writing exile gave her some of the distance with which to view the material with greater perspective. Following contemporary publishing practice, Ferber's Oklahoma story first appeared as a serial in a national magazine (*WHC*, November–December 1929 and January–May 1930) prior to its publication as a novel.

37. Edna Ferber, foreword to *Cimarron* (1963 Bantam/Pathfinder reprint of the 1930 edition). All subsequent quotes from the novel are taken from this edition.

38. When one of the Venables challenges the veracity of Yancey's description, to the family's further dismay, he goes on to characterize the state of her teeth: "broken and discolored like those of a woman of seventy. And most of them gone at the side" (18).

39. Parker 11.

40. Parker 134. See chap. 5 on "Mothering the Movies: Women Reformers and Popular Culture" for a detailed account of the WCTU's movie censorship program. Ferber may have targeted the overtly Christian affiliation of organizations like the WCTU as intrinsically bigoted; Parker does suggest that a "veiled anti-Semitism" inflected the organization's view of movie producers as "obsessed with profit" (143–44).

41. Maltby 46.
42. Parker 1. Parker offers a nuanced view of the WCTU and similar groups' "social and political agenda," disputing previous characterizations of their membership as "Victorian prudes" interested in repression and as nativists supporting extreme assimilationist policies. She also problematizes earlier scholars' arguments in support of such groups' feminism or protofeminism (8–10).
43. Ferber claimed again in her second autobiography that from 1921 to 1961, "the novels I wrote were novels of protest. Loving protest, but protest nonetheless" (*A Kind of Magic* 262).
44. "Oklahoma Culture in 1898," *Cimarron News*, 4 April 1930, Ferber Papers, Box 5, Folder 10.
45. Ferber, *Treasure*, 340.
46. Tilghman, "Among Oklahoma's Literary People," *Harlow's Weekly*, Ferber Papers, Box 5, Folder 10.
47. Vestal, "Oklahoma Is Setting of Edna Ferber's New Book," Ferber Papers, Box 5, Folder 10. For defenses of Ferber in Kansas papers, see two editorials, "Genius," in the *Wichita Eagle*, which lauds the novel for its tribute to the pioneer woman who "made Oklahoma"; and "Mugwump Musings: In Defense," from the *Concordia Blade-Empire*, Ferber Papers, Box 5, Folder 10. Although unsigned, the writer of the latter piece was apparently a friend and protégé of William Allen White, who sent Ferber a copy of the editorial.
48. *Daily Oklahoman*, cited in "Oklahoma Culture in 1898," *Cimarron News*, 4 April 1930, Ferber Papers, Box 5, Folder 10. Later, one film reviewer commented that "several of our book critics patronized [the novel] a bit with the implication that it was a movie scenario between best-selling covers" (Cohen, "The New Photoplay").
49. Ferber, *Treasure*, 340.
50. Editorial, *Bartlesville News*, Ferber Papers, Box 5, Folder 10. Ferber may have been wounded by this characterization, but in a note to her publicist Dan Longwell that is attached to the clipping, she responded flippantly: "Well, Big Boy, I'll blatt to the cock-eyed world that I found a publisher as dumb-witted as myself even if Bartlesville doesn't like my little epic. Return this, Dan dear. I want to give readings from it" (Ferber Papers, Box 4, Folder 12).
51. "Edna Ferber Says Characters Are Imaginary Ones," *Wichita Eagle*, 14 March 1930; anonymous review of *Cimarron*, *Wichita Eagle*, 23 March 1930; see also "The Adult Youngster," editorial, *Wichita Eagle*, 17 March 1930, Ferber Papers, Box 4, Folder 12.
52. Letter from E. W. Marland, 31 March 1930, Ferber Papers, Box 4, Folder 12. This and other correspondence implies that Ferber had met Marland during her May 1928 trip to Oklahoma.
53. *BFI Companion to the Western* 251–52.
54. Maltby 41.
55. See Crafton 133–42, also his discussion of "thermionics" 23–61. The Radio Pictures advertisement and accompanying caption is found on 24.
56. Significantly, the *Cimarron* project was cultivated by William LeBaron, a seasoned producer who spent several years at Paramount during the 1920s and thus would have been well aware of the features and functions of the "epic" Western. The

Oscar-winning scenario was written by Howard Estabrook, who also had been at Paramount, where he adapted the popular 1930 version of Owen Wister's *The Virginian*.

57. This two-sheet poster for *Cimarron* can be found in Crafton (370). The reproduction here is derived from an original negative held by the Wisconsin Center for Film and Theater Research in Madison.

58. Ferber, *Cimarron*, 146–48, 188–90, 227–29. Ferber may well have intended Sol Levy as a kind of allegorical figure referencing the "nonnative" motion picture producers. Several aspects of the character support such a reading: his origin in the mercantile business, his success in building a thriving company much patronized by the inhabitants of Osage, and especially his critical support of the *Oklahoma Wigwam* through hard times by constantly providing advertising revenue—all the while remaining a socially and culturally liminal figure subject to scapegoating and stereotyping by the community.

59. See advertisements in *Variety* just before *Cimarron*'s release, 7 January 1931, 15–17; 14 January 1931, 23–26; 21 January 1931, 13–16.

60. RKO ran two-page ads for *Cimarron* in every issue of *Variety* from 7 May 1930 to 7 January 1931, when four-page ads appeared. For details on the exhibition settings, see reviews in New York, Chicago, and Los Angeles dailies found in the Ferber Papers, Box 23, Folder 3.

61. Reviews in *Time* and *Commonweal*.

62. Reviews in the *New Yorker*, *Editorial Telegram*, *Photoplay*, *Literary Digest*, and the *New York Times*.

63. Review in *Variety*.

64. Undated telegram from William LeBaron to Ferber, probably sent to her sometime near the end of 1930 (Ferber Papers, Box 1, Folder 2).

65. See "Richard Dix and 'Cimarron' Role." According to this publicity piece on Dix, the actor notes that Ferber saw a "preview" of the film and liked it.

66. Ferber, *Treasure*, 339–40.

67. The torn invitation, now carefully taped together, is in Ferber Papers, Box 4, Folder 13.

68. Crafton 184, 552, 554. *Cimarron*'s negative cost was $1,433,000, but it only made $1,122,000 in domestic (U.S. and Canada) theater rentals.

69. Corey Ford [John Riddell], *In the Worst Possible Taste*, 28–38. The sketch about Ferber revises a parody entitled "Macaron, as if by Edna Ferber," which had appeared earlier in the October 1930 issue of *Vanity Fair*. Ford was the resident parodist and sometime fiction writer for *Vanity Fair* and under the pseudonym "John Riddell" also acted as its book review editor. A frequent contributor to the *New Yorker* and the *Saturday Evening Post*, he was considered a member of the New York "Smart Set." Ford often denied in print rumors that he and "John Riddell" were one and the same, probably because given his social circle he would have come into frequent contact with the celebrities and artists he lampooned. See *Vanity Fair* editorial "A Ford of Literature" 31.

70. Williams, *Covarrubias*, 18–22, 44–45, 54, 71–72.

71. The legend and caricature appear on unnumbered pages in the middle of the "American Booty" sketch in *In the Worst Possible Taste*.

Works Cited

"The Adult Youngster." *Wichita Eagle,* 17 March 1930 [n.p.].

"Art: Pioneer." *Time,* 28 March 1927, 20–21, 28.

Bazin, André. "The Western, or the American Film *par excellence.*" Trans. Hugh Gray. *What Is Cinema?* Vol. 2. Berkeley: University of California Press, 1971, 140–48.

Bigelow, Frederick. *A Short History of the "Saturday Evening Post": An American Institution in Three Centuries.* New York: Curtis Publishing Company, 1927.

Buscombe, Ed. *The BFI Companion to the Western.* New York: Da Capo, 1988.

Chappel, Deborah. "American Romances: Narratives of Culture and Identity." Ph.D. diss., Duke University, 1991.

Cimarron. Dir. Wesley Ruggles. Perf. Richard Dix (Yancey Cravat), Irene Dunne (Sabra Cravat), Estelle Taylor (Dixie Lee), Nance O'Neil (Felice Venable), William Collier Jr. (the Kid), Roscoe Ates (Jesse Rickey), George E. Stone (Sol Levy), Stanley Fields (Lon Yountis), Robert McWade (Louis Hefner), Edna May Oliver (Mrs. Tracy Wyatt), Nancy Dover (Donna Cravat), Eugene Jackson (Isaiah). RKO, 1931.

Cohen, John S. Jr. "The New Photoplay." *New York Sun,* 26 January 1931 [n.p.].

Cohn, Jan. *Creating America: George Horace Lorimer and the "Saturday Evening Post."* Pittsburgh: University of Pittsburgh Press, 1989.

Crafton, Donald. *The Talkies: American Cinema's Transition to Sound, 1926–1931.* New York: Scribner, 1997.

"The Current Cinema." *The New Yorker,* 7 February 1931, 63.

Edna Ferber Papers. State Historical Society of Wisconsin, Madison, Wisc.

"Edna Ferber Says Characters Are Imaginary Ones." *Wichita Eagle,* 14 March 1930 [n.p.].

"Emerson Hough's Dying Message." *Literary Digest,* 12 July 1923, 25–26.

Everson, William. *A Pictorial History of the Western Film.* New York: Citadel, 1969.

Fenin, George N., and William K. Everson. *The Western from Silents to the Seventies.* 2d ed. New York: Grossman, 1973.

Ferber, Edna. *Cimarron.* 1930. New York: Bantam/Pathfinder, 1963.

———. *A Kind of Magic.* New York: Doubleday, 1963.

———. *A Peculiar Treasure.* New York: Doubleday, 1939.

Field, Louise Maunsell. Review of *The Covered Wagon,* by Emerson Hough. *New York Times Book Review,* 11 June 1922, 26.

Film Daily. *1932 Film Daily Yearbook.* New York: Film Daily, 1932.

"A Ford of Literature." *Vanity Fair,* March 1931, 31.

Ford, Corey [John Riddell]. *In the Worst Possible Taste.* New York: Scribner, 1932.

———. "Macaron, as if by Edna Ferber." *Vanity Fair,* October 1930, 63, 103–4.

Furlong, Charles Wellington. "Emerson Hough—Tourist and Writer." *Boston Evening Transcript,* 5 May 1923, 3.

Gilbert, Julie Goldsmith. *Ferber: A Biography of Edna Ferber and Her Circle.* New York: Doubleday, 1978.

Grover, Dorys Crow. "W. H. D. Koerner & Emerson Hough: A Western Collaboration." *Montana* 29, no. 2 (April 1979): 1–14.

Hall, Mordaunt. "A Cinematic 'Cimarron.'" *New York Times,* 1 February 1931, sec. 8:5.

———. "Oklahoma, Then and Now." *New York Times,* 27 January 1931, 20.

Hardy, Phil. *The Overlook Film Encyclopedia: The Western*. Woodstock, N.Y.: Overlook, 1994.

Hough, Emerson. *The Covered Wagon*. New York: Grosset & Dunlap, 1922.

———. "The Covered Wagon." *Saturday Evening Post*, 1 April–20 May 1922.

———. *The Passing of the Frontier: A Chronicle of the Old West*. Chronicles of America Series. Vol. 26. New Haven: Yale University Press, 1918.

———. "Traveling the Old Trails." *Saturday Evening Post*, 15 July–25 August 1919.

Hutchinson, W. H. "Packaging the Old West in Serial Form." *Westways*, February 1973, 19–22.

"Inside Stuff: Pictures." *Variety*, 25 November 1921, 41.

Johnson, Carole McCool. "Emerson Hough and the American West: A Biographical and Critical Study." Ph.D. diss., University of Texas at Austin, 1975.

Kenaga, Heidi. "'The West Before the Cinema Invaded It': Famous Players–Lasky's 'Epic' Westerns, 1923–25." Ph.D. diss., University of Wisconsin–Madison, 1999.

Malloch, Douglas. "A Comrade Rides Ahead: To the Memory of Emerson Hough." *Current Opinion*, August 1923, 225.

Maltby, Richard. "The Production Code and the Hays Office." In *Grand Design: Hollywood as Modern Business Enterprise, 1930–1939*. Ed. Tino Balio. New York: Scribner, 1993.

"Marland Praises Women Pioneers." *New York Times*, 26 February 1927, 32.

Moley, Raymond. *The Hays Office*. Indianapolis: Bobbs-Merrill, 1945.

"Mugwump Musings: In Defense." *Concordia Blade Empire*, 30 April 1930 [n.p.].

Mulrooney, Frank. "The Sunbonnet and the Sombrero: Pioneer Feminism and Feminist Pioneers in the Early Novels of Edna Ferber." Ph.D. diss., University of South Florida, 2000.

"Oklahoma Culture in 1898." *Cimarron News*, 4 April 1930 [n.p.].

Parker, Alison. *Purifying America: Women, Cultural Reform, and Pro-Censorship Activism, 1873–1933*. Urbana: University of Illinois Press, 1997.

Pelswick, Rose. "Film from Ferber Novel an Epic Production." *Editorial Telegram*, 26 January 1931 [n.p.].

"The Pioneer Woman" [editorial]. *New York Times*, 29 April 1930, 26.

"The Pioneer Woman Praised by Hoover." *New York Times*, 23 April 1930, 4.

"Planting Cities with a Two-Gun Editor." *Literary Digest*, 21 February 1931, 28.

Radway, Janice. *A Feeling for Books: The Book-of-the-Month Club, Literary Taste, and Middle-Class Desire*. Chapel Hill: University of North Carolina Press, 1997.

———. "The Scandal of the Middlebrow: The Book-of-the-Month Club, Class Fracture, and Cultural Authority." *South Atlantic Quarterly* 89, no. 4 (1990): 703–36.

Review of *Cimarron* [film]. *Commonweal*, 18 February 1931, 440–41.

Review of *Cimarron* [film]. *Photoplay*, February 1931, 54.

Review of *Cimarron* [film]. *Time*, 2 February 1931, 40.

Review of *Cimarron* [film]. *Variety*, 28 January 1931.

Review of *Cimarron* [novel]. *Wichita Eagle*, 23 March 1930 [n.p.].

"Richard Dix and 'Cimarron' Role." *New York Times*, 25 January 1931, sec. 8:6.

Savage, Kirk. *Standing Soldiers, Kneeling Slaves: Race, War, and Monument in Nineteenth Century America*. Princeton, N.J.: Princeton University Press, 1997.

Shaughnessy, Mary Rose. *Women and Success in American Society in the Works of Edna Ferber*. New York: Gordon Press, 1977.

Slotkin, Richard. *Gunfighter Nation: The Myth of the Frontier in Twentieth-Century America.* New York: Harper Perennial, 1992.

Tebbel, John. *George Horace Lorimer and the "Saturday Evening Post."* Garden City, N.Y.: Doubleday, 1948.

Tilghman, Zoe A. "Among Oklahoma's Literary People." *Harlow's Weekly* [n.d., n.p.].

"To Honor Pioneer Women." *New York Times,* 17 April 1930, 5.

"A True Romancer of the West." *Outlook,* 9 May 1923, 832.

Vestal, Stanley. "Oklahoma Is Setting of Edna Ferber's New Book." *Dallas Morning News,* 30 March 1930.

Welter, Barbara. "The Cult of True Womanhood, 1820–1860." *American Quarterly* 18 (1966): 151–74.

White, G. Edward. *The Eastern Establishment and the Western Experience.* Yale Publications in American Studies 14. New Haven, Conn.: Yale University Press, 1968.

Williams, Adriana. *Covarrubias.* Austin: University of Texas Press, 1994.

"The Woman with a Sunbonnet." *Literary Digest,* 9 April 1927, 26–27.

Wylder, Delbert. *Emerson Hough.* Southwest Writers Series 19. Austin, Tex.: Steck-Vaughn, 1969.

Yale University Press. *The New Historians: A Booklet About the Authors of the Chronicles of America.* New York: Yale University Press, 1920.

"Yale's Movie Version of American History." *Literary Digest,* 4 March 1922, 38.

Young, Stark. "The Pioneer Women." *New Republic,* 16 March 1927, 98–100.

Anzia Yezierska and the Marketing of the Jewish Immigrant in 1920s Hollywood

LISA BOTSHON

When Jewish immigrant author Anzia Yezierska arrived in Hollywood in 1921, she stepped off the transcontinental train into a cloud of waiting paparazzi. Wearing a worn blue serge suit, Yezierska stared wide-eyed at the Hollywood luxury that was offered her and blushed at all the attention she received. Samuel Goldwyn, who had bought the film rights to her first collection of short stories, *Hungry Hearts*, had brought her to Hollywood to play the part of the Goldwyn Company's resident Jewish immigrant ingenue, and Anzia Yezierska, at least initially, appeared to be an excellent candidate for such a role.

This scene of Yezierska's arrival in Hollywood was created by a combination of southern Californian publicity machinery and her own self-promotion. Like many popular writers of her day, Yezierska participated in her own reinvention. The "Sweatshop Cinderella," as she was sometimes called, helped to imagine the Jewish immigrant for the American middlebrow readers of the early twentieth century. However, as might be imagined, her agenda was not always in line with that of the Hollywood studios.

Goldwyn's hiring of Yezierska coincided with a boom in the representation of Jewish immigrants in American popular culture. During the 1920s the nation experienced a growing unease about immigrant entry and assimilation, and a concomitant rise in the commercialization of ethnicity. The representation of the Eastern European Jewish immigrant became caught in the sway of these competing ideas. In American popular culture

Jews were portrayed as the miserly and manipulative racially inferior dregs of Europe, but they also came to represent the ideal Every Immigrant, holding the promise of American opportunity. Complicating the imaging of the Jewish immigrant in the twenties was that a significant number of Jewish immigrants occupied positions of cultural control in Hollywood: Jewish movie moguls such as Samuel Goldwyn, Adolph Zukor, and William Fox made a great impact on the way in which Jews were portrayed on the silver screen. Likewise Anzia Yezierska, whose short stories depicting the Jews of New York's Lower East Side ghetto propelled her to fame, was able to leave her own mark on the American imagination.

The marketing of the Jewish immigrant was never straightforward. The representation of Jewish immigrants on the silver screen could inspire ticket buyers eager to view the way "the other half lived"; on the other hand, it also could provoke anti-Semitism or anti-immigrant sentiment. A ghetto film might play successfully in ghetto movie houses, or the film itself could be condemned for negative stereotyping. Lester Friedman maintains that Jewish ghetto films "tried to make Americans less nervous about Jews, and Jews more conscious of themselves as Americans" ("Conversion" 48), but while this formulation is valid, it doesn't account for the ambivalence inherent in such a process. Hollywood's almost relentless insistence on representing the Jewish immigrant as icon housed simultaneous doubt; the fiercely independent Yezierska's makeover into romantic ingenue barely covered the worldly woman's wrinkles, and the happy assimilationist ideology of the ghetto films could break down on the level of narrative and dialogue. In exploring Anzia Yezierska's experience in Hollywood and the production of the film *Hungry Hearts* based on her work, this essay addresses the ways in which the mass-marketed Jewish immigrant, which appeared to be a smooth package on the surface, often unraveled around the edges.

The Immigrant Jew in the American Imagination

Representations of Eastern European Jews proliferated in early-twentieth-century American culture in virtually every possible popular genre, from newspapers, to cartoons, to songs, to vaudeville. Old paradigms stigmatizing Jews abounded; film historian Kevin Brownlow cites a report of the Anti-Defamation League printed in 1913: "Whenever a producer wishes to depict a betrayer of public trust, a hard-boiled usurious money-lender, a crooked gambler, a grafter, a depraved fire bug, a white slaver or other villains of one kind or another, the actor was directed to represent himself a Jew" (*Behind* 376).

Despite the prejudices and hostilities these immigrants faced, however, they were also celebrated for a certain exotic and romantic appeal. The Eastern European Jewish immigrant experience, the Jewish people, and the Lower East Side ghetto they inhabited were of great cultural interest to other Americans. The Lower East Side was seen equally as a locus of intellectual and creative activity, the site in which undercivilized immigrants could be seen practicing foreign lifeways, and a place in which new sociological and social work techniques could be practiced. Contemporary Jewish author Abraham Cahan, in his 1917 novel *The Rise of David Levinsky*, wrote that the ghetto

> was the great field of activity for the American University Settlement worker and fashionable slummer. The East Side was a place upon which one descended in quest of esoteric types and "local color," as well as for purposes of philanthropy and "uplift" work. To spend an evening in some East Side cafe was regarded as something like spending a few hours at the Louvre; so much so that one such cafe, in the depth of East Houston Street, was making a fortune by purveying expensive wine dinners to people from up-town who came there ostensibly to see "how the other half lived." (284)

The ghetto, then, was not only a site in which immigrant Jews lived and worked, struggling with the realities of poverty and pressures to Americanize, but also a kind of showcase where the immigrant Jew was on parade for native-born Americans. Cahan's passage depicts an early understanding of the way in which ghetto Jews commanded the American fascination for the primitive.

Yezierska and the Hollywood Experience

While Cahan's *Rise of David Levinsky* lends credence to Michael Rogin's speculation that "the multiethnic New York slums brought savagery to the heart of civilization" (122), the journey of the immigrant Jew from inexperienced greenhorn to acculturated American also carried a great deal of symbolic weight in the popular media at a time in which immigration was a contested issue in the United States. Because Eastern European Jews came to the United States already ostracized, made themselves highly visible in American culture, and pressed hard to achieve assimilation in the face of losing their own culture, they became, as film critic Thomas Cripps writes, an "icon of the ritual of Americanization" (197). The story of a radically oppressed group coming to this country and ultimately struggling with the pressures to become not just U.S. citizens but *Americans* illustrated for many the time-honored story of an America that offered a place to live as well as a place to make oneself over as a better person.

Primed by authors of the previous decade such as Cahan and Mary Antin, who helped to popularize the immigrant narrative, the literary market readily accepted Jewish-American writer Anzia Yezierska, who captivated readers with depictions of life's struggles in the tenements of New York's Lower East Side. Yezierska had immigrated to the United States as a child from Eastern Europe around 1890 and had a varied career as a factory worker, actor, and home economics teacher before she gained fame as a writer of short stories that dealt with the lives of ghetto Jews. During the twenties she was often praised for the "realism" of her fiction, a style that combined haunting portraits of substandard living conditions with emotive immigrant speech. Thomas Ferraro notes that her books "were promoted as an insider's guide to 'how the other half lives'" (547). Laura Wexler similarly contends, "Yezierska has often been read nostalgically, as a local color writer, and sentimentally, as a primitive voice from the ghetto" (160).[1] Both Ferraro and Wexler usefully demonstrate the dangers of sustaining such readings; Wexler in particular warns that sentimental readings of Yezierska's work have often resulted in a corresponding dismissal. Nonetheless, it is essential to remember that Anzia Yezierska herself encouraged such readings, which enabled her popular success.

Yezierska recognized the marketability of the stories in which she described the impoverished and anguished lives of Lower East Side inhabitants who strove to achieve upward mobility. She was also aware that her very existence as a former Hester Street immigrant would allow her a certain privileged access to publication. Mass interest in the immigrant story led major journals and publishers to seize upon her early work with relish. By the time she published her short stories as a collection in 1920 with Houghton Mifflin, her work had already appeared in the pages of popular magazines such as the *New Republic, Metropolitan,* and *Century.*

Hearst columnist Frank Crane, one of her early supporters, perceived Yezierska's work as symbolic of the recent trend in immigrant authorship and saw her ethnic identity as her real strength. At the dawn of her fame Crane was to write: "I got a new slant on America from Anzia Yezierska. She walked into my office one day and brought the Old World with her.

She had not said three words before I saw farther into the heart of Russia and Poland than I had ever been able to do by reading many heavy books. She was Poland. She was the whole turgid stream of European immigration pouring into our home country" (quoted in Schoen 36). Crane's response to her work was very much in line with the ghetto cult, which saw the Old World immigrant not merely as an exotic specimen but as being able to bring a fresh perspective to native-born Americans. The support of men like Crane was indicative of the larger trend in popular literature to lionize the immigrant narrative, which linked the literary marketplace with the ideal of American pluralism.

The public taste for the immigrant narrative also meant that Yezierska's career depended on the promotion of the author as a young single immigrant fresh from the tenements. In this guise Yezierska appealed as a "real-life" romantic heroine. She was considered "the personification of the happy ending that Hollywood [had] been turning out" (*Red Ribbon on a White Horse* 54).[2] Film historian Benjamin Hampton notes that during this period, "the fascination of the screen drew flocks of young women to the studios. Their minds were filled with the glamorous stories of success that appeared constantly in newspapers and magazines" (209). The ingenue Yezierska embodied the fulfillment of the feminized Hollywood dream, a real-life Cinderella story.[3] The young immigrant was an ideal romantic heroine, for she was symbolic of the Hollywood dream, in which a poor factory girl could become a glamorous celebrity, and she also symbolized the larger American dream, in which a determined individual who started with nothing could work his or her way to economic success.

However, the success of Yezierska *qua* immigrant author was dependent on editing out those details of her life that did not correspond to the general public's understanding of an already established paradigm. Many facts of Yezierska's life were particularly ill suited for public display. Her first marriage had ended when she insisted on a platonic relationship. Her second was on the rocks by the time she arrived in Hollywood, and she had been accused of abandoning her small daughter. In addition, she had dabbled in socialism, lived on the fringes of Greenwich Village life, and read radical authors like Havelock Ellis. If part of the appeal of the immigrant icon was that she was a little naive and innocent and carried an Old World tradition with her, which might evoke a comfortable nostalgia from her audience, the real-life Yezierska was hardly an appropriate model. In fact, Alice Kessler Harris has called her "revolutionary" for her independence and individualism (ix).[4]

Nevertheless, Yezierska the ingenue needed to exist so that Yezierska the author could make a good living, and she entered into self-promotion with what appears to be a great deal of savvy. Shortly after the publication of *Hungry Hearts*, several film companies began bidding for the rights to her book. She eventually signed on with Goldwyn, who offered her $10,000 for her collection of short stories. Published accounts of Yezierska's first market triumph traded on her ingenue persona. In one article, "This Is What $10,000 Did to Me," originally published in *Cosmopolitan* in 1925 during the height of her literary career, Yezierska writes of herself just before she was offered the Goldwyn contract. The first paragraphs emphasize her poverty and contrast her starving artist–immigrant lifestyle with the wealth she sees on Fifth Avenue. The poverty angle is key, and with it she is able to portray herself as "crazed with want" (264) when she receives a "surprise" telegram from Goldwyn offering her "the unheard of sum of ten thousand dollars" for the rights to her book (265). The article continues in the Cinderella style that delighted her audience and describes the poor immigrant's bedazzlement over Hollywood excesses such as limousines, fresh flowers, and a room in a luxury hotel.

Ironically, Yezierska's success at self-promotion was ultimately self-destructive. Once she had acquired material wealth she could not maintain her immigrant "fresh from the sweatshops" status. The acknowledgment that she had received an enormous sum of money for her book meant that her persona as impoverished immigrant was destabilized. Yezierska's narrative then twisted to accommodate the image of immigrant-with-wealth, which is quite disjunctive from, and did not generate the same commercial interest as, immigrant-in-want. Thus the voice with which she narrates her success story in "This Is What $10,000 Did to Me" reflects her unease with her newfound riches in Hollywood. The last part of the article portrays a newly rich woman struggling with the burden of wealth—a burden because it disrupts her immigrant self and doesn't leave her with a model with which to replace it. Explicit in this narrative is the realization that "you can't be an immigrant twice" (269). Snagged in a catch-22, Yezierska cannot remain an immigrant author once she has achieved the success she seeks.

The publicity in which Yezierska engaged once she arrived in Hollywood was also the source of great ambivalence. The headlines that appeared soon after her arrival cemented the very image she helped to construct: "Immigrant Wins Fortune in Movies," "Sweatshop Cinderella at the Miramar Hotel," and "From Hester Street to Hollywood." However, she writes, "there was a picture of me above those captions, but I couldn't recognize myself in it, any more than I could recognize my own life in the newspapers' stories of my 'success'" (*Red Ribbon* 40).

Yezierska's retrospective displeasure with her publicity was partly based on the fact that in Hollywood she had decreasing control over her own public persona. Out of New York, out of her element, Yezierska's ambivalences about publicizing her immigrant self in Hollywood become manifest in a sway of contradictions, sometimes within the same paragraph. For example, Yezierska relates the story of a Hollywood promoter who wants to capitalize on the story of the ambitious immigrant. He tells her, "We'll add Hollywood's touch. . . . If you have anything to offer, Hollywood can use it. Hollywood, the golden city of opportunity, the first to recognize genius whether it comes from Russia, Poland, or even the United States." She responds, "But all my previous interviews were distortions"(*Red Ribbon* 79–80). He then asks her how old she is, and she makes a point of billing herself as thirty, even though she was close to ten years older at the time. Here Yezierska's struggles with the pressures of self-promotion are evident. In one sentence she is protesting the way in which the publicity misrepresents her, and in the next she is reconstructing herself yet again, hanging onto the image of the youthful immigrant. Near the end of her chapter on her Hollywood years, she admits, "As long as I remained with Goldwyn I was in a glass-house with crooked mirrors. Every move I made was distorted, and every distortion exploited to further the sale of *Hungry Hearts*" (*Red Ribbon* 81). The author cannot successfully marry her public image with her actual state of being. That her "autobiography" contains an extensive rehash of her short stint in Hollywood (a period of mere months) reflects her battle over the control and maintenance of her public immigrant self.

Goldwyn did not hire Yezierska to function solely as the studio's poster immigrant, however. In addition to buying the film rights to *Hungry Hearts*, he offered the author $200 a week to work on the screenplay. It is important to remember that during this period in Hollywood women still outnumbered men in the screenwriting profession.[5] In fact, women (like Jews) were found in virtually every aspect of the film industry, which hints at Hollywood's feminized status in its early years.[6] While screenwriting had never been (and still is not) a particularly admired profession within the industry, it was nonetheless essential to the production of a successful film, and proven screenwriters were often given huge salaries. Yezierska joined the roundup of what Goldwyn termed his "Eminent Authors," which included popular women writers such as Elinor Glyn, who created the "It" girl, and best-selling novelist Gertrude Atherton.[7]

It remains unclear what Yezierska thought would happen with her work in Hollywood. Most work that was bought by the studios underwent great transformations. Even screenplays produced solely for studio use were usually altered in some way. Sonya Levien, a scenarist with a similar Jewish immigrant background to Yezierska's (and also something of a friend), advised writers who sold their work to Hollywood to "do themselves a favor and avoid seeing the results of the continuity process" (Ceplair 50).[8] Yezierska, however, tried to get as involved as she possibly could in the production of *Hungry Hearts*.

It was Goldwyn's intent to create one unified narrative out of several of her stories that were mostly thematically connected; thus her work would have to be seriously transformed. Yezierska worked diligently on the creation of the scenario and praised the efforts of her collaborator, Julian Josephson. She recalled saying to him, "Why do authors complain that Hollywood distorts their books, slaps on ready-made puppets to take the place of real characters? . . . Your scenario has built up my character sketches into a story that everyone can understand" (*Red Ribbon* 48). Yezierska writes of being moved by the work of the actors and the sets, which were realistic renditions of a Russian shtetl and a tenement apartment (*Red Ribbon* 48, 52).

However, other events in the production of the film were disturbing to her. The Goldwyn company was experiencing serious rifts concurrent to the editing of *Hungry Hearts*. Samuel Goldwyn had just been ousted from the company and had been replaced by his rival Frank Godsol.[9] It was then, in the fall of 1921, that Jewish humorist Montague Glass was hired by Godsol to add titles to the film. According to Kevin Brownlow, many of the people originally involved with the film, including E. Mason Hopper, the director, and Paul Bern, were less than happy with Godsol's interference. Godsol insisted on cutting almost three reels of the film and required that "all positive offcuts be sent to New York," presumably for his approval (Brownlow, *Hungry*, 123).

That the studio was embroiled in its own power struggles reinforced that Yezierska, a mere writer, would be left out of much of the decision making for the film. Glass, the author of the popular *Potash and Perlmutter* stories, had been selected by the studio executives because of his success at conveying Jewish humor.[10] However, Yezierska records her meeting with Glass with hostility and writes, "there was only the swift clash of antagonism between us." This man, she contends, "turned out his caricatures of Jews like sausage meat for the popular weekly and monthly magazines. Americans reading his Potash and Perlmutter stories thought those clowning cloak and suiters were the Jewish people" (*Red Ribbon* 81). Yezierska's concerns were not without merit; Glass's representation of Jews in the popular media differed substantially from hers. In addition, the studio was once again exerting control over the project without her input. They believed that the addition of a few laughs and Glass's name would aid in the marketing of the film.[11] For Yezierska, though, this was akin to "murder[ing] it with slapstick" (*Red Ribbon* 82).

Although Yezierska had no tolerance for the likes of Montague Glass, Goldwyn telegrams show that Glass was quite admiring of the work that had gone into *Hungry Hearts*.[12] Glass, extravagant in his praise of the initial screening of *Hungry Hearts*, said that it was "a perfect human document" and "the finest picture he ever saw" (quoted in Brownlow, "*Hungry*," 122). The telegrams show that "he could not suggest a single improvement" and that "he also commented about the fine judgment shown in the spoken titles" (122). Nonetheless, Glass was hired by the company to rework the very titles he had praised. Apparently, he added a good number of titles to the film—so many, in fact, that the studio was appalled and thus recut two versions of the film, one with all of his titles and one using only some. They were relieved when Godsol approved the second. The surviving film is presumably this second version cut by the studio. Though the intertitles occur in different fonts, it is unclear where the initial cuts were made or which titles are in fact Glass's. That the film continued to be worked and reworked meant that it emerged in theaters a different production than had been originally anticipated.

Hungry Hearts—The Movie

Although the wide release of a Hollywood motion picture featuring Jewish immigrants may seem like an anomaly today, the production of *Hungry Hearts* followed two decades of filmmaking that depicted the Jewish immigrant. Lester Friedman notes that "between 1900 and 1929 alone, approximately 230 films featured clearly discernable Jewish characters," a substantial number of which concerned immigrant themes (*Hollywood's Image* 9).[13] Patricia Erens contends that over three dozen films focusing on the Jewish ghetto were released by major studios in the twenties alone, which inspires her to create a genre term —the "Ghetto Film" (77). While some of the earliest films often relied on comedic or villainous typecasting, by the 1920s ghetto films largely strove to present Jewish immigrants in more nuanced ways.

David Weinberg and Thomas Cripps find the ghetto silents regrettably assimilationist.[14] Friedman concurs that these films "often begin by accentuating the differences of Jews—speech, dress, custom, diet—[but] they usually end by proclaiming their more important similarities to other Americans—love of family, financial distress, generational differences. Peculiarity, therefore, is quickly eliminated as a major issue. Only superficial, outward elements distinguish Jews from their neighbors; inner strengths bind them to all Americans" (*Jewish Image* 52).[15] Indeed, in employing marks of Jewish difference, the ghetto film does trade on the spectacle of the exotic and/or evoke nostalgia for European tradition. In addition, pat resolutions of narrative conflict do tend to promote upward mobility and secularism over the preservation of Jewish culture. Yet, rather than understanding this formula as uniformly assimilationist, I would suggest that the ghetto film finds it difficult to maintain this ideology and that a great deal of ambivalence about the imaging of Jewishness is built into the genre. The film version of *Hungry Hearts* is an excellent case in point. While it first appears to be a somewhat facile tale of immigrant struggle and success in the New Land, it also reveals a profound unease in the representation of Jewish immigrants in the United States.

The filmic *Hungry Hearts* is a compilation of three of the most well-crafted and moving short stories published in Yezierska's original collection: "The Lost Beautifulness," "Where Lovers Dream," and "How I Found America." Each reveals a complex understanding of the conflicts faced by Jewish immigrants in the United States and portrays believable situations—the tyranny of a successful Jewish landlord over greenhorn tenants, the emotional costs of upward mobility, and unexpected realizations about what it means to be a "real American." Some of the stories are cynical or ironic; others are painful; none are happily resolved. At best, Yezierska's protagonists look forward to something better for themselves, but the reader never knows if they accomplish their goals.

At first glance *Hungry Hearts* appears to be a dilution of Yezierska's work. It opens with the Levin family living in a Russian shtetl; Abraham, the gentle patriarch, teaches Jewish law to the village children. However, they are soon persecuted by the Cossacks, who wish to prevent Jewish religious instruction. Upon reading a letter from a fellow villager who has made it in New York, the Levins, prompted by Hanneh, the mother, and Sara, the oldest daughter, decide to emigrate to America. Initially taken aback by the crowded living conditions of the ghetto, they settle in.

Here the story fragments in order to follow each character in his or her own pursuit of American-style happiness. The dedicated scholar Abraham attempts to set up a pushcart business, Hanneh is set upon creating an "American" kitchen, and Sara, longing for romance, responds to the overtures of the Jewish landlord's lawyer nephew, David Kaplan. Each of these plots moves through its own crisis. Abraham loses his pushcart. Rosenblatt, the landlord, upset with his nephew's intent to marry a greenhorn, not only prohibits the marriage of Sara and David but also raises Hanneh's rent when he sees her new kitchen. Here Hanneh becomes the star as she, in response to Rosenblatt's unfairness, takes an axe to her kitchen and is then hauled to court. All is resolved in the American courtroom, where David comes to the aid of Hanneh and is reunited with Sara, and the judge rules against the avaricious Rosenblatt. The last scene depicts the Levin family suddenly transported to the suburbs, where the picket fence is white, the little Levins play in the yard, Abraham reads his Hebrew text on the front porch, and the successful assimilated couple, Sara and David, smile for the camera.

It would be easy enough to criticize the film version of *Hungry Hearts* as a sanitized acculturation narrative that bears little resemblance to Anzia Yezierska's work. Hanneh's destruction of her kitchen and the following courtroom scene, for example, are based on the short story entitled "The Lost Beautifulness." The impact of Yezierska's original conception relies on the contrast between the new immigrant's (Hanneh) contribution to the nation in the form of her enlisted son and the nation's heartless judicial system. Hanneh, starved for months as she attempts to keep up with the landlord's rent increases, gets her day in court, but the judge rules in favor of the landlord. Then, Hanneh, in a moment of great passion, destroys her kitchen. A moment of irony arises at the end of the story, as her son, on whose shoulder "was the insignia of the Statue of Liberty . . . bestowed by the United States Government" (*Hungry Hearts* 96), comes home to discover his evicted mother and all their worldly possessions dumped outside in the rain. But the film does not take on such ironies. In what has become a trademark of Hollywood filmmaking, the court scene is given great drama; the wronged hardworking mother is avenged, David and Sara are reunited, the evil landlord is punished, and the American justice system is shown to have the utmost objectivity and integrity. Thus Hollywood seems to simultaneously resolve the problems of the immigrant and bolster nationalist sentiments.

Nonetheless, the neatness of this patriotic assimilation narrative is complicated by an overburdened plot, an uneven narrative structure, and the use of a Yiddish-American patois. Ghetto films are particularly notable for the way in which plotlines are piled on the assemblage of characters. *Hun-*

gry Hearts takes on Eastern European religious oppression, poverty, upward mobility, literacy, slumlords, romance, and a court case (not to mention subplots among the neighbors), all of which are resolved in a little over an hour. Other ghetto films such as *Humoresque* (1920) and *His People* (1925) presented their audiences with similar profusions of themes, rendering their Jewish immigrant characters into virtual allegories for the larger American immigrant experience.[16] But the abundance of storylines reaches almost absurd proportions, betraying an anxiety inherent in these depictions and prompting one to question the manic vigor with which the Jewish immigrant is iconized.

The abrupt ending of *Hungry Hearts* also gives one pause. The pretty young couple in the suburbs bears little resemblance to the careworn immigrant daughter who tries to hide her greenhorn stockings, or to the barely-out-of-law-school youth bullied by his avaricious uncle. There is nothing in the preceding scene (the triumphant court case) to prepare the audience for this radical transition. The disruption in narrative could be attributed to the disruptions that were concomitantly occurring in the studio; conflicting directives may have resulted in messy continuity editing. Even so, the obvious fissure between courtroom and suburb points to the possibility that the film even has the *wrong* ending. How can a film that climaxes with a *Yiddeshe* mama winning a lawsuit filed by her landlord logically conclude with a modish American couple? With so little connecting the end to the rest of the film, the assimilation scene carries little weight.

It is perhaps in the dialogue intertitles where *Hungry Hearts* most actively resists an assimilationist reading. Here is where Yezierska's writing is most directly used, and it is through the intertitles that this film distinguishes itself from others of its genre. Films like *Humoresque* or *His People* employ occasional Yiddish words and make gestures toward representing the hybrid language of the Lower East Side. But Yezierska's work on *Hungry Hearts* rendered it uniquely able to represent the linguistic interchange between American English and Yiddish. Her fiction draws a great deal of impact from what the characters say and how they say it. A unique blend of English and Yiddish, which some critics call *Yidgin*,[17] her characters' utterances reveal a linguistic hybridization essential to representing the immigrant experience.

In an early exchange in the film set in Russia, the family discusses the possibility of emigrating to the United States:

HANNEH: Gottuniu! If only we could lift ourselves to America—the golden land!

ABRAHAM: Meshugeneh Yidini! Where's the money for ship-tickets?
HANNEH: Money? I could sell the shirt from my back—only to go to
America!
SARA: Let us sell anyhow our fur coats. It must be always sunshine in
America![18]

There are two distinctive elements working within this dialogue. The first
is the incorporation of Yiddish words, such as *gottuniu* and *meshugeneh.*
The second is the way in which the spoken English is stylized, as if based
upon a translation using Yiddish grammar. However, as twenties critic
Alter Brody has shown, Yezierska's "translation" is not direct but rather a
literary device designed to create the effect of an immigrant language.
Despite the authentic sound of Yezierska's dialogue, hers were in fact *literary* renderings of the language immigrants spoke. This is particularly significant for the scenes set in Russia, as here the Levins are not yet
immigrants. Yidgin dialogue, a hybrid language created to illustrate an
immigrant linguistics, does not have a realistic place in the immigrant's
country of origin. In Russia the Levins would have been speaking to each
other in a fluent Yiddish, which would most aptly be "translated" into standard English. The choice to portray the Levins as speaking Yidgin in Russia sets them up from the beginning of the film as *immigrant* Jews, already
marked by the hybridization of the American experience.

Alter Brody, writing in 1926, criticized literary Yidgin in general for its
lack of realism and "crude . . . local color" (206–7). Though he recognized
that it could take different forms, Brody saw this language as "purely imaginary" (205) and suggested that Jewish authors such as Yezierska employed
it to reduce Yiddish-speaking immigrants to ignorant buffoons. "The
American public finds anything that is not American either irresistibly
comic or profoundly pathetic," he argued (207). Brody, under the impression that Yezierska and similar authors were maligning the complex and
sophisticated language of Yiddish, could not see that the importance of
Yidgin is its very hybridity. Though he was right to point out the dangers
of representing Yiddish speakers through Yidgin in that any stylization of
a cultural form may be subject to the problems of stereotyping and conde-
scension, he did not accept that Yidgin was important to the immigrant
narrative for the way in which it signified the process of cultural mixing.
What Brody seems to be registering in this critique is a more deep-seated
anxiety over the loss of a "pure" Yiddish. Significantly, this parallels the
anxiety already present in American culture over the penetration of standard American English by immigrant languages. That a commercial film

like *Hungry Hearts* could use Yiddishisms such as *meshugeneh* in its titles becomes a larger issue when one considers the fact that many non-Jews probably understood these words by its release in 1922, indicating that "American English" had already been influenced by immigrant languages. The film's dialogue, then, is important for its portrayal not only of the Americanization of the immigrant but also of the "immigrantization" of America.

While the structure and titles of *Hungry Hearts* demonstrate some of the ways in which the ghetto film's portrayal of Jewishness is far from uniform, so too does the casting reveal the complexity of representing the Jewish immigrant on film. Finding the appropriate actress to play Sara, the female romantic lead, appears to have been the most difficult decision. While Sara was hardly the showiest role, the female romantic lead was important for the universalizing aspects of the film; it would be Sara with whom the young women audiences, regardless of ethnicity, would identify. At least three Jewish girls were tested for the part; one, the daughter of a rabbi, was deemed "too American" (Brownlow, *Behind*, 396). A Russian Jew named Ethel Kaye initially got the part.

The studio considered women of different ethnic backgrounds for the more demanding role of Hanneh, the mother. A Gentile character actress was discussed as it seemed possible that she could learn "Jewish mannerisms" but then rejected as it seemed unlikely that she could acquire these mannerisms before the shooting. Russian-Jewish stage actress Sonia Marcel was then selected on the advice of Anzia Yezierska. Bryant Washburn, a young actor who had been in several light comedies, was chosen to play the part of the lawyer, David Kaplan, and was justified by the studio as "the only juvenile leading man we know who acceptably photographs Jewish" (quoted in Brownlow, *Behind*, 396).[19] The casting, then, was contingent on acquiring actors who would convey already understandable Jewish traits. In other words, in order to make a Jewish film, the producers needed actors who fit certain stereotypes attributable to Jews, regardless of their own ethnicity.

Though shooting for *Hungry Hearts* began in September 1921, it soon was halted as Ethel Kaye had, according to studio head Abe Lehr, "lost something that makes her acceptable" (quoted in Brownlow, *Behind*, 397). It is unclear exactly what Kaye had lost, but she was replaced by Gentile actress Helen Ferguson, a woman who was thought to look Jewish, suggesting perhaps that Kaye did not (unlike Washburn) "acceptably photograph Jewish." Soon after the firing of Kaye, Sonia Marcel was also let go. Though she clearly had a particular Jewish appearance, it was not quite the look the studio was seeking for Hanneh. Lehr wrote to Goldwyn: "She is photographically almost impossible for this part because of hard straight mouth and hawk nose that even in slightest profile gets over hardness which makes her repellent in her sympathetic scenes. . . . Her personality is negative and instead of giving us simplicity of peasant Jewess she is giving us intensity of an intellectual dressed in peasant's clothes" (quoted in Brownlow, *Behind*, 397). As is suggested by Yezierska's own Hollywood persona, the intense intellectual Jewish woman was not a marketable commodity. The "Long Suffering Mother" (termed by Patricia Erens) needed to be traditional, nostalgically comforting. Russian-Jewish actress Rosa Rosanova, a veteran of the Yiddish theater, was eventually chosen by Goldwyn and Yezierska to replace Marcel.[20]

Significantly, the ethnicity of the actors themselves was secondary to the way in which they were believed to look to mass audiences. That one actress was rejected for appearing more Irish than Jewish, that one actress was thought to be able to acquire Jewish mannerisms, and that an actor was accepted for "photograph[ing]" Jewish indicates the way in which "authenticity" was relative to film as representation.[21] For the producers of *Hungry Hearts*, "authenticity" was about conveying preexisting ideas of Jewishness on screen rather than creating new definitions or employing Jewish actors. It was about reinscribing the visible signifiers of Jewishness that descended from old stereotypes.

All of the primary actors in *Hungry Hearts* were eventually chosen, at least in part, for their ability to *look* convincingly Jewish. One of the criteria used to ensure a Jewish look was the size and shape of the actors' noses. Sander Gilman argues that the nose is one "'striking feature' which marks the Jew as different, what marks the Jew as visible" (176). The relative conspicuousness of the actors' noses in the film indicates the importance of portraying Jewish characters as visibly different, as visibly Jewish. This takes on extra significance because *Hungry Hearts* is a silent film, a genre in which the face and figure of the actor take precedence over anything he or she could say. The imaging of the Jewish face, then, is as necessary to the plot of the Jewish silent film as any other part of the narrative.

The importance of the Jewish face in *Hungry Hearts* surfaces in a promotional piece published in the April 1922 issue of *Motion Picture Classic*. Entitled "Helen's Hungry Heart," the article is a first-person narrative by Helen Ferguson accompanied by glamour shots as well as portraits of her dressed as her character Sara. Ferguson's description of the way in which she broke into the acting business resembles Yezierska's account of her own literary ascent.[22] What is most striking, however, is the end of the article, where the plug for *Hungry Hearts* emerges. "I want you all to see it," Ferguson writes. "It is a story of the struggle of the Russian Jews in America, and while I'm not a Jewess, and have always hated the little hump on my nose, I now love it because it brought me the part I love so" (78). In this, her only endorsement of the film in the article, Ferguson simultaneously acknowledges her Jewish-signifying nose for its cinema market value and makes clear both her own non-Jewishness and her discomfort with "the little hump" for its ethnic significance. Ferguson prefers to portray herself as one who can, but does not have to, perform Jewishness. Her newly commodified Jewish signifier (nose) only becomes acceptable in the marking of its inauthenticity.[23]

The Jewish nose becomes a real issue in the film *Hungry Hearts*, as it is one of the important factors in fashioning an authentic Jewish look.[24] Bryant Washburn's ability to "photograph Jewish" may indeed have hinged on the fact of his substantial (though not humped) nose, and there is no doubt that Rosa Rosanova, the woman finally picked to play Hanneh, also came facially prepared. Abe Budin, a real-life Jewish delicatessen owner for whom Helen Ferguson had worked in order to prepare herself for the role of Sara, was chosen to play the supporting role of Sopkin the Butcher. The ever-smiling round meat man was very well-endowed nose-wise, as was Otto Lederer, who played his friend Gedalyeh Mindel.[25]

The Release of *Hungry Hearts*

Despite all efforts to create an "authentic" Jewish film, *Hungry Hearts* was not to be uniformly marketed as such. It was hoped that *Hungry Hearts* would be equal in blockbuster status to its ghetto film predecessor, *Humoresque*, but the publicists were clearly hesitant to mark it as Jewish. One of the earliest promotions for the film, published a full year and a half before its release, called *Hungry Hearts* "A Great Drama of the Melting Pot" (*Motion Picture News*, 2 July 1921, 154), which succeeded in lending the film a universal quality.

The "exploitation" given the film before its opening in New York also capitalized on its universalist immigrant story. *Motion Picture News* reported in its late December issue that "a woman and a boy were hired to dress up in Russian peasant costume, carrying large red hearts on which the showing of 'Hungry Hearts' at the Capitol was advertised" (23 December 1922, 3201).[26] In addition, thousands of candy hearts and shopping bags with slogans were distributed in stores. Grosset and Dunlap issued a reprint of Yezierska's book with film stills. That actors were hired to dress up in "Russian peasant costumes" to parade around the streets of New York did not necessarily mark the film as a Jewish picture. It is unlikely that midtown New Yorkers would have recognized the specificity of the actor-immigrants' origins by their costumes. Rather, this ploy emphasized that *Hungry Hearts* was an immigrant film and of interest for its coming-to-America narrative.

Anzia Yezierska herself was brought into the marketing of *Hungry Hearts*. Her commercial viability as a fresh young immigrant author was replayed in New York prior to the release of the film. An unidentified author for the *New York Tribune* wrote, "Probably as romantic a figure as contemporary American literature affords is that of Ansia [*sic*] Yezierska, who landed at Ellis Island fifteen years ago as a frail, young Polish-Jew immigrant girl, and who has won her way through dreary hours in sweatshop and scullery to a place among the successful authors of the day. . . . Miss Yezierska's great discovery is 'There is justice in America.' And that is the motif of her picture, 'Hungry Hearts'" (2).

The writer as representative young immigrant girl who had made it big in Hollywood was a malleable public figure. The *Tribune* portrayed her as an enthusiastic author, pleased with the results of her Hollywood experience: "'It [the film] has been wonderfully done,' she said, 'but I think that is because the members of the cast really lived the story. They felt it. I cannot tell you how deeply I was impressed by the spirit of actuality that was evident while Mr. Hopper was directing the players in their parts'" (2). Only three days later *Motion Picture Classic* showed yet another side of the writer. In an interview "transcribed by Faith Service" Yezierska says that she found Hollywood smothering, and that she was aghast at the final version of the film: "And then imagine for me the horror of finding that after my work was done huge Ogres had the power to meddle with the inviolate idea that had been wrought with pain and agony. Little bits of human heart–pictures that took me weeks and months to portray truthfully—*were cut out*. A happy ending was appended. A happy ending! To my story. What a ghastly anti-climax" (86). While it is likely that Yezierska was less than satisfied with the happy ending tacked on to *Hungry Hearts*, it is hard to believe the entirety of the article in *Motion Picture Classic*, a fairly popular fan magazine. First, it seems as though the "transcriber" employed his or her own language to try to approximate Yezierska's. "Human heart–pictures," for example, sounds suspiciously like the Yezierskian rhetoric used in advertising campaigns rather than like Yezierska herself. Near the end of the interview Yezierska delivers a parable about

Christ and keeping faith, which is almost laughably suspect. Anyone following the tale of the young Jewish immigrant girl in other publications would find it difficult to believe that she had suddenly converted to Christianity.[27] Nonetheless, this maneuver, orchestrated as yet another publicity stunt, reinforced the (Christian) universality of the Jewish immigrant through the persona of the public Yezierska. The combination of the *Tribune* and *Motion Picture Classic* articles, which both came out around the time of the New York premiere of *Hungry Hearts*, suggests that the author's real views of the film, as the author's real self, did not much matter; publicity alone, particularly that which drove home the idea that foreignness such as Jewishness could be Americanized, was of greater value.

The use of Yezierska in this publicity campaign further functioned to reassure readers and potential viewers of the assimilability of immigrants by presenting her as an ideal immigrant, particularly in the demonstration of her enthusiasm for the American system and her knowledge of Christianity. Anyone following the ad campaign for *Hungry Hearts* would have no real idea what the film was about, but they could feel comforted to know that the Jews in Hollywood were making truly "American" pictures.

Hungry Hearts opened to mixed reviews and never became the blockbuster the studio had hoped for. Newspaper reviewers found it overblown and sentimental, albeit watchable, and there are no records of the opinions of the ordinary viewers who saw it. Although the film was not a great success, Hollywood continued to represent the Jewish immigrant for wide American audiences in the 1920s.[28] Anzia Yezierska made another stab at the Jewish immigrant film in the mid-twenties with her novel-turned-film, *Salome of the Tenements*, and continued to produce immigrant fiction for another decade. However, the hullabaloo over the "Sweatshop Cinderella" and the thrill over the treasures of the Lower East Side lost their momentum by the thirties. Stars for the moment like Yezierska, who had ridden the wave of Jewish immigrant popularity but who were ultimately unable to transform themselves as the excitement of the Jewish immigrant in American popular culture waned, faded as well. Nevertheless, Anzia Yezierska's pursuit of fame as an immigrant author and the concomitant Hollywood impulse to represent the Jew as the ideal immigrant both reveal an important struggle with the complexities of cultural representation in the United States.

Notes

1. Ferraro and Wexler are especially significant as they move away from the wave of critics who a bit too zealously scripted Yezierska as a protofeminist after she was

first reprinted in the 1970s and 1980s. Ferraro points to the way in which Yezierska's varied approaches toward upward mobility have often been elided; Wexler reinvokes the significance of Jewish memory. Another important perspective is offered by Walter Benn Michaels, who demonstrates an implicit antiassimilationist ethic present in Yezierska's 1925 novel, *Bread Givers*.

2. *Red Ribbon on a White Horse* is hereafter cited as *Red Ribbon*. While *Red Ribbon*, written decades after Yezierska had already faded from public view, is treated as an autobiography, it is widely regarded as a semifictional work. I use it here as it provides the most comprehensive discussion of her time in Hollywood.

3. According to Ben Hampton, the Cinderella story "continued through this period to occupy a prominent position among box-office attractions" (224).

4. See Alice Kessler Harris and Henricksen for an elaboration of Yezierska's free-thinking ways.

5. According to the much-cited Writers Guild of America figures, the ratio was ten to one. See McCreadie and Acker, for example.

6. Anthony Slide has commented, "During the silent era, women might be said to have virtually controlled the film industry" (9). This seems somewhat exaggerated, but it is indicative of a different gender balance than was to be found in Hollywood even a decade later.

7. See Berg for a more extensive discussion of the Eminent Authors project, which was designed to lend the studio literary "class" and ultimately resulted in failure.

8. Levien, who had been a magazine editor before she became a screenwriter, had bought one of Yezierska's earliest stories for *Metropolitan*. Henricksen claims that Levien "virtually started Anzia's career" (123).

9. This company was to become Metro-Goldwyn Mayer (MGM), whereas Samuel Goldwyn then formed the Samuel Goldwyn Company. For an expanded discussion of Goldwyn's ousting, see Lewis's article, "Include Me Out," and Berg.

10. A few years later Glass's *Potash and Perlmutter* stories were to be made into films by the Samuel Goldwyn Company. Frances Taylor Patterson, a scenarist and instructor at Columbia University in the 1920s, attributed the appeal of these films to titles "which recorded with comic accuracy the garbled grammar of the ghetto" (61).

11. Glass had by this time made a name for himself as a "Jewish dialect specialist." According to J. Hoberman, Glass wrote the titles for, among other things, *The Perfect Thirty-Six* (1914), a German film in which the young Ernst Lubitsch appeared as "an enterprising yet bungling Jewish apprentice or clerk" (47n).

12. In addition, Kevin Brownlow feels that Yezierksa's account of her meeting with Glass is inaccurate. Though she writes in *Red Ribbon* that she had met Glass in California, Brownlow believes that if she had met him at all it would have been in New York. He further suggests that the whole meeting might have been a fabrication (*"Hungry"* 123). Whether or not this account is true, it is important for the way in which it portrays Yezierska's discomfort with this marketing strategy for her film.

13. Such films received scant critical attention until the 1980s. Friedman's *Hollywood's Image of the Jew* (1982) and Patricia Erens's *The Jew in American Cinema* (1984) are the two most extensive works that catalogue the representation of Jews in Hollywood films. However, they were preceded by several significant essays from the seventies—most notably those by Thomas Cripps and David Weinberg.

14. Weinberg in particular notes, "The price of social integration continues to be the rejection of all cultural ties" (68).

15. It is worth mentioning that Yiddish ghetto films made during this period, which were directed primarily at Jewish audiences, seem to reflect more cultural conflict and disruption than their Hollywood cousins. See Hoberman for an excellent overview of Yiddish film.

16. The original *Humoresque* (a deethnicized remake with Joan Crawford was released several decades later), based on a story by Fannie Hurst and directed by Frank Borzage, was the first blockbuster ghetto film of the decade. The story involves a poor Jewish boy who, encouraged by his mother, makes a name for himself as a great violinist. Wounded in the war, he finds he is unable to play upon his return home but miraculously his arm is healed through his love for a childhood sweetheart. *His People*, directed by Edward Sloman, concerns the trials and tribulations of the Cominskys, a ghetto family. Morris, the adored oldest son, cruelly denies his family in his quest for upward mobility while his younger brother, who is kicked out of the house for being a boxer, works behind the scenes to help his parents. The family is happily reunited in the end.

17. Alter Brody and Sally Drucker, among others.

18. This passage is copied directly from the only extant copy of *Hungry Hearts* known to exist. The surviving print, discovered in 1978 in England, is missing about 15 minutes of its original footage. It is housed at the British Film Institute in London. All other references to the film are from this print.

19. Apparently not all reviewers agreed with this assessment of Washburn once the film was released. In one review of *Hungry Hearts*, a *Variety* author writes, "It was a grave error to cast Bryant Washburn as the young lover. Here was a play of foreign flavor, and they chose for its romantic foreground an actor who is familiar to all fandom as a smart modern hero, entirely out of the atmosphere of the story and production" (1 December 1922, 34). This remark points to the hazards of typecasting. Obviously, in this reviewer's mind one could not successfully meld "foreign" (and significantly Washburn plays an *acculturated* Jewish American, not an immigrant) with "smart [and] modern." It also bears remarking that this reviewer confuses Hanneh with Sara throughout the piece.

20. Rosanova, who performed the role of Hanneh admirably in *Hungry Hearts*, continued to play the role of the Jewish ghetto mother throughout the twenties in films such as Edward Sloman's *His People* (1925), the interethnic *The Shamrock and the Rose* (1927), and *The Younger Generation* (1929), based on a story by Fannie Hurst.

21. Though one might expect otherwise, the review of *Hungry Hearts* in the *American Hebrew* was complimentary of the non-Jewish actors. "Bryant Washburn and Helen Ferguson, although Gentiles," writes reviewer Harry Sabbath Bodin, "have caught the proper spirit of the picture and are a convincing pair of Jewish lovers" (8 September 1922, 387). This underscores the acceptability of performing Jewishness in Hollywood films for at least part of the American Jewish community.

22. Though Ferguson claims that hers "is not a fairy tale of the studios" and that she had no "great artistic 'urge'" to become an actress, her story resonates as a classic Cinderella tale (24). Ferguson writes that she began acting because of her fami-

ly's financial distress, though this seems unlikely, particularly because of the economic tenuousness of such a career, as well as her self-admitted stream of initial failures. The main current of her narrative reads like a rags-to-riches story, which is similar to the way in which Yezierska marketed herself as an uneducated immigrant fresh from the sweatshops.

23. Possibly Helen Ferguson's nose made her more acceptably "foreign" (Jewish) looking to the *Variety* reviewer who panned Washburn (see note 19 above): "Helen Ferguson was much better. She *looked* the part and played it sympathetically" (emphasis mine).

24. One colleague, upon viewing *Hungry Hearts* for the first time, exclaimed that there was "certainly a lot of nose in this film." Subsequent casual viewers were inclined to agree.

25. Otto Lederer was to play similar Jewish roles in later films such as *The Jazz Singer* (1927), in which he appears as Yudelson, the Cantor's meddlesome friend.

26. The Capitol Theater was located at 51st Street and Broadway in New York, far from any of the city's ghettos. Films shown there were often accompanied by lavish live productions.

27. The article, an amalgam of odd quotations attributed to Yezierska, is further perplexing as it features a large photograph identified as "a scene from the poignant drama of the Ghetto, 'Hungry Hearts'" (41) that does not seem to bear any relation to the film.

28. The 1927 film *The Jazz Singer* is one of the most well-known examples, but the list also includes the comic Potash and Perlmutter episodes (also produced by Goldwyn) as well as the above-mentioned *His People* (1925) and *The Younger Generation* (1929). See Erens and Friedman for surveys of this period.

Works Cited

Acker, Ally. *Reel Women: Pioneers of the Cinema, 1896 to the Present.* New York: Continuum, 1991.

Antin, Mary. *The Promised Land.* 1912. New York: Houghton Mifflin, 1946.

Berg, A. Scott. *Goldwyn: A Biography.* New York: Knopf, 1989.

Bodin, Harry Sabbath. "Review of *Hungry Hearts.*" *The American Hebrew*, 8 September 1922, 387.

Brody, Alter. "Yiddish in American Fiction." *American Mercury*, February 1926, 205–7.

Brownlow, Kevin. *Behind the Mask of Innocence.* Berkeley: University of California Press, 1990.

———. "*Hungry Hearts*: A Hollywood Social Problem Film of the 1920s." *Film History* 1, no. 2 (1987): 113–25.

Cahan, Abraham. *The Rise of David Levinsky.* 1917. New York: Penguin, 1993.

Ceplair, Larry. *A Great Lady: A Life of the Screenwriter Sonya Levien.* Lanham, Md.: Scarecrow, 1996.

Cripps, Thomas. "The Movie Jew as an Image of Assimilation, 1903–1927." *Journal of Popular Film* 4, no. 3 (1975): 190–207.

Drucker, Sally Ann. "Yiddish, Yidgin, and Yezierska: Dialect in Jewish-American Writing." *Yiddish* 6, no. 4 (1987): 99–113.

Erens, Patricia. *The Jew in American Cinema*. Bloomington: Indiana University Press, 1984.

Ferguson, Helen. "Helen's Hungry Heart." *Motion Picture Classic*, April 1922, 24.

Ferraro, Thomas. "'Working Ourselves Up' in America: Anzia Yezierska's *Bread Givers*." *South Atlantic Quarterly* 89, no. 3 (1990): 547–81.

Friedman, Lester. "The Conversion of the Jews." *Film Comment* 17, no. 4 (1981): 39–48.

———. *Hollywood's Image of the Jew*. New York: Frederick Ungar, 1982.

———. *The Jewish Image in American Film*. Secaucus, N.J.: Citadel, 1987.

Gilman, Sander. *The Jew's Body*. New York: Routledge, 1991.

Hampton, Benjamin B. *History of the American Film Industry from Its Beginnings to 1931*. 1931. New York: Dover, 1970.

Henricksen, Louise Levitas. *Anzia Yezierska: A Writer's Life*. New Brunswick, N.J.: Rutgers University Press, 1988.

Hoberman, J. *Bridge of Light: Yiddish Film Between Two Worlds*. New York: Schocken, 1991.

Hungry Hearts. Dir. E. Mason Hopper. Perf. Bryant Washburn, Helen Ferguson, E. A. Warren, and Rosa Rosanova. Based on the book of the same name by Anzia Yezierska. Goldwyn, 1922.

Kessler Harris, Alice. Introduction to *Bread Givers* by Anzia Yezierska. New York: Persea, 1975.

Lewis, Arnold, and Kevin Lewis. "Include Me Out: Samuel Goldwyn and Joe Godsol." *Film History* 2, no. 2 (1988): 133–53.

McCreadie, Marsha. *The Women Who Write the Movies: From Frances Marion to Nora Ephron*. New York: Birch Lane, 1994.

Michaels, Walter Benn. *Our America: Nativism, Modernism, and Pluralism*. Durham, N.C.: Duke University Press, 1995.

Patterson, F. T. *Scenario and Screen*. New York: Harcourt, 1928.

"Review of *Hungry Hearts*." *New York Tribune*, 9 November 1922, 5:2.

"Review of *Hungry Hearts*." *Variety*, 1 December 1922, 34.

Rogin, Michael. *Blackface, White Noise: Jewish Immigrants in the Hollywood Melting Pot*. Berkeley: University of California Press, 1996.

Schoen, Carol B. *Anzia Yezierska*. Boston: Twayne, 1982.

Service, Faith, transcriber. "A Message of Faith from Anzia Yezierska." *Motion Picture Classic*, November 1922, 41.

Slide, Anthony. *Early Women Directors*. New York: A. S. Barnes, 1977.

Weinberg, David. "The 'Socially Acceptable' Immigrant Minority Group: The Image of the Jew in Popular Films." *North Dakota Quarterly* 40, no. 4 (1972): 60–68.

Wexler, Laura. "Looking at Yezierska." In *Women of the Word: Jewish Women and Jewish Writing*. Ed. Judith R. Baskin. Detroit, Mich.: Wayne State University Press, 1994.

Yezierska, Anzia. *How I Found America: Collected Stories of Anzia Yezierska*. New York: Persea, 1991.

———. *Hungry Hearts and Other Stories*. 1920. New York: Persea, 1985.

———. *Red Ribbon on a White Horse*. 1950. New York: Persea, 1987.

IV

WOMEN
AND
CONSUMPTION

"An Unwonted Coquetry": The Commercial Seductions of Jessie Fauset's The Chinaberry Tree

SUSAN TOMLINSON

> Nervously situated in the overlapping liminal spaces of our own lives in the marketplace, we are subjectivities born of tension. Rather than multiple and fragmented, perhaps we find ourselves buoyed up by the contradictions that let us imagine—or assert—our autonomy for the economic order that, more than ever, defines us.
> —Nina Miller, *Making Love Modern*

In a 1932 interview with Marion L. Starkey published in *Southern Workman*, Jessie Fauset described the practical side of balancing her writing career with making a living through her high-school teaching, and expressed the frustrations of time and energy constraints. Fauset revealed that she wrote most of her 1931 novel *The Chinaberry Tree* while on summer recess, having studied magazine romance fiction "to analyze and isolate the germ of popular writing" (217). She also admitted her attempts to achieve a commercial success that would free her to write full-time as well as her ongoing struggle to overcome white publishers' and readers' expectations of "Harlem dives . . . race riots . . . and picturesquely abject poverty" (218). This struggle might explain two of Fauset's commercial strategies—enlisting the popular white novelist Zona Gale to write the book's foreword, and borrowing popular literary models—that contribute to the novel's hybridity as an antiromance romance novel that manipulates and even mutates the popular "germ" in order to undermine and ultimately reinscribe it.

The Chinaberry Tree, Fauset's third novel, represents the battle for thematic supremacy between the structure and politics within the text and the social and commercial forces outside it. As in her previous novels, *There Is Confusion* (1924) and *Plum Bun* (1928), Fauset uses the conventions of popular domestic fiction to represent the politics of gender, race, and class and their roles in identity formation and self-determination. However, *The Chinaberry Tree* represents an even less certain relationship to the generic constructions it adopts. Fauset's least urban novel—the first and only one set outside a major city—*The Chinaberry Tree* is thematically Fauset's most urbane, dealing explicitly with sexual desire, hypocrisy, adultery, and incest, not with a gasping, pearl-clutching prurience but rather with a knowing sobriety that daringly assumes a level of sophistication in the readership it courts. *The Chinaberry Tree* appeals to mainstream society while interrogating principles of social organization. Although its publishers marketed the novel as a representation of exemplary black life, the text satirizes the moral cowardice and superficiality of black social leaders. *The Chinaberry Tree* challenges the injustice and inhumanity of class distinction, only to posit a new social pyramid that marries an organic aristocracy with social and professional success.

The commercial transparency of Zona Gale's introduction suggests the lengths to which Fauset was willing to go to sell the book, specifically to a white audience. By 1931 Fauset had accepted that a predominantly black readership does not a best seller make, and as the Depression set in, readers of all races were less inclined to purchase books. The original Frederick A. Stokes edition of *The Chinaberry Tree* is literally packaged to appeal to white readers unfamiliar with the black middle class. Fauset depicts in all her novels female protagonists who conspicuously consume luxury beauty products and whose material, emotional, and sexual insecurities make them particularly vulnerable to those products' appeal. Indeed, these depictions exemplify Kathy Peiss's analysis of beauty culture as "a system of meaning that helped women navigate the changing conditions of modern social experience" (6). The reader can gauge, in fact, a Fauset heroine's dependence on her femininity and her investment in the heterosexual economy by the qualitative and quantitative descriptions of products on her dressing table. Fauset's narrative representation of advertising—the packaging of products to appeal specifically to female consumers and, in turn, the self-packaging of those consumers to appeal to men—mirrors the advertising strategies she and her publishers employed to sell this novel.

"What goes on within the walls which the more advanced classes of colored Americans have built about their private lives—a separate citadel which few white Americans ever penetrate?" The aura of mystique and exclusivity and the promise of a revelation in the front-jacket teaser replicate the advertising techniques used to sell the "feminine mystique" in which middle-class women are trained to encase themselves for success on the marriage market. The production of *The Chinaberry Tree* as an object to be coveted, handled, and ultimately purchased mirrors the very objectification and social pressure toward self-objectification with which Fauset's female protagonists struggle and which her novels simultaneously promote and subvert. The jacket blurb discursively mirrors the harshest realities of the marriage economy: the "advanced" middle classes of blacks, like respectable (white) women, protect themselves from white (male) penetration; however, the logic runs, the reader as consumer can purchase the right to enter that world, to penetrate those fiercely guarded walls. The message here is not subliminal. Analyzing the novel's commercial representation and its elicited critical reception enables us to think about how Fauset's struggle for artistic recognition and remuneration corresponds to her protagonists' struggles to balance the development of their identities with their need to adapt to a society that discourages that development. In short, Fauset goes to great lengths to sell a version of *The Chinaberry Tree* that does not exist. The exotic, never-before-told story promised on the jacket does not match the novel it encases. The slippage between *The Chinaberry Tree* as product and as text symbolizes both the narrative tension between romantic myth and sexual reality as well as Fauset's own ambivalence toward the genre she appropriates.

In her introduction, whose rhetorical logic merits almost as close a reading as the novel it promotes, Gale adopts the voice of fair-minded American liberalism to draw the attention of its social peers to the existence of the black bourgeoisie. She first emphasizes the exclusivity of this community, while decrying the need to affirm its existence, and implicitly stresses its class superiority to many whites, who "serve them in shops and in traffic" (vii). She then employs a false delicacy, suggesting her own and the reader's impertinence to look at, to invade, and to penetrate this cloistered world of black respectability. In this rhetorical gesture, Gale resembles a circus ringmaster or cabaret emcee; while appealing to the reader's fine sensibilities (respect for privacy, the dignity of social ritual) she establishes and authorizes the reader's position in the spectacle. The reader, she implies, is about to enter the "real" world of this novel, a world so real that she may feel like an intruder.[1] Gale's introduction foregrounds the exceptionality of the novel's depicted community and barely alludes to the novel's themes, so that the text is made to resemble a sociological study rather than a work of fiction. By its penultimate paragraph, Gale's introduction pleads the case of the black bourgeoisie, affirming that constituency's dignity by stressing the shame of the white reader's assumed ignorance. "It seems an impertinence. . . . It seems an impertinence. . . . Above all it seems an intrusion. . . . [Ergo] they merit" (viii). She measures each black cultural, professional, and intellectual achievement by the degree of white unawareness of it, morally compelling the reader to educate herself about these people.

In Gale's introduction to her friend's novel, Fauset herself resembles less a novelist than a native informant in an anthropological study. "[Fauset] has shown in her novels," Gale writes, "men and women *of the class to which she herself belongs*, with her wide interests and her American and European experiences" (viii; emphasis added). Gale validates Fauset as supremely positioned to tell this story as a world-traveled member of the community. Gale discursively privileges Fauset's middle-class status over her role as an artist, locating Fauset's competence in her authentic class position rather than in her literary talent. Gale's assumed role in promoting *The Chinaberry Tree* is reminiscent of Lydia Maria Child's influence in securing the publication of Harriet A. Jacobs's *Incidents in the Life of a Slave Girl*.[2] In light of Fauset's struggle to be taken seriously as an artist by her peers and the extent to which her class position continues to overdetermine her work's critical reception, Gale's virtual erasure of the literary aspects of the novel is poignantly ironic.

In his review of *The Chinaberry Tree* for the *New York Herald Tribune*, the Harlem Renaissance novelist Rudolph Fisher points out Gale's misrepresentation and tactfully (or tactically) assumes that Fauset herself had no part in it.

> There is [an] important implication to throttle, because it throws a false light on this and other Fauset novels. . . . How Miss Gale could have so soon after their appearance forgotten "Quicksand," "Passing," "The Fire in the Flint," . . . "The Blacker the Berry," and "Nigger Heaven" is curious. If the central characters in these novels had been examples of "the uneducated Negro," the books would never have been written. Miss Fauset therefore must not be judged as having cornered the market on the more literate black subject. She herself would be the last to claim that. (6)

Fisher's intervention implies that Gale's ideal reader is someone unfamiliar with black literature and by extension with black people, for her introduction effectively denies the existence of Fauset's literary peers and hinges on the book's uniqueness. Fisher takes Gale's introduction at face value as a fact-based contextualization of *The Chinaberry Tree* within American literature rather than as a deliberate appeal to white fascination with the secret lives of black people. Gale misrepresents not only *The Chinaberry Tree*'s position within black literature but also the novel's themes and primary characters.

The Gale-Fisher debate over representing *The Chinaberry Tree* to potential readers exposes the larger cultural and political conflict over value, specifically the use-value of the black middle-class subject to diverse political constituencies. The cultural marketplace privileged the very existence of a novel about a refined, successful black woman and her community over the novel's "subjectivity," that is, how and to what ends its author depicts that subject. Gale's foreword implies that *The Chinaberry Tree*'s value hinges on its exceptionality; the novel is special, not like other black novels. Fisher, on the other hand, challenges not only the veracity of that claim but also its purported significance; Fauset's novel makes sense only in relation to its literary community, the cultural context that Gale's argument denies.

Despite its author's and publisher's attempts to commercialize it, *The Chinaberry Tree* strains to burst through its critical wrappings. Gale's discussion may apply to *There Is Confusion*, which emphasizes its central family's counterstereotypical bourgeois identification. Yet with *The Chinaberry Tree*, Fauset breaks her own rules, representing class and cultural diversity within the black community and employing at times the very devices she previously eschewed. For example, Gale writes that Fauset "forgoes the color, the richness, the possibility of travesty and comedy and the popular appeal of the uneducated Negro with his dialect and idiom, his limited outlook" (vii). Quite the contrary—*The Chinaberry Tree* is, in fact, Fauset's only novel to feature comic "darkies." The figures of Johnathan and Johnasteen Stede, working-class blacks, represent old-fashioned values of labor, personal dignity, and loyalty. At the same time, Johnasteen's social and physical awkwardness and Johnathan's malapropisms and constant peckishness render both characters figures of fun, comic relief from the complex trials of the fully developed, more readily assimilated primary characters.

Fauset's repeated and excessive descriptions of her more aesthetically and culturally favored protagonists' dress and toilette draw attention to themselves; few critics have failed to comment (usually negatively) on what the late Barbara Christian called Fauset's "voluptuously reported" (46) lifestyle details. These extravagances are more than appeals to a popular female audience and more than reflections of the author's appreciation of fragrance and frills. Far from getting carried away by her own depictions, Fauset inscribes characters who get carried away *by* the values these prod-ucts and their pursuit represent and *from* those values that distinguish their household in a repressed and stagnant community. These descriptive extravagances erupt so frequently and predictably that the narrative imbal-ance they engender suggests a deliberate inscription of thematic imbal-ance. *The Chinaberry Tree*'s readers learn not only what cosmetics Melissa uses but also what tools she uses to apply them. We know that the girl plans to serve beans in green ramekins to her half-sibling fiancé and when and where she plans to buy them on sale. (In offering the domestically ignorant reader a definition of *ramekin* and its suggested uses, Fauset seems to parody the worst excesses of uplift didacticism.) Beyond brushing her eyelashes and rearranging her dishes, Melissa's self-definition and future plans remain unclear and are further obscured by the text's litany of household clutter.

Feminist scholarship has exposed the crass misogyny behind canonical dismissals of *The Chinaberry Tree*, exemplified by Robert Bone's much-quoted quip about the novel's being "about the first colored woman in New Jersey to wear lounging pajamas" (102) and subtler but equally simplistic dismissals of the novel as "genteel melodrama" (Young 206). We might now read beyond the elaborate domestic depictions to their textual and extratextual meanings, the cultural symbolic register they bring to the text. As Jean Radford reminds us in her analysis of popular romance fiction's ability to speak to its readers' contradictory subjectivities, "The repressions and repetitions in the textual system cannot be constructed merely as flaws, but are representations of the always existing conflicts in our inner and outer worlds" (14). This psychoanalytic approach to Fauset's work, par-ticularly the richly repetitive and self-contradictory *The Chinaberry Tree*, enables us to analyze how Fauset used repetition and excess to represent thematic disorder and how those formal "flaws" in the text itself reveal the disordered social context into which Fauset was writing.

The critical conversations about Fauset protagonists' grooming and housekeeping rituals have enabled a generation of Fauset scholars to con-sider the author's use of recognizably "feminine" or "popular" subjects to examine and challenge class and gender ideologies. In her groundbreaking 1981 critical biography of Fauset, Carolyn Wedin Sylvander interprets Fauset's lengthy descriptions of fashion and decor both as appeals to female readers "who might otherwise be terrified by serious fiction" and as demonstrations of Laurentine's and Melissa's efforts to appear respect-able. "Emphasis on proper appearance," she writes, "is overcompensation, in a sense, for the moral laxity assumed to be characteristic of the Black woman." Sylvander goes on to suggest that Fauset's elimination of these descriptions once the women have found loving, trustworthy men implies that the author's earlier emphasis of these matters is a strategic device rather than a stylistic flaw (202).

Sylvander's analysis opens an important space for considering the class-inflected generational dynamics within the Strange family and Fauset's own use of class-based assumptions to represent these dynamics. Sal Strange was a servant in the Halloway household before she became involved with her employers' son. Laurentine, the relationship's issue, has risen in status as a locally renowned and sought-after dressmaker who employs two assistants. As a member of a burgeoning constituency of self-made women, like Maggie in There Is Confusion, Laurentine is subject to the pressure of female commodification, a condition from which her economic independence excludes her but by which her new class affiliation constructs her. Laurentine's overcompensation serves, then, as a sign of her social insecurity, the extent to which her class ascendance has left her unsure of how to represent herself to and move within society. Laurentine and Melissa wrap themselves not only in the products geared to middle-class women but also in the very myths that sell those products, the images of womanliness promised in those products.

Her characters' reliance on commercial myths of femininity demonstrates Fauset's exploitation of advertising rhetoric to represent the gendered cultural spaces that both she and her fictional subjects occupy. Jennifer Wicke's analysis of advertising as literature's "shadow partner" (3) enables a reading of The Chinaberry Tree's "advertising impulse" (2), that is, the text's relentless depictions of feminine self-fashioning, grounded in commercial images of gender identity: "To look at [Melissa's dressing table] always amused Laurentine. She herself could have been taken for a Parisian model, her elegance, her freshness, her discreet use of discreet scents and powders. . . . Melissa had creams, cleansing ones, tissue-building ones—of all things with her gorgeous youth!—vanishing creams, tints for darkening the eyelids, tiny brushes for eye lashes, tweezers to shape her eyebrows, pastes for finger-nails, powders in several tints" (127). Through cataloging the contents of Melissa's dressing table, Fauset materializes the younger woman's faith in scents and soaps (all the perfumes in Jersey) to cleanse her of disrepute, and both women's self-representation through the products they choose. Fauset assumes her readers' fluency in the semiotics of beauty culture while critiquing the industry's incitement and exploitation of what Simone Weil Davis calls the "anxiety about one's inherent odiousness" (10). Laurentine's comparison of Melissa's haphazard collection of implicitly ill-chosen cosmetics with her own tasteful choices contrasts the teenager's social desperation and pretense (suggested by paints and tints) with the older cousin's class-coded toiletries. Unlike Joanna in *There Is Confusion*, Laurentine is not an ascetic; in her desire to present a tasteful, upmarket image she prefers products advertised as tasteful and upmarket.[3]

Elizabeth Ammons rightly argues that Fauset's own stable bourgeois assumptions are evident in these descriptions (213) as her characters, in order to achieve their desired status, must abandon their conspicuous ways.[4] Perhaps the impact of another aspect of the author's identity reveals itself more immediately in her characters' self-commodification, particularly Laurentine's. A month before resigning from the literary editorship of the *Crisis*, Fauset wrote to NAACP chairman Joel Spingarn for assistance in finding new work. Her letter reveals the difficulties of securing suitable employment for even this most educated and accomplished of women. Having reminded Spingarn of her two (Ivy League) degrees, Phi Beta Kappa membership, and excellent French, she advises him also of her typing skills but admits to an ignorance of shorthand (78–79). The letter reveals the desperation harrowing to any reader familiar with Fauset's life and work. What for Fauset must have been an excruciatingly humiliating need to ask a powerful white man for help ("Please," she writes to Spingarn, "do not think I'm making no effort to help myself") illustrates the financially vulnerable reality behind the artistic, intellectual, and social prominence.[5] Fauset, who was forty-three at the time, asserts her "loyal and honest" traits over her unique professional expertise. Keen not to return to teaching, this noted race woman offers that "if the question of color should come up I could of course work from home."

Ultimately, Fauset returned to teaching. She married Herbert Harris in 1929, two years before *The Chinaberry Tree*'s publication. Until she was in her early sixties Fauset worked full-time; her letters to friends reveal a woman with little time left over from her editorial, teaching, and household responsibilities to write, and little money to travel and to continue her already advanced education.[6] As a woman who remained unmarried until she was forty-seven, Fauset had little intimate knowledge of the leisured woman's lifestyle, and despite—or because of—her financial constraints, she must have taken pride in the self-sufficiency that she attributes to her similarly independent heroines. Laurentine Strange is Fauset's most mature and financially successful protagonist to date; unlike *There Is Confusion*'s Maggie and *Plum Bun*'s Angela, she supports herself more than adequately and hardly needs a meal ticket. Fauset's subjectivity, combined with her representation of Laurentine's independence and moral certainty, lends a noticeable tartness to the protagonist's overwrought courtship strategies.

As in her earlier novels, Fauset's detailed depictions of her protagonist's preparation for sexual combat (and subsequent defeat) serve to produce in the female reader an identification with the character and to reveal both the reader's and character's vulnerability to, complicity with, and underestimation of their social constructedness. As Ann duCille argues, "such dressing scenes . . . often unfold in the form of double-edged, revealing details that cut through to the underside of the garments, leaving the characters exposed, vulnerable—almost as if the very act of dressing the body is an undressing of the soul" (98). Following Ammons's reading of Fauset's parodic descriptions of her characters' overinvestment in showy materialism, duCille considers these depictions to be Fauset's social commentary on her characters' class desires.

Kimberley Roberts's analysis of Harlem Renaissance prostitution imagery provides a useful context for Laurentine's feminine self-representation.. Writing on the fiction of Nella Larsen and Claude McKay, Roberts notes that "as the prostitute makes [the] triad [of sexuality, economics, and color] most literal—in that she makes herself sexually desirable and different from the 'respectable' woman through her colorful appearance in order to seek sex—she opens up a space for the analysis of the commodification of the exotic/erotic during the Harlem Renaissance as well as of the class and gender oppression forced upon Harlem society by the dicta of the bourgeois black elite" (109). The construction of Laurentine's self-betrayal as a dalliance with marriage as a fundamentally economic arrangement continues and deepens Fauset's exploration of the commodification of women in *Plum Bun*. Laurentine, desperate to appear respectable, struggles to strike that fine balance between virgin and whore called "marriage material" and slumps rather hopefully toward the latter.

In an early date-dressing scene, Laurentine puts on an impeccably cut outfit with a mink collar and reasons that if her dressmaking business continues on its course, "she would be able to treat herself to an entire coat of the beautiful fur. But it would be fun, it would be marvelous to receive such a coat from Phil" (35). Even more telling than the commodification issue is Laurentine's struggle to reimagine herself not as a woman who earns a living by making and selling clothes but rather as a woman for whom men buy clothes, particularly furs. In order to enter this marriage economy, Laurentine will have to forgo the pride of being able to clothe herself, to keep herself warm, for the convention of allowing a man to take care of her as well as of modeling for society his income in an expensive coat. The deliberateness of this image, with regard to Laurentine's fashion career and in light of her mother's legacy, cannot be overestimated. Having inverted constructions of wife and mistress in the parents, Fauset posits in the daughter an awareness of the commercial aspects of marriage and a rejection of Sal's unwitting iconoclasm.

Laurentine produces and markets images of affluent womanhood; she fashions other women's as well as her own self-presentation. To the literal reader—and later, to the text's resident ideal reader, Mrs. Ismay—Laurentine, characterized always by her elegance and self-restraint, also functions as what Simone Weil Davis calls the product's "vehicle," the figure whose persona represents and enhances the product's image (112). Beyond blurring the distinction between producer and vehicle, Laurentine, by dressing herself, destabilizes her role as a consumer who buys, or buys into, others' images of correct femininity. Her fur-coat fantasy represents the extent to which the marriage economy obliges her to "pass" or disappear into what Davis calls "thing status" (112), or pure vehicle status, as a woman who will wear clothes bought for her to advertise her social position and her husband's financial success. In order to achieve bourgeois feminine perfection, Laurentine must transform herself from fashion's producer to its trademark.

In a construction of marriage that privileges the social institution over the spiritual expression, female sexual desire becomes both excess and liability. Fauset's critical reputation for Victorian primness notwithstanding, *The Chinaberry Tree* is an earthy novel. Sal has had socially proscribed sex with Halloway, Judy has had sex with lots of "big, hard, sweaty, black fellows" (15), and Harry Robbins publicly manhandles Melissa while older men appraise her body and gait. The calculated barrenness of Laurentine's feelings for Hackett stands out in this novel that depicts all manner of sexual energy. The possibility for and interest in physical contact, much less sex, is written out of Laurentine's interest in Hackett as Fauset depicts her protagonist's desire for a kiss as the desire for social validation. "She had so wanted his kiss—bestowed with love, with ardor, with respect. Yet she knew that his reticence had really been the finest expression of that respect" (40). The lack of sexual desire, in this formula, confirms esteem. Fauset implicitly critiques this erasure of female desire and of sexual interest from the marriage economy by depicting Laurentine's self-doubt and by representing the protagonist's suppression of her own desire to conform to conventional models of respectability. The conflicting signals of her date-wear mirror the mixed messages, ideological discord, and contradiction that inscribe a woman's subjectivity in courtship ritual.

Zona Gale's introduction addresses the white female reader; the novel itself appeals to this reader, but its most explicit and innovative appeal is to a black female constituency. Laurentine Strange is not a doctor's daughter, an Old Philadelphian debutante, or a college graduate; as the illegitimate daughter of a maid and the son of the family she served, Laurentine is a working-class seamstress who builds her own successful dressmaking business. Majestic beauty and uncommon style aside, however, she is hardly the standard heroine of ladies' fiction, for her social origins are not merely humble but socially debased. The text brandishes this product of an interracial extramarital affair as not only a suitable but also a logical romantic heroine. The narrative moral economy that privileges natural love over social convention and legitimacy posits Laurentine as the idealized female subject. *The Chinaberry Tree* claims the romantic novel for black American women, whose access and relation to the conventions extolled in this genre are overdetermined by the legacy of slavery. By casting as her heroine a black woman whose social position is neither sanitized, condemned, nor obscured but rather is central to the plot and justified, even celebrated by the narrative ethic, Fauset speaks directly to the female reading subject previously erased (at best) by this genre. A feminist reading of *The Chinaberry Tree*, perhaps more so than of Fauset's other novels, requires us to consider the subjectivities of Fauset's imagined readers, the role of popular culture in private as well as communal identity formation, and as a site of pleasure, not just ideological indoctrination. *The Chinaberry Tree* is a pleasurable text; part of this reader's pleasure in reading the innumerable depictions of household furnishings, clothing, and toiletries lies in recognizing Fauset's unconcealed delight in writing them. Fauset's own interest in female popular culture is evident in her detailed representations, which demonstrate that this politically committed professional woman considered fabric and fragrance, too, fertile topics for literature.

In order to accept Gale's assertion that the novel focuses on the exclusive society of educated blacks, one must read *The Chinaberry Tree* as a class-based rescue drama in which Laurentine Strange, cast adrift from the natural aristocracy of which she is a member, languishes in obscurity, scorned by her inferiors, until she is discovered by her real peers and restored to her deserved position. Hackett is the wrong love interest, and Laurentine's interest in him embodies the wrong desires. Fauset represents Laurentine's attempts to gain social respectability as a revenge fantasy; by marriage to one of the richest black men in town, she might queen it over the Red Brook snobs and win their acceptance if not their veneration. This socially motivated interpretation of marriage runs counter to the text's ethos; Laurentine betrays her own values of emotional honesty and self-reliance by fantasizing about the coat Hackett might purchase for her. She symbolically prostitutes herself, donning a form-fitting (but high-necked) red dress in an attempt to vamp him into marrying her, believing that through marriage to this successful ash-collector's son, she might scale the social heights. Meanwhile, however, in the proverbial kingdom not that far away, is the real bourgeoisie, represented as far too grand and secure for petty snobbery and endowed with the taste and culture to appreciate Laurentine's innate nobility.

This reading rationalizes the relatively late emergence of the Browns, the Ismays, and Dr. Denleigh, whose education (they are all, unlike Red Brook's self-styled social denizens, college graduates) and professional and cultural superiority not only expose Red Brook's social provincialism but also provide an exalted milieu in which Laurentine might flourish. *The Chinaberry Tree* thus becomes a class melodrama; Laurentine is noticed, wooed, and finally won by the bourgeoisie. She herself effects this rescue by embodying a feminized attitude in relation to her masculinized pursuers.

Initially, Laurentine's internalized shame leads her to refuse the bourgeoisie's advances. Assuming that all middle-class "respectable" blacks are as intolerant as those who scorned her family, Laurentine refuses Mrs. Ismay's patronage, claiming that her white customers might object. Fauset eroticizes Laurentine's cool reserve and unapproachability and particularly Mrs. Ismay's response: "She had meant to order only one [dress] but this girl's bearing, her real queenliness . . . confused her" (56). Laurentine makes herself irresistible by showing no interest in this woman's society; rather, she passively allows herself to be pursued and cajoled. Lurking rather slinkily in a parked car, Mrs. Ismay comes almost to resemble a stalker: "She straightened up from the cushions against which she had been lolling and crossing the pavement met Laurentine as she passed, still nonchalant and self-possessed, through the gates. The doctor's wife touched the girl's hand fleetingly, her arm slid round her waist. 'Miss Strange,—Laurentine—do come home with me and spend the afternoon'" (84). Laurentine's cool dissemblance in front of Hackett attracts Mrs. Ismay, propelling her out of the car and into a contrived meeting with her prey. Fauset inscribes in this exchange between the imperious younger woman and the practiced older one a physical intimacy at once seductive and familiarly primal. Mrs. Ismay seduces Laurentine into her bourgeois fold and away from the peasantry Sal represents. The flirtatious physical (touching Laurentine's waist) and social ("I shall be all alone") liberties she takes contrast starkly and provocatively with Sal's almost wincing fear of her daughter. At the same time, this confrontation, this mirror-stage moment of class- and commercial-bound recognition exemplifies what Simone Weil Davis describes as "the pleasure of performance and the erotics of the commodity braid[ed] together inextricably with the anxiety incited by that same culture to motivate and fuel such stagings" (13). Fauset eroticizes Laurentine's initial rejection, Mrs. Ismay's persistence, and both women's ultimate recognition of Mrs. Ismay as Laurentine's ideal consumer—the very embodiment of leisured black femininity.

The infamous lounging pajamas make their first appearance in an extended "girl talk" scene between Laurentine and Millie Ismay. Through the characters' gush over fabric and tailoring, Fauset represents female culture as a space in which women develop and articulate intimacy and mutual recognition. "Laurentine would hold the cloth up against Mrs. Ismay's skin and drape with her magic fingers the stuff into marvelous fold and line, employing an enthusiasm and liveliness of interest such as she rarely manifested to her customers" (146). As critics like Alison Lurie and Valerie Steele have argued of a semiotics of fashion, Fauset's characters' dressing speaks a language of social engagement. Clothing gives Laurentine and Mrs. Ismay the opportunity to touch and to scrutinize each other, a space in which to perform their familiarity with one another and to communicate their shared (and mutual) interest. With the woman whose social position once intimidated Laurentine, the dressmaker can now relax as a social peer rather than a tradeswoman. The commercial space—shifted from Laurentine's dress shop to Mrs. Ismay's dressing room—offers an erotic space, a site where product and pleasure become indistinguishable.

Later when Laurentine does, like Cinderella, go to the symbolic ball—that most bourgeois of social rituals, the small dinner party—and meets Denleigh, the requisite prince is displaced as seducer by the Ismay household, where "a hazy veil of sunlight hung over the darkened dining room, affording a hazy background to what, it seemed to the young guest, must be a dream" (87). Fauset breathlessly depicts the Ismay household as familiar, enveloping, and embracing in its "lack of restraint the utter feeling of peace and content" (87). The bourgeoisie, embodied in its sanctum sanctorum, the home, welcomes its rightful chatelaine. The dining table becomes the site of Laurentine's social consummation.

This analysis of *The Chinaberry Tree* foregrounds the notion of female consumerism as a means of making or projecting a self-image; crucial to any reading of the novel is a consideration of its protagonist's profession. Laurentine's success as a *modiste* depends on her ability literally to sell good taste—the casual but luxurious elegance exemplified by the lounging pajamas—to affluent New Jersey matrons. Moreover, Laurentine's clientele is exclusively white until she agrees to sell to Mrs. Ismay, who ultimately introduces Laurentine to her future husband and symbolically initiates Laurentine into the black upper-middle class. That Laurentine originally worries that black patronage might compromise her business implies the extent to which the style—the elegance that she sells—hinges on a black-white exchange: a white "taste" shaped and manufactured by an exotic, excluded black gaze and labor. Mrs. Ismay's patronage breaks a color barrier and suggests yet another level of exchange—a black-originated style refined, authorized, and commercialized by white consumption.

Fauset's admitted attention to the literary marketplace enables us to recognize Laurentine Strange as a popularized inscription of the author's own professional struggle and cultural legacy. As a dress designer rather than a writer, Laurentine—like Fauset—embodies Nina Miller's definition of the modernist woman writer as "a subject, a producer, and (directly or indirectly) an icon of popular culture" (4). Laurentine's commercial success hinges on her self-representation as a woman whose innate style and artistic talent authorize her to make and sell taste to other women. The reader imagines Laurentine as a lonely, socially excluded schoolgirl studying fashion magazines from which she gleans not only how to make herself appear refined—what kind of figure to cut—but also how to buy the cloth that cuts that figure. The "germ" of fashion that Laurentine isolates is the relationship between her own identification with images of bourgeois womanhood and her ability to reproduce and sell that identification—as much as the image itself—to other women.

Perhaps we might read this economy of Laurentine Strange's dress business as a synecdoche of *The Chinaberry Tree*'s commercial seduction, the extent to which the text itself is captivated by the commerce it depicts and the advertising strategies used to promote it. Fauset's own description of studying the *Saturday Evening Post* to "isolate the germ" of popular fiction suggests honing strategies to apply to her work as well as taking possession of the genre's essence in order to mutate it. We must also consider how gendered, racialized, and class-informed readings further captivate and mutate *The Chinaberry Tree*, especially in light of critical mutations of

Fauset's literary reputation as a bourgeois apologist. If Zona Gale's introduction authorizes the novel's representation of the mores of the black bourgeoisie to an imagined white bourgeois readership, perhaps that commercial authorization indirectly but convincingly authenticates the novel's use value to an upwardly mobile black readership. Such a didactic, embarrassingly Booker-T.-Washington, "topsheets and toothbrushes" approach to uplift was no doubt the furthest thing from Fauset's political values and literary project. However, that very conduct-book appeal may have inadvertently emerged as the novel's most effective selling point to a black readership. As Stuart Hall reminds us, "in the study of popular culture, we should always start here: with the double-stake in popular culture, the double movement of containment and resistance, which is always inevitably inside it" (228). *The Chinaberry Tree* both embodies Hall's dialectic and nudges it even further back to Fauset herself, the producer who remains a cultural worker and, one hopes, a cultural work-in-progress.

Notes

1. I liken Gale's rhetorical strategy to that of a ringmaster or emcee because of the way she deliberately blurs her representation of what is to follow and of her own and the readers' position vis-à-vis the spectacle.
2. Harriet Jacobs tried for years to find a publisher for her autobiography and wrote to Child for help. The manuscript finally found a publisher, Thayer and Eldridge, who insisted that Child write the preface. For further accounts of Child's role in promoting Jacobs's narrative and in editing the text to appeal to a white female readership, see Jean Fagan Yellin's introduction to Jacobs's *Incidents in the Life of a Slave Girl, Written by Herself* and Carolyn L. Karcher, *The First Woman in the Republic: A Cultural Biography of Lydia Maria Child* (Durham, N.C.: Duke University Press, 1994).
3. Peiss's discussion of women's cosmetic choices as a means of expressing class identity and desire examines how "scent, color palettes, and packaging carried elusive but legible signs of status." Laurentine's cosmetics represent her identification with upper-class women, to whom "high-priced or imported brands with light scent and natural tints" were marketed (190).
4. In *The Coupling Convention,* duCille takes issue with Ammons's assertion that Fauset's depictions of conspicuous consumption reveal her own class biases, and argues "that it is the *characters'* not Fauset's, class pretensions and standards of propriety and decency that are at issue here" (99; emphasis in original). I feel compelled to address what I consider a false distinction here because it is crucial not only to my own argument but also to the basis of all reassessments of Fauset's work since Sylvander's biography. Ammons's point draws attention to the fact that Fauset's female protagonists, contrary to most critical misreadings, do not share her class position but rather aspire to it. While reevaluations of

Fauset cannot go far enough, it seems, to redress the false assumption that Fauset was simply a bourgeois propagandist, it is important to recognize that Fauset's work undermines and challenges class constructions at the same time as it necessarily, as a cultural product, reflects its own investments in those constructions. Part of the challenge of Fauset's work (and its reward) is in examining how Fauset, a middle-class subject and political activist, balanced, at times more successfully than others, both influences in her writing voice.

5. Kevin Gaines offers an insightful reading of this slippage in his discussion of Alice Dunbar-Nelson's diary, which, he writes, "provides a document of painful truths masked by dissemblance, as the record of [Dunbar-Nelson's] daily life captures the complex relationship between public and private life for many privileged blacks. The pressures of genteel poverty fed the gnawing doubts she harbored about her self-worth, public life, and leadership status, doubts she was disinclined to raise in public" (213).

6. In her 20 April 1924 letter to Langston Hughes, Fauset confided her plans for an extended trip to Europe, which she imagined would be her last. She makes light of her financial straits: "Of course the money is the main thing. I am saving every penny—but oh I do love pretty clothes! I didn't care such a lot about them when I was a girl in the high school, but as a grown-up woman! However, I want to travel and to write even more than I want the pretty things so I guess I'll accomplish them."

Works Cited

Ammons, Elizabeth. "New Literary History: Edith Wharton and Jessie Redmon Fauset." *College Literature* 13 (Fall 1987): 207–18.

Bone, Robert. *The Negro Novel in America*. Rev. ed. New Haven, Conn.: Yale University Press, 1965.

Christian, Barbara. *Black Women Novelists: The Development of a Tradition, 1882–1976*. Westport, Conn.: Greenwood, 1980.

Davis, Simone Weil. *Living Up to the Ads: Gender Fictions of the 1920s*. Durham, N.C.: Duke University Press, 2000.

duCille, Ann. *The Coupling Convention: Sex, Text, and Tradition in Black Women's Fiction*. New York: Oxford University Press, 1993.

Fauset, Jessie Redmon. *The Chinaberry Tree: A Novel of American Life*. Introd. Zona Gale. New York: Frederick A. Stokes, 1931.

———. Letter to Joel Spingarn, 26 January 1926. Schomburg Center for Research in Black Culture, New York. In Carolyn Wedin Sylvander. "Jessie Redmon Fauset." *Afro-American Writers from the Harlem Renaissance to 1940*. Ed. Trudier Harris and Thadious M. Davis. Detroit, Mich.: Gale Research, 1987, 78–79.

———. Letter to Langston Hughes, 20 April 1924. Langston Hughes Papers, James Weldon Johnson Memorial Collection, Beinecke Rare Book and Manuscript Library, Yale University.

———. *Plum Bun: A Novel without a Moral*. 1928. Introd. Deborah E. McDowell. Boston: Beacon, 1990.

————. *There Is Confusion.* New York: Boni and Liveright, 1924.

Fisher, Rudolph. "Where Negroes Are People." Review of *The Chinaberry Tree*, by Jessie Fauset. *New York Herald Tribune Books*, 17 January 1932, 6.

Gaines, Kevin K. *Uplifting the Race: Black Leadership, Politics, and Culture in the Twentieth Century.* Chapel Hill: University of North Carolina Press, 1996.

Hall, Stuart. "Notes on Deconstructing 'The Popular.'" In *People's History and Socialist Theory.* Ed. Raphael Samuel. London: Routledge, 1981, 227–40.

Jacobs, Harriet. *Incidents in the Life of a Slave Girl, Written by Herself.* Ed. and introd. Jean Fagan Yellin. Cambridge, Mass.: Harvard University Press, 1987.

Karcher, Carolyn. *The First Woman in the Republic: A Cultural Biography of Lydia Maria Child.* Durham, N.C.: Duke University Press, 1994.

Lurie, Alison. *The Language of Clothes.* New York: Random House, 1981.

Miller, Nina. *Making Love Modern: The Intimate Public Worlds of New York's Literary Women.* New York: Oxford University Press, 1998.

Peiss, Kathy. *Hope in a Jar: The Making of America's Beauty Culture.* New York: Holt, 1998.

Roberts, Kimberley. "The Clothes Make the Woman: The Symbolics of Prostitution in Nella Larsen's *Quicksand* and Claude McKay's *Home to Harlem.*" *Tulsa Studies in Women's Literature* 16 (Spring 1997): 107–30.

Radford, Jean. "A Certain Latitude: Romance as Genre." *Gender, Language, and Myth: Essays on Popular Narrative.* Ed. Glenwood Irons. Toronto: University of Toronto Press, 1992, 3–19.

Starkey, Marion L. "Jessie Fauset." *Southern Workman* 61 (May 1932): 217–20.

Steele, Valerie. *Fashion and Eroticism: Ideals of Feminine Beauty from the Victorian Era to the Jazz Age.* New York: Oxford University Press, 1985.

————. *Fetish: Fashion, Sex, and Power.* New York: Oxford University Press, 1996.

Sylvander, Carolyn Wedin. *Jessie Redmon Fauset, Black American Writer.* Troy, N.Y.: Whitson, 1981.

Wicke, Jennifer. *Advertising Fictions: Literature, Advertisement, and Social Reading.* New York: Columbia University Press, 1988.

Young, James O. *Black Writers of the Thirties.* Baton Rouge: Louisiana University Press, 1973.

The Wages of Virtue: Consumerism and Class Formation in Fannie Hurst's Back Street

STEPHANIE BOWER

Critics, by and large, have not been kind to Fannie Hurst. Reviewers of her era dismissed her as the "sob-sister of American fiction" and relegated Hurst, in the words of one particularly vicious review, to the purview of the "overpainted little shopgirl whose alleged mind can travel no further than the distance from the first to the last page of the worst tabloid" (Salpeter 612). Though some critics likened the intensity and scope of her work to that of Balzac, Zola, and Dreiser, most found fault with its crude and overdrawn sentimentality. Indeed, Hurst's own autobiography seemingly endorses this verdict (even as it reverses its valuation) insofar as it takes as an ongoing concern her anxious intuition that popularity comes at the cost of "literary stature." "Rather be a classical failure than a popular success" goes the refrain that haunts her when comparing herself to such contemporaries as Willa Cather and Ernest Hemingway (*Anatomy* 259). Nor have more recent critics done much to challenge Hurst's self-assessment. Critical attention has focused almost exclusively on cinematic adaptations of her novels, locating in some of these films a subversive subtext absent from the novels themselves. Studies in melodrama, for example, have found in Douglas Sirk's version of *Imitation of Life* (1933) an ironic rendition of bourgeois ideology that subverts the false moralism of Hurst's text. For Jon Halliday, "Sirk fight[s]—and transcend[s]—the universe of Fannie Hurst" (9–10). Even feminist critics who dispute the implicit misogyny of such claims have not revisited the novels themselves; their identification of resistance to patriarchal narratives is similarly located within such adaptations.

An overview of *Back Street* (1930), one of Hurst's most popular books, confirms the middle-class moralism with which she is charged: a career woman is undone and finally destroyed by her love for a married man. In this reading, the punishment Hurst metes out for her heroine's sexuality accords with the assumption that such deviants pay a moral if not a material price for their transgression. I argue here that another reading of the novel emerges when we position it within contemporary debates about gender and consumption—a reading that makes visible Hurst's critique of the gender roles at the heart of middle-class authority. Instead of endorsing bourgeois ideology, Hurst's narrative undercuts the privilege granted to its hallowed spaces. For the fallen woman in Hurst's novel does not in fact follow the trajectory familiar to readers from other novels and films; unlike those heroines, who use their sexuality to negotiate their social ascent, acquiring along the way the diamonds and furs that signal their upper-class status and their moral degeneration, Ray Schmidt ends up more as Angel in the House than mistress; the home she maintains for her lover is an idealized enactment of middle-class domesticity. Thus Hurst dramatizes an imagined identification between fallen woman and wife that some commentators locate within a gendered model of consumerism. According to this logic, once women are rendered as economically dependent upon men—consumers rather than producers—their bodies become their only means of assuring prosperity or even survival, translated into a sexual economy that flattens out the moral distinctions between the (middle-class) wife and the (upper-class) mistress or (lower-class) prostitute. By displacing virtue from wife onto mistress, Hurst calls into question the model of femininity by which the middle class identifies itself and claims its authority. Yet I suggest here too that Hurst accomplishes this critique through an anti-Semitic framework; consumerism in this novel is not only gendered but also racialized, so that Ray escapes the condemnation otherwise accorded her because her lover is Jewish. Race, in this reckoning, secures the class categories endangered by the redemption of the fallen woman.

Golddiggers and Parasites

By the early twentieth century, the "fallen woman" familiar to audiences and readers from eighteenth- and nineteenth-century melodramas had taken on a new guise as the golddigger or, as she was called early in the period, the "female parasite." Instead of following the fallen woman's usual descent into ignominy and death, the parasite usually prospers from vice; if Stephen Crane's *Maggie* (1893) stands as the parodic culmination of the earlier type, Dreiser's *Sister Carrie* (1900) might serve as her twentieth-century incarnation, the financial success she enjoys at the end of the book (courtesy of her male admirers) prefiguring a rash of books and films that feature women who use their bodies as social currency. Novels such as David Graham Phillips's *Susan Lenox: Her Fall and Rise* (1917) and Anita Loos's *Gentlemen Prefer Blondes* (1925), and films such as *Baby Face* (1933) and *Red Headed Woman* (1932)—all to a greater or lesser extent feature heroines who translate their sexuality into fame and fortune. Set within this cultural landscape, Hurst's tale of a woman who trades a lucrative career to live tucked away with barely enough money for food and rent, all in the name of love for a married man, stands as an anomaly. Ray's affair yields not a Manhattan penthouse but a modest apartment where she acts out a nineteenth-century ideal of middle-class domesticity; this reversal of expectations, I suggest, calls attention to an implicit identification between wives and mistresses generated within a newly emergent discourse of gender and consumption.

After the widespread availability of mass-produced household goods transferred production from the household to the factory, middle-class women became defined primarily through their role as consumers, a form of economic agency recognized but largely disparaged in contemporary writings. Richard Ohmann's account of the emergence of mass culture during this period argues, for example, that the "displacement of home production amounted also to a redefinition of gender, especially for women. . . . From acting as part of a semi-autonomous productive unit, women gradually gave up parts of their works and skill to industrial capitalists. . . . Women's productive activities were devalued and made almost invisible, because left out of the new money economy. But women as consumers were visible indeed" (76–77).[1] With women's participation rewritten as dependence, more and more commentators remarked upon the consequent shift in the socioeconomic axis of middle-class marriage. Without independent means of making a living, marriage was now imagined, in the words of satirist and cultural commentator H. L. Mencken, as "the best career the average woman can reasonably aspire to" (55). Here, Mencken's typically trenchant phraseology posits an identification between the housewife and the prostitute implicit within the economic reconfiguration of middle-class women's roles: the relegation of women to the (allegedly) nonproductive role of consumer establishes an economy wherein women's only assets—their bodies—are necessarily and inevitably translated into currency.

Equally if not more disturbing for many social critics, though, were the desires generated by this consumer economy. As responsibility for household consumption devolved onto the middle-class housewife, her desires became increasingly essential to a smoothly running economy. However, an economy phantasmically fueled by female desire places conflicting demands upon this housewife. On the one hand, her purchases reinforced class difference by using taste, or the proper selection of commodities, to demarcate class position. Elaine Abelson writes that "as money translated into possession, a new sense of class identity was forged, not in production but in consumption. The 'right' purchases became signals, albeit temporary, of group cohesiveness" (33). On the other hand, the gratification of these desires endangered such distinctions, since the moral authority of the middle class was grounded in character traits—self-control and restraint—notably at odds with the culture of consumption (Lears 13). The fact that consumerism was imagined as a gendered activity made class affiliations even more precarious, since as the "golddigger" makes clear, women's desire for commodities was often implicitly sexualized. That is, the consumer items displayed so enticingly at newly designed department stores were imagined to be capable of seducing housewives and working girls alike, tempting them into actions incommensurable with conventional standards of "ladylike" behavior.

This imagined conflation between wife and prostitute haunts contemporary accounts of gender, consumption, and marriage. For example, Charlotte Perkins Gilman's influential treatise *Women and Economics* harnesses the scandalous implications of this identification in order to make a rhetorical point. Her description of the "female parasite" defamiliarizes the sexual economy of the middle class by rendering women's consumption as a kind of pathology. As Gilman puts it: "While [women's] power of production is checked, [their] power of consumption is inordinately increased by the showering upon [them] of the 'unearned increment' of masculine gifts. For the woman there is, first, no free production allowed; and, second, no relation maintained between what she does produce and what she consumes" (118). Women's "natural desire to consume," detached from the "power of production" that maintains the system's equilibrium, metamorphoses into an "unnatural appetite," an "inordinate" capacity for desire without relation to economies of need or even of value. In this account, the correlation between economic dependency and "sex-attraction" collapses the distinction between the "transient trade" on the "open market of vice" (prostitution) and the "bargain for life" (marriage) (63). Given the era's identification of prostitution with the lower class, Gilman's description of marriage as another form of vice erodes one of the hallmarks of middle-class privilege, yet the outraged tone of the passage ultimately affirms the distinction she seeks to deny. That is, the identification is so hyperbolic, so deliberately provocative, that it works as much to call attention to the differences between the positions as to link them together.

Female desire, deemed so dangerous in Gilman's account for its ability to disrupt a natural balance between production and consumption, occupies such a large place in the cultural imagination of the period precisely because it conflates sexuality and consumerism. The desiring female shopper, so necessary to a consumer-driven economy, is sexualized not only because she relies upon her "sex-attraction" to fund her purchases but also because material desires meld so easily into sexual ones. In another account of marriage, Ellen Key, a Swedish "sexologist" whose books came to define the "modern" marriage for many Americans, carves out middle-class authority by formulating a model of desire that differentiates it from the immorality attributed to the upper and lower classes. "Great love," the highest state of being in Key's formulation, "arises only when desire of a being of the other sex coalesces with the longing for a soul of one's own kind" (74). Unlike in previous ages, when such longing belonged exclusively to men, now women "will no longer be captured like a fortress or hunted like a quarry; nor will she like a placid lake await the stream that seeks its way to her embrace. A stream herself, she will go her own way to meet the other stream" (82). Key defines this transmogrified desire by contrasting it with the "two lowest expressions of sexual division . . . sanctioned by society, namely *coercive marriage and prostitution*" (24), practices she later identifies with the upper and lower classes: "Marriage had to cease to be a trade among the upper classes, as prostitution still is among the hungry lower classes" (96). If the upper class produces the "kept wife, fashionable and full of pretension" (126), whose "need of maintenance" perverts the "importance of womanly love's selection for the spiritual and bodily improvement of the race" (145–46), the lower class lacks the "control of sensuality" necessary to "develop the deeper feelings of love" (112). What emerges from these strategic juxtapositions is a class defined in opposition to these excesses, produced through its identification of a female desire neither physical (the "coarse and greedy" hungers of the lower class) nor material but spiritual.

In her 1911 collection *The Morality of Women*, Key claims for women an

"erotic temperament" that clearly differentiates the woman of the twentieth century from the "passionlessness" ascribed to her foremothers. Here,
too, she attempts to cleanse such desires by denying their affinity with
marriages performed for "worldly or merely sensual motives" (*Morality* 9).
By contrast, the erotic unions she heralds involve a perfect reciprocity, an
"erotic completeness of the individually developed woman . . . which
causes her always to wish more fervently to cherish the personality of the
man as entirely as it is her happiness and her pride to be able to give her
own" (14). Yet underlying such claims for women's "erotic completion" is
a note of anxiety, sounded most clearly in her oxymoronic slogan for this
"new ideal": "self-assertion in self-surrender" (54). The fantasy this slogan
articulates—women claiming their "erotic temperaments"—is contained
by its method of implementation, a surrender of the self akin to nineteenth-century idealizations of feminine self-sacrifice. Self-assertion legitimized through self-sacrifice; this impossible economy testifies to the deep
ambivalence about women's desires and the simultaneous attempt to promote such desires through their abnegation. The appeal of this fantasy is
evidenced as well in Gilman's nostalgic evocation of a prior evolutionary
state where women's "true" nature could be revealed, where "love" and
"self-interest" were recognized as fundamentally antithetical, and where
"birth brought death." If women's "unceasing demands" currently imperil
the future of the race, Gilman uses the image of a mother who sacrifices
all for her child to imagine the end of such dangerous desires, a "sacrifice
through love" that can remove their taint only by erasing their bearer (98).
The end of desire, longingly evoked by both Key and Gilman, can be
accomplished only with the end of the desiring subject.

So far, then, we can see the ways that the shift to a capitalist mode of
production imaginatively dependent upon female desire generates discom-
forting resemblances between the sexual economy of the middle-class wife
and that of the upper-class mistress or lower-class prostitute. Commentators such as Gilman and Key invoke and disclaim this identification, recon-
figuring middle-class authority within a model of feminine self-sacrifice.
Fannie Hurst, too, invokes this identification in her portrait of a mistress
who functions as a wife and a wife who functions as a mistress. Her title
entices potential readers with its sordid suggestiveness, promising the voy-
euristic pleasures of dimly lit alleyways frequented by cheap harlots and
their desperate clientele. Yet the back street of this novel turns out to be a
comfortable, well-furnished flat in a prosperous section of Manhattan, one
lovingly overstuffed with all the trappings of home, from hand-embroi-
dered "lace mats and tidies" daintily covering chairs and tables to the smell

of "homey foods" "lurking in portieres and plushes," which give the place a "lived-in atmosphere" (162). Unlike Gilman and Key, however, Hurst renders the middle-class ideal as a house of horrors, calling attention to the virtual necrophilia latent within "self-assertion in self-surrender."

Hurst's novel begins in the 1870s, yet her heroine, Ray, epitomizes a new era; her job is described as a source of financial, social, and personal fulfillment. Working at her father's store, Ray becomes a successful and sought-after businesswoman with earnings sufficient to guarantee her livelihood; even when the store closes following her father's death, she easily obtains another more lucrative position in New York City, where she quickly earns bonuses and promotions. Once in New York she enjoys the "public excitements of hotel-lobbies, race-tracks, variety theaters," which to her are the "staff of life" (135), explaining to her roommate, "Like good times. Like to gamble. Enjoy a horse-race and can't help it. Like clothes. Loud ones" (141).

Such transgression is short-lived, however, for the allure of newfound freedom cannot withstand the compulsions of the heart, and six years later when Ray encounters Walter Saxel, previously a suitor but now a married man, she almost immediately agrees to become his mistress. At Walter's urging, Ray rents an apartment to avoid the publicity of restaurants and hotels, and there they establish the cozy domicile they will occupy for the next thirty years. Despite her long enchantment with the public sphere, Ray takes to her flat like a fish to water, decorating every nook and cranny with handmade "small gay tassels" and developing "out of the Zeus of past experiences, a talent for cookery" (161). Her flat becomes "her kennel" that beckons her during the "long, chilly intervals between leaving and returning" (161), exerting so powerful an attraction that she barely demurs when Walter asks her to quit her job and make herself continually available for the stolen lunches and hasty dinners he manages to spend with her. If, as Lea Jacobs suggests in her study of fallen women films from the 1920s and 1930s, the heroine's sexual transgression is often rendered visible within the stylistic vocabulary of modernity, here Hurst deliberately reverses this code by placing her fallen heroine within the trappings of a nineteenth-century bourgeois ideal (52–84). In so doing, Hurst visually relocates the (immoral) sexual economy of the mistress from the penthouses of the rich into the parlors of the middle class.

In only a few short months, the streets that previously seemed to Ray to be full of excitement and adventure now seem "big and exposed and unfriendly." The gaze of male passersby, previously so pleasurable, now incites only terror and revulsion: "Eyes that stole her privacy—hard small eyes and probing eyes that roved and roved all over her until the flesh felt desiccated" (189). If the sensual eroticism she previously enjoyed from this display seems a small price to pay for the rewards of being with the man she loves, a more serious price is exacted when she loses her ability to support herself. Through a disastrous misunderstanding, one of Walter's trips to Europe leaves Ray temporarily destitute, but instead of relying upon her previous capacity for "up and getting" (205), Ray sits helplessly waiting for Walter's return, unable to "get back her legs" or to "learn to walk in these regions again" (206). To pay her bills Ray takes up china painting, an occupation women's magazines such as *Good Housekeeping* recommended for the wife who sought a little supplemental income without endangering her respectability by working outside the home. In an ironic twist, her apartment, supposedly the location of domestic health and happiness, becomes a "tomb" (205), and starvation looms not because of the low wages she earns while working in the public sphere but because of the utter incapacity she experiences in the private. Though Ray embraces her new life with the same ardent passion she lavishes on her lover, Hurst emphasizes how this domesticity virtually imprisons her, inscribing her within smaller and smaller spaces until she can barely breathe and rendering the public sphere so inhospitable that she cannot enter it even to save her own life.

If Ray fulfills wifely functions in her exclusive habitation of the private realm, Walter's wife Corinne fulfills those of a mistress in her preoccupation with public pursuits. Unlike Ray, who is blissfully happy with Walter no matter his degree of wealth or success, Corinne fervently desires the social status his meteoric rise to the top will achieve for her and her children. She is consumed with "lust for the position and power and wealth of her husband and children," which becomes "the animating force of her life" (237). Like the other "kept women" living in Ray's apartment building, who skillfully manipulate their lovers to extract "furs, jewels, and the gay accouterments of indiscretion" (259), Corinne too "traffick[s] in reciprocity and demand[s] of her husband in return for what she gave," basing her marital dealings "on a plane almost as simple and tangible as book-keeping. Debit. Credit. Give what you must. Take all you can get" (252). Echoing turn-of-the-century feminists like Gilman, Hurst describes the fundamental affinity between wives and their competitors, linked despite their mutual animosity, both dependent upon men for their economic sustenance even though one trades upon her virtue and the other upon her vice. Only Ray refuses to reduce her "incalculable passion" (253) to the dry columns of an accountant's balance sheet, yet her repudiation of the economic exchange underlying her relationship means that she is constantly underpaid for her services; that is, her insistence upon defining her relationship in terms of romantic love instead of marketplace values does not remove her relationship from the marketplace but merely ensures that she will never be able to successfully negotiate a fair exchange.

The gambling tables of the French resort Aix-les-Bains enact this economic dependency in the hideous spectacle of the women who crowd around the shoulders of the big spenders, hoping that some benevolent man on a lucky streak will toss the crumbs from his winnings into the surrounding group of outstretched, grasping hands. By the end of the novel, after Walter has died without providing for Ray in his will, this desperate struggle to "clutch for spoils" (350) becomes a matter of life or death, yet once again Ray rejects the material realities that underlie the ideology of romantic love, this time with fatal consequences. With only a few centimes left to her name, Ray quells her repugnance for such a degrading spectacle and resolves to fight with the women in the pack for the small tidbits thrown her way, "to peck as they pecked—shove as they shoved—push as they pushed" (480). Her determination pays off when she catches 500 francs tossed by a distracted youth, but after she grabs the money she realizes that the identity of her unknowing benefactor is none other than Walter's youngest son, Arnold. Instead of acknowledging the reality of her relationship with Walter—an exchange of flesh for money—Ray tries to transform money into flesh, insisting that Arnold's money can be transmuted as if by alchemy into the flesh of her dead lover, a living memento of their love for one another: "Here was something more directly from the flesh of the flesh that had been Walter. Five hundred francs as if from the dead hand of Walter, by way of the live hand of his son. Catch me giving these up. . . . Catch me" (481). By denying the economic exchange at the heart of her relationship, Ray turns her own living body into a corpse, dying from starvation, clutching to her bosom the francs that could guarantee her survival.

Ray chooses to die rather than accept the sexual economy that links together wife and mistress. But instead of idealizing Ray's death with etherealized descriptions of her demise, as we might expect from sentimental conventions that turn self-sacrifice into "self-assertion" and death into a kind of spiritual apotheosis, Hurst emphasizes in gruesome detail Ray's bodily deterioration. Over and over we hear about Ray's thinning hair, which can no longer keep the dye she uses to hide the gray, or the thinning neck that makes her "take on that plucked look of old eagles" (267). By the end of the novel, her breasts have turned into "two drooping wrinkled sacs," and she has developed Parkinson's-like tremors which she can only keep controlled by wearing a jeweled hat that alerts her to her own trembling (349). Such emphasis on her physical decay undermines a nostalgic evocation of the Angel in the House insofar as it exposes this middle-class feminine ideal as a (failed) masquerade. Hurst's novel thus reconfigures the domestic body as monstrous spectacle, dislodging readers from their initial identification with Ray's eroticized submission and her adherence to domesticity.

Consumption and "the Jew"

That Walter Saxel is Jewish is neither incidental to his character nor insignificant in the novel's plot. Most obviously, his obligation to marry inside his faith triggers the events of the novel by preventing him from making Ray his wife. Yet more importantly, Hurst's portrait of Walter relies upon a network of competing, even conflicting racist stereotypes that alter Hurst's critique of the feminine ideal at the heart of bourgeois ideology. For in Hurst's rendering it is Walter's cultural difference that determines both Ray's parsimony and his wife's extravagance; the pathological poles of miserliness and enervating luxury are both understood, in other words, as Jewish cultural traits rather than essential attributes of a consumer economy. I have argued above that female consumerism necessitates a redefined locus of authority to shore up middle-class privilege. If the golddigger's ascent endangers class distinctions by suggesting that wealth and morality might not always be conjoined, so too Walter Saxel's mobility endangers racial categories by making assimilation available through purchasing power. That is, in the cultural imagination of the era, the golddigger and the Jew trace similar trajectories: both are positioned as social climbers whose ability to acquire the trappings of the well-to-do disrupts class and racial divisions. By deflecting transgression from the golddigger to the Jew and containing this transgression within the fact of cultural difference, Hurst uses the seemingly inalterable qualities of race to stabilize the blurriness of class.

Fannie Hurst discusses her Jewish identity in her autobiography, *Anatomy of Me* (1958). In that book, Hurst calls attention to the internalized anti-Semitism learned within the "middle-western world of assimilated German Jews," where Judaism had to be downplayed if not concealed lest it endanger the "middle-class respectability" to which her parents aspired (*Anatomy* 18–19). When faced with the "richus" or "race prejudice" that separates her family from neighbors, classmates, and business associates, her parents blame Russian Jews for calling attention to the marks of cultural difference. She says, "It was to be many a day before I could look upon an orthodox Jew with sideburns and a long flapping coat, without a snide sense of embarrassment for him and myself!" Aware of her own vulnerability to anti-Semitic stereotypes, Hurst comes to blame Jews for their confirmation of them: "Let a Jewish woman appear under an unseemly load of jewels and furs, even though she be only one of a group of women of many races and persuasions, similarly bedecked, and it was she whom I singled out for criticism. Despite the fact that the great financial tycoons of America are not Jews, I deplored the implications that they were." For Hurst, "it took a Hitler to blast out of regarding the Jew and his problems objectively" (350–51).

What is intriguing is the way Hurst identifies Jewish difference within a set of contrasting costumes: Jewish people are identified by their Orthodox garb and by the "jewels and furs" of the white American. Either Jews are marked as alien, or they distinguish themselves by being too American. The paradox contained within this contrast enacts the fundamental instability that Daniel Itzkovitz locates within representations of Jews at the turn of the century. "As exacting as early-twentieth-century American accounts of Jewish difference often become, they are most striking, taken as a whole, for their inability to arrive at a solid notion of 'the Jew.' Jewishness kept slipping within and among the categories of race, nation, religion and culture, and the criteria for affiliation and disaffiliation . . . were very vulnerable to contestation" ("Secret" 180).

In *Back Street*, Hurst knits together biological and cultural readings of Jewishness in her portrait of Walter and his family. Hurst consistently characterizes what she terms "the kernel of race" (265) as an instinct toward "solidarity" that excludes Gentiles like Ray. According to Ray, Walter and his race are "Snug. Right. Tight" (130); she says of Walter and his son that "the blood that bound the two was thicker than water; it was the thick coagulated blood that bound clans and made imperishable a certain heritage of Jewishness" (293). Hurst's reference to "blood" in this context renders Judaism as biological destiny, an immutable physiological fact that translates into a set of cultural characteristics. This reading of Jewish identity effectively dooms Ray and Walter's romance, so that Ray is forever shut out from "this mammoth tower of race" (81). What it also accomplishes, though, is to shift blame for anti-Semitism from Anglo-American society to the Jewish community; Jewish "solidarity" becomes responsible for the systematic exclusion of Jewish people. At one point in the novel, frustrated by her exclusion from Walter's life, Ray thinks to herself: "These solid

Jews. These sticklers for one another. These tight units of kith and kin, which are more ostracizing than ostracized" (189).

Within this paradigm of biology translated into cultural difference, Ray's selfless love for Walter acquires a somewhat different valence because it positions Walter as an unsuitable, even unnatural, object of her devotion. In the racist scheme provided by nativists such as Madison Grant, miscegenation necessarily entailed the degeneration of the white American (especially when it involved white women and "dark" men): "Whether we like to admit it or not, the result of the mixture of two races in the long run, gives us a race reverting to the more ancient, generalized and lower type . . . the cross between a white man and a negro is a negro . . . and the cross between any of the three European races and a Jew is a Jew" (Grant 16). As Ray thinks when Walter decides to marry a Jewish woman, "Intermarriages were a risk. Just as easy for a man to make up his mind to fall in love with the right girl as with the wrong. On the other hand, why should anybody not born a Jew elect to be a Jew? People born Jews turned Gentile, but who ever heard of a Gentile turning Jew?" (80). By emphasizing the biological basis of Jewish identity and thereby invoking hierarchies of racial difference, Hurst alienates readers from Ray's otherwise admirable acts of self-sacrifice, the selfless devotion so idealized within Gilman and Key.

This alienation intensifies when Hurst identifies Ray's self-sacrifice with stereotypes about the miserliness of Jews. Ray's deprivations and almost self-destructive self-denial occur not simply because she thinks of others before herself but also because Walter consistently refuses to provide her with the means necessary for even a modest lifestyle. And at different moments in the novel Hurst identifies this fiscal conservatism as a biological characteristic of his race. From the very beginning of their romance, Ray notices that Walter is "not a foolish spender" and attributes this to the fact that he is one of "those boys" (52). Once he sets up Ray in her own tiny apartment, he allots her so small a budget as to effectively hoard her for himself. He says at one point, "Try to understand, dear. Of course, I could deck you with diamonds. But I won't! I want you like this—mine alone—simple—plain. If I'm a selfish dog, I'm a selfish dog" (310). Indeed, his reluctance to expend any of his increasingly prodigious resources on Ray becomes almost pathological, perhaps signaling a kind of atavism often associated with races identified as primitive or degenerate. And Ray explicitly links this tendency toward miserliness with biology when she speculates that Walter's refusal to allow her to become pregnant originates within the tendency toward "withdrawal" identified with "the kernel of race" (265). The linkage between this "withdrawal" and the haven Ray creates for Walter transfers the associations from a racialized construction of hoarding onto a middle-class domestic ideology so that this ideology is itself figured as an atavistic remnant of a previous era.

If Walter's parsimonious treatment of Ray signals a kind of hoarding linked with Jews in the racist vocabulary of the period, the extravagance that characterizes his spending on his family fits in with another, seemingly contradictory stereotype about Jews. Ray's deprivations are consistently set against descriptions of the lavish lifestyle of Walter's family, confirming another popular representation of Jews as fat and pampered parasites. Daniel Itzkovitz documents the era's tendency to associate Jewish men with physical degeneracy that translates into economic nonproductivity: "For many turn-of-the-century American writers, Jewish relations to economic productivity became the primary means by which to understand Jewish male bodily difference" (187). But in Hurst's novel, Walter's consumption is located within the descriptions of Corinne, who grows plumper as the novel progresses. In fact, Walter's increasing prosperity is measured by the jewels and furs Corinne displays, just as it is her relentless ambition that impels his rise to the top. Over and over Corinne is defined by her "magnificent registered pearls" and her "superb chinchilla wrap, for which [Walter] had paid thirty-five thousand dollars at a Paris exposition" (312). In Ray's resentful reveries, these commodities come alive—"flawless, pink-fleshed pearls in which [Walter's] family trafficked with such munificence" and "a tender little baby fur, off an animal that could never have hurt you while it lived"—as if to register both the transformation of living flesh into commodity form and the Jew's role in performing this transaction. By persistently identifying consumerism with Corinne, Hurst thereby locates consumption within the body of the Jewish woman.

Miser and spendthrift: such paradoxical representations surface as well in the depiction of Walter's success. For even though Walter keeps Ray as a living embodiment of a bygone era—her apartment a kind of museum of nineteenth-century style and ideals—Walter and his family come to epitomize twentieth-century modernity. That is, if Ray remains virtually static during the novel's movement into the twentieth century, Walter becomes identified with the forces of modernity, his finger on the pulse of America's emergent commercial culture just as his children follow "the syncopated rhythm" (279) of the Jazz Age. Warren Susman's influential characterization of modern culture as one defined by a "culture of personality" as opposed to a "culture of character" is salient here insofar as it helps to explain Walter's move from small-town banker to international financier, a move made possible within a consumer culture that gives him access to a social set defined by purchases rather than by essence. It is important to point out in this regard the way that Walter's success is represented within the very stereotypes that Hurst later disclaims. Walter, for example, becomes one of the "great financial tycoons" typically identified as Jewish in the cultural imagination of the era. His work as an international banker gradually involves him in world economic and political events, positioning him "beside men upon whose judgment the destiny of America in world war was to be decided" (186). This rendering of the Jew as both atavistic primitive (in his miserly treatment of Ray) and exemplar of modernity confirms contradictory stereotypes about Jews at the same time as it registers Hurst's anxious relationship with a modern world imagined as fundamentally alien.[2]

Walter's entrance into the theater of world events also confirms a representation of Jewish identity described by Daniel Itzkovitz as a kind of performativity or "chameleonism." According to Itzkovitz, Jews of the era were imagined in terms of their ability to adapt or assimilate into white America, to use imitation as a vehicle of social mobility. For Itzkovitz, "Jewish performativity seemed to signal the dangers of consumer capital without the comfort and clarity of absolute difference that *Plessy's* racial distinction seemed to offer. If the Jew could become White, then anyone could become 'a Jew'" ("Passing" 40). Yet, as Itzkovitz argues, this representation of Jewish identity does not erase difference so much as locate difference within the Jew's phantasmic ability to erase difference; in Itzkovitz's words, "the Jew was most Jewish, that is, when not Jewish at all" ("Passing" 39). In the cultural imagination of the period, in other words, Jewish performativity became an essential and immutable marker of Jewish identity. I suggest that Hurst similarly contains Walter's mobility by emphasizing the gaps in his assimilation, the space of otherness that makes him a perpetual outsider in the world he inhabits. In spite of his financial and political prominence, Ray notices that Walter never seems entirely comfortable within such lofty society. When she spies Walter in conversation, for example, she notes, "A screwed expression invariably came into his features when he spoke of the banking-house whose traditions he was succeeding in carrying alone. The look of a man not sufficiently sure of himself, or the stability of achievement, to relax. The look of a man who suspects his success to be bigger than he is" (283). Here, Ray's perspective emphasizes Walter's perpetual discomfort with his position; her inner knowledge of his insecurities calls attention to the gap that prevents his full participation in that world, a gap perhaps best explained by the racial identity that marks him as different. For all his wealth and prominence, then, Walter is finally unable to assimilate into white upper-class society.

Once we read Walter's story as one of a failed passing, we might start to sketch out tentative connections between *Back Street* and another of Hurst's best sellers, *Imitation of Life* (1933); both the novel and the two cinematic adaptations have attracted much recent critical commentary for their representation of black/white relations. In fact, Ray's story is very similar to that of Bea Pullman, the protagonist in *Imitation of Life*, who also justifies transgressive behavior within the rhetoric of self-sacrifice. Throughout the novel, Bea worries over the career she creates for herself after her husband dies, fearful lest the disreputable position of a woman working outside the home taint her daughter's chances for social success. But with both her daughter and her father dependent upon Bea's earnings, such respectability is a luxury she can't afford, and she steadfastly forgoes any personal life in the task of their support. If the reiteration of this sacrifice indemnifies her against charges of unwomanly behavior, it also justifies the financial success she achieves at the end of the book, success visualized within the social mobility and consumptive practices identified, as I have argued, with the golddigger. Here again Hurst cleanses sexualized economies by racializing her depiction of consumerism, this time substituting African Americans for Jews. For the key to Bea's success comes in her relationship with an African-American woman, Delilah, another single mother who gives Bea the recipes and the inspiration for her lucrative restaurant chain. Hurst depicts Delilah as the stereotypical "mammy" familiar from plantation mythology: abject, servile, obese, and devoted to the preservation of white supremacy. Indeed, it is precisely this stereotype that fuels the restaurant's popularity, since Bea effectively commodifies the simple-minded warmth and physicality evoked within Delilah's image: "The heavy cheeks, shellacked eyes, bright, round, and crammed with vitality, huge upholstery of lips that caught you like a pair of divans into the luxury of laughter, Delilah to the life beamed out of that photography with sun power!" (105). The primitive energy communicated through this caricature proves especially appealing as an antidote to the anonymity and alienation of the city; the vitality projected onto blacks is seen as a refuge from modernity.

Delilah's resistance to the practices of modernization takes shape as well in her studied resistance to consumption; at one point she even likens Bea's decision to sell some of their old furniture to a slave auction. Delilah's nostalgic evocation of a time and a place outside industrialization draws upon the same set of racist associations as does Hurst's portrait of Walter in *Back Street*: both representations position racial others as more primitive, almost atavistic in their distance from the consumerism that characterizes the modern world. Just as in *Back Street* Hurst sets in motion dialectical representations of Jews as a means of displacing anxiety about this consumer economy, so too does she use a similar dialectic in her por-trait of Delilah's daughter, Peola, a mulatta who finally decides to renounce her mother and "pass" after sterilizing herself (to avoid the possibility of detection) and swearing her mother to secrecy. Peola articulates a model of race premised upon performance rather than biology; she is dependent upon the forces of modernization and consumption her mother finds an unnatural violation of "de Lawd's" law: "I seen her pap suffer tryin' to pass. Lord'll gimme strength for sparin' his chile dat sufferin' an' pain. . . . Ain't dat de way, though? All dese pale Northern niggers spendin' their las' pennies to git Gawd's kink out of dat hair, and all de white ladies spendin' dars to git Gawd's kink into thars. I's seen too much white-nigger heart-ache in mah time" (142). Mammy and mulatto: the racist narratives attached to each figure give voice to the wishes and fears engendered by a consumer economy—the desire for a state outside desire and for the phan-tasmic fullness embodied within Delilah's physical girth, on the one hand, and, on the other, the anxiety and attraction attached to Peola's plasticity, her ability to purchase the bodily modifications that enable her passage from one race to the other.

In the novel, unlike in the films, Peola's passing entails her disappear-ance from the narrative. Delilah's garish funeral does not bring her daugh-ter's return or her repentance, as it does in the cinematic remakes, but her virtual erasure accomplishes a similar objective insofar as it writes passing as a form of figurative death. Hurst thereby constructs a metaphoric equiv-alence between "passing" as white and "passing" away, a metaphor made literal in Peola's voluntary sterilization. In *Imitation of Life* as well as in *Back Street*, then, Hurst stages dramas of failed assimilation as both counter and complement to the class and gender transgression of her white heroines. The correspondence Hurst constructs between blacks and Jews complicates Michael Rogin's influential paradigm, wherein the immobility attached to blackness enables a corresponding fluidity for Jew-ish characters, who accomplish the movement into whiteness by differen-tiating themselves from black Americans. Reading *Back Street* in tandem with *Imitation of Life* suggests, by contrast, the way that Jewishness can function as a marker of difference that stabilizes gendered conceptions of class. Jewishness is rendered meaningful not in opposition to blackness but as a means of warding off challenges to white middle-class authority experienced within a consumer economy. Not only does this suggest the way that Hurst explores the spaces of difference between whites and Jews, but it also suggests that Hurst's depiction of Peola might enact a displaced representation of Jewish assimilation—Hurst's own unresolved identifications with Jewish identity worked out within the axis of black/white relations.

It should be clear that Hurst's novels do not present a simpleminded or monolithic endorsement of bourgeois morality. Reading them in the context of contemporary debates about consumption, class, and gender restores the network of identifications and disavowals that channels sympathy to her heroines. Such currents of feeling are more complicated than previously acknowledged: the sympathy that extends from reader to heroine can function as an implicit endorsement of transgressive behavior but only by associating transgression with the racial others who represent the heroine's most meaningful attachments. Reading the novels next to each other exposes the correspondences that chart the ways black and Jewish identities are entangled for Hurst and, more broadly, within the nation's cultural imagination. Hurst's representation of Jewishness deflects her critique of bourgeois ideology by rendering the sexual economy that transforms Ray into a living corpse a product of Walter's pathological miserliness rather than the natural consequence of an economy that positions middle-class women as domestic consumers. In other words, that Walter is Jewish works to cleanse or recuperate the sexual economy of the middle class by marking the translation of women into commodities as a product of Jewish difference. Further, Walter's social ascent and his identification with modernity create a curious parallelism with conventional representations of the golddigger; in my reading of the novel, Hurst invokes this plot yet displaces it from the golddigger to her Jewish lover so that it is he, not she, who moves up the social ladder laden with diamonds and furs. Race, in this reckoning, works to naturalize class distinctions endangered by modern conceptions of identity insofar as it provides a means of differentiating the mistress from the wife, the upstart from the upper class.

Notes

1. For other accounts of the role of women as consumers, see Horowitz and Ewen.
2. Juliet Steyn notes this contradictory representation of the Jew in her article "Charles Dickens' *Oliver Twist*: Fagin as a Sign." She describes the way that Jews seem to

symbolize the ills of modernity and at the same time to represent something that is out of place in the modern, civilized world (50).

Works Cited

Abelson, Elaine S. *When Ladies Go A-Thieving: Middle-Class Shoplifters in the Victorian Department Store*. New York: Oxford University Press, 1989.

Ewen, Stuart, and Elizabeth Ewen. *Channels of Desire: Mass Images and the Shaping of American Consciousness*. New York: McGraw Hill, 1982.

Gilman, Charlotte Perkins. *Women and Economics*. 1898. New York: Harper Torchbooks, 1966.

Grant, Madison. *The Passing of the Great Race*. New York: Charles Scribner's Sons, 1916.

Halliday, Jon. *Sirk on Sirk*. London: Secker and Warburg, 1972.

Horowitz, Daniel. *The Morality of Spending: Attitudes Toward the Consumer Society in America, 1875–1940*. Baltimore: Johns Hopkins University Press, 1985.

Hurst, Fannie. *Anatomy of Me: A Wonderer in Search of Herself*. New York: Doubleday, 1958.

———. *Back Street*. New York: Cosmopolitan Book Corporation, 1930.

———. *Imitation of Life*. New York: Harper and Brothers, 1933.

Itzkovitz, Daniel. "Passing Like Me." *South Atlantic Quarterly* 98, nos. 1 and 2 (Winter/Spring 1999).

———. "Secret Temples." In *Jews and Other Differences: The New Jewish Cultural Studies*. Ed. Jonathan Boyarin and Daniel Boyarin. Minneapolis: University of Minnesota Press, 1997.

Jacobs, Lea. *The Wages of Sin: Censorship and the Fallen Woman Film, 1928–1942*. Berkeley: University of California Press, 1995.

Key, Ellen. *Love and Marriage*. New York: G. P. Putnam's Sons, 1911.

Lears, T. J. Jackson. *No Place of Grace: Antimodernism and the Transformation of American Culture, 1880–1920*. Chicago: University of Chicago Press, 1981.

Mencken, H. L. *In Defense of Women*. New York: Alfred Knopf, 1920.

Ohmann, Richard. *Selling Culture: Magazines, Markets, and Class at the Turn of the Century*. London: Verso, 1996.

Rogin, Michael. *Blackface, White Noise: Jewish Immigrants in the Hollywood Melting Pot*. Berkeley: University of California Press, 1996.

Salpeter, Harry. "Fannie Hurst: Sob-Sister of American Fiction." *Bookman* 73 (August 1931).

Steyn, Juliet. "Charles Dickens' *Oliver Twist*: Fagin as a Sign." In *The Jew in the Text: Modernity and the Construction of Identity*. Ed. Linda Nochlin and Tamar Garb. London: Thames and Hudson, 1995.

Susman, Warren I. "'Personality' and the Making of Twentieth-Century Culture." In *New Directions in American Intellectual History*. Ed. John Higham and Paul K. Conkin. Baltimore: Johns Hopkins University Press, 1979.

Shopping to Pass, Passing to Shop: Consumer Self-Fashioning in the Fiction of Nella Larsen

MEREDITH GOLDSMITH

Representatives of the rising black middle class, Nella Larsen's African-American heroines are preoccupied with the interrelation of consumption and self-transformation. Helga Crane, of *Quicksand* (1928), shops to pass, using consumption as a tool to claim a coherent identity within the African-American middle class, while Clare Kendry and Irene Redfield, co-heroines of *Passing* (1929), pass to shop, exploiting their light skin to take advantage of segregated leisure. Using the tools offered by a burgeoning consumer culture to alter how their bodies are perceived, Larsen's protagonists simultaneously manipulate their bodies to gain access to objects of elite consumption. Fashioning identities through the material apparatus of clothing, makeup, and decor, Larsen's heroines appear to embrace willfully inauthentic, performative selves.

In this essay I argue that the social performances of Larsen's characters provide an important insight into the split between agency and social construction that theorists have described as characteristic of performativity. Judith Butler's efforts to clarify the involuntary nature of performativity in *Bodies That Matter: On the Discursive Limits of "Sex"* encapsulates the dilemma of Larsen's characters. Responding to criticism of the notion of performativity articulated in *Gender Trouble*, she writes:

> If I were to argue that genders are performative, that could mean that I thought that one woke in the morning, perused the closet for some

more open space for the gender of choice, donned that gender of that day, and then restored the garment to its place at night. Such a willful and instrumental subject, one who decides *on* its gender, is clearly not its gender from the start and fails to realize that its existence is already decided *by* gender. Certainly, such a theory would restore the figure of a choosing subject—humanist—at the center of a project whose emphasis on construction seems to be quite opposed to such a notion. (x)

Throughout *Bodies That Matter*, Butler struggles to distinguish performativity from the consumerist theatricality of her example, the agent who "chooses" an identity as if it were a garment. However, the slippage between self-conscious theatricality—in which consumerism emerges as a mode of racial and gender identity construction—and performativity, a system in which the reiteration of "regulatory norms" (Butler 2) of such categories calls subjects into being, is precisely the problem that Larsen's novellas explore. In addition, my analysis points to a lacuna in theories of performativity around questions of class; as her own work on Larsen demonstrates, Butler's theory of performed identities argues backward from gender to sexuality and race. The relative absence of class from psychoanalysis—one of Butler's major sources—might account for this exclusion; one might also argue that class, unlike race and gender, is not written on the body and thus need not be taken into account. However, Larsen's fiction suggests that class is performed and policed just as rigorously as are gender, race, and sexuality; her characters manipulate dress, adornments, and object culture to metonymize their desires for middle-class position, African-American selfhood, sexual fulfillment, and feminine beauty. Through the reading of costume, decor, color, and light, I examine both the pleasures and the consequences of Larsen's characters' efforts at class, racial, and gendered self-fashioning.

Repositioning Nella Larsen with respect to the middlebrow literature and culture of the 1920s illuminates her work in a number of ways. Larsen, probably more so than any other author discussed in this book, has been associated with "high" modernism. While Larsen's stylistic experimentation might seem to exclude her from the category of middlebrow literary expression, bringing her work into juxtaposition with that of more popular writers of the era elucidates the tensions and continuities between "middlebrow" and "modern." Larsen's efforts, and those of her characters, to attain positions among the black haute bourgeoisie entailed a rejection of a nascent black middlebrow culture that developed in tandem with and parallel to its Anglo-American counterpart. Thus, reading Larsen's fiction in parallel with middlebrow women's fiction exposes not only the friction within the developing black middle class of the 1920s but the fierceness with which that position was guarded. In addition, reading Larsen within the middlebrow context reveals her concern, shared by a number of popular women writers, with the possibilities for women offered by the burgeoning consumer culture of the era. A variety of 1920s popular and middlebrow women's novels explore the opportunities and limitations of consumer self-fashioning—among them Edna Ferber's *Fanny Herself* (1917), Anzia Yezierska's *Salome of the Tenements* (1923), Dorothy Canfield Fisher's *The Home-Maker* (1924), and Jessie Fauset's *Plum Bun* (1929). As Larsen's fiction shows, however, the acceptance of consumerist theatricality subjects African-American middle-class women to a particular set of risks. African-American women in the early twentieth century felt particular pressure to avoid the labels of "exotic" and "primitive." As part of his principle of "sober economy," for example, Booker T. Washington urged an aesthetic of primness upon middle-class black women, imposing dress codes on the teachers and students at the Tuskegee Institute and Fisk University.[1] More generally, the ascendance of the heroine as consumer runs the risk of reproducing women's role in a culture dependent upon what feminist anthropologist Gayle Rubin calls "the traffic in women" (177), which reduces women to objects of exchange and reinforces homosocial bonds between men. Middle-class women offered no possibilities of productive labor may become, in Charlotte Perkins Gilman's phrase, "priestesses of consumption" (118), increasingly dependent on their husbands to supply the capital for their consumer habits. As the heroines of Larsen's fiction appropriate selfhood through performance, they risk losing their class position through uncomfortable proximity with the figures of the actress and the prostitute, women who are defined by, but manipulate, their own commodity status and who were frequently racial and ethnic minorities. However, as the rise of consumer culture offered women new access to the public sphere,[2] narratives of female consumption lend particular insight into the yearnings of middle-class women for political and social autonomy. By forging narrative economies in which bourgeois African-American women must constantly vacillate between the role of consumer and that of object of consumption, Larsen's fiction provides a particularly compelling example of how black middle-class female selfhood may be both enabled and endangered by the possibility of consumerist masquerade.[3]

The Consuming Desires of Helga Crane

Larsen's childhood experiences of racism, nativism, and class disenfranchisement fueled the desires of Helga Crane, the heroine of *Quicksand*, to attain a middle-class African-American identity through consumption. Born in the 1890s, Larsen was the daughter of a white Danish immigrant mother and a black father, believed to have emigrated to the United States from the Danish Virgin Islands. Before Larsen was three, her mother was married to another white Dane, leaving Larsen as the only black member of a white household.[4] Whether out of compassion or disdain, Larsen's mother and stepfather sent her to a boarding school associated with Fisk University and then to the university itself; her contact with her family appears to have ended in her teenage years. After a brief career as a teacher at Fisk, where she deeply resented the codes for dress and behavior that Washington imposed, Larsen briefly married Elmer Imes, a scion of the African-American elite. After a bitter divorce, Larsen returned to her career as a nurse and remained estranged from her family for the rest of her life. At her death in 1960, her sister denied her existence. Perhaps because of a personal history shot through with racial, class, and ethnic conflict, Larsen became deeply committed to attaining middle-class security—a desire repeatedly voiced, yet rarely realized, by her heroines.[5]

The conflict between fantasies of middle-class desire and bodily realities of race and gender drives Helga Crane's narrative. The child of a white immigrant mother and a black father, Helga is stifled by the homogenous atmosphere of Naxos, the Tuskegee-inspired black college where she teaches. Helga longs passionately for beauty, attempting to craft a "commodity aesthetic" by arranging herself and her world; however, when she has the opportunity to do so, she is reduced to commodity status through her frequent association with the very objects she desires. As Jean-Christophe Agnew explains, a "commodity aesthetic" implies a collapse of boundaries between the self and the desired object, "celebrat[ing] these moments when the boundaries between the self and the commodity world collapse in the act of the purchase. Such an aesthetic regards acculturation as if it were a form of consumption and consumption, in turn, not as a form of waste or use, but as deliberate and informed accumulation" (135). By focusing on the moment of collapse of boundaries between self and other, Agnew fails to call attention to the consequence of such a fragmentation of the self, especially for nonwhite and female subjects. Once Helga senses the failure of her commodity aesthetic, she marries a preacher and returns to the rural South, believing that marriage, children, and sexuality will fulfill her sense of longing. With the closure of the novel, the realities of reproduction trump Helga's dreams of consumer desire; trapped in a claustrophobic cycle of pregnancy and childbirth, Helga is left with nothing but the fantasy of "freedom and cities" (135).

Considering Helga's narrative in the context of middle-class women's roles as both consumers and objects of consumption illuminates a set of issues in the novel usually given scant critical attention. Several critics have explored at least one facet of Larsen's use of color imagery, for example, but few have focused on Larsen's extensive and complicated poetics of color.[6] In addition, almost no critical attention has been devoted to Larsen's dense and textured descriptions of costume, light, art objects, and decor. Yet the modern department store, perhaps the most important consumer institution of the 1920s, supplies the backdrop for Larsen's lush poetics of color and description. Early-twentieth-century innovations in the production of color, glass, and light revolutionized department store merchandising, thus accelerating the rise of consumer culture. In contrast to the relatively stable color system that prevailed in most of the nineteenth century, by the 1880s advances in the dying process offered over one thousand shades and hues; neon lighting and mass-produced plate glass theatricalized the experience of shopping. Window trimmers were encouraged not to merely arrange piles of objects, as had been characteristic of Victorian displays, but to create coherent scenes of luxurious living, tableaux that focused more intensely on objects than on the characters who used or wore them. Display designers organized the shopwindows of major department stores by color, exploiting the range of hues in one color, or created vibrant contrasts by using a different color in each window of the store.[7] In *Quicksand*, Larsen uses the color vocabulary of the 1920s to underscore the especially liminal position of African-American middle-class women with respect to the burgeoning consumer culture.[8]

Like the window trimmers, Larsen uses color to create a harmonious interplay between the bodies of her characters and the signifiers of bourgeois sophistication that they crave. In addition, however, she enlists color imagery to code her characters within a feminine trajectory of sensuality, marriage, and reproduction. Larsen's characters self-consciously manipulate bodily surfaces to convey interior states. When Helga quits Harlem for Denmark, for example, she chooses "as a symbol" of her decision a "cobwebby black net [dress] touched with orange" in which she resembles "something about to fly" (56). Larsen consistently links the colors green and red to her heroines' sexuality; the name of Helga's husband, the Reverend Pleasant Green, signifies both the erotic thralldom that draws Helga to him and the fecundity that will characterize Helga's married life. Red carries conventional associations of uncontrolled female eroticism: having mistakenly wandered into church wearing "a clinging red dress," Helga is characterized by the women surrounding her as "a scarlet woman," "a pore los' Jezebel" (118), as if Helga's costume were identical with her sexual desires. The name of Irene Redfield, the heroine of *Passing*, literalizes through its juxtaposition of red and green the heroine's conflict between her own desires and her commitment to the roles of mother and wife. Advancing the heroines' sexual conflicts through color, Larsen offers us a way of seeing that operates in tandem with the consumer aesthetics of the era.

Rather than creating an opposition between beautiful object and body, Larsen fuses the two, applying the new color vocabulary of the era to her characters. Challenging the racist aesthetic coded into the binary of white and black by creating a multihued spectrum of racial coloration, Larsen presents both her light- and dark-skinned black characters in the vocabulary of art and tasteful commodities. Faces range from "ivory" to "alabaster" to "mahogany"—materials used for decorating wealthy bodies or furnishing homes of the well-to-do. "Tea" and "biscuits," food for the upper middle class, figure Helga Crane's feet and Brian Redfield's fingers. The students at Naxos appear in shades of "ebony, bronze, and gold." At a nightclub in Harlem, Helga marvels "for the hundredth time" at the various "gradations within this oppressed race of hers. A dozen shades slid by. There was sooty black, shiny black, taupe, mahogany, bronze, copper, gold, orange, yellow, peach, ivory, pinky white, pastry white" (59).[9] In the equation of "shade" and "person," Larsen aestheticizes and celebrates the diversity of Harlem; even as she does so, however, she risks reifying its subjects as commodities for audience consumption.

The aesthetic of the shopwindow dominates *Quicksand* from its first scene, in which Helga Crane frames herself with commodities. The interplay of light and shadow focuses the reader's attention on Helga:

Only a single reading lamp, dimmed by a great black and red shade, made a pool of light in the blue Chinese carpet, on the bright covers of the books which she had taken down from their long shelves, on the white pages of the opened one selected, on the shining brass crowded with many-colored nasturtiums beside her on the low table, and on the oriental silk which covered the stool at her slim feet. . . . This was her rest, this intentional isolation for a short while in the evening, this little time in her own attractive room with her own books. (1)

Contrasts emerge, however, between the woman as consumer and arranger of art, and woman as art object, as the narrator goes on to admire Helga's "skin like yellow satin," "well-turned limbs," and "sharply cut face." Helga initially seems a model of bourgeois feminist self-possession; with "her own attractive room" filled with "her own books," she establishes selfhood through the ownership of things. Despite her felicitous taste, however, the decorative rhetoric that surrounds Helga suggests that she too is a potential and alluring object of possession. In this tableau, Larsen intimates that Helga's narrative will vacillate between the two poles of woman as consumer and woman as object of consumption.[10]

Larsen contrasts Helga's elegance with the factory-like milieu of Naxos,[11] the black college where she teaches. Larsen characterizes the students of the college as "products" (3); the college, Helga tells us, is "a machine," "a big knife with ruthlessly sharp edges ruthlessly cutting all to a pattern" (4). Helga's passion for elegant clothes in sensual, "queer" colors—"dark purples, royal blues, rich greens, deep reds"—and "soft, luxurious" fabrics (18), Larsen explains, has always been at odds with the aesthetic of sober economy on which Naxos is founded. Helga's dissatisfaction with Naxos, we learn, has been amplified by a white minister who has come to the school to preach a version of Washington's critique of consumption: "he hoped, he sincerely hoped, that they wouldn't become avaricious and grasping, thinking only of adding to their earthly goods . . . it was their duty to be satisfied in the estate to which they had been called, hewers of wood and drawers of water" (3).

Helga is desperate to restore to Naxos's black female students the love of color that she believes to be part of their "inherent racial love of gorgeousness" (18). "One of the loveliest sights Helga had ever seen," Larsen writes, "had been a sooty black girl decked out in a flaming orange dress, which a horrified matron had next day consigned to the dyer. Why, she wondered, didn't someone write *A Plea for Color*?" (18; author's italics).[12] Despite the primitivist overtones of her sentiments, in her desire for "a plea for color," Helga craves not only a diversity of colors in art and clothing, but an appreciation of heterogeneity within the race as well. In her view, the "sooty black girl" can be just as beautiful as the amber-hued Helga if her beauty is properly framed. Watching one of her few friends at the school, she wonders "just what form of vanity it was that had induced an intelligent girl like Margaret Creighton to turn what was probably nice live crinkly hair, perfectly suited to her smooth dark skin and agreeable round features, into a dead, straight, greasy, ugly mass" (14). The contrast between "live" and "dead" is significant; if the hair, a synecdoche of self, can be deadened through an internalization of white standards of beauty, the consequences to the psyche seem equally threatening.[13] Helga rejects the assimilation to the white ideals supported by Naxos's dress and style regulations, choosing the elite consumables she craves as a means to craft an autonomous aesthetic.

In her attempts to reclaim individual beauty and style, however, Helga has no choice but to enter a pattern of pecuniary emulation like that described by Thorstein Veblen in *The Theory of the Leisure Class*, in which she must imitate the spending patterns of leisure-class women. As a teacher—an exemplary middle-class profession—Helga's efforts to recuperate the material goods she lacks and the spiritual fulfillment she seeks require that she masquerade as a woman of means. First buying her way out of the Jim Crow car of the northbound train, she spends her money too quickly in Chicago on "things which she wanted, but did not need and certainly could not afford," including a book and a "rare old tapestry purse" (35, 32). In making these purchases, Helga compensates for feeling rejected by her white uncle and his new wife, who have refused to see her. Using these objects as both frame and mask, she can imaginatively possess the sense of history she lacks and simultaneously emphasize her own sense of beauty and rarity. Forced into competition with her white middle-class relatives who have rejected her, Helga uses material objects to reinforce a tenuous sense of self.

However, Helga's shopping risks reiterating the status of woman as an object of consumption. For this reason, her consumerism parallels her association with prostitution, a trope recurring throughout the novel. Overqualified for domestic work and undertrained for more professional forms of employment, "it seemed that in that whole energetic place nobody wanted her services. At least not the kind that she offered. A few men, both white and black, offered her money, but the price of the money was too dear. Helga Crane did not feel inclined to pay for it" (34). Larsen's exploitation of metaphors of price and value embodies Helga's vacillation between consumer and object of consumption. Even as her economic situation draws her dangerously close to prostitution, in which her "services" would become a commodity for sale, Larsen constructs Helga as a consumer, with her sexuality turned into payment for the money men would offer her. Helga's consuming habits provide a means to control the way her body is perceived, thus serving as the only alternative to her intense bodily self-consciousness.

Helga's struggle to occupy a black female middle-class subject position puts her in the company of two characters in the novel who reference the rise of black middlebrow culture. Mrs. Hayes-Rore, who enters the novel only to convey Helga from Chicago to Harlem, exemplifies elite critiques of middlebrow culture. Despite her relatively minor status in the novel, however, Mrs. Hayes-Rore lends important insight into the emergence of African-American middlebrow culture. A black clubwoman and speech-maker, Mrs. Hayes-Rore engages Helga as a secretary and charges her with condensing and editing her speeches. As a member of the Board of the YWCA in Chicago where Helga seeks employment, her means of and interest in uplift cast her firmly in the middlebrow tradition. First charac-terized as a mere "lecturing female" (35) to whom Helga believes herself superior, Mrs. Hayes-Rore's professional persona excludes her from the role of leisure-class lady, signaled in her ill-fitting "five-years-behind-the-mode-garments" that contrast sharply with Helga's fashionable outfits (35). Echoing critiques of the middlebrow by such acerbic figures as H. L. Mencken, Helga quickly realizes that Mrs. Hayes-Rore's speeches lack originality: "Ideas, phrases, and even whole sentences and paragraphs were lifted bodily" (38) from the works of great orators on the race ques-tion. As Helga and Mrs. Hayes-Rore develop what is the briefest but per-haps the most genuine friendship Helga experiences in the novel, Helga learns to appreciate her directness. However, the bluntness of the class arriviste—Mrs. Hayes-Rore is the widow of a newly rich South Side polit-ico—soon gives way to an unexpected reticence; Helga learns that Mrs. Hayes-Rore would prefer not to speak of Helga's heritage of miscegena-tion. Their mutual failure to connect suggests the fragility of the class posi-tions of both women: to acknowledge Helga's working-class, miscegenous origins would threaten to unseat Mrs. Hayes-Rore's own hard-won place in the bourgeoisie.

Next, Helga encounters Anne Grey, who becomes her mentor among the Harlem elite. In her depiction of this character, Larsen uses commod-ity aesthetics to show the sense of belonging to an American haute bour-geoisie that Harlem's elite enjoys; simultaneously, however, she demonstrates a middlebrow liminality regarding the cultural divide white and black New Yorkers negotiated in the 1920s. Anne has achieved the harmonious interplay between her body and physical space that Helga craves, appearing excluded from the nexus of consumer and consumed.

Ensconced in Anne's home, Helga is struck not only by the beauty of her things, but also by their voluminousness:

> Beds with long, tapering posts to which tremendous age lent dignity and interest, bonneted old highboys, tables that might be by Duncan Phyfe, and others whose ladder backs gracefully climbed the delicate wall panels. These historic things mingled harmoniously and comfortably with brass-bound Chinese tea-chests, luxurious deep chairs and davenports, tiny tables of gay color, a lacquered jade-green settee with gleaming black satin cushions, lustrous Eastern rugs, ancient copper, Japanese prints, some fine etchings, a profusion of precious bric-a-brac, and endless shelves filled with books. (44)

Despite the quantity of Anne's possessions, Helga does not characterize her as vulgar because her "mingling" of styles signifies Anne's successful entry into an Anglo–African-American middle class. In its interplay of vivid colors and Orientalist motifs, the description of Anne's space repeats certain elements of Helga's rooms, but here Larsen adds "historic things" metonymizing the American past, emphasizing the sense of tradition that Helga lacks. Moreover, Anne's membership in the black elite seems to lend her the bodily self-confidence Helga does not possess: in Helga's view, Anne "possessed an impeccably fastidious taste in clothes, knowing what suited her and wearing it with an air of unconscious assurance" (45).

Anne's superb taste in decor, which for Helga suggests a black middle-class history she has been denied, masks the extent to which the black middle class functions as both intermediary and wedge between the white elite and the black masses. Through the character of Anne, Larsen shows the racializing of the high and popular culture divide in early-twentieth-century American culture, for Anne resides on an uncomfortable boundary between white high and African-American cultural expression. "Ap[ing]" the "clothes," "manners," and "ways of living" (48) of the white upper classes, she regards black popular culture with contempt. As Larsen writes: "Like the despised people of the white race, she preferred Pavlova to Florence Mills, John McCormack to Taylor Gordon, Walter Hampden to Paul Robeson" (49). Larsen underscores Anne's hypocrisy by underscoring her allegiance to white artistic culture, even as she elevates the black race as an abstract identity. Anne emerges as a more sophisticated version of what Helga found so distasteful at Naxos: the mimicry of Anglo-American mores, interests, and aesthetics in an attempt to construct an autonomous black bourgeoisie.[14]

In an effort to extricate herself from this stifling world, Helga quits Harlem for her Danish relatives, believing that to be adored for her otherness will assuage the "lack somewhere" (7) she has always felt. Helga's foray into white European culture forcefully demonstrates, however, that her efforts to differentiate herself from black America must come at a price that eventually proves "too dear" (34). As Larsen positions Helga as the leisure-class consumer she has longed to become in her years of aesthetic deprivation, she simultaneously marks Helga's white relatives' desires to craft her as exotic primitive.[15] Helga realizes quickly that in Denmark she is to be "a decoration. A curio. A peacock" (73); her Danish relatives promote her, and thus their own social status, by clothing her in exotic styles and fashions reminiscent of blues divas (duCille 94–97) and Josephine Baker, whose image hovers on the margins of the Copenhagen section of the novel (Wall 103). Significantly, Baker and the blues performers Helga resembles here successfully leapfrogged class boundaries and rose from working-class origins to enormous wealth. In contrast to Helga, Baker at least was able to balance the ways in which she was commodified by the white audiences and critics of twenties Paris with her status as both consumer and producer.[16] In Denmark, however, as Helga acquiesces to her status as commodity, Larsen alerts the reader to her heroine's dilemma through the wildly excessive clothes her relatives purchase for her:

> There were batik dresses in which mingled indigo, orange, green, vermilion, and black; dresses of velvet and chiffon in screaming colors, blood-red, sulphur-yellow, sea-green and one black and white thing in striking combination. There was a black Manila shawl strewn with great scarlet and lemon flowers, a leopard-skin coat, a glittering opera-cape. There were turban-like hats of metallic silks, feathers and furs, strange jewelry, enameled or set with odd semi-precious stones, a nauseous Eastern perfume, shoes with dangerously high heels. (74)

One might argue that the "black and white thing in striking combination" is exactly what her Danish relatives would like her to be. They encourage her to "capitalize on her difference" (Wall 101), to exaggerate her blend of racial heritages. Larsen repeats the same images she uses earlier to characterize Helga's aesthetic, but exaggerates them: Orientalist motifs become "nauseous" and explicitly primitive, reducing Helga to a souvenir of exotic colonial adventures like the leopard whose skins make her coat. Whereas both Helga and Anne excel at creating a harmonious interplay of color, here colors are "mingled" to intoxicating effect. The "screaming" colors

Aunt Katrina and Uncle Poul urge upon her overwhelm the subtlety Helga seeks in her aesthetic arrangements. Through Helga's clothes, Larsen foreshadows that Helga's accession to consumerism is inseparable from the evacuation of selfhood characteristic of the commodity.

Although for the first time in her life she has the money and the comforts she has always desired, Helga now has little to fill her time but shopping and arranging herself aesthetically. Finally a member of the leisure class, Helga initially revels in the sensuous pleasures she has been denied. In Chicago she had skipped meals to buy accessories; in Denmark, "an endless and tempting array" of food satisfies her cravings (77). Though she is not much of a skater, the "attractive skating-things" (78) she can wear mitigate a few tumbles. In striking contrast to her previous experience as a consumer, however, here Helga makes no decisions: her aunt and uncle select her costumes, organize her social schedule, and promote a series of possible suitors. Helga's sense of her own objectification by the white Danes is underscored by the word that falls "freely, audibly" (73), from their lips—*Den Sorte*, Danish for "the black." Here, Larsen demonstrates the destructive potential within Helga's desire to aestheticize herself and her world. Having previously argued that blacks should feel pride in the heterogeneity of their colors, here she is reduced to no more than a color.

The closure of the Denmark section of the novel makes clear the extent to which Helga's efforts to control the ways in which she is represented have come at the expense of an increasing ambivalence toward the materiality of her own body. Significantly, Helga realizes that low and high cultural representations of the black body are almost identical in their rendering of blackness. At a vaudeville performance, for example, Helga is appalled by a pair of black performers who sing ragtime tunes while "pounding their thighs, slapping their hands together, twisting their legs, waving their abnormally long arms, throwing their bodies about with a loose ease" (83). The explicitly sexual language Larsen uses here, stressing the sinuosity and flexibility of black bodies, signals Helga's anxiety about the possible similarity between these bodies and her own. Helga displays a comparable ambivalence when Axel Olsen, her artist suitor, depicts her as an exotic primitive in a portrait. Although Larsen never steps outside Helga's point of view to describe the portrait in detail, Helga interprets it as "not herself at all, but some disgusting sensual creature with her features" (89). Despite the resonance of Olsen's portrait with Picasso's and Matisse's paintings of African women, Helga glimpses the similarity between Olsen's portrait and the vaudeville performers—both read race, and Axel explicitly reads Helga, in terms of sexuality. That the only viewer of the painting who shares Helga's disgust is the white Danish maid, Marie, only illuminates the precariousness of Helga's position. Identification with a working-class woman (who, significantly, shares the name of Larsen's mother) would unsettle Helga's middle-class position. While Larsen briefly offers a moment of cross-class identification, it swiftly dissipates as Helga seeks to reclaim a sense of her beauty and rarity by returning to Harlem.

The novella's title, *Quicksand*, however, reminds us that changes in location inevitably fail to heal Helga's anxiety and ambivalence. As the novel moves toward its conclusion, Larsen introduces both the continuity and the tension between erotic and consumer desires, for Helga begins to believe that sexuality will provide the solace she has been seeking. As suggested by the etymological link of the word *consumption* to the word *consummation* (Bowlby 20), consumerism implies an absorption of the purchased object by the self, an erotically charged but temporary suspension of boundaries. Having rejected Olsen's marriage proposal and realizing she has lost a chance at love with the erudite Dr. Anderson, principal of Naxos, Helga undergoes a religious conversion and marries a Southern preacher, the Reverend Mr. Pleasant Green. Larsen represents Helga's embrace of religion as a capitulation to the sexual desires she has repressed throughout her past. Having wandered into a church, she is horrified, then entranced, by the press of bodies, which recalls the vaudeville dancers in Denmark; her resistance swept away, she yields to the "brutal desire to shout and sling herself about" (113).[17] In the orgasmic release that accompanies her conversion, Helga allows the Reverend to accompany her to her hotel; the two are married in the "seductive repentance" (118) of the next morning. Eroticism initially replaces consumerism, as Helga admits to herself that "things . . . hadn't been, weren't enough for her" (116).

In the shift from consumption to consummation, Helga welcomes for the first time complete peace of mind. As she claims to herself that she has transcended the world of things, her religious convictions and sexual satisfaction mitigate "the choppy lines of the shining oak furniture" and "the awesome horribleness of the religious pictures" (121). Significantly, Larsen figures Helga's newfound comfort as "anaesthetic" (118), suggesting not just the soothing of pain but the muting of her sensitivity to art. Attempting to aestheticize her surroundings by "subduing [their] cleanly scrubbed ugliness . . . with soft inoffensive beauty," Helga abjures her previously sensuous tastes, now regarding them as "fripperies" (121). Offering rural black women a form of aesthetic redemption and renouncing her own desires, Helga at first appears to have resolved the opposition between consumer and consumed that has characterized the entire novel.

In the final section of the novel, however, Larsen emphasizes the contrast between the material self-fashioning of the black middle-class female self and the bodily realities of rural black women. The lives of the "dark undecorated" (121) women Helga encounters in Alabama are organized by a seemingly endless cycle "of births and christenings, of loves and marriages, of deaths and funerals" (121). Far removed from the tableaux of urban department store shopwindows, to them Helga is simply an "uppity No'the'nah" (119). The presence of Clementine Richards signals the new irrelevance of Helga's aesthetic. As if Axel Olsen's painting of Helga had sprung to life, Clementine is "a strapping black beauty of magnificent Amazon proportions and bold shining eyes of jet-like hardness. A person of awesome appearance. All chains, strings of beads, jingling bracelets, flying ribbons, feathery neck-pieces, and flowery hats" (119). While in their primitivist characteristics the representations of Helga in Denmark and Clementine in the South seem markedly similar, these two efforts at black female self-fashioning differ significantly. Where the "barbaric bracelets" (70) and wildly colored clothes Helga's Danish relatives urge on her increase her sense of immobility, Clementine is all motion—"jingling bracelets" and "flying ribbons" (119). Where Helga's white audience fetishistically views her body as a series of discrete parts—"superb eyes . . . color . . . neck column . . . yellow . . . hair . . . alive . . . wonderful" (71)—the physically imposing and sexually autonomous (as Larsen's labeling her an "Amazon" suggests) Clementine resists such anatomization. Divorced from an urban world of surfaces, Clementine seems to have absorbed the pleasures of bodily self-fashioning without assuming its risks.

With the closure of the novel, the conflict between middle-class consumerist fantasy and working-class bodily reality escalates even further. Wishing that her body could again become a static art object, "something on which to hang lovely fabrics" (123), Helga now moves with "lumbering haste" (125), weakened from her repeated pregnancies. Worn out from the birth and death of her fourth child, she fantasizes a return to the bourgeois world of "freedom and cities" (135). However, the abstract ideal of freedom is represented by the specifics of elite commodity culture: "clothes and books . . . the sweet mingled smell of Houbigant and cigarettes in softly lighted rooms filled with inconsequential chatter and laughter and sophisticated tuneless music" (135). Helga claims she will "retrieve all these agreeable, desired things" (135) but succumbs to her postpartum weakness instead.

One might suggest that it is the inexorability of consumer desire that Larsen's novel documents so compellingly, for in both the form and content of the novel, Larsen creates an aesthetic lens through which her heroine is only visible when framed by commodities. In the gap between the novel's last two paragraphs, the narrative voice shifts out of Helga's consciousness into that of a distant narrator. While Helga has dreamed of the objects of elite consumption, the novel's last paragraph declasses her, stripping her of her individuality. As Larsen writes: "And hardly had she left her bed and become able to walk again without pain, hardly had the children returned from the homes of the neighbors, when she began to have her fifth child" (135). With its first word, *And*, its repetition of the word *hardly*, and its use of the pronoun *she* rather than Helga's name, the final sentence underscores the cyclical, impersonal nature of Helga's reproductive state. In the earlier portions of the novel, Helga has manipulated the practices of consumption and adornment as a means of individualizing her body and simultaneously of differentiating it from the material realities of working-class female black life depicted in the final section. However, the last line of the novel, with its generalizing nature, transforms Helga's body into part of the mass of rural black women in labor.[18] With this grim closing gesture, Larsen signals the triumphs of the material realities of race, class, and gender over the tools of bourgeois identity formation Helga has struggled so poignantly to claim.

Passing and the Class Politics of Bodily Style

In contrast to *Quicksand*, in which passing as middle class emerges as an attempt to appropriate a coherent racial identity, the racial masquerade of *Passing* permits the appropriation of class identities. Whereas in *Quicksand*, Larsen demonstrates through the character of Helga Crane the risks to the self of controlling one's bodily representations through performative self-fashioning, *Passing* enacts these risks through its style, metonymizing the black female body through representations of the material world: colors, light, objects, and decor. While *Passing* does not use consumption as metaphor of self in the consistent manner of its predecessor, the critique of consumption Larsen provides in *Quicksand* complicates the sexual and racial repression many readers have located in this novella. The "aches" and "passions," the "wild desires" (145) of the heroines, have not only an erotic inflection but a consumerist one as well.[19]

Passing maps the efforts of competing heroines, Irene Redfield and

Clare Kendry, to control representations of the middle-class black female body. The two are former childhood friends, the first a comfortably affluent Harlem dweller and the second a formerly impoverished orphan whose passing has enabled her to vault class boundaries. Clare occupies a shadowy racial borderland, masquerading as a white woman in her marriage to the wealthy Jack Bellew, yet making sorties into Harlem to recover the black world she has lost through passing. Allowing her husband to call her "Nig" (170) and joking about a possible touch of the tar brush (171), she performs a version of near-white femininity for her husband. Irene herself is involved in the merchandising of blackness through her race work; in close proximity with the white intellectual elite, for whom Harlem may serve as literary or political material, she is eager to promote an unexoticized, unthreatening version of middle-class black femininity.[20] Each heroine is thus engaged with the relationship between racial passing, class mobility, and self-commodification; however, Clare accepts, while Irene denies, the relationship between these terms.

Irene and Clare renew their acquaintance through a chance meeting in the segregated rooftop tearoom of Chicago's Drayton Hotel. Irene has repaired there in a state of near-collapse after an unsuccessful shopping trip; six stores have failed to yield the sketchbook she has promised her son. Larsen's setting of the scene suggests the dizzying and threatening possibilities inherent in a consumer world of surfaces, in which "the glass of the shop-windows threw out a blinding radiance" (146). Irene initially appears an unsophisticated consumer, a woman who will shop all day in infernal heat to please a child and end the day unsatisfied (146). Clare appears to have made more felicitous choices; clad in a "fluttering dress of green chiffon whose mingled pattern of narcissuses, jonquils, and hyacinths was a pleasant reminder of cool spring days," she has selected things that were "just right for the weather, thin and cool without being mussy, as summer things were apt to be" (148). As Irene and Clare engage in mutual inspection, Larsen stages the first scene in the class competition that is to structure their relationship. Despite Clare's air of careless wealth, Irene judges her frank smile "just a shade too provocative" for the waiter who comes to take her order.[21] Clare's comfort with the waiter suggests that her security in her class position cannot be dislodged by inappropriate familiarities; as we learn, however, it may simultaneously have to do with her own working-class background. As Irene recalls her childhood acquaintance with Clare, Larsen reveals the class strata within the African-American community of early-twentieth-century South Side Chicago: "Clare had never been exactly one of the group, just as she'd never been merely the janitor's daughter, but the daughter of Mr. Bob Kendry, who, it was true, was a janitor, but who also, it seemed, had been in college with some of their fathers" (154). The awkwardness of Irene's locution emphasizes the ambiguity and difficulty of claiming class positions within the race. Bob Kendry's class position, Irene suggests, is just as contingent as Clare's and, like Clare's, dependent on secrets and repression. Irene's father, for example, refuses to tell his son how Kendry lost his class status and advises him instead "to be careful not to end in the same manner as 'poor Bob'"(154). Clare, it appears, has performed a reverse version of Bob Kendry's downward slide, manipulating racial identity as a means of transcending class divisions.

Leisure-class consumer spaces in which bodies are on display become sites for passing; simultaneously, however, they objectify the subjects who circulate through them. Irene gazes at Clare as if she were the inhabitant of a show window, underscoring the motivations behind both women's efforts to pass. Each is passing, Irene for a day and Clare for life, to enjoy the pleasures of the white elite. Irene justifies her passing to herself as a magical self-transformation in which she has no agency: "It was, she thought, like being wafted upward on a magic carpet to another world, pleasant, quiet, and strangely remote from the sizzling one that she had left below" (147). On the other hand, Clare is aware that her passing contains much more dangerous possibilities. Having crossed the color line to marry Jack Bellew, a man "with untold gold" (159), Clare passes despite, if not because of, the constant risk of exposure. That consumerism becomes a site for both the pleasures and dangers of passing is suggested in Clare's description of being snubbed by her black childhood friends in a department store: "once I met Margaret Hammer in Marshall Field's. I'd have spoken, was on the very point of doing it, but she cut me dead. . . . I assure you that from the way she looked through me, even I was uncertain whether I was actually there in the flesh or not" (154). Clare's statement makes vividly clear the possibilities for both self-extinction and -gratification in the act of consumption. "The cut" administered by Margaret Hammer engenders complete self-effacement and an ironic reversal: where Clare has passed to eradicate her sense of invisibility as a working-class black woman, she is now reduced to complete invisibility as a leisure-class white woman.

Jacquelyn McLendon notes that the women spend the afternoon trading signs of "whiteness and middle-class status" (113) to reinforce their developing homosocial bond. Smoking, which literalizes the link between consumption and bodily absorption, constitutes one of these signs. Cigarettes serve as a synecdoche for consumption in early-twentieth-century culture, for as Oscar Wilde writes in *The Picture of Dorian Gray*, "cigarettes are the perfect type of the perfect pleasure. They are exquisite, and they leave one unsatisfied" (8). Rachel Bowlby observes that cigarettes were "one of the most ubiquitous and widely advertised late nineteenth-century commodities," and "could connote the indolence of the beautiful life of the dandy but also . . . the sexually transgressive associations of the independent 'new woman'" (7, 8). Connoting both the dandy's sense of style and the New Woman's freedom, here, cigarettes also mark the clandestine erotics of Irene and Clare's relationship and the class privilege that permits such pleasures: less attractive and tasteful women, as we learn later in the novel, do not smoke. Cigarettes also lend themselves to Larsen's poetics of color; the smoke in which Irene and Clare wrap themselves blends light and dark, metaphorizing their passing and veiling their mutual attraction. Blurring the boundary between body and commodity, transforming black and white into ambiguous gray, smoking concretizes the aesthetics of passing and consumption.

Larsen's depiction of the near-white female body underscores the class valences of racial passing. Nowhere are the class implications of passing clearer than in her portrait of Gertrude Martin, a childhood friend who has also married a white man. The circumstances of Gertrude's passing are different from Clare's: her white husband knows her origins, as do most of her friends.[22] Gertrude's sartorial style, or lack thereof, places her in a vastly different category from that which Clare and Irene occupy. While Gertrude's racial passing is successful, her class passing is in doubt:

> Gertrude . . . looked as if her husband might be a butcher. . . . She had grown broad, fat almost, and though there were no lines on her large white face, its very smoothness was somehow prematurely ageing. Her black hair was clipt, and by some unfortunate means all the live curliness had gone from it. Her overtrimmed Georgette crepe dress was too short and showed an appalling amount of leg, stout legs in sleazy stockings a vivid rose-beige shade. Her plump hands were newly and not too competently manicured—for the occasion, probably. (167)

Gertrude's bad bob—which Larsen implies has endured chemical straightening procedures—her shoddy manicure, and her ill-fitting dress bespeak failed class emulation. Each aspect of Gertrude's body suggests the failure of her efforts to rise above her class; marriage to a butcher appears to have

ruined her youthful beauty. Moreover, the colors Larsen uses to characterize Gertrude are stark and ugly compared with the subtle shading of Irene
and Clare. Larsen rarely marks her characters with the labels "black" and
"white"; for her to do so is the sign of contemptuous disinterest. Successful passing comes to be associated with upper-middle-class blacks like
Irene and Clare, for despite Clare's poor upbringing, she was born with
"that dim suggestion of polite insolence with which a few women are born
and which some acquire with the coming of riches or importance" (161).

As the comparison between Clare, Irene, and Gertrude demonstrates,
class competition dominates Irene's imagination, and she is repeatedly
frustrated by Clare's refusal to observe class boundaries. As with Anne
Grey in *Quicksand*, Irene's anxiety hints at an embattled black bourgeoisie
reluctant to sacrifice its own hard-won position; however, Irene's behavior
registers even more explicitly the gradations within the African-American
middle class. In a characteristic moment of denial of her own impulses,
Irene claims that "it wasn't she assured herself, that she was a snob, that
she cared greatly for the petty restrictions and distinctions with which what
called itself Negro society chose to hedge itself about" (157). Both Irene and
her husband Brian work to claim their role in the black middle class
through their defense against those above and below. As Irene is galled by
Clare's comfortable mingling with the maids Zulena and Sadie (208),
Brian loathes his "sick," and implicitly poor, patients, with their "smelly,
dirty rooms" and "filthy steps in dark hallways" (186).

Larsen's depiction of the Negro Welfare League ball, a charity event
staged by affluent Harlemites, provides a setting for the class competition
in which the Harlem bourgeoisie is engaged. The charity ball suggests the
efforts of the black middle class to perform its uplift work for poorer blacks
to the gaze of the white elite. As an organizer of the ball, Irene demonstrates her investment in the marketing of palatable images of black Harlem for a white audience; she discourages Clare from attending the ball
with the suggestion that she might be taken for "a lady of easy virtue looking for trade" (199). Irene's attempt to distance herself from Clare thus
serves as an ironic miniaturization of the class conflict that affects the
black bourgeoisie as a whole. When Clare arrives at the Redfield home to
prepare for the party, Irene feels painfully inadequate in comparison with
her friend: "Clare, exquisite, golden, fragrant, flaunting, in a stately gown
of shining black taffeta, whose long, full skirt lay in graceful folds about
her slim golden feet; her glistening hair drawn smoothly back into a small
twist at the nape of her neck; her eyes sparkling like dark jewels. Irene,
with her new rose-coloured chiffon frock ending at her knees, and her

cropped curls, felt dowdy and commonplace" (203). Larsen's description sets up an ideal to which Irene implicitly believes she should aspire. The repetition of adjectives has the air of an advertisement, and Clare herself speaks in the flattering language of an ad, causing Irene to remark to herself on her overuse of superlatives (204, 209). While Larsen renders Clare as a static object, description without action, her description of Irene renders her painfully embodied; one can sense her embarrassment even in her exposed knees. Through references to her short pink dress and cropped hair, Larsen transforms Irene into a slightly more sophisticated version of Gertrude Martin, emulating the successful passer in vain. Clare's "exquisite" beauty, which facilitates her pass, undermines Irene's sense of class position, the one thing in which she feels secure.[23]

Throughout *Passing*, Larsen uses the consumption of objects as a symbol for the securing of black middle-class femininity; as the novel draws to a close, the proliferation of those objects prefigures Clare's demise. At the party at which Irene becomes convinced of Brian's infidelity, Clare is clothed in colors that recall her racial liminality, "cinnamon-brown" accented with "amber" and "a little golden bowl of a hat" (220). What at first appears a simple description of a cloche comes back to mind moments later, as Irene, with "rage boil[ing] up in her" (221), either smashes or drops to the floor a delicate china teacup. The "white fragments" at her feet prefigure the near-white fragments into which Clare's racially ambiguous body is soon to fragment. Arguably, one might also hear an echo of James's *The Golden Bowl* (1905) in this scenario.[24] At this juncture, Irene, like Maggie Verver in James's novel, believes that she has secured an understanding of her husband's infidelity, symbolized in James's novel by the flaw in the gilt bowl, once believed to be golden. Maggie smashes the golden bowl—and thus the fiction of her husband's fidelity—by finding its hidden flaw. By replacing the golden bowl with the white china teacup, Larsen recasts James's metaphor in racial, class, and gendered terms, as the smashing of the teacup symbolically destroys Clare's near-whiteness, Irene's bourgeois gentility, and the history of miscegenation that both women share. As Irene attempts to justify her act to her white friend Hugh Wentworth: "It was the ugliest thing that your ancestors, the charming Confederates ever owned. I've forgotten how many thousands of years ago it was that Brian's great-great-grand-uncle owned it. But it has, or had, a good old hoary history. It was brought North by way of the subway. Oh, all right! Be English if you want to and call it the underground" (223). In smashing the teacup, Irene symbolically obliterates her own history of slavery (implied in Larsen's reference to the "underground," a trope on the underground railroad) and miscegenation (suggested in the slippage between "your ancestors" and "Brian's great-great-grand-uncle"). Yet through her use of the teacup, delicate and infinitely breakable, as a symbol of black middle-class female history, Larsen makes clear the tenuousness of the black middle-class femininity Irene works to maintain.

While for Clare and Irene, racial passing comes to serve as the opposite face of bourgeois consumption, Larsen presents one character who can enjoy class privilege and remain unaffected by the desire for racial transformation. As Irene's merger of passing with conspicuous consumption initiated the two women's first encounter, it also brings on the novel's denouement. Arm in arm with the darker-skinned Felise Freeland on a shopping trip in a midtown Manhattan street, Irene experiences a comfortable homosocial bond, in contrast to her feelings while in physical proximity with Clare. The women collide with Jack Bellew, who instantly discerns the truth. Surveying him "with the cool gaze of appraisal she reserved for mashers" (226), Irene moves on, explaining to her friend, "I don't believe I've ever gone native in my life except for the sake of convenience, restaurants, theatre tickets, things like that. Never socially I mean, except once. You've just passed the only person that I've ever met disguised as a white woman" (227). Here, the trajectories of consumerism and passing, imbricated throughout the novel, work at cross-purposes. Irene admits to passing to enjoy the pleasures of segregated consumerism, despite its risks of public exposure and humiliation. However, her enjoyment of these pleasures is tainted by the same risks that heighten it. Frightened by the certain results of her encounter with Bellew, Irene gives up her shopping trip, while Felise returns to admiring a coat in a shopwindow.

How might we understand Felise Freeland, who, in her own words, "queers" (227) Irene's passing by showing her color in relation to Irene's? Her name alone signifies unambiguous security in her black identity; her confidence contrasts with the vexing liminality of the mulatta. While Felise, too dark to pass, is unembarrassed about exposing Irene, she takes unqualified pleasure in consumerism. Felise counsels Irene to recover from a low mood through "buy[ing] yourself an expensive new frock, child. It always helps. Any time this child gets the blues, it means money out of Dave's pocket" (219). Clare's desire for "things" has caused her to deny her racial identity through a marriage that constantly harbors the risk of exposure; Irene's claim that she only passes to enjoy segregated leisure, given what we see of her activities, suggests that she may pass more often than she cares to admit. Only Felise, who, like Clementine Richards in *Quicksand*, is a minor character given almost no narrative attention, appears to have acknowledged the pleasures of consumerism without fantasizing about its transformative possibilities. In contrast to Irene's metaphorizing of literal upward motion into upward mobility at the Drayton, no "magic carpet" "wafts" (147) Felise's guests up to the top of her Harlem apartment building. Their color notwithstanding, they all go up by what Brian calls "nigger-power" (236). Significantly, Felise's apartment may only be reached through walking up stairs, through physical labor; she maintains an awareness of the materiality of the body that Irene has lost in her fantasy of racial and class transformation.

The color spectrum Larsen creates in *Passing* narrows dramatically with the novel's final chapter. A snowstorm covers Harlem; seemingly innocent contrasts of black and white in fact foreshadow Clare and Bellew's final encounter. Before the Freelands' party, Irene watches as snow fills in the "ugly irregular gaps" on the sidewalk; as Clare and Irene enter the Freelands' apartment building, they keep to the cement path that "splits" the "whiteness" of the garden. The complementarity of black and white, which Larsen has exploited from the very beginning in her depiction of Clare ("ebony" eyes in an "ivory" skin, for example), returns with an ominous difference.

Bellew, having discovered Clare's association with the Redfields, storms the Freelands' party and denounces Clare as "a nigger, a damned dirty nigger!" (238). Even in the moment of Clare's public exposure, Larsen represents her as an aesthetic object; despite the fact that the fictions of her life have just been shattered, Clare stands calm and "composed" (238). As Clare jumps, falls, or is pushed through the window, Irene registers the implications of her loss in a way that reifies Clare even further: "Gone! The soft white face, the bright hair, the disturbing scarlet mouth, the dreaming eyes, the caressing smile, the whole torturing loveliness that had been Clare Kendry. That beauty that had torn at Irene's placid life. Gone! The mocking daring, the gallantry of her pose, the ringing bells of her laughter" (239). Irene verbalizes the fragmentation of Clare's body as it smashes against the sidewalk in her reduction of Clare to a series of parts for the whole. Larsen distributes the synecdoches of Clare's difference onto the darker-skinned members of the party, who, like Clare, undergo a bodily transformation: "the golden brown" of Felise Freeland's "handsome face" has "changed to a queer mauve colour" (241). Brian's "lips" are "purple and trembling" (241). The color purple, of which mauve is a shade, has signified Clare's exoticism from the first page of the novel, when Irene opens the letter that announces Clare's return to New York. In her final juxtaposition of color schemes, Larsen transfers the symbolic colors of race and class passing onto Brian and Felise, the characters who cannot pass. For Irene, who can choose whether or not to pass, "everything" goes "dark" (242). The consumerist aesthetic that Clare and Irene have crafted fails to represent the realities of race and gender that overshadow them, and the color Clare has brought to Irene's monochromatic life is finally subsumed in the polarities of black and white.

Conclusion

Larsen's own life attested to the struggle of black female middle-class self-representation in the 1920s. Resenting the Washingtonian aesthetic of sober economy for the banal homogeneity it imposed, she nonetheless realized the risks to black women posed by the self-conscious celebration of difference. In her catapult to fame, Larsen embraced aestheticism and consumer pleasures, yet she finished her life in the lower-middle-class profession of nurse, returning to both the Washingtonian ethos of second-class citizenship and the uniforms she scorned in her years at Fisk and Tuskegee. Larsen's characters negotiate similar poles, simultaneously engaging methods of radical self-fashioning and showing the failure of such efforts.

Considering Larsen against the backdrop of middlebrow women's writing and the efforts of African-American intellectuals to articulate models for the black bourgeoisie prompts a reconsideration of the politics of consumption in her work. Despite the lure of the commodity aesthetics in Larsen's work, it is worth remembering that the vacillation between consumer and commodity Larsen's characters experience depends upon the erasure of black middle-class women's labor. As black middle-class women entered the public sphere in the early twentieth century, the positions of clubwoman, teacher, and nurse were among the few professional options available. One might view Larsen's middle-class "race women" like Mrs. Hayes-Rore or Irene Redfield, despite the author's depiction of their hypocrisy and repression, as the survivors of the Harlem Renaissance. Examining them in the context of middlebrow literary and cultural movements of the 1920s underscores their productivity as well as their weaknesses. Viewed from this perspective, the efforts of Clare Kendry and Helga Crane to forge racial and class identities through consumption underscore the limitations of consumerist theatricality in the relative absence of—and perhaps as compensation for—productive intellectual and aesthetic work for black women. While *Quicksand* and *Passing* poignantly document the allure of self-aestheticization for black middle-class women in the 1920s, they simultaneously remind us of the costs at which the ephemeral, intense beauty of Larsen's art and life were achieved.

Notes

1. Booker T. Washington advocated modest consumption, as exemplified in his belief in the "gospel of the toothbrush," and sharply criticized "showy" blacks who used installment plans to buy items they could not afford (113, 174–75).
2. See Felski's analysis of consumption as a means of increasing women's object status. Despite her pessimism on this score, Felski considers the entrance of women into the public sphere through consumption as an opportunity for increased agency and, ultimately, political power.
3. Doane provides a useful account of women's position between consumer and commodity.
4. See Davis and Larson. Both authors, but particularly Davis, construct Larsen's primary trauma as her "abandonment" by her mother, Marie Larsen. Hutchinson ("Nella"), however, by reconstructing Larsen's relationship with her mother, has shown how the compression of Larsen's mixed-race heritage into a homogenous narrative of African-American history ignores important elements of her personal history.
5. Locating Larsen in the context of "middlebrow moderns" helps bring her class investments, long buried in the critical conversation, to light. Much of the following supports Carby's contention that *Quicksand*'s importance lies in its status as perhaps "the first text by a black woman to be a conscious narrative of a woman embedded within capitalist social relations" (171). For an essay that has many parallels with both Carby's and my own, see Rhodes.
6. Hostetler provides the most extensive analysis; see also McDowell (xviii–xix, xxvii–xxix).
7. See Leach (65) and Abelson (41–44). As Abelson explains, many female shoplifters reported feeling "seduced" into theft by the theatricality of the displays. Among the most influential window trimmers was L. Frank Baum, who wrote *The Art of Decorating Dry Goods Windows* (1900) at the same time as *The Wizard of Oz* (1900). For an analysis of Baum's poetics of color, which might be read provocatively against Larsen, see Culver.
8. Both Ferber and Canfield Fisher use the department store as a site for the exploration of middle-class women's economic and aesthetic autonomy. The heroine of Ferber's *Fanny Herself* (1917), whose special talent lies in the arrangement and description of objects, rises to power as a department store buyer; Nell Willing and Evangeline Knapp of Canfield Fisher's *The Home-Maker* (1924) claim autonomy within their marriages through work in department store advertising and sales, respectively. The roles of department store buyer and window trimmer are particularly pertinent for women, as they allow women to occupy the roles of producer and consumer/arranger of goods simultaneously.
9. Michie reads this catalogue, and Larsen's representation of light-skinned black

women in general, as part of a pattern of "sororophobic contrasts," female attempts to disidentify from other women. Such contrasts are implicit in the class conflicts I treat in this essay.

10. Interpreting this first scene in light of the journey trope in African-American fiction, Hostetler argues that the tableau imprisons Helga in the first of many social spaces she must escape to live without hypocrisy (37).

11. As several critics have noted, "Naxos" is an anagram for Saxon. In her wordplay, Larsen suggests that black imitation of white culture produces a distorted mirror image, whereas Helga consumes in an effort to create an autonomous aesthetic. As Banta observes, Larsen calls upon a Taylorist vocabulary of mass production to differentiate Helga from the Naxos pupils (7, 277).

12. Both Hostetler and Dittmar argue that Helga's desire to beautify the women around her allegorizes the position of the frustrated female artist.

13. Hair is a particularly powerful symbol of identity in African-American narratives. In James Weldon Johnson's *Autobiography of an Ex-Colored Man*, for example, the narrator marks his decision to pass for white by shaving his mustache.

14. Larsen's critique of Anne's taste suggests her affinity with some of Jessie Fauset's characters, who share a liminality with respect to the boundary between high and popular culture. On Fauset, consumption, and the middlebrow, see Susan Tomlinson's essay in this volume.

15. On white audiences' ostensible craving for the exotic primitive in black culture, see Douglas (98–99); Huggins (84–136); and Lewis (224–29). Hutchinson offers an important critique of the trope of exoticism in African-Americanist literary criticism (*Harlem*).

16. Wall gives a detailed analysis of the similarities between Helga and Baker (103–11), underscoring that the difference between the two lies in Baker's ability to manipulate her image as exotic primitive, whereas Helga acquiesces to it. Debra Silverman also contextualizes Helga's status as exotic primitive against Baker. On Baker's consumer habits, see Rose (113, 131, 143); on her love of sumptuous clothes, many of which she designed herself, see Baker and Chase (120–21, 275).

17. On Larsen's representation of the conversion scene in relation to nineteenth-century theories of the spontaneous agency of the crowd, see Esteve.

18. As Cutter argues, the stifling end of *Quicksand* leaves us, in Barthesian terms, as consumers of the text, whereas the ambiguity of the conclusion of *Passing* transforms us into textual producers. My thinking departs primarily from Cutter's in that the binary of consumption and production creates a false opposition that early-twentieth-century understandings of consumer culture do not fully support.

19. Many critics have commented on the erotic dynamics of Clare and Irene's relationship. McDowell has read the novel as a narrative of repressed lesbian desire. Blackmer offers an interesting reading of Irene's anxieties around Clare as a form of "lesbian panic," arguing that Larsen critically revises the erotic triangle of Gertrude Stein's *Melanctha*. Blackmore has located male homoerotic impulses in the representation of Brian Redfield, who considers sex "a joke" and yearns to flee Manhattan for Brazil.

20. DuCille offers the best reading of the complementarity of Clare and Irene, arguing that the dialectical relationship between the two women figures the dialectic of the Harlem Renaissance itself: modernism versus late Victorianism, free love

versus marriage, passing versus race pride. In duCille's reading, Clare's return to Harlem suggests a yearning for the respectability she has lost in crossing to the white world.

21. As Brody suggests, Irene's response to Clare's behavior may have to do with the fact that the waiter is black (1058).

22. Gertrude appears only once in the novel, at the tea party where Irene discovers Jack Bellew's hatred of blacks. In their mutual dupe of Bellew, Gertrude and Irene function as what Robinson calls "in-group clairvoyants" (716), the third parties necessary for a successful pass.

23. Brody also underscores the element of class competition in *Passing*, suggesting that Clare's rags-to-riches narrative might be read as the "embodiment of Irene's bourgeois fantasies" (1060).

24. As Davis notes, Larsen read James for her librarians' exams at the New York Public Library; ironically, then, the Jamesian intertext symbolizes not only Larsen's efforts to claim access to an elite literary tradition but also her position in the black middle class, exemplified by the profession of librarian. While Lay, McLendon, and Wall have noted parallels between Larsen's work and that of James and Wharton, the possibility of self-conscious revision has yet to be considered.

Works Cited

Abelson, Elaine. *When Ladies Go A-Thieving: Middle-Class Shoplifters in the Victorian Department Store.* New York: Oxford University Press, 1989.

Agnew, Jean-Christophe. "A House of Fiction: Domestic Interiors and the Commodity Aesthetic." In *Consuming Visions: Accumulation and Display of Goods in America, 1880–1920.* Ed. Simon Bronner. New York: W. W. Norton and Co., 1982, 133–55.

Baker, Jean-Claude, and Chris Chase. *Josephine Baker: The Hungry Heart.* New York: Random House, 1993.

Banta, Martha. *Taylored Lives: Narrative Productions in the Age of Veblen, Taylor, and Ford.* Chicago: University of Chicago Press, 1994.

Berlant, Lauren. "National Brands/National Body: *Imitation of Life*." In *Comparative American Identities: Race, Sex, and Nationality in the Modern Text.* Ed. and introd. Hortense Spillers. New York: Routledge, 1991, 110–40.

Blackmer, Corinne. "African Masks and the Arts of Passing in Gertrude Stein's *Melanctha* and Nella Larsen's *Passing*." *Journal of the History of Sexuality* 4 (1993): 230–63.

Blackmore, David. "The Unusual Restless Feeling: The Homosexual Subtexts of Nella Larsen's *Passing*." *African American Review* 26, no. 3 (1992): 475–84.

Bowlby, Rachel. *Shopping with Freud.* London: Routledge, 1993.

Brody, Jennifer DeVere. "Clare Kendry's 'True Colors': Race and Class Conflict in Nella Larsen's *Passing*." *Callaloo* 15, no. 4 (1992): 1053–65.

Bundles, A'lelia. "Madam C. J. Walker." *American History* (July/August 1996): 42–47, 56.

Carby, Hazel. *Reinventing Womanhood: The Emergence of the Afro-American Woman Novelist.* New York: Oxford University Press, 1987.

Christian, Barbara. *Black Women Novelists: The Development of a Tradition, 1892–1976.* Westport, Conn.: Greenwood, 1980.

Culver, Stuart. "What Manikins Want: *The Wonderful Wizard of Oz* and *The Art of Decorating Dry Goods Windows.*" *Representations* 21 (1988): 97–116.

Cutter, Martha. "Sliding Significations: Passing as a Narrative and Textual Strategy in Nella Larsen." In *Passing and the Fictions of Identity.* Ed. Elaine K. Ginsberg. Durham, N.C.: Duke University Press, 1996, 75–100.

Davis, Thadious. *Nella Larsen, Novelist of the Harlem Renaissance: A Woman's Life Unveiled.* Baton Rouge: Louisiana State University Press, 1994.

Dittmar, Linda. "When Privilege Is No Protection: The Woman Artist in *Quicksand* and *The House of Mirth.*" In *Writing the Woman Artist: Essays on Poetics, Politics, and Portraiture.* Philadelphia: University of Pennsylvania Press, 1992, 133–54.

Doane, Mary Ann. *The Desire to Desire: The Woman's Film of the 1940s.* Bloomington: Indiana University Press, 1987.

Douglas, Ann. *Terrible Honesty: Mongrel Manhattan in the 1920s.* New York: Farrar, Straus, and Giroux, 1995.

duCille, Ann. *The Coupling Convention: Sex, Text, and Tradition in Black Women's Fiction.* New York: Oxford University Press, 1993.

Eckert, Charles. "The Carole Lombard in Macy's Window." In *Fabrications: Costume and the Female Body.* Ed. Jane Gaines and Charlotte Herzog. New York: Routledge, 1990, 100–121.

Esteve, Mary. "Nella Larsen's 'Moving Mosaic': Harlem, Crowds, and Anonymity." *American Literary History* 9, no. 2 (1997): 268–86.

Felski, Rita. *The Gender of Modernity.* Cambridge, Mass.: Belknap Press of Harvard University Press, 1995.

Gilman, Charlotte Perkins. *Women and Economics.* 1898. New York: Harper and Row, 1966.

Hostetler, Ann. "The Aesthetics of Race and Gender in Nella Larsen's *Quicksand.*" *PMLA* 105, no. 1 (1990): 35–46.

Huggins, Nathan. *Harlem Renaissance.* New York: Oxford University Press, 1971.

Hutchinson, George. *The Harlem Renaissance in Black and White.* Cambridge, Mass.: Belknap Press of Harvard University Press, 1995.

———. "Nella Larsen and the Veil of Race." *American Literary History* 9, no. 2 (1997): 329–49.

Larsen, Nella. *"Quicksand" and "Passing."* Ed. Deborah McDowell. New Brunswick, N.J.: Rutgers University Press, 1986, ix–xxxv.

Larson, Charles. *Invisible Darkness: Jean Toomer and Nella Larsen.* Iowa City: University of Iowa Press, 1993.

Lay, Mary. "Henry James's *The Portrait of a Lady* and Nella Larsen's *Quicksand*: A Study in Parallels." In *The Magic Circle of Henry James.* Ed. Amritjit Singh. New York: Envoy Press, 1989, 73–84.

Leach, William. *Land of Desire: Merchants, Power, and the Rise of a New American Culture.* New York: Pantheon Books, 1993.

Lewis, David Levering. *When Harlem Was in Vogue.* New York: Oxford University Press, 1981.

McDowell, Deborah. "Introduction to *Quicksand* and *Passing.*" New Brunswick, N.J.: Rutgers University Press, 1986.

McLendon, Jacquelyn. *The Politics of Color in the Fiction of Jessie Fauset and Nella Larsen.* Charlottesville: University of Virginia Press, 1995.

Michie, Helena. *Sororophobia: Differences Among Women in Literature and Culture.* New York: Oxford University Press, 1992.

Piess, Kathy. *Hope in a Jar: The Making of American Beauty Culture.* New York: Metropolitan Books, 1998.

Rhodes, Chip. "Writing Up the New Negro: The Construction of Consumer Desire in the 1920s." *Journal of American Studies* 28, no. 2 (1994): 191–207.

Robinson, Amy. "It Takes One to Know One: Passing and Communities of Common Interest." *Critical Inquiry* 20 (1994): 715–36.

Rooks, Noliwe. *Hair Raising: Beauty, Culture, and African American Women.* New Brunswick, N.J.: Rutgers University Press, 1995.

Rose, Phyllis. *Jazz Cleopatra: Josephine Baker in Her Time.* New York: Vintage, 1989.

Rubin, Gayle. "The Traffic in Women: Notes Toward a Political Economy of Sex." *Toward an Anthropology of Women.* New York: Monthly Review Press, 1975.

Tate, Claudia. *Psychoanalysis and Black Novels: Desire and the Protocols of Race.* New York: Oxford University Press, 1998.

Thornton, Hortense E. "Sexism as Quagmire: Nella Larsen's *Quicksand.*" *College Language Association Journal* 16 (1973): 285–301.

Veblen, Thorstein. *The Theory of the Leisure Class.* 1899. New York: Penguin, 1978.

Wall, Cheryl. *Women of the Harlem Renaissance.* Bloomington: Indiana University Press, 1995.

Washington, Booker T. *Up From Slavery.* 1901. New York: Penguin, 1990.

Notes on Contributors

LISA BOTSHON is an assistant professor of English at the University of Maine at Augusta where she teaches American literature and women's studies. She has published on a number of American popular women writers of the twenties and is completing a book on the New Woman and the politics of race and ethnicity.

STEPHANIE BOWER teaches courses in American and gender studies at Claremont McKenna College. She has published essays on Frank Norris, Willa Cather, and Theodore Dreiser, and she is finishing a manuscript on prostitution and social formation in turn-of-the-twentieth-century American culture.

DONNA CAMPBELL is associate professor of English at Gonzaga University. She is the author of *Resisting Regionalism: Gender and Naturalism in American Fiction, 1885–1915* and articles on Edith Wharton, Sarah Orne Jewett, Mary Wilkins Freeman, and other women writers. Her current project is a book on the second generation of women regionalist writers.

SARAH CHURCHWELL is a lecturer in American literature at the University of East Anglia. She has published several articles on Sylvia Plath and Ted Hughes, as well as an article about Marilyn Monroe and biography. She also publishes short fiction and reviews regularly for the *TLS* and for the *Observer*. She is presently at work on two books: "Dead Metaphors," a study of the biographical reconstruction of famous dead women, and "Artistic Pretensions," a study of American celebrity authorship in the 1920s.

DOMINIKA FERENS teaches at the Department of English, University of Wroclaw, Poland. She earned a Ph.D. in English from the University of California, Los Angeles. Her research focuses on Asian-American literature, popular fiction, and ethnography. Her book *Edith and Winnifred Eaton: Chinatown*

Missions and Japanese Romances was published by the University of Illinois Press in 2002.

MEREDITH GOLDSMITH is an assistant professor of English at Whitman College and recently held a Fulbright Fellowship in Zagreb, Croatia. She has published on American women writers, ethnic American literature, African-American literature, and South African literature. Currently, she is working on a book manuscript entitled "Acting the Part: Staging Race and Gender in American Women's Fiction."

JAIME HARKER is the managing director of the Western Pennsylvania Writing Project in the English Department at the University of Pittsburgh. She received her Ph.D. from Temple University. Her publications include work on contemporary Japanese literature, sentimental writers of the 1850s, and popular women writers of the 1920s and 1930s. Her essay on Dorothy Canfield is part of a larger study entitled "America the Middlebrow: Women Writers, Liberalism, and Middle-Class Authorship, 1920–1940."

MAUREEN HONEY is a professor of English and women's studies at the University of Nebraska at Lincoln, where she teaches courses in women's literature and popular culture. She is the author of *Creating Rosie the Riveter: Class, Gender, and Propaganda During World War II* and the editor of *Breaking the Ties That Bind: Popular Stories of the New Woman, 1915–1930, Bitter Fruit: African American Women in World War II, Shadowed Dreams: Women's Poetry of the Harlem Renaissance,* and a reprint of *The Job* by Sinclair Lewis. She is the coeditor of *Double Take: A Revisionist Harlem Renaissance Anthology* and *"Madame Butterfly" by John Luther Long and "A Japanese Nightingale" by Onoto Watanna: Two Orientalist Texts.*

HEIDI KENAGA teaches film, literature, and television at the University of Memphis. She received her Ph.D. from the University of Wisconsin–Madison. Her work on aspects of American cinema and culture during the 1920s has appeared in several anthologies in the United States and the U.K., including *Race and the Production of Modern American Nationalism* and *Film and Popular Memory.* She is currently working on a book project entitled "Marketing a Usable Past: Prestige Westerns and Historical Commemoration, 1923–31."

JOAN SHELLEY RUBIN is a professor of history at the University of Rochester. The author of *Constance Rourke and American Culture* (1980) and *The Making of Middlebrow Culture* (1992), she is at work on a book entitled "Poetry in Practice: American Readers and the Uses of a Literary Genre," for which she received a Guggenheim Fellowship.

SUSAN TOMLINSON is an assistant professor of English at Fairfield University, where she teaches courses in late-nineteenth- and early-twentieth-century American literature, the Harlem Renaissance, and the New Woman. She is completing a book on Jessie Redmon Fauset and feminine performativity.

DEBORAH LINDSAY WILLIAMS is an associate professor of English at Iona College in New York, where she teaches American literature and women's studies. She has published a number of articles about American and British women writers and is the author of *Not in Sisterhood: Edith Wharton, Willa Cather, Zona Gale and the Politics of Female Authorship* (2000). She has edited and written the introduction to a collection of Zona Gale's Friendship Village short stories, which is forthcoming from the Feminist Press.

Index

Page numbers in italic refer to illustrations.

Abelson, Elaine, 247
ACLU. See American Civil Liberties Union
  (ACLU)
Addams, Jane, 47
Addington, Sarah: "The Tornado," 97–98
Advertising, in magazines, 135–64
African Americans, 16–17; consumer role of,
  265; difficulties faced by, 104; equal
  rights, views on, 58; lives, portrayal of,
  228; suffrage movement and, 62 n.9. See
  also The Chinaberry Tree (Fauset); Harlem
  Renaissance; Passing (Larsen); Quicksand
  (Larsen)
The Age of Innocence (Wharton), 90
Aldrich, Bess Streeter: A Lantern in Her
  Hand, 30
American aesthetic, creation of, 41
American Civil Liberties Union (ACLU), 58,
  62n. 13
American Indian Magazine, 99
American Mercury, 136, 137
Ammons, Elizabeth, 6
Anatomy of Me (Hurst), 254
Anti-Defamation League, 204
Antin, Mary, 206
Anti-Semitism, 187, 204, 246
Arnold, Matthew, 73
Art as Experience (Dewey), 113
Asian Americans, 104. See also "Japanese"
  novels
Atherton, Gertrude, 209

Baby Face (film), 247
Back Street (Hurst), 17, 245–62
Baker, Bryant, 175, 185

Barreca, Regina, 16in. 10
Bartlesville News, 183
Batker, Carol, 6
Bazin, André, 167
Bern, Paul, 210
The Big Trail (film), 185
"Bird Girl" (Bretherton), 92–93
Boas, Franz, 66
Bodies That Matter: On the Discursive Limits
  of "Sex" (Butler), 263–64
Bodily style, 277–85
Bok, Edward, 118
Bone, Robert, 232
Bonfire (Canfield), 118
Book-of-the-Month Club, 119; history of, 9;
  institutions epitomized by, 116; mergers,
  18; satire of, 162n. 17; stewardship of, 14
Bourne, Randolph, 55, 60
Bowlby, Rachel, 16, 280
The Breaking Point (Rinehart), 9
Bretherton, Vivien: "Bird Girl," 92–93
The Brimming Cup (Canfield), 14, 112, 117,
  120–30
Bromfield, Louis, 196n. 36
Brownlow, Kevin, 204, 210
Burnett, Frances Hodgson, 9
But Gentlemen Marry Brunettes (Loos), 154,
  162n. 17
Butler, Judith: Bodies That Matter: On the
  Discursive Limits of "Sex," 263–64; Gender
  Trouble, 263–64
By the Shores of Silver Lake (Wilder), 28

Cahan, Abraham, 205
Campbell's Soup advertisement: Harper's
  Bazaar, 144

Canfield, Dorothy, 111–34; *Bonfire*, 118; *The Brimming Cup* (Canfield), 14, 112, 117, 120–30; pragmatist influence, 112–15; *The Squirrel Cage*, 117; *Why Stop Learning?*, 116–17

Cather, Willa, 158, 245; Hurst, Fannie, meeting with, 10; *My Mortal Enemy*, 90; *The Professor's House*, 90

Catt, Carrie Chapman, 47

Chambers, Robert W.: *The Common Law*, 90

Child, Lydia Maria, 112, 230

The Chinaberry Tree (Fauset), 11, 16, 227–43

Christian, Barbara, 231

Cigarette smoking, 279–80

Cimarron (Ferber), 12, 15, 27, 29–31, 33–34, 41, 167–201 passim; film version, 168

Class formation, 245–62

Collier's, 90, 121

The Common Law (Chambers), 90

Consumerism, 245–62; shopping, 263–90

Consumption, 16

Correll, Mrs. Irwin, 71

Cosmopolitan, 90, 99, 208

Cosmopolitan regionalism, 45–63

Cott, Nancy F., 89, 97

Covarrubias, Miguel, 191–92

The Covered Wagon (Hough), 172, 179, 190; film version, 168, 172

Crane, Frank, 206–7

Crane, Stephen: *Maggie*, 247

Cripps, Thomas, 206, 212

Crisis, 99, 234

Culture and Anarchy (Arnold), 73

The Custom of the Country (Wharton), 159

Daily Oklahoman, 182

Damon-Moore, Helen, 112, 118

Daniels, Roger, 79

Davis, Simone Weil, 15, 233–34, 236

Dawn O'Hara (Ferber), 25

Deland, Margaret, 90

Delano, Edith Barnard: "Henry's Divorce," 96–97

Delineator, 97–98

Department stores, 279, 286n. 8

Depression, the, 190

Dewey, John, 14, 113–14

The Dialectic of Modernism (North), 5, 8, 10

The Diary of Delia (Eaton), 77

Diverging Roads (Lane), 40

Douglas, Ann, 5, 8, 13, 126; *The Feminization of American Culture*, 10

Dreiser, Theodore: *Sister Carrie*, 247

Du Plessis, Rachel Blau, 94

DuBois, W. E. B., 114

duCille, Ann, 235, 241n. 4

Dunbar-Nelson, Alice, 242n. 5

Durant, Will: *The Story of Philosophy*, 139

Eastern European Jewish immigrants. *See* Immigrants, Jewish

Eaton, Edith, 5, 67, 69

Eaton, Winnifred, 5, 13, 65–84, 98; *The Diary of Delia*, 77; *The Heart of Hyacinth*, 68, 70–71, 74–76; *His Royal Nibs*, 81; *A Japanese Blossom*, 68, 70; *A Japanese Nightingale*, 74, 76–77, 102–3; *Marion: The Story of an Artist's Model*, 101–2; *Me, A Book of Remembrance*, 81; *Miss Numè of Japan*, 67, 68, 70–74; *Tama*, 66–67, 77–79

Ellis, Havelock, 80, 207

Emma McChesney and Company (Ferber), 25

"Epic" Westerns, 168, 185

Erens, Patricia, 211, 217

Etiquette (Post), 139

Everybody's Magazine, 117

"Fallen woman," 246. *See also Back Street* (Hurst)

Fanny Herself (Ferber), 5, 265, 286n. 8

Fass, Paula, 97

Faulkner, William, 158

Fauset, Jessie: *The Chinaberry Tree*, 11, 16, 227–43; Hughes, Langston, letter to, 242n. 6; *Plum Bun*, 100–101, 228, 234, 235, 265; "The Sleeper Wakes," 99–100; *There is Confusion*, 228, 231, 233, 234

Federal Trade Commission, 168

"Female parasites," 246–54

Feminism: New Woman fiction, in periodicals, 87–109; popular feminism, in periodicals, 111–34

The Feminization of American Culture (Douglas), 10

Ferber, Edna, 25–44, 90; caricature, *192*; *Cimarron*, 12, 15, 27, 29–31, 33–34, 41, 167–201 passim; *Dawn O'Hara*, 25; *Emma McChesney and Company* (Ferber), 25; *Fanny Herself*, 5, 265, 286n. 8; *Giant*, 36–40; *A Peculiar Treasure*, 30; Pulitzer Prize, 10, 26; *Roast Beef, Medium*, 25; *Saratoga Trunk*, 35–36; *Show Boat*, 5, 41; *So Big*, 26

Ferguson, Helen, 216–18

Ferraro, Thomas, 206

Fetterley, Judith, 50

Films, 15. *See also* Hollywood; *specific film*

Finney, Gertrude: *The Plums Hang High*, 30
Fisher, Dorothy Canfield, 5, 14, 90, 159; *The Home-Maker*, 265, 286n. 8; influence of, 7
Fisher, Rudolph, 230–31
Fitzgerald, F. Scott, 10, 139, 161n. 13; *The Great Gatsby*, 8, 147
Foote, Stephanie, 54
Ford, Corey: *In the Worst Possible Taste*, 191
Fox (film studios), 168, 185
Fox, William, 204
Franzen, Jonathan, 18–19
Frazer, Elizabeth: "The Sob-Lady," 92
Free Land (Lane), 27–42
Friedman, Lester, 204, 211
Friendships, portrayal: magazines, 98
Friendship Village, 45–63 passim

Gale, Zona, 5, 9, 13, 45–63; *The Chinaberry Tree* (Introduction), 11, 227–31, 236, 241; *Heart's Kindred*, 48–49, 59, 60; *Miss Lulu Bett*, 46; *Mothers to Men*, 51; *Peace in Friendship Village*, 47, 52–55, 58–59; Pulitzer Prize, 10; *Uncle Jimmy*, 9; "What Women Won in Wisconsin," 45
Gender Trouble (Butler), 263–64
Gentlemen Prefer Blondes (Loos), 7, 14, 135–64, 247
Georgi-Findlay, Brigitte, 27
German Jewish culture, 5
"Ghetto Film," 211
Ghettos, Jewish, 205–6
Giant (Ferber), 36–40; film version, 39–40
Gibson, Charles Dana, 90
Gilman, Charlotte Perkins, 248–50, 265
Gilman, Sander, 217
"The Girl Who Slept in Bryant Park" (Lockwood), 95
Glass, Montague: *Potash and Perlmutter*, 210–11, 221n. 10
Glimpses of the Moon (Wharton), 9
Glyn, Elinor, 209
Godsol, Frank, 210–11
"Golddiggers," 246–54, 261
The Golden Bowl (James), 282
Goldwyn, Samuel, 16; Yezierska and, 203, 204, 208, 210
Good Housekeeping, 14, 90, 92–94, 252
Grant, Madison, 256
The Great Gatsby (Fitzgerald), 8, 147
Gregory, John: *Pioneer Woman*, 32
Grey, Zane, 15, 170–71, 183
Griffis, William, 79
Gross, Terry, 18
Guillory, John, 150

Hall, Stuart, 241
Halliday, Jon, 245

Hampton, Benjamin, 207
Harding, Warren G., 118
Harlem Renaissance, 5, 99; experimentalism, 16; prostitution imagery, 235
Harper's Bazaar, 14–15; Campbell's Soup advertisement, 144; *Gentlemen Prefer Blondes*, 135–64; hats, advertisements, 146
Harris, Alice Kessler, 207
Harris, Herbert, 234
Hays, Will, 169
The Head of the House of Coomb (Burnett), 9
Hearst's, 101, 206
The Heart of Hyacinth (Eaton), 68, 70–71, 74–76
Heart's Kindred (Gale), 48–49, 59, 60
Heidi (Spyri), 9
Hemingway, Ernest, 161n. 13, 245
"Henry's Divorce" (Delano), 96–97
Heterodoxy, 47, 61n. 4
His Royal Nibs (Eaton), 81
Holloway, W. J., 175
Hollywood, 15, 205–11; immigrants, Jewish, marketing of, 203–24. *See also specific films*
Holmes, Oliver Wendell, 159
The Home-Maker (Fisher), 265, 286n. 8
Hoover, Herbert, 175, 185
Hopper, E. Mason, 210
Hough, Emerson, 170–71, 176, 183; *The Covered Wagon*, 172–73, 179, 190; Koerner, collaboration with, 195n. 23; *The Passing of the Frontier*, 171–72, 175
The House of Mirth (Wharton), 41
Household Magazine, 99
Hudson River Bracketed (Wharton), 6–7
Hughes, Langston, 242n. 6
Hull, Edith, 15
Humoresque (Hurst), 15, 222n. 16
Hungry Hearts (Yezierska), 16, 203, 204, 208–9; film, 211–20
Hurley, Patrick, 175
Hurst, Fannie, 5, 9, 11; *Anatomy of Me*, 254; *Back Street*, 17, 245–62; Cather, Willa, meeting with, 10; *Humoresque*, 15, 222n. 16; *Imitation of Life* (Hurst), 5, 245, 259–60; *The Vertical City*, 9
Hutchinson, George, 113
Hutner, Gordon, 112
Huxley, Thomas, 66
Huyssen, Andreas, 7–8, 138
Hwang, David Henry, 82n. 5

Imitation of Life (Hurst), 5, 245, 259–60
Immigrants, Jewish, 203–24; in American imagination, 204–5; Hollywood and, 205–20

Incidents in the Life of a Slave Girl (Jacobs), 230
In the Worst Possible Taste (Ford), 191
The Iron Horse (film), 168
Itzkovitz, Daniel, 255, 257, 258

Jacobs, Harriet A., 241n. 2; *Incidents in the Life of a Slave Girl*, 230
James, William, 14, 113
A Japanese Blossom (Eaton), 68, 70
The Japanese Nation in Evolution (Griffis), 79
A Japanese Nightingale (Eaton), 74, 76–77, 102–3
"Japanese" novels, 65–84. *See also* Eaton, Winnifred
Jewish Americans, 17, 184, 192; identity, 258; immigrants, marketing of, 203–24; stereotypes, 254–61. *See also* Anti-Semitism
Johnson, Carole McCool, 171
Josephson, Julius, 210

Kaplan, David, 216
Kaye, Ethel, 216
Kerr, Sophie, 90, 106n. 14; "The Tyrant," 95–96
Key, Ellen: *The Morality of Women*, 249–50
Kirchwey, Freda, 127
Kirkland, Edward, 142
Koerner, W. H. D.: Hough, collaboration with, 195n. 23; *Madonna of the Prairie* (Koerner), 173, 174, 192
Kroeger, Brooke, 10

La Follette, Robert, 47–48, 50
Ladies' Home Journal, 89, 95, 96–97, 118
Lane, Gertrude Battles, 90, 117, 118
Lane, Rose Wilder, 25–44 passim; *Diverging Roads*, 40; *Free Land*, 27–42; *Let the Hurricane Roar*, 27–28
A Lantern in Her Hand (Aldrich), 30
Lape, Noreen Groover, 67, 69
Larsen, Nella, 17, 263–90; *Passing*, 263, 277–85; *Quicksand*, 263, 266–77
LeBaron, William, 190, 197n. 56
Lehr, Abe, 216–17
Leimbach, August: *Madonna of the Trail*, 32
Lesbians, 287n. 19
Let the Hurricane Roar (Lane), 27–28
Levien, Sonya, 210
Lewis, Sinclair, 41, 131, 132n. 4; *Main Street*, 120–22
Lewis, Wyndham, 159
Limitless lands myth, 40
Ling, Amy, 70

"Little House" series, 25, 28–29
Locke, Alain, 114
Lockwood, Scammon: "The Girl Who Slept in Bryant Park," 95
Lofroth, Eric, 9
Long, John Luther: *Madame Butterfly*, 102; *Miss Cherry-Blossom of Tokyo*, 71–72
Long, Ray, 90
Longwell, Dan, 197n. 50
The Long Winter (Wilder), 28
Loos, Anita, 10; advertisement in *Harper's*, 155; *But Gentlemen Marry Brunettes*, 154, 162n. 17; *Gentlemen Prefer Blondes*, 7, 14, 135–64, 247; and magazine publishing, 14–15
Lorimer, George Horace, 170, 172
Loti, Pierre: *Madame Chrysanthème*, 71
"The Lotus Eater" (Mason), 94
Lower East Side (New York City), 205–6

McCall's, 90, 118, 121
McClure's, 117
Macdonald, Dwight: "Masscult and Midcult," 3–4
McLendon, Jacquelyn, 279–80
Madame Butterfly (Long), 71, 82n. 5, 102
Madame Chrysanthème (Loti), 71
Madonna of the Prairie (Koerner), 173, 174, 192
Madonna of the Trail (Leimbach), 32
Magazine culture, 13–15; and advertising, 135–64; and New Woman fiction, 87–109; and popular feminism, 111–34; prices paid for serialization, 117–18, 161n. 13
Maggie (Crane), 247
Main Street (Lewis), 120–22, 132n. 4
Making Love Modern (Miller), 227
The Making of Middlebrow Culture (Rubin), 4, 117
Maltby, Richard, 185
Marcel, Sonia, 216, 217
Marion: The Story of an Artist's Model (Eaton), 101–2
Marland, Edward C., 173, 175, 184
Marland, Ernest W., 32
Mason, Grace Sartwell: "The Lotus Eater," 94
Mass culture, 4
"Masscult and Midcult" (Macdonald), 3–4
Matsukawa, Yuko, 67
Me, A Book of Remembrance, (Eaton), 81
Melanctha (Stein), 287n. 19
Mena, Maria Cristina, 98
Mencken, H. L.: Loos and, 136, 140, 156,

16111. 11; marriage, on, 247; middle class, on, 130–31; *Smart Set Criticism*, 3, 162n. 22

Mendel, Gregor, 65

Metro-Goldwyn-Mayer, 221n. 9

Michaels, Walter Benn: nativism, 32–33; *Our America: Nativism, Modernism, Pluralism*, 8–9, 25

Midcult, as threat, 4

Middlebrow, defined, 3

Miller, Nina: *Making Love Modern*, 227

Miss Cherry-Blossom of Tokyo (Long), 71–72

Miss Lulu Bett (Gale), 46

Miss Numè of Japan (Eaton), 67, 68, 70–74

Modernism and mass culture, 7–8

Monroe, Marilyn, 135

The Morality of Women (Key), 249–50

Mothers to Men (Gale), 51

Motion Picture Classic, 217–20

Motion Picture Producers and Distributors of America (MPPDA), 169, 181, 185

MPPDA. *See* Motion Picture Producers and Distributors of America (MPPDA)

My Mortal Enemy (Cather), 90

Myres, Sandra L., 27

NAACP. *See* National Association for the Advancement of Colored People (NAACP)

Najmi, Samina, 67

National American Woman Suffrage Association (NAWSA), 47

National Association for the Advancement of Colored People (NAACP), 58, 62n. 13, 99, 234

National Women's Party, 47

Nativism, 32–33, 171, 256

NAWSA. *See* National American Woman Suffrage Association (NAWSA)

New Woman character: feminist New Woman fiction, 87–109

New York Herald Tribune, 230

New York Tribune, 219, 220

New York World, 48

Nineteenth Amendment, 45, 61n. 1

Norris, Kathleen, 90

North, Michael: *The Dialect of Modernism*, 5, 8, 10

O. Henry Award, 26

Ohmann, Richard, 247

Oklahoma: Pioneer Woman monument, 171–73, 175, 176, 180, 184; "Spirit of the Oklahoma Pioneer," 185

Oscars (awards), 190

Our America: Nativism, Modernism, Pluralism (Michaels), 8–9, 25

Pacifist movement, 48–49

Paramount (film studios), 168, 185

Parker, Alison, 181

Passing (Larsen), 17, 263, 277–85

The Passing of the Frontier (Hough), 171–72, 175

Paul, Alice, 47

Peace in Friendship Village (Gale), 47, 52–55, 58–59

A Peculiar Treasure (Ferber), 30

Performativity, 263–64

Perloff, Marjorie, 32–33

Peyser, Thomas, 12

Phillips, David Graham: *Susan Lenox: Her Fall and Rise*, 247

Pictorial Review, 89, 90

The Picture of Dorian Gray (Wilde), 280

Pioneer Woman (Gregory), 32

Pioneer Woman monument, 171–73, 175, 176, 180, 184

Plum Bun (Fauset), 100–101, 228, 234, 235, 265

The Plums Hang High (Finney), 30

Post, Emily: *Etiquette*, 139

Potash and Perlmutter (Glass), 210–11, 221n. 10

Pragmatism, 112–15

Prairie Madonna, 12, 26, 27, 32

The Professor's House (Cather), 90

Prostitution imagery, 235

Pryse, Marjorie, 50

Pulitzer Prize, 10, 26

Quantic, Diane, 28

Quicksand (Larsen), 17, 263, 266–77

Quindlen, Anna, 18

Race relations, 80

Racial and ethnic groups, 5, 265

Racial nativism, 171, 256

Racism, 98–99, 101

Radway, Janice, 9, 14, 115, 119, 169

Reader's Guide to Periodical Literature, 79–80

Red Headed Woman (film), 247

Red Ribbon on a White Horse (Yezierska), 207, 221n.2

Reynolds, Paul R., 115, 117

Rinehart, Mary Roberts, 9, 90

The Rise of David Levinsky, 205

RKO Corporation, 167–68, 186–90; poster, 187

Roast Beef, Medium (Ferber), 25

Roberts, Kimberley, 235
Rogers, Will, 175, 185
Rogin, Michael, 205, 260
Roosevelt, Eleanor, 7
Roosevelt, Theodore, 15, 170, 183
Rosanova, Rosa, 218, 222n. 20
Rosenberg, Rosalind, 89, 97
Rubin, Gayle, 265
Rubin, Joan Shelley, 9, 159–60; *The Making of Middlebrow Culture*, 4, 117
Russell, Bertrand, 159

Salome of the Tenements (Yezierska), 220, 265
Santayana, George, 158
Saratoga Trunk (Ferber), 35–36
Saturday Evening Post, 170, 240
Savage, Kirk, 174
Self-fashioning, 17, 263–90
Sensational Designs: The Cultural Work of American Fiction (Tompkins), 10
Sexual selection, 68
Shapiro, Laura, 31
Shopping, self-fashioning and, 263–90
Show Boat (Ferber), 5, 41
Sirk, Douglas, 245
Sister Carrie (Dreiser), 247
"The Sleeper Wakes" (Fauset), 99–100
Smart Set Criticism (Mencken), 3, 162n. 22
So Big (Ferber), 26
"The Sob-Lady" (Frazer), 92
Southern Workman, 227
Spaulding, Carol Vivian, 67
Spencer, Herbert, 66, 73
Spingarn, Joel, 234
"Spirit of the Oklahoma Pioneer," 185
Spyri, Joanna, 9
The Squirrel Cage (Canfield), 117
Starkey, Marion L., 227
Stein, Gertrude: *Melanctha*, 287n. 19; *Three Lives*, 149
The Story of Philosophy (Durant), 139
Stowe, Harriet Beecher, 112
Suffrage movement, 62 n.9; opposition to, 118
Sui Sin Far. *See* Eaton, Edith
Susan Lenox: Her Fall and Rise (Phillips), 247
Susman, Warren I., 138, 257
"Sweatshop Cinderella," 203, 208, 220
Sylvander, Carolyn Wedin, 232–33

Tama (Eaton), 66–67, 77–79
Terrible Honesty (Douglas), 5, 8
The Theory of the Leisure Class (Veblen), 270
There is Confusion (Fauset), 228, 231, 233, 234

Three Guineas (Woolf), 49
Three Lives (Stein), 149
"Time-Children" (Lewis), 159
Tompkins, Jane: *Sensational Designs: The Cultural Work of American Fiction*, 10
"The Tornado" (Addington), 97–98
"The Tyrant" (Kerr), 95–96

Uncle Jimmy (Gale), 9
United Artists (film studios), 168

Van Vechten, Carl, 158
Van Vorst, Marie, 158
The Vanishing American (film), 168
Vanity Fair, 136, 158
Veblen, Thorstein: *The Theory of the Leisure Class*, 270
The Vertical City (Hurst), 9
Vogue, 142
Vorse, Mary Heaton, 90

Washburn, Bryant, 216
Washington, Booker T., 112, 265, 286n. 1
Watanna, Onoto. *See* Eaton, Winnifred
WCTU. *See* Women's Christian Temperance Union (WCTU)
Weinberg, David, 212
Welter, Barbara, 173
Western historical narratives, 167–201
Wexler, Laura, 206
Wharton, Edith, 158; *The Age of Innocence*, 90; *The Custom of the Country*, 159; *Glimpses of the Moon*, 9; *The House of Mirth*, 41; *Hudson River Bracketed*, 6–7, 9; and magazine publishing, 13–14
"What Women Won in Wisconsin" (Gale), 45
White, William Allen, 121, 176, 182
Why Stop Learning? (Canfield), 116–17
Wicke, Jennifer, 15, 141
Wilde, Oscar: *The Picture of Dorian Gray*, 280
Wilder, Laura Ingalls: "Little House" series, 25, 28–29; *The Long Winter*, 28; *By the Shores of Silver Lake*, 28
Winfrey, Oprah, 18–19, 111
The Winning of Barbara Worth (film), 168
Wisconsin, 45–46
"Wisconsin Idea," 48
Wister, Owen, 15, 170
Woman's Home Companion, 89, 90, 95–96, 117–18, 177
Women's Christian Temperance Union (WCTU), 181
Women's magazines, 13–14

Women's Peace Party (WPP), 48, 60–61
Woolf, Virginia, 4, 116; defines middlebrow, 139; *Three Guineas*, 49
Woollcott, Alexander, 159
World War I, 48–49
WPP. *See* Women's Peace Party (WPP)
Wright, Richard, 112
Wyckoff, Elizabeth, 118
Wylie, Elinor, 158

Yates, Elizabeth, 119
Yezierska, Anzia, 5, 11, 203–24; Hollywood experience, 205–11; *Hungry Hearts*, 16, 203, 204, 208–9, 211–20; *Red Ribbon on a White Horse*, 207, 221n.2; *Salome of the Tenements*, 220, 265

Zukor, Adolph, 204